Adelbert Ames, the Civil War,

and the

Creation of Modern America

CIVIL WAR SOLDIERS AND STRATEGIES
Brian S. Wills, Series Editor

Richmond Must Fall: The Richmond-Petersburg Campaign, October 1864
HAMPTON NEWSOME

Work for Giants: The Campaign and Battle of Tupelo/Harrisburg, Mississippi, June–July 1864
THOMAS E. PARSON

"My Greatest Quarrel with Fortune": Major General Lew Wallace in the West, 1861–1862
CHARLES G. BEEMER

Phantoms of the South Fork: Captain McNeill and His Rangers
STEVE FRENCH

At the Forefront of Lee's Invasion: Retribution, Plunder, and Clashing Cultures on Richard S. Ewell's Road to Gettysburg
ROBERT J. WYNSTRA

Meade: The Price of Command, 1863–1865
JOHN G. SELBY

James Riley Weaver's Civil War: The Diary of a Union Cavalry Officer and Prisoner of War, 1863–1865
EDITED BY JOHN T. SCHLOTTERBECK, WESLEY W. WILSON, MIDORI KAWAUE, AND HAROLD A. KLINGENSMITH

Blue-Blooded Cavalryman: Captain William Brooke Rawle in the Army of the Potomac, May 1863–August 1865
EDITED BY J. GREGORY ACKEN

No Place for Glory: Major General Robert E. Rodes and the Confederate Defeat at Gettysburg
ROBERT J. WYNSTRA

From the Wilderness to Appomattox: The Fifteenth New York Heavy Artillery in the Civil War
EDWARD A. ALTEMOS

Adelbert Ames, the Civil War, and the Creation of Modern America
MICHAEL J. MEGELSH

ADELBERT AMES, *the* CIVIL WAR, *and the* CREATION *of* MODERN AMERICA

Michael J. Megelsh

THE KENT STATE UNIVERSITY PRESS

Kent, Ohio

To my wife, Chara—my joy.

© 2024 by The Kent State University Press, Kent, Ohio 44242
All rights reserved
ISBN 978-1-60635-467-4
Published in the United States of America

No part of this book may be used or reproduced, in any manner whatsoever, without written permission from the Publisher, except in the case of short quotations in critical reviews or articles.

Cataloging information for this title is available at the Library of Congress.

CONTENTS

Acknowledgments   vii

Introduction   1

1 From the Rockland Waterfront to the Potomac River   12

2 Fresh Lieutenant to Seasoned Colonel   26

3 Colonel Ames, His Regiment, and Smallpox   47

4 Boy General   64

5 Futility along the James River   85

6 The Final Struggle for Victory   108

7 Travels Abroad   132

8 A Military Man Wearing Political Hats   148

9 Senator from Mississippi   167

10 The Height of the Party and the Height of Prejudice   189

11 A Governor and Reconstruction on Trial   212

12 Life Refusing to Slow   233

Conclusion   257

Notes   264

Bibliography   292

Index   305

ACKNOWLEDGMENTS

John Donne's "No Man Is an Island" is not only a heralded piece of literature but also relatable to the process of writing a book. It takes immense effort and focus to complete a manuscript for publication. The process of doing so takes individual perseverance, yet support from others is vital. Just as Donne reminds his audience that humanity is interconnected, the art of writing a book highlights that interconnectedness. Without the help of other people, this book does not exist.

I want to thank the people of Smith College in Northampton, Massachusetts, for all their help. Their assistance in providing resources, images, and a warm welcome to their campus and special collections was a privilege. It truly was a way to feel closer to Adelbert Ames and his family.

Taylor Plimpton, a descendant of Adelbert and Blanche Ames, provided essential help in gathering information and assisting me in obtaining permissions to use images belonging to the Ames family in this book. His uncle, Oakes Plimpton, was also an invaluable contributor. I enjoyed conversing back and forth about all things Ames. Their family and its legacy are hopefully honored properly with this book.

I wish to extend thanks also to Steven Woodworth and Brian Melton. Both Civil War historians I hold in high esteem, they were the first scholars to assist me in the process of bringing Ames's conduct and service to a twenty-first-century audience. I also with to thank Kathryn Braund, Keith Hebert, David Carter, and Matt Malczycki, all of whom helped me and guided me as a doctoral student at Auburn University. My further gratitude goes to Stewart Bennett and

Jim Witte for their support and valuable advice. And most of all, I wish to extend my utmost thanks to Ken Noe. His mentorship and support over the years means a great deal. His willingness to welcome me as his mentee, along with his patience as I maneuvered through the ups and downs of academia and writing, will always mean so much to me.

Josh Shiver and Dan Cone provided great assistance during the early stages of my work. They offered critique and helped with editing. I am truly thankful for them. In addition, I want to thank Peter Thomas, Andrew Baker, and Dan Campbell for their friendship and encouragement during the entire process of bringing Ames's story to light. May our exploits echo through history.

Lastly, I am humbled by and appreciative of the love and support of my family. As I read about Ames, his ancestors, and his descendants, I saw a family full of strong men and courageous women. Those attributes of strength and courage proudly apply to my family as well. I am grateful to my mother and father for the lessons they shared and the examples they offered to me. I am thankful for my sisters—knowledgeable, brave, and brilliant—and for my brother, who is dedicated, bold, and honorable. Without them, my life has far less light. My wife, Chara, is a blessing I do not think I will ever deserve. Her love, patience, support, and wisdom is matchless. She brings joy and stability. The Lord has given me a great many things more than I deserve, and I am appreciative for all the people in my life until the very end.

INTRODUCTION

On October 31, 1931, Adelbert Ames turned ninety-six years old. Outliving nearly all of his friends, colleagues, family members, and enemies, the elderly man relished his peaceful life. Although advanced in years, he remained in relatively good health. The body of the old general ached, and his sight was not what it was before, but his eyes still had the same piercing glare and his mind still produced a flash of wit as when he was a senator representing Mississippi sixty years earlier. His speech was coherent, and he spoke clearly and lucidly.

Ames preferred to spend his days reading and writing now, and he liked going on outings. In the summer, he would leave the chilly winters of his native New England and travel to Florida, where he would play golf as often as he could. On Halloween, 1931, one newspaper noted his birthday and reminded its readership that Ames was a celebrity: he was now the last surviving Union general. He also was a relic of a distant era that seemed archaic compared to the bustling technology of the 1930s. Although his days now focused on enjoying his twilight years, Ames's life had been far from mundane. In fact, the newspaper observed that, on his birthday, "Gen. Ames looked back . . . upon a life crammed full of action and from a memory rich in anecdote . . . of famous men and famous battles that shaped his country's destiny."[1]

His mind carried the memory of many experiences, while his body also bore evidence of his exploits. Ames had a scar on his right thigh from a wound he received seventy years prior as a junior officer fresh out of West Point. On the afternoon of July 21, 1861, 1st Lieutenant Ames collapsed upon the ground, struck by a musket ball in his leg. Warm blood oozed from the wound, its temperature comparable to that of the midsummer day along Bull Run in northern Virginia. Suffocating heat and sultry humidity, paired with the smoke from the guns that Ames commanded in the Fifth US Artillery Battery, created a stifling environment. Around the young officer and his men a battle raged, nearly engulfing them. Although wounded, Ames propped himself up and continued to bark orders as he and his comrades faced an onslaught of Confederate infantrymen approaching their position.

Leaning his maimed body on an artillery caisson to direct his men, the pain was excruciating. The projectile responsible was likely a .69-caliber smoothbore round. While it was not as devastating as a rifled Minié ball that could smash through bone and sinew, it was still capable of disastrous effects. The lack of accuracy of the bullet further made it errantly enter the human body. Instead of passing through, a smoothbore round tended to lodge within its target, creating a twisted path as it tore through muscle and sometimes bone before nestling within the victim. According to reports, however, this round actually passed through Ames's thigh. Despite such a wound, at First Bull Run Ames demonstrated the attributes that defined his life and his many careers. He would survive that battle and many others, both in the military and in the post–Civil War American politics of Reconstruction. Ames lived to be a few years shy of 100, while so many of his contemporaries died many years before him.

This book provides the first modern biography of Adelbert Ames depicting his life in its entirety. It weaves together a multitude of fields—antebellum politics, the Civil War, Reconstruction, the long civil rights movement, postwar banditry on the Great Plains, American tourism culture, international politics, the rise of twentieth-century US imperialism, and the historiography of the Civil War—in order to understand such a multifaceted life. Few figures can boast of having their story intertwine all these fields, but Ames's does exactly that. This study helps expand Civil War–era scholarship and functions as a tale about the transformation of the United States into a modernizing nation through the life of a man born on the humble shores of Maine.

In bringing together all these historical elements, this book makes several arguments. Ames was a valuable commodity to the Union army, not just a peripheral contributor. He epitomized the type of midlevel commander who helped Federal forces achieve victory on the battlefield. While generals such as Ulysses S. Grant, William Tecumseh Sherman, and Philip H. Sheridan directed their armies during successful campaigns, it was their midlevel commanders such as Ames who executed their orders on the front lines while commanding thousands of men.

Additionally, Ames was the most talented and successful of the famed "boy generals" who entered the ranks of the Army of the Potomac's upper command echelon in 1863. A collective group of Union officers (most West Point graduates) who became brigadier generals midway through the war, their rise represented the changing of the old guard and the introduction of new, aggressive, and bold generals commanding brigades, divisions, and sometimes, as with Ames, corps. His accomplishments, diverse skills, combat experience, leadership of the now legendary Twentieth Maine Regiment, and efforts that earned him the Medal of Honor make the case that Ames shined as the greatest boy general of all.

Yet Reconstruction-era politics shaped Ames's legacy to a greater extent than his military career. This work supports recent scholarship that disputes earlier interpretations of Ames as a corrupt carpetbagger on the make in Mississippi. To the contrary, Ames was not a dishonest public figure but ardently tried to do his best. As the state's military governor, US senator, or elected governor, Ames encountered both success and failure. Dedicated to the Constitution and enforcing federal law, the Republican Ames also championed decency in office. Furthermore, he worked to apply a modern, capitalist economic plan to a rural, depleted southern state suffering from the aftereffects of civil war. Above all else, he prioritized the defense of formerly enslaved persons, championing their civil liberties and economic freedom against oppressive Democratic forces. During his time in Mississippi, Ames demonstrated the same bravery he had shown on the battlefield in order to maintain law and order and to give all of the state's residents a chance to rebuild their communities and their lives.

Still, Ames's term as a US senator and his gubernatorial administration suffered notable failings. Some grew from his personality. Ames was temperamental and a perfectionist. He did not always exercise good judgment during a political crisis, which could make him appear corrupt or tyrannical. He did not restrain tarnished officials from his party who took advantage of state finances. Those lawbreakers obstructed lawsuits and took part in making "carpetbagger" a byword for "corrupt and tyrannical" in Mississippi. Ames's ignorance of or his inability to stop them hurt his administration, his legacy, and most importantly the Magnolia State. Finally, he sometimes gave in to bouts of melancholy that, while understandable under his pressing circumstances, adversely affected law-enforcement officers, the legislature, local judges, and individual citizens. Thus, his political demise was not strictly external. Still, the political and social forces in Mississippi certainly would have crushed any northern-born Republican trying to promote equal rights and economic progress. Ames's fortitude in the face of such challenges is commendable. Nevertheless, his tenure as governor was an overall failure.

Ames was part of the arc of civil rights history in the United States, or the "long civil rights movement." American historian Jacquelyn Dowd Hall first coined this term early in the twenty-first century.[2] Although civil rights efforts of the 1950s and 1960s peaked in part because of social reforms stemming from the 1930s, Hall has argued that its timeline needs to expand beyond its more familiar periodization, typically 1954–68, also known as the "classical phase" of the civil rights movement. This has led to an ongoing debate, with some historians rejecting the idea of a long civil rights movement while others routinely begin discussions of civil rights in America with the foundational changes that occurred as far back as the 1860s and 1870s. Indeed, the civil rights movement predates the twentieth century, sparked by the Emancipation Proclamation in 1863 and fully initiated during Reconstruction with the implementation of constitutional rights for Black Americans. Ames was part of this. He took on the Ku Klux Klan in Mississippi—aiding in its temporary collapse—abhorred racism and slavery, and supported legislation protecting civil liberties. Ames elected to stand up for civil rights in the state, even though it likely cost him his governorship and political future. He was not just an early defender of civil liberties but a politician who staked his entire political legacy upon it. Ames thus deserves acclaim as an early civil rights advocate. His life and service suggest that acknowledging a long civil rights movement is helpful to better understanding the overarching story of civil rights in the United States. In short, Ames was part of the first wave of civil rights defenders in American history.[3]

Yet only two works have featured Ames as their central figure; both have limits. His daughter, Blanche Ames Ames,[4] published *Adelbert Ames: General, Senator, Governor, 1835–1933* in 1964. A complete biography covering her father's formative to final years, the massive work was previously the only source dedicated to Ames's entire life. A passion project, it contains much useful information but has drawn criticism for being essentially hagiographic and lacking objective analysis. In 1974 Harry King Benson completed a dissertation entitled "The Public Career of Adelbert Ames, 1861–1876," emphasizing Ames's time in the army and postwar politics. Benson argues that the general's public career ended with him as a victim of political adversaries, while his character was incorruptible. Part of the historical scholarship of the 1960s and 1970s that sought to revise the interpretation of what Reconstruction was and who carpetbaggers were, Benson's study nevertheless lacks breadth. Although both works are useful secondary sources, the current volume is the first to offer a fully comprehensive biography, including a more extensive account of Ames's military service.

Along with this lack of biographies, Ames has not attracted a massive scholarship with which to engage, whether agreeing, disagreeing, or splitting down the middle. Because he is thus moderately overlooked, this book seeks to establish a conversation, providing a standard account of his life, more so than to engage with a preexisting one. It also strives to add to multiple fields of study. Among these is how midlevel commanders and the boy generals functioned as conduits between army commanders and brigade and regimental leaders and their staffs. The book also offers an expanded interpretation of Mississippi's postwar struggles. Through Ames it analyzes the factors that led to the downfall of Reconstruction in that state and to an extent nationally. It also adds to the conversation about the long civil rights movement and whether his actions and service give credence to this school of thought. In doing these things, this study joins an extensive historiography and helps fill in current gaps through the telling of Ames's story.

More specifically, however, this biography builds upon the immense historiography of the Civil War era. It fosters a connection to voluminous previous scholarship while providing new insights, especially regarding the Army of the Potomac's officer corps, midlevel commanders, Reconstruction politics and occupation forces, and immediate-postwar Mississippi.

Historians to be sure have analyzed the Army of the Potomac, dissecting the attributes, conduct, and officers that composed this heralded Union field force. For example, any study that directly or indirectly involves the Army of the Potomac builds upon Bruce Catton's classic trilogy. His Pulitzer Prize–winning work chronicles the growth and evolution of that Union army.[5] More recently, historian Jeffry D. Wert has offered an authoritative single-volume study on the Army of the Potomac. Early defeats and a changing officer corps, which he analyzes to some extent, created a veteran army that would eventually thrive under the leadership of Grant in 1864. Ames's career trajectory and ascension through the officer ranks notably coincides with what Wert contends is a dramatic shift in Federal fortunes halfway through the war while emulating the maturation of the army Catton emphasizes in his trilogy.[6]

Other historians have focused more strictly upon the officer corps itself. In various ways John Eicher and David Eicher, Albert Castel and Brooks D. Simpson, and Ethan S. Rafuse all have described the conduct of Union generals, including what the officers in the Army of the Potomac did—and did not do—to achieve victory. Some have examined solely the Potomac Army's officers with impressive results. That army's generals, Stephen Sears contends, fought each other and the Lincoln administration as much as the Confederates. Yet when Grant assumed effective command, he was able to wrangle together a good contingent—including Ames, who ended his Civil War service as a major general—that helped him achieve success.[7]

Generals leading corps and divisions—the midlevel commanders in the Union army—directed thousands of men while also being beholden to their own superiors. They held sway over the battlefield yet were more personally invested in troop movements and often at risk of injury. From the Army of the Potomac, John Gibbon, Abner Doubleday, Gouverneur K. Warren, Hiram G. Berry, Henry Slocum, John Sedgwick, James S. Wadsworth, Francis Barlow, O. O. Howard, and Ames's former protégé Joshua L. Chamberlain, have all garnered significant attention. , From Dennis S. Lavery and Mark H. Jordan's biography of Gibbon to Thomas Barthel's life of Doubleday, writers have emphasized the merits of the subject individual's service within the context of the war.[8] Ames deserves similar attention because he was an equally important, if not more contributory, midlevel commander in helping achieve Union victory.

Just as some historians have worked to declare the noteworthiness of midlevel commanders, others have written about an injection of younger generals that helped pave the way for a different and more successful army effort. Among them, Samuel J. Martin has examined the life of aggressive boy general Hugh Judson Kilpatrick, historian Don E. Alberts has written about cavalry general Wesley Merritt, and Eric J. Wittenberg has highlighted Elon Farnsworth and his fateful charge at Gettysburg. But of all the boy generals, George Armstrong Custer has garnered the most attention. His flamboyant image and 1876 death at the hands of Plains Indians aside, Custer's courageousness during the Civil War has sparked interest from several scholars. Edward G. Longacre has analyzed his growth into a bold general. Daniel Davis and Eric J. Wittenberg have written about a heroism that bordered on pure recklessness. Another of these young leaders, Emory Upton, has received attention from David J. Fitzpatrick as well as Stephen E. Ambrose.[9] Ames's time in the military, and his age when earning his brigadier general's star, places him alongside these men.

Ames also connects with preexisting scholarship underscoring the noteworthiness of Mainers during the Civil War. His contemporaries Howard, Berry, and especially Chamberlain have received individual attention from academicians. Chamberlain, in large part due to his gallantry at Gettysburg and the central role afforded him in Michael Shaara's novel *The Killer Angels*, leads the way. Alice Rains Trulock and Thomas A. Desjardin are just two of the authors who have described his service and life, mentioning Ames only in passing as a key player in Chamberlain's development.[10] And intersecting with both Chamberlain and Ames, the Twentieth Maine remains one of the more famous regiments in the Union army. It too has received acclaim from historians, with each trying to give a unique take on how the unit is storied. John J. Pullen has written the seminal work on the regiment, while subsequent studies have offered new analyses that ultimately still conclude that the regiment was remarkable, tough, and able to answer grueling challenges.[11] But to best provide an answer as to why this regiment and Chamberlain, its commander at Gettysburg, were prepared to meet their challenges, Ames's leadership and guidance provides a foundational component.

Unlike many of his contemporaries, Ames continued to make his historical mark after the cannons and muskets fell silent. Ames's pertinence persisted into Reconstruction history. His experiences during these years touched upon many of the issues and topics facing the United States, including the military after the Civil War, the newly emancipated people, the so-called carpetbaggers, and the restoration of Mississippi to the Union. Ames continued to serve with the US Army after the war. The dilemmas of this period—the Ku Klux Klan, belligerent Democratic politicians, planter elites regaining control—all intersected with his postwar military service in Mississippi. As an early advocate of civil rights, Ames was involved with the stories of newly emancipated persons after the Civil War. Former slaves saw the potential for autonomy after the war. Against the difficulties in attaining that long-sought freedom, Ames worked alongside Freedman's Bureau agents during Reconstruction.[12]

Some white people in the postwar South were not locals but were actually northerners, relocating for political or economic benefit. The northern-born Ames was, by the simple if biased definition of the era, a "carpetbagger." But instead of lambasting carpetbaggers as simply corrupt, recent scholarship paints a more nuanced picture. Mentioning Ames alongside other carpetbaggers, Richard N. Current has made the case that not all northern-born arrivals were stereotypically corrupt and power hungry, lascivious landlords and political animals taking advantage of a wretched former Confederacy. Rather, some were respectable men and good leaders who had honorably served in the military during the war.[13]

The historiography of Mississippi during Reconstruction has benefited from revisionist and postrevisionist works reassessing what transpired in the state. William C. Harris and Michael Perman each notes that military occupation gave way to civil leadership, but both approaches were unable to impede the rising tide of 1870s conservative politics and the Democratic Party. A more recent work by Nicholas Lemann chronicles the demise of Reconstruction, discussing both the violence that occurred and Ames's shaky final year in Mississippi. These books ably describe some of the political and social impediments that Ames had to navigate in postwar Mississipppi.[14]

In general, Reconstruction-centric scholarship about Mississippi is relatively minimal, even though it was a state rocked with violence, unique legislative battles, and political ramifications. Before newer interpretations in the past several decades, James W. Garner's aging *Reconstruction in Mississippi* remained the authoritative source on the Magnolia State's political activities in the 1860s and 1870s. His Dunning School–inspired study justly has drawn criticism for its post-Confederate viewpoint. His analysis is reminiscent of an era when academics had a negative attitude toward civil rights legislation and Reconstruction. Yet as part of his research, Garner interviewed former governor Ames himself. So, to understand the direction Mississippi took during Reconstruction, a new look at Ames provides some clarity.

Adelbert Ames's life and relevance thus exists in a unique place. It is extensive, tying together multiple fields, and is uniquely situated in the timeline of American history. There are few figures of note who can boast of having participated and held some moderate sway in both the Civil War and Reconstruction and also lived deep into the twentieth century. Yet Ames's story requires charting a nuanced course. It would be easy to get bogged down in the marshy weeds of minutia about his daily activities. Concurrently, it is dangerous to inflate his service and deeds. Ames is not a figure worthy of being placed on a pedestal reserved for America's Founding Fathers, greatest philosophical minds, and courageous army commanders. Like much of what exists in the writing of history, the truth lies in between, and a thoughtful depiction of his life credits his accomplishments, makes his shortcomings known, and contributes to preexisting historical works.

Ames's life is chronicled in twelve chapters. Chapter one describes his formative years. Following a brief family history, Ames's years on the Maine coastline are explored, accentuating his developing personality traits and his family's philosophies and progressive politics. The chapter also notes the growing political strife within the nation as Ames leaves the Penobscot Bay shoreline and goes to West Point. It concludes with his interaction with West Point culture, graduation, and his transition to the US regulars as the country braced for a civil war.

The next five chapters describe Ames's conduct during the war. His Civil War service is essentially divided into two parts. The first, detailed in chapters two and three, recounts his first two years of service, charting his growth from a junior officer commanding a battery at the First Battle of Bull Run to a seasoned infantry colonel. Ames's gallantry and skill during these two years made him a respected young officer in the Army of the Potomac. This led to his appointment as colonel of the Twentieth Maine Volunteers, which had its harrowing baptism under fire during the Battle of Fredericksburg in December 1862.

The second part of Ames's military service, comprising the next three chapters, examine his conduct after his promotion to general. Chapter four highlights his leadership at Brandy Station and Gettysburg, arguing that his resoluteness helped the Union army hold Cemetery Hill on July 2, 1863. Ames afterward languished amid fledgling campaigns during the Union offensives in the spring of 1864, covered in chapter five. Even though he felt that he was being relegated to the side—he was in a way—this period notes his preparedness when called upon and his good judgment in the face of bad decisions by his superiors. Even during this lowly season, his superiors had great faith in the young general. Chapter six describes Ames's promotion to major general and his leadership during the too-often overlooked First and Second Battles of Fort Fisher, initially under the command of his future father-in-law, Maj. Gen. Benjamin Butler. The taking of Fort Fisher provided Ames with arguably his greatest military feat, yet according to Ames and some of his peers, the Mainer was overlooked by the press and his commanders—his role downplayed, the glorious victory credited to others.

Chapter seven reveals an important period of time that changed Ames's outlook on life. Still serving in the postwar army occupying the American South after the war, Ames managed to obtain a twelve-month leave of absence. During this time, the young American enjoyed a yearlong sojourn across the European continent. His numerous diary entries, spanning three journals, creates an intriguing travelogue describing European politics and travel culture while, more crucially, revealing Ames's own prejudices and developing emotional maturation.

The most frequently analyzed portion of Ames's career and life, his activities during Reconstruction, is the focus of chapters eight through eleven. Returning to the army after his sabbatical, Ames and his new command transferred to the tempestuous state of Mississippi in 1867. Chapter eight makes note of why Mississippi, and other southern states, were so violent in the postwar years. In this new environment Ames learned to navigate the waters of local culture. Chapter nine then details his transition from being a military leader to an elected official and protecting former slaves. Becoming a US senator in 1870, Ames had to adapt to his new role as a politician as he developed a growing commitment to civil rights, even when it drew ire and damnation from even his own colleagues.

Chapter ten details Ames's leadership as Mississippi's elected governor, when he created an emboldening and forward-thinking agenda for the state's future. Committed to an honorable administration, he tried to create an egalitarian and prosperous Mississippi rooted in protecting civil rights and free enterprise. That meant challenging the growing brutality and unruliness of the white populous and a resurging Democratic Party that refused to comply with the governor and his administration. For the first time in his life, Ames's confidence flagged. His struggles intensified as political enemies sought to topple Republicans and their efforts in Mississippi.

Ames's subsequent impeachment trial at the hands of his political enemies is the focus of chapter eleven. Captivating both the local and the national media, his impeachment trial became a contentious clash over Reconstruction itself, not just the governor's administration. A dramatic legal battle, the impeachment led to Ames's resignation from office, the end of Reconstruction in Mississippi, and the end of his political aspirations, which had seemed bright just a few years earlier.

The final chapter describes the remaining fifty years of Ames's life. From trying to stop Jesse James during a bank robbery to fighting in the Spanish-American War, Ames's post-Reconstruction excursions were full of perilous and intriguing events. This chapter bookends the biography with stories of his family life at a time when, rather than as a member of a young, upcoming generation, Ames was now the patriarch. It concludes the story of a life of an accomplished, courageous, flawed, temperamental, but gifted American.

Adelbert Ames was an actor whose actions and activities within the Civil War and Reconstruction merit analysis. Lamentably, he has been caught in a historical purgatory, not completely unknown or forgotten, but also not having garnered the same degree of attention he deserves. Most do not know anything about him, and even historians know of him only if moderately knowledgeable of the Civil War era.

Several factors likely contribute to this. Ames lacked a defining heroic moment on the battlefield, unlike his former subordinate Chamberlain. His most valiant moments as an officer were overshadowed by others in the same battle, as at Bull Run or Fredericksburg. Another factor is that his conduct was eclipsed when credit for success was redirected to superiors, as at Malvern Hill, Gettysburg, and Fort Fisher, itself a largely ignored Civil War event, often viewed as a sideshow to the drama at Petersburg.

It is also likely that his long connection to the unlikable Benjamin Butler has worked against him. Foundational scholarship about the Civil War incorrectly dismissed Ames's father-in-law as an inept bully, which may have tarnished Ames by proxy. Furthermore, having a legacy of being an ousted governor did not help justify his place in history with earlier historians. Even with newer interpretations portraying Ames in a more favorable light, he remains simply a carpetbagger to many, or just one of many Union generals who survived the war to others. Ultimately, he has fallen through the cracks of history.

Nevertheless, Ames is a figure worthy of historical exploration. His story is uniquely positioned in the nineteenth century. From Ames's life and career, one can gain a better understanding of not just the Civil War, Reconstruction, civil rights, or nineteenth-century history but also how these topics intertwine to create modern America. His participation and experiences embody the hardship, success, and failures of this transformative period in the United States, and how that era's legacy seeps into the present.

FROM THE ROCKLAND WATERFRONT TO THE POTOMAC RIVER

Adelbert Ames spent his formative years in the quiet coastal New England community of Rockland, Maine. With a population of 5,052 in 1850, Rockland was the largest town in Lincoln County. Lime-burning kilns and shipbuilders supported its stable economy. Rockland boasted an expansive library, a multitude of schools, and two weekly newspapers, the *Rockland Gazette* and the *United States Democrat*. It also featured eight churches, including Baptist, Methodist, Unitarian, and Episcopalian congregations—Ames belonged to the last.[1]

In this coastal community, Capt. Jesse Ames and his wife, Martha, welcomed their son Adelbert into the world on October 31, 1835, their second and last child. Described as a "venturesome people," the ambitious Ames family traced their ancestry back to Scotland and England, although they had lived in the Americas for six generations by the time of Adelbert's birth. Originally spelled "Eames," the family's earliest known patriarch was Anthony Eames, born in Dorset, England, around 1595.[2] He married a woman named Margery, whose maiden name remains unknown. According to family records and genealogical histories of New England, Anthony and Margery Eames arrived in North America in the 1630s, among the first settlers in the new Massachusetts Bay Colony. By 1636, they were in Hingham, Massachusetts, settled only three years earlier, just north of the border with the struggling Plymouth Colony.[3]

Capt. Anthony Ames—he had summarily dropped the initial "E" from the surname—soon made a name for himself in the Massachusetts colony as a deputy of the General Court from 1637 to 1638 and again in 1643. He later became the leader of the Hingham militia, or "trainband," in 1644. Tensions soon arose, however, between Ames and local leaders. Most of the townspeople originally lived in Norfolk, England, located in East Anglia over 100 miles northeast of London, and were religious dissenters seeking solace in North America. Ames, in contrast, hailed from the West Country. This difference in familial origin seems to have caused dissention with their neighbors. While Ames was popular enough to gain support from some of Hingham's citizens to lead the town's military force, others supported Bozoan Allen. Having lived in Hingham longer than Ames, Allen was perhaps more importantly an ally of Reverend Peter Hobart, the Norfolk native and highly respected clergymen who had shepherded a faction of East Anglians to America in 1635. The fractious squabble between the East Anglians and others intensified in 1645. At one point, Hobart threatened to excommunicate the persistent Ames, who refused to give in to the reverend's faction. Prominent religious leaders, meanwhile, attempted to sway public opinion over who should lead the militia. The divisive conflict ultimately attracted the attention of leading colonial magistrates in the Massachusetts Bay Colony, including Governor Thomas Dudley and John Winthrop, the former governor and founder of Boston. The militia dispute persisted until 1646, when Ames finally relented. Now elderly and having held prominent roles in the town for years, he relinquished all positions of leadership and, around 1650, moved south to the town or Marshfield, located in the rival Plymouth Colony. Not dismayed by his defeat, Ames soon rose to become a prominent citizen of his new community, serving as a deputy and thus proving that his abdication in Hingham was not a death knell for his public life.[4]

The family remained stationary for two subsequent generations until Captain Ames's great-grandson Ebenezer, born in 1711, moved his family north to North Fox Island in Penobscot Bay, later part of Maine. Ebenezer's son Mark Ames and grandson John Ames stayed there for most of their lives. Fishing and farming were the staple professions of the region, and the Ames family grew in number and in stature alongside the hearty and closely knit towns down the coast. John Ames's wife, Hanna, gave birth to Adelbert's father, Jesse, on February 4, 1808. Not long after Jesse turned eleven years old, the new state of Maine entered the Union on March 15, 1820. His children, including young Adelbert, would only know their community as being part of Maine and themselves as Mainers.[5]

Jesse Ames became a master mariner. Owning and operating multiple vessels, he navigated European seas, South America's Cape Horn, and the many islands of the South Pacific. A rugged yet trustworthy man, he garnered respect from his crews and held a significant influence over the development

Capt. Jesse Ames (Ames Family and Smith College)

of his youngest son. Family histories depict Jesse as a stalwart Mainer and a trusted leader in the community. He respected his men and prudently led by example, earning a reputation as a fair and judicial leader.[6]

Jesse moved his family from Fox Island to the seafaring community of East Thomaston in the autumn of 1835, soon after Adelbert was born. While still bordering Penobscot Bay, the town benefited his ventures more so than Fox Island. East Thomaston was a larger community that also featured a shipyard, which produced a significant number of vessels for a relatively small production center. Like many of the villages and communities in the growing area, the town did not possess its original name for long. The citizens changed the name of their town to Rockland after it was incorporated in 1850, when Ames was fifteen years old.[7]

The virgin forest and natural resources that surrounded Rockland helped its industry blossom. In the 1700s, when residents in the region were still loyal to the British crown, the people sent straight and strong oak and pine trees for ship masts, grain from their bountiful wheat harvests, and fish from their well-stocked waters across the Atlantic Ocean to England. Years later, now operated by independent US citizens, those same commercial enterprises continued to flourish. Timber, grain, and cod industries helped Rockland thrive, as did quarrying deep deposits of pure limestone. Dozens of lime kilns burned in the town by the mid-1800s. The updated kilns introduced in the 1850s were forty feet tall and made from solid granite, which helped manufacturing soar. For the rest of the nineteenth century, Rockland produced more than a million casks of lime annually, which in turn required the cooperation of all facets of the town's economy. Ships brought wood from the islands nearby to fuel the kilns, craftsmen made wooden barrels to hold the powdered limestone, and farmers provided food for the growing number of townsfolk laboring along the Maine coastline.[8]

The shipping industry, in which Ames's father participated, also grew rapidly. Crafting vessels ranging from schooners to barques, Rockland's shipbuilders rivaled the production of larger ports. In 1854 alone the town constructed twenty ships comprising 17,365 tons. One lionized vessel built in 1853, the *Red Jacket*, broke records for speed, including the fastest transit from Australia to Liverpool and back. Captain Ames commanded another vessel, the *David Kimball*, weighing 500 tons. Just like the lime kilns, shipping connected all the industries in Rockland and kept the town vibrant with the influx of international goods and a growing prominence along the coastline. Although tucked away in the northeastern United States, seemingly remote from the large cities of America and the world, Ames grew up in an economically strong and nationally and internationally connected seaside community that boasted substantial financial capital.[9]

As a child, young "Del," as his family called Adelbert, watched as Jesse held positions of authority with poise and strength. Like most Ames sons, he tried to imitate his father. From an early age he craved a higher education as he attended the local public school. Intelligent and thoughtful, Adelbert also was known for being jovial; cracking jokes was commonplace for him. Although the sea captain's son usually was disciplined and capable, he also displayed a vivacious but foolish youthful energy. He notably had a penchant for mischief, according to his family. Adelbert would spend unsupervised time around the docks with the rough men who frequented there. He listened to the boisterous tales of old sailors on the wharves and was enamored by their stories of vicious storms, slave ships, and the threats of pirates in distant seas.[10]

Sometimes, Adelbert's antics frightened his parents, especially his mother. He frequently roamed Rockland with other young men, hovering around the harbor during his early teenage years. Sometimes this led to fights with other young men in East Thomaston, which his family feared presaged a future of lawlessness and delinquency. One of the supposed ways in which they tried

Martha Tolman Ames (Ames Family and Smith College)

to keep the young Adelbert out of further trouble was by encouraging his love of music. His mother enticed him to remain at home by singing songs. But it was not just his love for music that finally trumped any interest in leaving for the docks. Tapping into the young man's fierce competitive nature and the desire to display talents, his father took Adelbert and his older brother, John, hunting for waterfowl and fishing in the Maine wilderness.[11]

Literature was important too in the Ames home. On cold winter evenings, the family held reading sessions, with Captain Ames doing the yeoman's work. From the Bible to Scottish poetry, he and other family members would read aloud some of the clan's most treasured snippets. Young Del apparently loved especially *Aesop's Fables*. The *Federalist Papers* were also popular in the Ames household. Jesse revered the political philosophies espoused in the writings of James Madison and Alexander Hamilton, and his sons came to agree. The Ameses reverenced the United States and took pride of the family's military service. Often, they discussed their ancestors' participation in the American War for Independence and again during the US naval war against the Barbary Pirates.[12]

Not surprisingly, his family openly discussed politics. Adelbert's uncle, David Ames, often would visit and discuss local and national issues with Captain Ames. Jesse and his sons were Whigs and often disagreed with Uncle David, a Democrat who admired Jeffersonian politics. The Democratic Party had more operatives and a large voting base in Maine, but to Jessie's delight, the Whig Party clobbered this political establishment in 1840, giving the nation a Whig president in William Henry Harrison and Maine a Whig governor in Edward Kent. Captain Ames was one of dozens of local officers who helped coordinate the Whig convention that year and played a part in securing the state's seven electoral votes for Harrison. But the Whig success was short lived. Harrison died after only three months in office and was replaced by an anti-Jackson Democrat, John Tyler. Furthermore, state Democrats ousted Kent in the next election, thanks in large part to the Whigs receiving the lion share of the blame for a treaty with Great Britain to resolve Maine's boundary dispute with Canada. Whigs in the state believed their interests had suffered even if Anglo-American diplomacy successfully avoided a war. Although Jesse did not appreciate Democrats controlling Augusta, the lack of organization in the Whig Party exasperated him and other members across the state even more.[13]

While the Ames family shared and expressed a variety of different partisan views, their disdain for slavery united them. Maine increasingly became a hotbed for single-issue politics. Just as his parents and neighbors, Adelbert never saw slavery as acceptable. According to a family historian, "Sea captains who stooped to loading their ships with slaves and importing them from Africa were held in virulent contempt by Captain Ames and his associates."[14] The annexation of Texas in 1845 incensed antislavery politicians in Maine, including not only the entire Whig Party but also factions from Uncle David's antislavery wing of the Democrats. Six of the state's congressmen, including four Democrats, voted against the resolution, while only one Democrat voted in favor. The Mexican-American War, which began in 1846 when Adelbert was eleven years old, saw most Mainers and their legislature support the Wilmot Proviso, which they believed would impede the growth of slavery in the United States. Named after Pennsylvania Democratic congressman David Wilmot, the proposed bill sought to prevent the expansion of slavery into newly acquired land seized from Mexico during the war. The Maine legislature, with backing from the governor, notably passed a resolution in 1847 supporting the proviso. "The sentiment of this State is profound, sincere, and almost universal that the influence of slavery upon productive energy is like the blight of mildew," the resolution declared. "That is it is a moral and social evil, it does violence to the rights of man, as a thinking, reasoning, and responsible being. Influenced by such considerations, this State will oppose the introduction of slavery into any territory which may be acquired as indemnity for claims upon Mexico."[15]

A young Adelbert Ames (Ames Family and Smith College)

Adelbert Ames, according to family accounts, initially was fairly indifferent when it came to slavery, even though he never viewed it favorably. Jesse and Martha Ames, however, were quick to stress the moral severity of slavery, which eventually changed their son's mind. In addition, he had learned in his academic studies that the Supreme Court of Massachusetts interpreted the "free and equal" clause in the US Constitution to mean that an enslaved person was free from the obligation of service and thus should be free from slavery. That belief carried over into Maine's creation and separate statehood from Massachusetts in 1820. Before long, Adelbert fully became an antislavery man alongside his parents and most in Maine, a state that served as the last stop for many slaves seeking freedom by way of the Underground Railroad. Applauding the speeches of Daniel Webster and holding Harriet Beecher Stowe's *Uncle Tom's Cabin* in high regard, the young Ames grew to detest the institution of slavery immensely once he had a keen understanding of its history and brutality.[16]

Adelbert eventually witnessed the activities of southern slave markets firsthand. It was not uncommon for Jesse Ames to take members of his family with him on trips around the world. Martha, for example, sailed with her husband during a humanitarian voyage, delivering corn to Irish ports during the Great Famine. Adelbert and his mother sailed with Jesse regularly. Serving as a cabin boy, the youngest son ventured around Cape Horn around the age of fourteen. He visited ports on both the European and African continents and saw the islands of the South Pacific. With his father instructing him, Adelbert learned mathematics, geography, and navigation in real-world scenarios. This arguably instilled in him the discipline and interest in learning that would encourage aspirations to join the military. Yet while seeing the wide world was enthralling, encountering southern cities, slave ships, and slave markets in places such as New Orleans repulsed young Ames. Even if he was not concerned about the legal ramifications of slavery, or even the possibility of Black Americans gaining legal equality, he nonetheless found slavery off-putting.[17]

While Adelbert gained practical experience sailing with his father, he displayed an ability to excel in the classroom as well. The young man had high aspirations for his education and dedicated himself to self-study. He also mastered formal education at local private institutions in Maine. But his ultimate goal was to attend the US Military Academy at West Point. Acceptance to the school was difficult to obtain, yet it was exactly the place where the ambitious young man wanted to enroll. His family's military history and the reputation of the institution spurred his interest. In 1856, after his twentieth birthday, Adelbert Ames was accepted into West Point, primarily due to his uncle's friendship with a state representative and future Maine governor, Republican Abner Coburn. While he did not use "political strings to pull or to hasten his own advancement," the young man did benefit from his family being politically active in local Republican politics following the collapse of the Whig Party in 1854.[18]

Ames arrived at West Point prepared to join an institution already steeped in a tradition that brought both praise and denunciation. The administration and faculty at the academy were keen on making engineering and science as invaluable to a young cadet as military exercises. Beginning in 1817, West Point superintendent Sylvanus Thayer had embraced French curriculums from the *Ecole Polytechnique* to guide the instructors teaching cadets. Although Thayer left West Point twenty-three years before Ames arrived, his legacy continued. Future antebellum superintendents did not leave such a consequential mark, but all came from engineering backgrounds, including Capt. John G. Barnard, who oversaw the academy the summer Ames arrived, and Richard Delafield, who replaced Barnard that autumn.[19] Ames immediately felt comfortable with his new surroundings. He eagerly applied himself to his work and education and quickly assumed a leadership role among the new cadets: "To Ames, West

Point was an inspiring experience and with enthusiasm and native drive he took leadership not only in military drills and maneuvers but also in his intellectual work."[20]

Critics charged that the system at West Point leaned too much into science and engineering while slighting strategy and weaponry, with military science confined to a cadet's senior year. Nevertheless, the academy purposely funneled its best students toward engineering, with all but one officer in the peacetime Engineer Corps a graduate of the academy. The intellectual demands of an infantry officer were less significant and in theory could be handled by an inferior graduate, but West Point men who had good to high marks were destined to serve with topographers or use their mathematical prowess to help artillery units hit their targets with precision. Some of the brightest minds who graduated never actually considered military strategy after leaving the banks of the Hudson. Instead, they worked on federal engineering projects, something more valuable than combat experience for the United States at a time when its regular army numbered 16,000 men. Graduating cadets were most likely to encounter combat while confronting Native Americans on the Great Plains and in the Southwest, where they found themselves assigned to cavalry or infantry.[21]

Crucially, Ames arrived in West Point as the institution was experiencing a radical metamorphosis. In 1856 the academy implemented a fifth year to its curriculum. Vigorously debated for years, Congress altered the program at West Point to allow more cadets to enter and to expand their training beyond engineering and mathematics. Opposed to making it even more arduous to gain admittance by having prerequisites, West Point alumnus and secretary of war Jefferson Davis also supported the move to expand the courses offered. Ames and his classmates would take more classes in history, geography, literature, English, and linguistics than their predecessors. While some new cadets floundered, Ames excelled. In 1857 his name appeared on the list of the academy's most distinguished cadets, and he received the cadet rank of corporal his first year. At the conclusion of that year, Ames ranked second in his class.

In an increasingly stern environment under Delafield's leadership, Ames thrived. Having already served at West Point from 1838 to 1845, Delafield had established a record of strictness. He zealously enforced regulations, punishing infractions severely. No letters or diaries by Ames exist from his time at West Point, but he doubtless did not appreciate the fire drills Delafield scheduled during cadets' rare moments of free time on Saturday afternoons. Nevertheless, Ames persisted with his studies and duties without falling behind.[22]

And it was easy to become overwhelmed at West Point. Upperclassmen harassed younger cadets, graduates from the antebellum era recalling having to stand up to arrogant classmates who looked down on them. At times fisticuffs ensued. Even seemingly mundane tasks could incite stress for Ames and his contemporaries. Cadets had roughly twenty minutes to scarf down their food at each of their three daily meals. They had to eat a breakfast of bread, butter, and hash or a diner of fibrous beef and boiled potatoes before they heard "squad rise," indicating that their mealtime had ended. In the classroom the young men had to maintain perfect posture; anyone who slouched in the classroom received a tongue-lashing from their instructor. Denis Hart Mahan, under whom Ames studied, was known to be particularly displeased if someone hunched over in his class. Father of famed naval theorist Alfred Thayer Mahan, the professor's nasal voice would shake a student from his stupor, after which he would sit up straight and pay attention.[23]

Although secluded from the rest of the nation—they were preoccupied with staying on top of their work as well—cadets at West Point followed key events taking place beyond the Hudson Valley. One of the more divisive court decisions in American history occurred during Ames's first year, and its effects reverberated around West Point's grounds. The Dred Scott decision of March 6, 1857, culminated a ten-year legal battle between enslaved man Dred Scott and his legal owner for his freedom. *Dred Scott v. Sandford* eventually arrived on the docket of the US Supreme Court, which decided on a 7–2 ruling that Scott—and by proxy all Black members of society—was not a US citizen and never could be one. Moreover, by defining enslaved African Americans as property and not as people (much less citizens), the ruling theoretically threw open the West to the expansion of slavery. Congress, the court argued, had no authority to limit slavery's expansion either. Chief Justice Roger B. Taney's majority decision tried to maintain the precarious balance between free states and slave states, but the outcome of the case only intensified cultural and political intensity in the United States.[24]

Attempts to insulate West Point from this and other political firestorms failed, even after the faculty banned student debate over slavery and sectionalism. From instructors to cadets, the tensions of the outside world leaked into their education and military training. After Dred Scott and the even more divisive raid by John Brown on Harpers Ferry, Virginia, in October 1859, it was nearly impossible for faculty to police political discourse. According to historian Wayne Hsieh, "violent fracases among cadets" were not uncommon.[25] The cadets were not the only ones. Commissioned officers, especially antislavery "free soilers," frequently found themselves tasked with following orders that they considered proslavery. Nevertheless, nationalist and Unionist fervor at the academy remained relatively solid. Even during Ames's period as a student, some southern-born cadets elected to support the Union over sectionalism. Among West Point graduates from 1800 to 1860, 43 percent from the Upper South and 12 percent from the Lower South chose to fight for the Union during the Civil War. Although neither group represented a majority of cadets from those regions, Ames's loyalty to the Union was also shared by many classmates from southern communities. Political tensions aside, Ames excelled at his academic work and academy duties. He became one of a handful of cadet captain his final year, boasting four bars on his collar.[26]

Ames put his quick and analytical mind to work in as many ways as possible. Shining in mathematics, engineering, artillery tactics, and mechanical draftsmanship, he devoted countless hours to his books in his final year in 1860. Although engineering reigned supreme, senior cadets such as Ames received strategic instruction for the infantry, artillery, and cavalry. All students at West Point also practiced military maneuvers as often as possible. The expanded curriculum created more chances for such instruction, and the number of practical drills skyrocketed. Infantry drills rose from 540 to 695 per year, artillery drills increased to 252 from 216, and fencing doubled from 108 to 216. Marksmanship and bayonet drills for the future officers also increased. Ames took to his lessons and instructions well.[27]

Yet despite his achievements, Ames—at least according to the Military Academy—was not a perfect student, but he came closer than most. Cadets received demerits for breaking rules or for unbecoming behavior such as being violent, disorderly, or continually lazy. Ames received only two demerits during his time at West Point, not for rambunctious behavior or disregarding orders but for "spending too much time reading and drawing," instead of dedicating himself to his work, and for not returning his books to the academy library at the proper time.[28]

Cadet Adelbert Ames (US Military Academy Library)

After five years of research and study, Ames graduated fifth in his class out of forty-five students. The senior class at West Point—Ames's group—graduated on May 6, 1861, while a second class graduated in June. Both groups produced bright, intelligent, and gifted young officers. The top-four graduating cadets received commissions in the engineers or the artillery. The army awarded fifth-placed Ames a commission as second lieutenant in the Second US Artillery Regiment. The Second Artillery had a prestigious lineage, serving with distinction in the Mexican-American War. Yet a number of cadets did not accept their commissions. The chaos of the national crisis came to a head that year, resulting in dozens of cadets changing their loyalties from the United States to the newly established Confederate States of America, severing the final threads that had kept the military's nationalistic identity together. Twenty-four of Ames's classmates resigned their commissions to fight for the South. Two of them, John Pelham and Thomas Lafayette Rosser, left West Point before they officially graduated to fight for the Confederacy. The defection of Rosser seemed surprising. While he would frequently clash against former classmates on the battlefield, Ames had never doubted his allegiance to the Union.[29]

Eight days after receiving his commission, Ames was promoted to first lieutenant. A week after this, the army sent him to Washington to assist in training recruits as part of a member of Capt. Charles Griffin's Battery D, Fifth US Artillery. This special battery consisted of four artillery pieces and seventy men. Originally stationed at West Point and garnering the moniker "West Point Battery," Griffin's men comprised capable and respected men siphoned from dragoon and other artillery attachments. On January 31, 1861, the battery had left New York and arrived in Washington, DC, where it was redesignated Battery D, Fifth Artillery and Griffin was promoted from first lieutenant to captain. Ames arrived there by May 12 to assume his duties as Griffin's second in command.[30]

His home state promptly tried to wrest him away from the regular army. Maine quickly raised volunteer regiments for the war, and Rockland produced four companies for the Fourth Maine Volunteer Infantry. Before Ames left for West Point, Hiram G. Berry, a native of Rockland and former mayor, created the Rockland Guard to serve as the local militia company. After the attack on Fort Sumter, Berry went to Augusta and received orders to recruit for the Fourth Maine. Naturally, he recruited the men who he knew from the militia. By May 8, the regiment, including the four companies from Rockland, had assembled just outside of that town, where its commissioned officers held an election to determine who should lead the regiment. They selected Berry as colonel and named Ames as their choice for lieutenant colonel. But they were to be disappointed. Whether Ames wanted to serve alongside fellow Mainers from Rockland—the evidence is murky—the War Department refused to allow the unit to take him from Battery D.[31]

Lieutenant Ames and other recent West Point graduates continued to train new recruits and do their utmost to prepare the masses of volunteer soldiers flooding the streets of the District of Columbia. Equally as numerous as the soldiers in Washington were the fireflies, which by the end of June were reported as being unusually copious. During these weeks, rain fell with regularity in the capital city and would sometimes drench the officers and enlisted men.[32] While senior officers in the Union attempted to develop an organized army, Ames and other highly educated junior officers provided disciplined and detailed instruction to the troops who would comprise the Federal fighting force.

The volunteers impressed Ames, who noted that they responded well to instruction. One regiment under his tutelage, the Twelfth New York Militia, stood out to the young officer. He wrote friend, colonel, and fellow Mainer Oliver Otis Howard describing the volunteers. "We have at least not less than thirty thousand troops here," Ames informed him. "The volunteers are intelligent looking men. In fact, I never saw finer looking men than taken in a body than they are."[33] He also revealed a New England bias when noting the stellar presentation of the First and Second Rhode Island Volunteer Regiments: "Their gentlemanly bearing—for they are all gentlemen—the happy adaptation to service—their intelligence, for they are the first society in the New England states—strike the beholder at once and he feels he is not in the presence of ordinary troops."[34]

Not every regular-army officer drilling the raw troops in Washington in 1861 had the same attitude toward volunteers as Ames did. Many did not mesh well with the citizen-soldiers they had to instruct. An air of elitism was rife among West Pointers and regulars, extending all the way at the top of the army. Brevet Lt. Gen. Winfield Scott, general in chief of the US Army, advocated that President Lincoln expand the size US regulars. Scott vehemently disagreed with the president's decision not to do so. His experience fighting British and Mexican troops had convinced him that American volunteers were subpar and incompetent, and the US regulars had come a long way since the end of the Mexican-American War in 1848. Most West Point alumnus shared Scott's views since volunteers did not have the years of training in military science they possessed. Fractures between strict officers and independent volunteers developed. Even more taxing was that only around 12 percent of West Point graduates who left the military prior to the Civil War came back to the military. Thus, impulsive and pompous junior officers fresh out of West Point, with little relatability to volunteers, had to prepare them for military service that was as alien to most of the raw recruits as the outer reaches of the solar system.[35]

As May gave way to June, Ames continued to drill volunteers on the basics of soldiering. During his time in Washington, he lived along Sixth Street, in close proximity to the White House, but did not enjoy these lodgings for long. On July 4 Battery D moved to the heights of Arlington, Virginia, across the Potomac River from the capital, and shortly thereafter marched to Fairfax. The unit did not encounter any Confederate forces during this first foray into Virginia, although the men and the entire Federal force they accompanied anxiously anticipated their first chance to fight.[36]

The young officer's appearance looked proper as Battery D left the capital. Ames had matured to a height of over six feet and possessed a lean, athletic build. His appearance looked professional, with a new blue uniform and sardine-box shoulder straps bearing the single-bar rank insignia of a first lieutenant. In contrast to his stylized haircut, with a part on the left side, Ames bore a thick mustache and a long goatee—brunette like his hair and making his cleanshaven cadet portrait look like another man. His hazel eyes had a glint of whimsy and adventure, which they retained through most of his life, yet they also had the intense glare of a motivated individual with a military education. Looking the part of a Union officer, Ames began to move with his comrades toward a Confederate army stationed roughly thirty miles from Washington, DC—near Manassas Junction, Virginia.[37]

FRESH LIEUTENANT TO SEASONED COLONEL

Both the Union soldiers and the folks back home believed that one major clash against Confederate forces in northern Virginia could bring the war to a swift conclusion. With that sentiment in mind, Ames and Battery D left the confines of Washington on July 16, 1861, as a part of Col. Andrew Porter's First Brigade of Col. David Hunter's Second Division, Army of Northeastern Virginia, commanded by veteran staff officer Brig. Gen. Irvin McDowell of Ohio. McDowell led two-thirds of his raw 35,000-man army—the largest in American history to that point—toward roughly 23,000 Confederate troops, commanded by Brig. Gen. P. G. T. Beauregard, camped near the strategic railroad station at Manassas Junction. He hoped to threaten the rear of the Confederate forces by cutting the railroad to the south and severing communications with Richmond. If the plan worked, the Rebel troops would at least withdraw from the area, and Washington could breathe easier. At best, the war might end.[1]

There were, however, many contingencies to McDowell's plan. Confederate troops to the west in the Shenandoah Valley, under Brig. Gen. Joseph E. Johnston, had to remain there to keep Beauregard at a numerical disadvantage and benefit the Union attack. Although McDowell was skeptical, Winfield Scott, the commanding general of the Federal army, promised that forces at Harpers Ferry under Maj. Gen. Robert Patterson could accomplish that goal. McDowell, meanwhile, needed his supply trains to run smoothly and his raw soldiers to march orderly and expediently, which was an immense task to ask of the rookie troops. Orders from Union officers fell on deaf ears as volunteers routinely separated from their units. Stragglers left their companies to pick blackberries, take breaks, and relieve themselves. Some pillaged homes, while others trudged along in the intense heat, trying to march with a properly erect military bearing. Ames and his battery at least were "professional soldiers" and marched competently compared to the volunteer regiments.[2]

McDowell grew alarmed on July 18 when rumors circulated that Johnston's forces were in route to Manassas Junction via railroad. This would mean that Patterson had failed. Indeed, Valley Confederates began reinforcing Beauregard, and McDowell's numerical superiority dwindled as Johnston's forces continued to flow east. With the opposing numbers approaching equivalency, McDowell proposed an immediate attack. At 2:30 A.M. on July 21, he ordered his troops forward. Their march toward the battlefield was congested, and their advance during the hot, dusty morning that followed was long and laborious. Vanguard regiments crossed Bull Run, north of the Confederate positions, and startled the enemy pickets. One Union general noted that this early portion of the battle consisted of feeble and tedious advances. By 5:15 A.M., artillery fire began, and its intensity multiplied within an hour.[3]

Ames and Battery D, armed with four Parrott rifles and two twelve-pound howitzers, did not participate in the initial phases of the battle. Captain Griffin later reported having to make a march of twelve miles to the field. As the engagement progressed, however, the battery, joined by Capt. James B. Rickett's battery from the First US Artillery, advanced through woods on the edge of the battlefield and moved their pieces within a thousand yards of the Confederate defensive line on Henry House Hill along the southwest–northeast Warrenton Turnpike. Once in position, Ames and his comrades dueled with Confederate cannoneers commanded by Brig. Gen. Thomas J. Jackson, soon to be nicknamed "Stonewall" because of his steadfast actions with his infantry brigade that day. Union infantry persistently pushed Confederate troops back, and McDowell ordered Ricketts and Griffin to lead their artillery crews to Henry House Hill itself, where the enemy determined to make a stand.

Supported by the Eleventh New York Volunteer Infantry, Griffin's Battery D redeployed at 11:30 A.M. and opened fire from its position near the western spur of the hill. His guns delivered a lethal and relentless barrage, silencing the Confederate batteries situated across the field. "At this time my brigade occupied a line considerably in advance of that first occupied by the left wing of the enemy," Colonel Porter noted. "The Battery [D] was pouring its withering fire into the batteries and columns of the enemy whenever they exposed themselves." He continued, "The batteries of Ricketts and Griffin, by their fine discipline, wonderful, daring and matchless skill, were the prime features in the fight." But while the artillerists neutralized the Confederate batteries, Ricketts's men came under heavy fire from sharpshooters. Further complicating the situation, Ricketts and Griffin operated independently of each other instead of working in unison. Furthermore, the artillerists were so close to enemy forces that they had trouble calculating the proper distance of their targets. Griffin then made a risky maneuver, sending two of his pieces

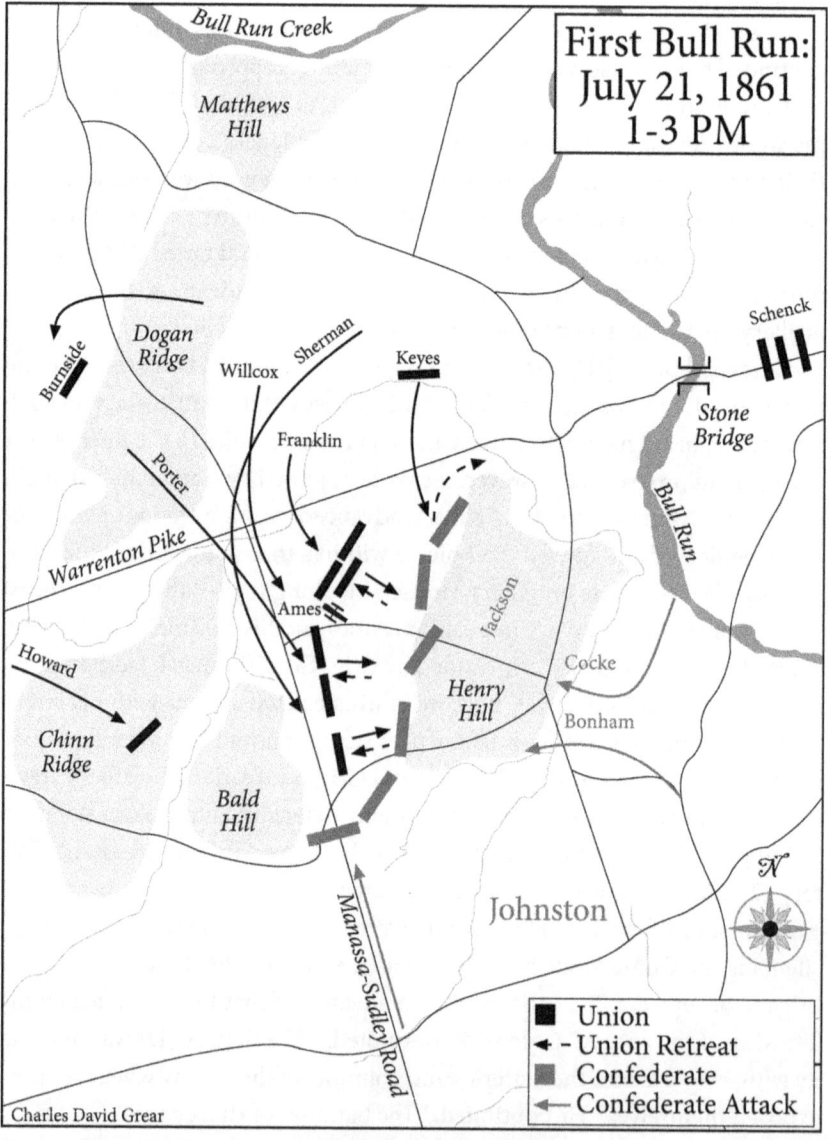

First Bull Run: July 21, 1861, 1–3 P.M. (Charles David Grear)

to the extreme right of the Union line on the hill. This divided his force and made his crews even more vulnerable.[4]

The proximity to Confederate soldiers jeopardized the safety of Griffin's unprotected artillerymen, and casualties mounted. During one of the first enemy volleys, a musket ball struck Ames in the thigh, dropping him to the ground. As noted by Griffin: "Lieut. Ames was wounded so as to be unable to ride a horse at almost the first fire; yet he sat by his command directing fire, being helped on and off the caisson during the different changes of front or position, refusing to leave the field until he became too weak to sit up."[5]

Griffin's battery suffered catastrophic losses. When a column of troops in blue uniforms approached from the woods to the right, the captain prepared to fire canister into the oncoming soldiers. But Maj. William F. Barry, Griffin's superior, assumed that the troops were Federal infantry coming to support the guns and ordered the battery to stand down. The artillerymen relaxed. A moment later a deadly volley ripped through the battery, felling men and horses. Instead of Union reserves, the men were Confederates wearing similar uniforms. The Thirty-Third Virginia Infantry, formed in the Shenandoah Valley and part of Jackson's brigade, dispersed Yankee infantrymen and artillerymen alike with their volleys. Col. Arthur C. Cummings, the Thirty-Third's commander, recalled, "Our orders were to wait until the enemy were within thirty paces, then to fire and charge with the bayonet." Although untested, his Virginians swarmed Griffin's battery. "No old regulars ever made a more gallant charge, though not a very regular one," attested the colonel. Making matters worse, Jackson sent two more of his regiments to take Ricketts's battery, which they promptly did. The Confederates also captured Ricketts, wounded four times and lying beside one of his guns, but Griffin and Ames managed to retreat. Ames's ongoing blood loss and refusal to leave nearly killed him. His leg bled out along with Union chances of victory that day.[6]

After rallying from a disastrous morning start, the Confederates drove the entire Union army from the field by evening. With Battery D suffering a significant loss of twenty-seven men and fifty-five horses, Griffin's survivors fled the field. A member of the Thirty-Third Virginia afterward wrote his parents "that part of the field, with the famous Griffin's Battery, was ours." According to Griffin, the confused retreat made it "impossible to take more than three field pieces from the field." More galling, the battery lost a fourth gun during the army's pell-mell withdraw, rescuing only one Parrott rifle and one howitzer. One historian wrote that the overall retreat was so disorganized that it was "nearly impossible to determine" the routes the fleeing regiments took. The roads northward, clogged with weary and woebegone troops, also featured astonished and distressed civilians. Washington socialites, who had come to watch the battle, found themselves surrounded by soldiers and discarded war materials in the meadows alongside the roadways. As the *Baltimore Sun* reported, "For a time, a perfect panic prevailed."[7]

After crossing Bull Run, Ames's men helped their lieutenant onto an ammunition wagon that bounced and listed but carried the young officer all the way back to Washington. Without springs, it only added to the misery of his injury and made the journey an excruciatingly painful one. Even after suffering significant losses in both manpower and field pieces, Battery D's commander could not help but praise the efforts of his unit. "I would state that my officers and men behaved in a most gallant manner, displaying great fearlessness, and doing their duty as becomes brave soldiers," Griffin wrote. He particularly praised Ames. The young lieutenant displayed determination and discipline in his first battle. Still, this opening fight at Bull Run was a demoralizing defeat for the North. "It is a sad duty to record a defeat accompanied with the loss of so many valuable lives," recalled a Union colonel. "But defeat should only make us more faithful still to the great cause."[8]

For the next several weeks, Ames slowly recovered from his wound in a military hospital in the District of Columbia. When it finally had healed and no longer incapacitated him, he left the hospital. Although the date of his release is unknown, Ames noted that by early October, he could move about without encumbrance. He could also go riding "at all times without inconvenience or harm." His letters home from Washington also highlighted the life of a junior officer, contained clever observations about politics, and displayed his increasing confidence. He enjoyed his comfortable winter quarters in the capital and having his father visit him at Camp Duncan, but he also despised the administrative minutia of filling out quarterly returns and other paperwork. Ames frequently wrote about spending time with notable Republican politicians, specifically John Rice and Lot Morrill of Maine, who might advance his career, even though he was keen on earning his promotions. The Mainer contemplated resigning his commission in the regular army and commanding volunteer troops from his native state. He also commented on the political attitudes of the nation, including the Confederacy. On one occasion, after talking with a paroled Union prisoner, Ames noted how the staunch animosity against Lincoln and the government in the South might only come from elites, that "the middle and lower classes were indifferent or partly sympathizing with the Union." His confidence grew during these months, many times bragging about senior officers praising him, his ability to train soldiers, and how his men will "make a noise if I can have my way."⁹

Writing home on October 3, Ames was jubilant. Gifts from his parents—a glass and pistol—brought him joy. He also was pleased to hear that his brother, John, was seeking a position in the Union army. Almost immediately upon his hospital discharge, the army sent Lieutenant Ames to Camp Duncan on the outskirts of Washington to train fresh recruits, just as he had done prior to Bull Run. On October 5, however, Ames officially received command of his own unit, Battery A, Fifth US Artillery, and promotion to brevet major in the US Volunteers. "I am in command of the battery," he wrote his parents. "The Captain [Griffin] has been promoted to Lieutenant Colonel on [Maj.] Gen. [George B.] McClellan's staff," he added, referring to the new commander of Federal forces at Washington, renamed the Army of the Potomac. "I shall be a Lieutenant commanding a battery." Ames reveled in the fact that the unit would now be known as "Ames's Battery." "I shall not have to ask my native state to do anything for me now," he declared. "General Barry, Chief of Artillery, came to see me at sunrise last Sunday morning for the purpose of telling me the gratifying news. . . . As I have received this position as a free gift from my superiors I shall exert myself more strenuously if possible than had it come by force."¹⁰

The promotion and assignment altered Ames's thinking about commanding volunteers. Although volunteer officers held higher ranks within those regiments, he and his fellow West Point graduates believed that they possessed more military intellect and skill as professionals and so deserved to command regulars. In one letter home at the end of 1861, Ames told his parents that he had asked a fellow Mainer, Maj. Seth Williams, the assistant adjutant general for the Army of the Potomac, to get a West Point graduate transferred to his battery for that exact reason. Ames, and many West Pointers of his ilk, thought it was worth forsaking the possibility of more rapid volunteer promotions than to command units in the field that purportedly lacked discipline and scattered like waterfowl at the site of a hunter.¹¹

Meanwhile, from September 1861 to March 1862, Ames and his new command helped defend Washington and the surrounding area during what was a dreary winter. The continued proximity of Confederate troops south of the Potomac River, coupled with political realities in Washington, forced McClellan to station troops to protect the capital. During this otherwise mundane period, Ames instilled military discipline within his unit and soon became known for unyielding consistency when training new soldiers.¹²

In quiet moments Ames took time to describe his gloomy state of mind while in Washington, making comments about more than just his life as an officer in the Union army. In December he lamented that his letter writing had been unsatisfactory, his correspondence affected by having his battery temporarily located at Camp Hooker, Maryland. Perhaps more indicative of his morale, he now believed that John—now married and with a family—ought to avoid going to war entirely (which he purportedly did).[13]

Social affairs that winter brightened his outlook to some degree. Ames, according to his contemporaries, was a handsome and dashing young officer who already could boast of valiant service and gallant conduct. Yet he purposely distanced himself from courtship and the possibility of marriage. Ames wrote home before Christmas that he had attended multiple weddings that winter and had served as "a groomsman for a couple of my friends." He enjoyed the festivities but disapprovingly described a "mania" that had taken over young officers in the army. The innumerable marital unions in 1861, in his opinion, adversely affected military service. "Such a step in such a time as this impairs a young officer's usefulness and advancement, so it will be a long day before we shall entertain any ideas of the kind." That Ames was not seeking courtship, however, did not mean that he was going unnoticed. On December 31, again writing to his parents on the eve of the new year, he admitted having received a letter from "Miss Lucy McLean, inviting me to resume our suspended correspondence. What could a young gentleman do under the circumstances but comply?"[14]

Still, Ames kept his mind largely on military affairs. With another campaign looming on the horizon, he impatiently waited for his opportunity to lead his battery in a large campaign. Although it was hardly a pitched battle, the battery did come under fire while at Camp Hooker. Writing home to his parents on December 4, Ames reported: "My men were frequently under fire, and I hope when they meet the enemy they will not disgrace me. Heretofore they have displayed the proper spirit, and if I have influence they will hereafter."[15]

With the exception of this brief skirmish, the young officer and his battery remained in the vicinity of Washington all winter. Ames wrote to his mother and father, "My health is excellent, and I have been laboring very, *very* hard." As he and his troops waited, the lieutenant felt the utmost confidence that his battery would develop into one of the finest in the army. In late December he boasted: "My battery is progressing finely. While confident, Ames repeatedly claimed that it was not vanity with which he described his command and their progress.[16]

McClellan began to assemble and better organize the newly christened Army of the Potomac into a massive, well-equipped, and well-organized fighting force. Although the army grew in numbers, McClellan hesitated to share with the administration any plans about his first major campaign as its commander. As impatient as Ames, President Lincoln issued General Orders No. 1 on January 27, 1862, requiring that McClellan make an advance by February 22. Lincoln wanted him to strike the Confederates stationed at Manassas Junction. In a lengthy letter of rebuttal, McClellan explained his objections to the president's order. "Although never formally revoked," he later recalled, "it is to be assumed that my letter produced, for a time at least, the desired effect." McClellan did not like the prospects of the overland attack that Lincoln wanted and divulged to the president his revised plans on February 2. Intending to outflank Confederate forces, the young major general wanted to transport his army by water to Urbanna, Virginia, march up the peninsula formed by the Rappahannock and York Rivers, cut off Johnston's troops at Manassas, and then advance to capture Richmond.[17] Even if the army failed to take the Rebel capital initially, McClellan assured Lincoln that the Army of the Potomac could entice the Confederate defenders "to come out and attack us" on ground of his choosing. Lincoln decried that suggestion. If the army took that route, it would leave Washington undefended against the Rebels at Manassas. McClellan's plan then began to disintegrate. Johnston withdrew his forces south from Manassas and across the Rappahannock River, negating any advantage that Urbanna offered. Upon learning of this, McClellan adjusted his plan, directing his army farther south to Union-controlled Fort Monroe on the Virginia Peninsula, formed by the James and York Rivers. With political pressures in Washington mounting and frustration among the troops growing noticeable, McClellan briefly pursued Johnston, turned back to the Potomac, and finally began to move his army downriver into Chesapeake Bay on March 17. Over the next two weeks, he transported thousands of troops to the Peninsula at Fort Monroe.[18]

"No one is more anxious for an advance than I," the impetuous young lieutenant wrote his parents. Ames recounted his joy that his battery had left the familiar confines of Washington along with his banal duties and concerns, which ranged from having to chronicle all of his military property to dealing with plaguy rumors that Congress was considering reducing the wages of officers. The only "action" he had experienced since McClellan took command was a duel between himself and the vermin in his tent. "A large rat has taken possession of my tent," he explained, "I ruling supreme during the day, and he during [the] night. He treats me badly—wakes me up at night, runs through the mud and then drags his tail over my pillow, walks on my letter paper, and pokes his nose into my affairs. . . . For his rudeness I am feeding him—bread and butter spiced with arsenic."[19] When the Peninsula Campaign finally commenced, Ames was more than prepared to participate.

Finally receiving orders to move out on March 10, Ames and his battery set off to fight Confederate forces instead of combating boredom and invasive rodents. As his command of 150 men proceeded toward Alexandria, he confidently wrote: "The war is, in my opinion, drawing to a close. These continued reverses must of necessity dishearten the rebels. They *must* yield sooner or later." His belief in his troops, and the army as a whole, was high. In a letter to his brother—an admirer of Union troops in the West—Ames admitted that there was little evidence to support his own faith. "You still believe 'we of the West' are more courageous than we of the East," he wrote. "Well, John, I have no particular desire to make you think the contrary—even if I could." While his brother confidentially praised soldiers in the western theater, especially after the fall of Forts Henry and Donelson, Lieutenant Ames reminded him that throughout history "the bravest men from most early periods have suffered the same way." Even the greatest European armies had at one time or another disorderly retreated. Thus, John should be "charitable" and not believe that all the brave and competent Union men were fighting west of the Appalachian Mountains. In due time Ames and the merit of the Army of the Potomac would present itself as it marched to take the Confederate capital of Richmond.[20]

By March 17, Lieutenant Ames wrote that he was in Alexandria, roughly 100 miles from the seat of Southern political power. "In fact, the greater part of the Army of the Potomac has assembled around this city for shipment to some point from which I presume we will make a straight line for Richmond," he informed his family. In another letter he remained full of conviction. "Our Northern army is better disciplined, more numerous, and more persevering than our hot-headed neighbors at the South," he wrote. "Perhaps I may not be in another battle *this* war," he continued, but a swift Confederate defeat would be "glorious news to our country" even if it did not provide battlefield glory for himself.[21]

As Ames he noted, the Confederacy had reason for concern. A massive Union army had mobilized against it and panic ensued among its people. The *Richmond Dispatch* nervously declared: "The enemy are at the gates. Who will take the lead and act, act, act?" As the Southern forces awaited the bayonets of McClellan's massive command, Ames and his battery boarded transports, steamed down the river and the bay, and went ashore at Fort Monroe.

The battery then moved into position outside of a town already known for its involvement in the American Revolution—Yorktown, Virginia.[22]

Confederate forces held the famous town behind extensive fortifications. Ames's superiors told him to dig in and await further instructions. McClellan, chagrined by the unexpected fieldworks as well as an unanticipated river cutting across his path, decided to set up a siege and pound the Confederates into submission with artillery. Ames speculated about the potential outcomes of the developing operation. "I am not permitted or rather orders forbid all persons writing about military operations in the field," he wrote to his family. "I can only tell you we are to have a siege here. Of this I am not certain; it is simply my opinion."[23]

Once the siege began on April 5, West Point–trained engineers suddenly were in high demand. Col. Henry Hunt, commander of the Union Artillery Reserve, ordered Lieutenant Ames to help oversee the construction of a section of the Federal earthworks while remaining in command of his battery. Although the lack of combat exasperated the young officer, Ames remained in relatively good spirits. Instead of complaining, he shared with his parents the names of his subordinates, the occupations of their fathers, and the local weather conditions, which he remarkably described as "delightful," given constant rain and deep mud. Union troops under Brig. Gen. William Farrar "Baldy" Smith broke through the Confederate defenses on April 16. McClellan, convinced that Maj. Gen. John B. Magruder, the local Southern commander, had more troops, "called him [Smith] back rather than reinforcing the breach." On May 5, after delaying the Federal advance for a month, Confederate defenders withdrew from Yorktown just before McClellan's planned assault. They left behind not only the town but also a Union army that had now developed logistical issues and began to emulate the hesitant idiosyncrasies of its commander. Ames for one did not appreciate the sluggish approach of the Army of the Potomac, yet he tried to remain positive. None of his letters in May 1862 point toward frustration or depression resulting from military operations thus far.[24]

Moving northwest from Yorktown, Ames and the Fifth Artillery plodded through mud and dust toward West Point, Virginia, having missed the bloody Battle of Williamsburg, fought by Johnston's rear guard. From West Point he wrote to his parents: "I have yet seen no fighting. . . . It is possible, however, that they may retire South, giving up Virginia without a struggle." Convinced that Confederate forces would falter in an outright battle against the Army of the Potomac, Ames remained confident that McClellan would draw them into a large-scale engagement. "We all have the greatest confidence in General McClellan—politicians notwithstanding," stated Ames. "A successful battle here will soon terminate the war."[25]

That decisive engagement did not come. The mismanaged two-day battle of Seven Pines (or Fair Oaks) took place on the outskirts of Richmond from May 31 into June 1. It was the closest battle fought to the Rebel capital and the first significant engagement for the Army of the Potomac. Yet it was inconclusive operationally, and Ames and his battery were not involved. Both sides incurred sizable losses, however. Union forces suffered 5,031 casualties, and the Confederates endured 6,134—including their commanding officer, General Johnston. Arguably the greatest ramification of the battle, Johnston's wounding allowed Gen. Robert E. Lee to assume command of what he soon rechristened as the Army of Northern Virginia.[26]

By early June, Ames's impatience was obvious. His parents, who had decided to leave the coast of Maine for the promising plains of Minnesota, could sense their son's frustration when they received his letters. "I must express my disappointment at my success," wrote the Mainer, "or because of want of success thus far; notwithstanding the many minor fights that have taken place since we started I have not been in one." As fellow classmates such as Edmund Kirby intrepidly led their commands on the battlefield, Ames resigned himself to the situation: "I probably shall not get into any [battles]. . . . I do not think I could be in a more secure [and safe] place than I am now." Two weeks later he remained in camp along the Chickahominy River east of Richmond. Ames bemoaned his current position and lack of action. "I have not been in any of the engagements that have taken place here," the ambitious young officer lamented on June 15. "And I think it very doubtful if I have the fortune to be in any. I am quite disgusted with my own ill luck." Ames was upset and his pride hurt. "I might as well be in St. Paul [Minnesota] so as far as fighting goes," he complained.[27]

While Ames stewed over his predicament, he still managed to wrest humor from the situation. His continued bachelorhood had prompted his Aunt Nancy to propagate a rumor. "I was informed recently that I was engaged to Miss Julia Hills!" he wrote. "I was quite surprised to hear it, as the thought never crossed my mind before. I suppose by what I heard that I have to thank Aunt Nancy. She evidently takes malicious delight in circulating improbable stories about her relatives."[28] Nevertheless, the young officer, supremely confident in his acumen and abilities, felt helpless in his current state. In an expedient turn of events, however, Ames and his battery became key participants in a pair of significant battles.

The Seven Days' Battles, fought between June 25 and July 1, 1862, culminated the Peninsula Campaign. On June 25, Union troops took up the offensive during a minor attack at the Battle of Oak Grove but gained little ground. During the Seven Days, Lee's initial goal was to destroy the Federal V Corps, under Brig. Gen. Fitz John Porter, isolated north of the flooded Chickahominy. The Battle of Mechanicsville (or Beaver Dam Creek) commenced on June 26. While a tactical victory for the Union army—V Corps repelled multiple Confederate attacks—it proved a strategic victory for Lee. Federal forces withdrew to Gaines's Mill at the end of the day, but Lee orchestrated a more successful attack there.[29]

Ames and his battery finally engaged the enemy on June 27 at Gaines's Mill, much to his delight. In a rare instance, the Confederate attackers outnumbered the Federal defenders. With the V Corps threatened on its right flank by Stonewall Jackson, and Porter unable to pull back the corps fast enough due to the high river and a lack of bridges, McClellan rightfully feared that a withdraw would expose the rear of the Union army. Thus, he ordered all available troops to reinforce the corps as the remaining Federal forces marched toward Malvern Hill, along the north bank of the James River. Porter, meanwhile, established a formidable semicircle defensive position along the north bank of the Chickahominy. With two divisions committed to this line and two divisions in reserve, Union troops adjacent to Dr. William F. Gaines's mill awaited the impending assault from six Confederate divisions. Of all of the scenarios to test the leadership and abilities of a young artillery commander, this was far from the easiest.[30]

To protect the troops south of the Chickahominy, Porter placed six reserve batteries on bluffs near James M. Garnett's farm. Ames detailed the actions of his command. Stationed near the farm, just next to Gaines's Mill, the lieutenant and his men waited along the banks of the Chickahominy. Ames's Battery A, possessing six light twelve-pound guns, received orders to move to a knoll behind Union earthworks in a wheat field near Garnett's farmhouse. At noon the unit came under heavy fire from what Ames estimated to be five Confederate batteries. His artillery brigade commander, Lt. Col. George W. Getty, estimated that Battery A faced twenty-four guns, or four batteries. In actuality, the two Confederate brigades, whose batteries bombarded Ames's position, possessed ten guns, but they were well commanded. In his after-action report, Ames noted the marksmanship of the Rebel gunners. "Their distances varied from 800 to 1,500 yards," he added. "After a cannonading of about an hour and a half they were silenced. Their loss is supposed to have been considerable." One opposing infantry regiment, the Twentieth Georgia Volunteer Infantry, suffered only two casualties, but its commander, J. B. Cumming, reported heavy fire raining down upon them from Union guns.[31]

Getty's report corroborated the viciousness of the Confederate barrage: "Whilst in position it [Ames's battery] was subjected to a terrific cannonade from the enemy." Lt. John L. Massie, a Confederate artillery officer who engaged Ames's battery, likewise described the Yankee volume of fire as "warm." With little to no cover, Massie's battery withdrew. Col. Stephen D. Lee, acting chief of artillery of General Magruder's division, also noted the effectiveness of the Union artillery on July 27, writing, "He [the Union artillery commander] replied with alacrity, showing he was still strong."[32]

As the afternoon heat intensified, Confederate troops under Maj. Gen. Lafayette McLaws moved against the Union line, but the heavy fire from Ames's and other Union gunners deterred their advance. "Finding the enemy in strong force occupying their works," McLaws reported, "the regiments were withdrawn." Later in the day all of the Union batteries except Ames's withdrew, leaving the young officer to command the last guns near Garnett's farm. An additional, yet brief, fight ensued during the sunset. Brig. Gen. Robert Toombs's brigade attacked the Union line around 7 P.M. while facing "galling fire from artillery and musketry." Lt. James Woolfolk's Ashland Virginia Artillery opened fire on Ames's battery from a distance of 600 yards. The duel lasted for ten minutes, but it was heated. One Confederate shell nearly killed a Union staff member when it passed just over his bed. Getty recalled that Battery A withdrew at nightfall. Ames beamed at the conduct of his men and his subordinate officers, highlighting his lieutenants for bravery and coolness under fire.

Confederate forces did not drive the Union troops from the field, but they did break the Union lines at Gaines's Mill. It was one of the costliest and arguably the most gruesome battle of the campaign. The Union army repulsed a slew of aggressive, yet discombobulated Confederate attacks on June 27 at multiple sites yet left the field that night. Porter praised his disciplined and courageous officers, including Ames. "Their [the troops] commanders were not excelled by those in any other corps in ability or experience; they had the highest confidence in each other, in the army, and in their own men, and were fully competent to oppose their able adversaries." The V Corps had fought valiantly against a Confederate onslaught but wisely withdrew that evening.[33]

Porter's command had crossed the Chickahominy to safety by the early morning of June 28. They burned the bridges after they passed over them, leaving behind their charred remains as well as nearly 900 dead soldiers north of the river. The V Corps had fought outnumbered, but McClellan exaggerated the severity of their numerical deficiency in his reports. Like the entire campaign, the higher command of the Army of the Potomac was rife with delusions and lethargic tendencies.[34]

Over the next three days, Lee pursued McClellan as the Federals raced toward the James, fighting three additional battles at Savage's Station, Glendale, and White Oak Swamp. Battery A, Fifth US Artillery did not participate in the combat but kept moving. As June ended, Ames and his men soon found themselves positioned at what would be the final battlefield of the campaign after rejoining the main Union column assembling around Malvern Hill. On this low plateau north of the James, McClellan regrouped his army. Awaiting the expected Confederate attack, the general formed his troops into a large defensive semicircle. Upon Ames's arrival late on the thirtieth, he received orders to position his guns along the River Road, which ran through the middle of the elevated terrain. Although supported by nearly 18,000 infantrymen, Ames and the other batteries along the crest of Malvern Hill were conceivably the most invaluable units on the field. The Union troops massed there looked daunting to the approaching Confederate regiments, especially because of the significant artillery presence facing an open field. On the morning of July 1, the Army of the Potomac had consolidated its defensive position on Malvern Hill, which looked like an "inverted U."[35]

Ames and his battery stood at the north part of the line. His men were flanked by soldiers and guns from the Third US Artillery, Sixth New York Light Artillery, and several other batteries. A total of thirty-one guns composed this portion of the line. Almost every portion of the Union position possessed some topographical advantage. The left and right flanks occupied steep terrain. In the middle, where Ames's battery was, the Union line did not benefit from steep elevation, but what it did have was a clear line of sight. Unobscured by trees or other obstructions, the artillerymen had a wide field of fire and could pummel any oncoming Confederate infantry.[36]

Skilled Yankee gunners and a defensible position, however, did not deter the Rebel force as the Battle of Malvern Hill began on July 1. Multiple factors hindered the Confederate attack. Troops under Magruder, the nemesis of Ames and the Union troops at Yorktown, arrived late because of improper road maps and inferior guides. Other Confederate units approached Malvern Hill slowly due to apprehension by commanders or because they had to gather their own artillery pieces, which were dispersed among the army from the previous battles. Nevertheless, Lee concluded that a decisive victory was possible. Discarded Union supplies and numerous stragglers along the approach to Malvern Hill convinced him that the Union army was demoralized. Although Federal and Confederate forces were nearly identical in terms of manpower, the Union army possessed far more artillery pieces than their foes. Some sources have suggested that the Federal artillery numbered 250 guns, with others indicate they had 171 in action on July 1 and 91 in reserve.[37]

Although outgunned, Confederate artillery barraged the Union center. When gaps appeared in the line, Rebel infantry then prepared to charge. At 1 P.M. Federal batteries returned fire and neutralized the effectiveness of Lee's pieces. From around 3 P.M. and into the evening, Lee sent multiple divisions against the Union positions. At times Ames and his men were under heavy musket fire, yet their six twelve-pound Napoleons continued to unleash a relentless barrage against the enemy troops. Again, and again Ames and his fellow gunners tore the attackers apart, leaving thousands of dead and wounded men on the field, piled up like cordwood. "Early in the afternoon the enemy charged a battery on our right," Ames reported, "but were entirely cut up, with the loss [of] their colors [flags]. In this instance of canister was very effective." Substantiating the ferocity of the barrage, Ames's West Point classmate Henry W. Kingsbury, operating his Battery D, Fifth US Artillery alongside Ames's command, recounted how the enemy lost their colors. "When they [Confederates] first formed I drew the attention of Lieutenant Ames to them. He, too, pointed some of his of guns on them."[38]

"During the battle," Ames laconically noted, "1,392 rounds of ammunition were expended." The salvos remained effective even after Ames's commanders withdrew the ammunition train from the battlefield. "Had not the ammunition train been removed, we would not have failed of ammunition at any time," Ames recalled. When Confederate troops tried to "turn our left," they experienced grueling losses. Ames praised his lieutenants and enlisted men for behaving coolly and courageously during the battle. He went on to boast, "Every private of the battery nobly did his duty." The Union force as a whole did too, but McClellan ordered the army to withdraw after the fighting ceased. Colonel Hunt, now one of the highest-ranking artillerymen in the Union army and a master tactician, had suggested a counterattack against the cut-up Confederates. Porter agreed, but McClellan ordered the army to entrench at its new base of operations at Harrison's Landing on the James, where the navy could safeguard the troops from additional bloody enemy assaults.[39]

The Union artillery performed superbly at Malvern Hill, and Ames received a great deal of praise for his conduct. In a report to Hunt, Getty described the events of the battle. A West Pointer himself—and an eventual major general in his own right—Getty lauded the conduct of and displayed admiration for Ames and his command: "At the Battle of Malvern Hill, July 1, Ames's Battery was posted on the right of the main road leading by the [Malvern] House, and with other batteries, was supported by the division of General Morrell. The battery remained on the field during the entire day, and was handled with great skill. . . . First Lieutenant Adelbert Ames, commanding Battery A, Fifth Artillery, deserves particular mention for his gallantry and skill at the battles of Chickahominy and Malvern."[40] Hunt, in his final report to army headquarters, likewise praised the officers and batteries of the Army of the Potomac. Highlighting junior officers, and specifically Ames, he wrote, "The conduct of these officers has been above praise." Due to Ames's meritorious service at Malvern Hill, he received another promotion. Now a brevet lieutenant colonel, the young man had emerged as a proven and recognized field officer.[41]

He also left his battery at this time. By mid-1862, with the Army of the Potomac stuck on the Peninsula at Harrison's Landing, President Lincoln recognized the need for more troops and authorized a call for an additional 300,000 volunteer soldiers. Needing veteran officers to command all those green recruits, the War Department relaxed its aversion to regular-army officers serving in volunteer regiments. Due to this influx of new soldiers, as well as his impressive war record, Ames found himself under consideration for a volunteer commission again. The battery commander knew that he could make more of a name for himself as an infantry officer, and he wrote to Maine governor Israel Washburn about getting a volunteer commission to achieve that end. Ames expressed an interest in leading Mainers and offered himself "as a candidate" for a colonelship.

Until such a commission came, Ames was reassigned to the Topographical Engineers following the Peninsula Campaign, remaining with that service for several weeks.[42] The Corps of Topographical Engineers had existed since 1838, but the need for officers trained for topographical duties was first recognized decades earlier by George Washington. Called "topogs," topographical engineers played a pivotal role in surveying lands for western settlement, railroads, and construction projects critical for nautical navigation in the Great Lakes region and the Mississippi River valley. At the start of the Civil War, the corps had grown to forty-five engineers but had rapidly declined to twenty-eight by 1862. The projects topogs worked on for the Union army included engineering research, field work, and helping with the distribution of updated maps. Ames never discussed any details about this portion of his military career. It was brief and inconsequential, and given his abhorrence of boredom, he probably loathed his time in the corps. Ames's expertise and rising reputation may have helped bolster the ranks of the Topographical Engineers, but the corps could not field a full company of enlistees. Although Ames probably would have received a transfer within the regular forces, he would soon accept a position with a volunteer regiment and leave the dwindling corps behind.[43]

In August, by order of the War Department, Ames took a permanent leave of absence from the regular army and went home to Maine to assume command of a newly formed regiment, the Twentieth Maine Volunteers. One of five new regiments from the state created under Lincoln's new call for troops, authorities established the Twentieth Maine to handle the overflow of recruits created in forming the other four. Like Ames, nearly every soldier who enlisted experienced the habitually inhospitable climate of the far Northeast. The rough livelihoods and lifestyles that the Mainers were accustomed to were not outlandish to their commander. On the contrary, the sights and smells of the North Atlantic, lime kilns, and pine forests they knew were equally familiar to their new colonel. Among the regiment's ranks, John L. Thorne, formerly a laborer, had worked whatever job he could in a lime mill or lumber yard in Brunswick. George Bailey was a woodsman in the Maine wilderness. Henry Gayer, forty-four years of age, had navigated the rugged Maine coastline as a sailor. Daniel Littlefield from Kennebunk farmed, same as Isaac Lathrop and a majority of the volunteers. Llewellyn Genthner was a blacksmith, while George Getchell of Waterville was a student at Colby College.[44]

The greatest contradistinction, however, between the new colonel and his troops was that Ames had a top-tier military education and was a polished army man who had seen action, as the scar on his leg from Bull Run confirmed. By the summer of 1862, he had known the life of a soldier for seven years. He was a West Pointer and a regular who was a perfectionist, highly motivated, and stressed attentiveness. In contrast, his new soldiers were relaxed and not at all straitlaced. While they were men hardened by life in the Maine woods or along the coast, none had ever experienced anything resembling the terror and carnage of combat or the vexatious rigidness of military discipline.

Arriving in Portland, Maine, in August 1862, Colonel Ames felt pressure from his superiors to provide the Union with a regiment of the highest quality—with roughly a month to accomplish it. The disciplined officer encountered his troops for the first time at Camp Mason, located on Cape Elizabeth south of Portland. Historian John J. Pullen has described how the recruits did not salute their new commanding officer but rather said, "How d'ye do, Colonel?" Such nonmilitary informality was rampant. While the men wanted to become soldiers, they had no notion of military affairs or conduct. They leaned against trees or walls when they were supposed to be on guard duty. Some stood in awkward positions with their legs crossed while on drill or standing at attention.[45]

Ames found his new troops rough and uncouth, with varying degrees of military competence. He supposedly fumed when they looked disheveled and declared, "This is a hell of a regiment!" He also roared at one soldier who was standing with his feet cockeyed. "For God's sake, draw up your bowels!" The men needed work, but Ames saw promise in them, even if military repute seemed improbable. They were able-bodied, patriotic volunteers who had experience with firearms. They simply needed proper, old-army instruction.[46]

That "old-army instruction" would have to come from Ames. Only one officer in the regiment, Maj. Charles D. Gilmore of Bangor, had any military experience. Gilmore had served in the Seventh Maine and saw action during the Peninsula Campaign. Since he was the lone veteran in the Twentieth, Ames's job proved more difficult. His second in command, Lt. Col. Joshua Lawrence Chamberlain of Brunswick, was an intelligent college professor, but his lack of military experience would require tutoring to acclimate him to military tactics and responsibilities. Not only would Ames have to train his rank and file himself, but his officers required intensive military instruction as well. The performance and even survival of his regiment was predicated on leadership, but the men charged to be leaders were as equally clueless as the men they were to lead. Getting them all prepared for combat was a difficult task that would test the patience of an ambitious and temperamental young colonel, who now placed immense pressure upon himself to succeed.[47]

With only three weeks to prepare the Twentieth Maine for active duty, Ames had to accelerate instruction for the enlisted men and officers. Wanting to prove that his versatile abilities to train and lead could apply anywhere, he quickly began to teach his raw troops the fundamentals of marching and maneuvering. At night, by the flickering light of lanterns, Ames and his inexperienced officers laboriously studied available military texts and maps in the colonel's makeshift officers academy.[48]

Joshua Lawrence Chamberlain (Library of Congress)

During regimental drills, both officers and enlisted men at first had difficulty mastering the most rudimentary, yet essential commands. Even the fife-and-drum contingent was incapable of carrying a tune or operating as a cohesive musical troupe (a shortcoming that would incite Ames's rage). As the regiment's training progressed, Ames thought he should hold a dress parade. In the process of assembling for the event, the fledgling music corps struggled. This caused immense chaos, "with much running to and fro and much discord under the theory of drumming and fifing, from the drum corps on flank, [and] much exhortation on the part of the line officers." The musicians then "broke loose" and started "to ramble down the line," which distracted the regiment. At this point Ames strained his vocal cords in shouting at one of his officers, "Captain [Isaac] Bangs, stop that damned drumming!" But Bangs apparently could not hear the colonel over the musical cacophony. Ames, now enraged, charged the regiment's drum corps with his sword drawn and made them disperse. "It was an unfair advantage," Ellis Spear recalled, "justifiable only on the ground of military necessity. The Colonel was armed and the drum corps had only drums and fifes. . . . Instantly they were routed and fled." The complexities of marching, forming columns, and the general movements a regiment needed to perform efficiently on the battlefield were too much for the recruits to master in such an abbreviated time.[49]

Many men in turn did not like their new colonel. More often than not, Ames addressed the troops in a traditional military manner if they failed their assignments—loudly and brashly. One soldier described him as a "savage man," and a number of other volunteers wished that he would find himself locked away in a prison. Nevertheless, Ames eventually produced positive results with his disciplined, if sometimes explosive, training. As Pullen notes, the men of the Twentieth Maine were raw materials with potential, and Ames did his utmost to prepare them as quickly as possible.[50]

August 1862 ultimately served as a test for both the new volunteers trying to adjust to military life and their ambitious young commander, who was prone to impatience and perfectionism. A twenty-six-year-old man in charge of nearly 1,000 men, Ames became a harsh and acerbic critic of both himself and his troops. Eventually, the regiment began to take the shape of a well-organized, hard-nosed unit. The Mainers would remain independent and sometimes skeptical of many of their officers and orders, but they began to put faith in some of their other officers and, when they received their uniforms, began to look like soldiers. Most importantly, as historian Henry King Benson writes, "a certain pride and *esprit de corps* began to emerge; eventually, even the regimental attitude towards Ames would change."[51]

The colonel still had doubts regarding his men, however. Officially mustered in to service on August 29, 1862, the Twentieth Maine had made significant strides since its conception.[52] While the results of the abbreviated training at Camp Mason still left plenty to be desired—especially for the perfectionistic Ames—the young colonel in fact had done a masterful job organizing and preparing 965 officers and enlisted men for war. Yet by his own high standards, the regiment still needed more instruction and better supplies. The men received neither and were summoned to join the Army of the Potomac immediately via a telegram from the Assistant Quartermaster's Office in Boston on the twenty-ninth.[53] Boarding the vessel *Merrimac*, the regiment left Portland on September 3; many soldiers would never again return to their native state.[54] After three days at sea, the regiment disembarked in Alexandria, Virginia, on the sixth.[55]

Once off the ship, the Twentieth Maine boarded a train bound for Washington, arriving the following day. There Ames again nearly lost total control of his temper. The regiment had yet to acquire its weapons, and so Ames marched the troops to the US arsenal. After receiving their new muskets and ammunition, the soldiers, according to Pullen, wanted to make a grand display as they marched to their camp at Fort Craig on Arlington Heights. The regimental band began to play as they marched, and the men were so enamored with their new weapons and the music that the "march turned into a frustrating draggle, with onlookers laughing and old soldiers jeering." No longer able to contain his emotions, and with his pride obviously hurt, Ames shouted, "If you can't do any better than you have tonight, you better all desert and go home!" The colonel could handle whizzing shot and shells better than he could humiliation.[56]

Assigned to a six-regiment brigade in the V Corps under the command of Brig. Gen. Daniel Butterfield, the raw troops of the Twentieth Maine found themselves alongside veteran and seasoned soldiers from across the North who, like Ames, had fought and bled during the Peninsula Campaign earlier that year. On September 12 Ames and his regiment participated in a forced march away from Washington. The choking heat quickly took its toll. Like many rookie soldiers, the Mainers cast aside their freshly acquired equipment, with heavy knapsacks often the first items they threw away. The regiment struggled the next day too. Many men suffered from blisters because of their new shoes. As Pvt. Theodore Gerrish of Falmouth, who enlisted at age sixteen, recounted, "These men were doubtless acquainted with fatigue before they entered the army, but this fearful strain in marching so many miles, in heavy marching order, for successive days, is too much for them."[57]

As the marching continued over the next several days, the regiment slowly toughened. During this time, Gerrish described his commanding officer: "The colonel is every inch a soldier. He is well mounted, and his eyes flash as brightly as the silver eagles upon his shoulders. That is Colonel Adelbert Ames, a graduate of West Point, and a soldier of the regular army. He was severely wounded at Bull Run is a native of Rockland, Maine, and one of the bravest officers in the army."[58]

The Twentieth Maine soon merged into the Army of the Potomac, marching through green fields and glens as they entered Maryland. With Confederate forces in close proximity, the anticipation of a forthcoming battle was high. Colonel Ames and his regiment marched northeastward, parallel to the Potomac River, toward the town of Sharpsburg.

COLONEL AMES, HIS REGIMENT, AND SMALLPOX

While Ames was home building the Twentieth Maine, Lee routed Maj. Gen. John Pope's Army of Virginia at the Second Battle of Bull Run, August 29–30, 1862. A Confederate army outnumbered by 20,000 men embarrassed and bloodied the larger Union force. After his success, Lee took the fighting north in the late summer of 1862, even as Ames brought his new regiment down to Washington. The Confederates invaded Maryland, and Union officials feared they would threaten large, industrial cities beyond that. On September 17 the Army of the Potomac and the Army of Northern Virginia clashed along Antietam Creek outside of Sharpsburg, Maryland. The most significant battle during the Maryland Campaign, total casualties at Antietam exceeded 22,700 men. Again, the Union army had a sizable numerical advantage, but Rebel troops benefited from being on the defensive. Federal assaults could not break through Lee's center for long or roll up his flanks, and the fortuitous arrival of Confederate reinforcements from Harpers Ferry helped save the Rebel army. The vicious battle ended in a tactical stalemate. Heavily outnumbered, Lee expected an attack the following day, but it never came. On September 18 he ordered his forces to leave Union soil and escaped back to Virginia.[1]

After the battle, critics attacked McClellan for—among other alleged failures—not employing his thousands of reserves. For most of the battle, Colonel Ames and his rookie Maine regiment remained in the rear with the rest of Col. T. B. Stockton's Third Brigade, First Division of Porter's V Corps: the Twelfth New York, Seventeenth New York, Forty-Fourth New York, Eighty-Third Pennsylvania, and a contingent of Michigan sharpshooters. Although the men did not fight, they watched multiple attacks take place on the opposite side of the creek. A few of the Mainers later asserted that they were indeed participants in the engagement because they had witnessed the fighting and its bloody consequences. Writing to his wife, Pvt. Hezekiah Long of Rockland described shots whistling over his head and declared that "every barn and church" he saw in the vicinity was full of wounded soldiers in agony. But Ames disagreed with such notions. He did not find that standing by in reserve equaled active participation in a battle. In a letter home to his parents on September 21, the young colonel exuded frustration. "As for being in the battles in this vicinity," he wrote, "I have to say—my officers think we were in (a little at least) but I do not think we were in enough to speak of it."[2]

Ames did not have long to wait, however. The Twentieth Maine officially took part in its first action three days after Antietam. On September 19 two regiments from the V Corps crossed the Potomac and engaged the Confederate rear guard, commanded by Brig. Gen. William N. Pendleton, at Boteler's Ford in present-day West Virginia. They managed to capture four Confederate field pieces that night. The two sides renewed the fighting the following day as Porter sent more troops against Pendleton. Also known as the Battle of Shepherdstown, the sharp engagement eventually saw both armies commit two divisions to the fight. During the battle, the Twentieth Maine incurred two wounded, and Lieutenant Colonel Chamberlain nearly died when a projectile killed his horse. Ames made little mention of the battle afterward. "We crossed the Potomac [River] near Shepherdstown where there was quite a little fight," he wrote his parents, adding that he intended to continue training the men regularly: "I do not imagine we shall have much fighting very soon. At least my regiment will be discipled when we do."[3]

The colonel was right to expect a lull in the fighting. After Antietam and Shepherdstown, the threat of Confederate invasion ended as Lee returned to Virginia. McClellan reported, "We may safely claim a complete victory" but did not pursue further. Instead, he complained to Washington that he needed more men, telling Lincoln, "This army is not now in condition to undertake another campaign nor to bring on another battle." The general wanted to replenish his veteran regiments, train new recruits, and safeguard recently recaptured Harpers Ferry first; the next campaign against Lee would have to wait. Lincoln, lamenting that Lee had slipped away, confessed to his secretaries that he did not think that McClellan intended to make any effort to strike a resounding blow to the mauled enemy army. A visit to the front confirmed his views, but the president also knew that he had to wait to deal with the Democrat McClellan until after the November elections.[4]

While the Army of the Potomac rested and the weather turned cold, Ames drilled his men. Many in the Twentieth Maine's ranks still viewed him as an overbearing, draconian disciplinarian. But others began to alter their perspective about their colonel. Hezekiah Long for one saw him in a favorable light following Antietam and Shepherdstown. Writing to his wife, Long told her, "You have probably heard that some of the Regt. here do not like Col. Ames very well as he swears at them sometimes, as for me I like him very well, and the rest of them are beginning to." Ames felt little attachment to his regiment, however, and perked up when he heard rumors about a promotion. He wrote his parents on October 10 that Brig. Gen. Hiram Berry was trying to get him promoted: "Gen. Berry still urges (or pretends to) my advancement. Whatever may be his motives, he aids me by word, by praise at least."[5] Ames received glowing support from Berry, but he did not receive the promotion. The colonel instead spent October and November drilling his troops and writing his about the current state of the army and the nation. "We of the military must be awake," the young Republican told his parents. "The fall election will be the crisis for the present. The feeling in the North between the two parties is becoming very bitter. The president must be rewarded." But the nation did not emphatically reward Lincoln or the Republican Party. While Republicans gained ground in the Senate, they lost twenty-seven seats in the House of Representatives, with Democrats winning important races in Pennsylvania and New York.[6]

Soon after the Union voted, the most senior officer in the Army of the Potomac lost his command. President Lincoln removed McClellan from his duties and replaced him with Maj. Gen. Ambrose E. Burnside on November 7. "With diffidence for myself, but with a proud confidence in the unswerving loyalty and determination of the gallant army now entrusted to my care, I accept its control, with the steadfast assurance that the just cause must prevail," Burnside announced to the army. The men responded with mixed emotions. Most considered Burnside a likable solider, while veterans knew him as an officer who had fought at First Bull Run and Antietam but, by most standards, was not exceptional. Soldiers had divided loyalties and still favored McClellan, but others thought that Burnside's promotion instilled optimism.[7]

After Burnside took command, the Maine-based campaign to secure a promotion for Ames entered a new phase. In a letter dated November 16 to Vice Pres. Hannibal Hamlin, a Maine native, Center Grand Division commander

Maj. Gen. Joseph Hooker, a native New Englander born in Massachusetts, wrote glowingly of the colonel:

> Young Ames was of my command last winter, in charge of a Battery, and I assure you gained my esteem and confidence for his intelligence, zeal, and devotion to duties. Since he has had the honor to command a Regiment he has displayed no less capacity and excellence. He is now of my Division and it would be my great satisfaction to have him advanced.... I know of no officer of more promise, and should he be promoted I feel no doubt but that he will reflect great credit upon himself and his state. You will have no cause to regret any assistance you may be able to render this young officer.[8]

A week later a second letter to Vice President Hamlin recommended Ames for promotion. General Berry genuinely respected the young colonel's aptitude and talents. Moreover, the death of Maine native Brig. Gen. Charles Davis Jameson on November 6, 1862, provided an opening for a generalship in the Army of the Potomac. Berry believed that Ames would both make their state proud and provide the army with a gifted young leader.

> I find no name that stands higher than that of Colonel Ames of the 20th [Maine]. I am well aware that his appointment to a higher position at this time may be considered hurried and premature by some—still in the present emergency of our country such considerations should not avail. Colonel Ames is a soldier and a good one. He has already won a name, by his bravery and skill on the battle-field, that any man may well be proud of.... He has the benefit of an excellent Military education, is brave, intelligent, intrepid, and devoted—and is also an excellent disciplinarian.[9]

Ames drew additional support from within his regiment. Both Lieutenant Colonel Chamberlain and Major Gilmore wrote to Governor Washburn, Republican of Maine, about the situation on November 15. They acknowledged that Hooker and Berry had suggested Ames for promotion, and both favored the change: "The past services of Col. Ames in this war are as great and as honorable as those of any other officer in the army. And among military men no one sustains a higher reputation."[10]

Meanwhile, under immense pressure from Washington, Burnside made his preparations to attack Lee. Hoping to confuse the Rebel commander about his true intentions for the fall of 1862, Burnside's plan included marching the Army of the Potomac southeast toward the town of Fredericksburg, Virginia. There the army would cross the Rappahannock River, running parallel to the east–west flowing Potomac River, using pontoon bridges to replace the spans destroyed earlier in the year. Once across the Rappahannock, the army could threaten Richmond, taking advantage of the Richmond, Fredericksburg, and Potomac Railroad to shuttle troops toward the Confederate capital. Most importantly, Burnside wanted to mask his movement and protect the right flank of his columns during the process. On November 13 he asked Maj. Gen. Henry W. Halleck, general in chief of all Union armies, for definite approval for his plan. Halleck responded the next day, telling him that the president assented to the strategy. Lincoln emphasized, however, that the movement could only succeed if Burnside moved rapidly.[11]

Setting out on November 15, Burnside's advance columns arrived at Falmouth—across the river from Fredericksburg—two days later. The pontoon bridges the men needed to span the Rappahannock did not arrive from Washington on time, however. According to a report from the Fiftieth New York Engineers, the order for pontoons did not arrive until the afternoon of November 12. The best they could do was start moving thirty-six pontoons toward Falmouth on Sunday the sixteenth. While Burnside paused, Lee deduced what he was doing and acted quickly. "On the 21st, it became apparent that Burnside was concentrating his whole army on the north side of the Rappahannock," Lee reported. He hurried Lt. Gen. James Longstreet and his corps to occupy both the town and the high terrain immediately outside of Fredericksburg. Lee later noted that Longstreet's men could not deter Burnside if Union troops managed to get across the river, and so he ordered Lt. Gen. Stonewall Jackson's troops to Fredericksburg as well. Jackson covered 200 miles at the same time Burnside, Ames, and the Union army only had to march 36 miles to travel to reach the Rappahannock. On November 23 Longstreet's divisions arrived, and Jackson's men reached the locale by the twenty-ninth.[12]

Ames and his regiment waited on the northern banks of the Rappahannock in increasingly frigid temperatures, languishing with Burnside's entire army. The colonel no doubt felt the chill December winds even under the layers of his wool uniform and coat as well as underneath his full facial hair. Before a battle even took place, the weather cost Ames two of his men. Sleeping in tents lined with logs, two Twentieth Mainers reportedly froze to death. Pvt. Theodore Gerrish, who nearly died from exposure himself, remembered, "We

buried some of the bravest of our men there [Falmouth]—noble fellows, who hoped that if they were to die for the country they might have the privilege of dying on the field of battle, but that boon was denied them."[13]

After scouting the river, Burnside chose to cross directly at Fredericksburg before all of Lee's army arrived. He wrote Halleck, "I think now that the enemy will be more surprised by a crossing immediately in our front than in any other part of the river." The army commander assured the general in chief that he had made precautions to protect the crossings and that his division commanders agreed with his plan. On December 11, Union engineers began to construct bridges across the Rappahannock. Due to the expert marksmanship of Confederate sharpshooters stationed in Fredericksburg, construction delays mounted. In response, Hunt's artillery pummeled the town to silence the marksmen. Although the barrage did little to deter them, Capt. Samuel T. Keene of Rockland, commanding Company G, Twentieth Maine, wrote that the cannonading was terrific, even though they were resting in a field far removed from the bombardment. Burnside and Hunt concurred that they needed to set up a bridgehead across the river. If they could get Union infantry into the town, the soldiers could clear out the Rebel marksmen house to house. Hunt ordered the artillery to open fire again. This half-hour barrage

Skinkers Neck on the Rappahannock below Fredericksburg, VA, by Alfred R. Waud, 1862 (Library of Congress)

resulted in Confederate defenders scurrying for cover. When the cannonade concluded around 3:30 P.M., Union infantry traversed the river, some crossing via pontoons while others rowed across in three boats. Fierce street fighting continued for hours before Confederate troops withdrew. At 6:30 P.M. Burnside wired Halleck: "Our troops now occupy Fredericksburg. . . . I expect to cross the rest of my command tomorrow." Over the next two days, infantry divisions marched into the town and across adjacent fields along the river. On December 13 Ames and his regiment arrived in Fredericksburg.[14]

By the time Burnside had gathered his army, Lee had 80,000 troops along the ridges and hills on the southern side of the Rappahannock. Longstreet's line held the Confederate left, extending five miles. It featured copious artillery batteries on Taylor's Hill, Howison Hill, and Marye's Heights. In front of the last, a sunken road and stone retaining walls formed a well-protected defensive trench. South of Marye's Heights, past a potentially dangerous gap in the Confederate line, Jackson's men held Prospect Hill. Although it was not steep, woods that spread in front of it shielded Jackson's men and his artillery from Federal forces. To reach the Confederate defenses, Union brigades would have to cross open fields, mostly devoid of cover, with enemy batteries positioned to rake the terrain with lethal fire.[15]

Burnside planned a two-pronged attack, although its details never became clear to his subordinates. Maj. Gen. William B. Franklin's 60,000-man wing would concentrate its attack on Jackson's men. Troops in the II and V Corps would participate in diversionary attacks to the north against Longstreet. Franklin asked Burnside how and when to prepare his troops for their assault, which required coordination with the rest of the army, especially since Franklin's men would have to dislodge Jackson's four infantry divisions. Burnside, however, was reticent. Instead of responding to Franklin on the evening of December 12, he did not share orders until early the next day, and even then they were vague. He told Franklin to send out "a division at least" and avoid the "possibility of a collision of our own forces" because of the morning fog.[16]

December 13 began with a misty morning and low visibility. According to historian Robert K. Krick, the temperature was warmer than the previous days and not as bitterly cold. Franklin, who by now had little faith in Burnside, interpreted his orders as conservatively as possible, sending only Maj. Gen. George G. Meade's division against Jackson's position. Meade's division moved toward the enemy line around 8:30 A.M. but paused because of the fog. In the early afternoon his men briefly managed to crack through Jackson's line before the Confederates closed the breach. Meade complained that Birney's and Brig. Gen. John Gibbon's divisions did not reinforce him fast enough to capitalize on the breakthrough. Burnside's vague orders and Franklin's extreme caution prevented any success on the Federal left.[17]

Burnside assumed that Franklin was making a stronger effort on the left as he sent his right forward. On the outskirts of Fredericksburg, the Union II and V Corps began their futile attacks through town against Longstreet's men at 11 A.M. "As they [Union troops] came within reach," Longstreet recalled, "a storm of lead was poured into their advancing ranks and they were swept from the field like chaff before the wind." Even though the Confederate infantry and artillery were unloading their ordnance with astounding volume and ferocity, fresh Union troops continued to march forward in waves. "Hardly was this attack off the field," Longstreet continued, "before we saw the determined Federals again filing out of Fredericksburg and preparing for another charge." The battlefield, littered with the dead and the dying, would force the final waves of Union troops at dusk to maneuver over thousands of casualties, impeding their advance.[18]

Ames and the Twentieth Maine were part of those final, futile efforts. As the afternoon began to wane, the regiment received orders from their division commander, Charles Griffin, now a brigadier general, to move forward with the rest of the First Division. Ames led the march, with Lieutenant Col-

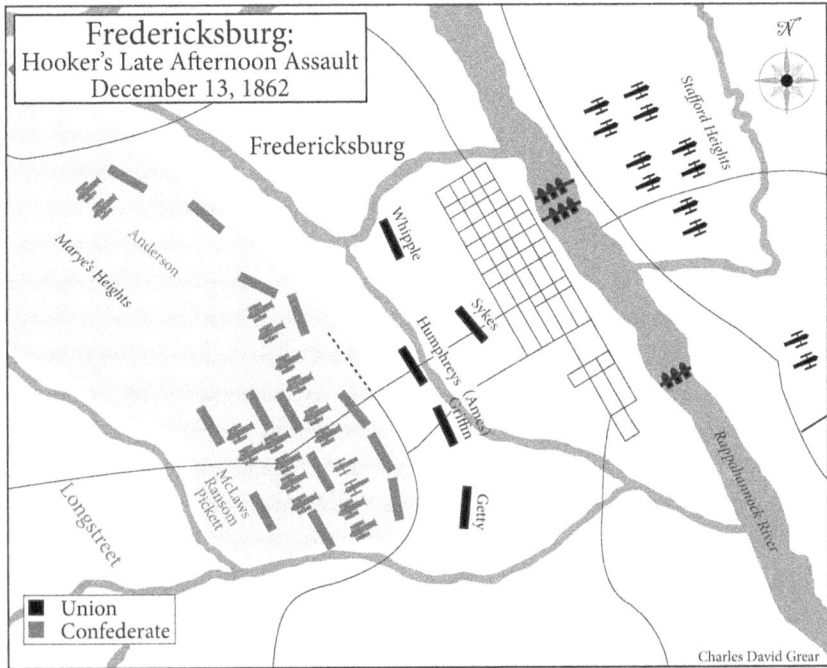

Fredericksburg: Hooker's Late-Afternoon Assault, December 13, 1862; Ames's Twentieth Maine was part of Griffin's division (Charles David Grear)

onel Chamberlain beside him, still a dutiful pupil. Leading up to the battle, Ames had continually taught tactics to Chamberlain most evenings. If the Twentieth Maine's enlisted men faltered, at least Ames could now count on his officers to lead them properly.[19]

Waiting along the corridors of Fredericksburg's war-torn streets, Ames received orders that the Third Brigade was to advance. Capt. Ellis Spear wrote after the war that the colonel was solemn and resolute. "The only word I heard from Colonel Ames at that time excepting necessary orders, was 'This is earnest work,'" the Mainer from Warren claimed. He also noted that Ames was "quiet, [had a] composed bearing, [and] inspired confidence" even though he was younger than many of his fellow officers.[20]

The Twentieth Maine awaited the bugler's call. Upon hearing the signal blasted through the winter air, Ames turned toward his regiment and yelled over the cacophony of battle, "Forward the Twentieth!" Two of the New York regiments on Ames's right did not hear the bugle call, however, and stayed put. The Twentieth Maine surged toward Marye's Heights, but with their right flank exposed.[21]

Private Gerrish described not only withering fire during the advance but also the men's high morale. Fredericksburg "was our first baptism of fire that our regiment ever received, but with the inspiration derived from such a man as Colonel Ames, it was a very easy thing to face danger and death." As the Twentieth Maine advanced, Capt. Victor Maurin's Louisiana Donaldsonville Artillery moved to the front of Marye's Heights and enfiladed the Union line. Chamberlain recalled the deadly skill of the Louisianan gun crews: "The artillery fire wreaked havoc. Crushed bodies, severed limbs, were everywhere." He claimed that Ames turned to him and whispered, "God help us now."[22]

Crossing over railroad tracks, breaking through fences, and passing through a wide drainage ditch brimming with two feet of icy water, the Mainers' columns began to break apart. Ames and his fellow officers did their best to quickly reestablish lines of battle as the cannonade roared. As Chamberlain recalled, Ames motioned him to the right flank while the colonel "went to the front, into the storm."[23]

As the regiment pushed forward through the hail of lead, Capt. Robert G. Carter of the Twenty-Second Massachusetts described the Twentieth Maine's advance behind him. "Once I looked over my shoulder," he wrote, "I saw the Twentieth Maine, which was in our division, coming across the field in line of battle, as upon a parade, easily recognized by their new state colors, the great gaps plainly visible as the shot and shell tore through the now tremulous line. . . . It was a grand sight," he continued, "and a striking example of what discipline will do for such material in such a battle."[24]

Carter went on to describe Ames: "Shortly after, a tall, slim colonel coolly walked over our bodies. 'Who commands this regiment?' he asked. Our colonel responded. 'I will move over your line and relieve your men,' he [Ames] quietly rejoined. It was Colonel Adelbert Ames. . . . We fell back through the lines a few yards. The Twentieth Maine swept forward, and as it was its first engagement the rattle and roar instantly grew furious."[25]

With no support on their right during the entire attack, the Twentieth Maine continued its advance. "On we pushed up slopes slippery with blood," Chamberlain remembered, "miry with repeated unavailing tread. We reached the final crest, before that all-commanding, countermanding stone wall." As darkness fell on the battlefield, Ames directed his men to open fire. Both sides exchanged volleys at rapid rates. Unharmed Mainers dropped down on the soil to avoid the slaughter as the enemy returned fire. Lying on their stomachs alongside mangled corpses, Ames and his regiment now faced a blistering exchange of gunfire as dead grass—and the droplets of blood from fallen comrades—clung to their uniforms. Chamberlain recalled: "The situation was critical. We took warrant of supreme necessity. We laid up a breastwork of dead bodies, to cover our exposed flank. Behind this we managed to live through the day."[26]

The Twentieth Maine received orders to hold fast as the night grew colder and visibility waned. With no relief coming their way, Ames and his officers did their best to keep the regiment intact and protected. According to Colonel Stockton, the officers of his brigade received orders "that we must hold our positions until 10 o'clock next day, when the Ninth Corps would attack." Stockton made note of the precarious position of Ames and his command. "The enemy's sharpshooters were very vigilant and had evidently obtained such a position that they could almost fire upon the men when lying down." The Twentieth Maine thus spent the entire evening on the cold, dangerous battlefield. Bullets from the unrelenting Confederate defenders during the night thudded into the corpses that provided shelter for the living. Meanwhile, safely secured in Fredericksburg from the night air, Burnside's subordinates snapped at each other while their commander refused to consider a retreat.[27]

The morning of December 14 dawned mild, the grass dewy and bloody. Ames and his regiment had not moved, remaining static like statues. Blackened with power residue and having survived the traumatic evening, the stranded Mainers who had lasted the night battled between 200 and 300 Confederate skirmishers attempting to move closer to the weary Union soldiers. Cpl. Nathan S. Clark wrote in his journal that Confederate riflemen peppered the regiment, and "their sharpshooters killed a few of our men." Nonetheless, Ames and his troops, with the aid of the other regiments marooned on the battlefield, turned the enemy back all day with their own sporadic volleys. "Had to lay flat all day," Captain Keene recalled. "As soon as a man shew himself was popped at." When darkness fell once again, the survivors of the Twentieth Maine—cold, exhausted, and surrounded by corpses—continued to hold their advanced position.[28]

The Union high command finally ordered all troops to desist that evening; Burnside had given up on continuing the battle. When the orders reached the Twentieth Maine, however, the men did not immediately return to Fredericksburg. Covered with mud and using only their bayonets, the Mainers buried their dead in shallow graves, erecting small headstones using broken musket butts. As an aurora borealis made flowing patterns of vivid light in the night sky, the regiment finally withdrew to the confines of Fredericksburg, passing corpses of men and horses encircled by ammunition cases and discarded weapons. Captain Keene, a lawyer by trade, wrote in his journal that the regiment sought out and occupied vacated houses. Able to find a sofa to sleep on, Keene, a devout Christian, had a reason to rejoice that he and his men were no longer outside.

The next day Ames received orders to move the Twentieth Maine again and form a picket line on the cusp of the city. Still fearing a potential attack from the Confederates, particularly Jackson's regiments, the Mainers' prepared for the worst. Fortunately, an attack never came, and the regiment moved across the river after dark.[29]

The regiment suffered four dead and thirty-two wounded, a remarkably small sum considering the blistering volleys of musketry and artillery they received from Marye's Heights, their exposed flank, and remaining two nights under fire.[30] Historian Harry King Benson writes: "Under the most difficult conditions, the 20th Maine had received its baptism of fire and proven its mettle. In the process, the men of the regiment gained a new respect for their commander." The Battle of Fredericksburg induced a sense of pride and accomplishment within the unit, if not in Burnside and the army as a whole. Ames was proud of the valor and conduct of his regiment. He wrote home boasting that while his men had doubts in him, "at that battle the feelings in the regiment changed completely. I was the only Colonel in the brigade who went in front of his regiment and *led* his men into the fight." He went on to say, "My men now have confidence in me; and the battle taught them the necessity of discipline." The Mainers were no longer a rabble of inexperienced lumberjacks and fisherman who needed reprimanding, Ames concluded, but soldiers who had fought admirably and deserved his respect.[31]

Local newspapers printed similarly enthusiastic reports from the national press about the Twentieth Maine for the home folks. The *Portland Daily Press* lauded the regiment and their creditable behavior. "The coolness and bravery with which it [Twentieth Maine] met the murderous fire of the enemy is said to have been unusual," the paper reported. "Col. Ames showed himself a fearless and skillful officer as was expected." But while the Mainers reveled in their heroism, the brutal defeat marked a low point for the morale of the Army of the Potomac as a whole. The army, "always better than its commanders, always ready to 'stand in the evil hour,' suffered defeat at the hands of their southern foe."[32]

After Fredericksburg the Twentieth Maine partook in a fruitless reconnaissance expedition to Richards and Ellis Fords in late December. The men saw nothing of interest along the river and suffered no casualties. When January 1863 arrived, Burnside tried orchestrating another river crossing. After his first plan fell apart, he decided to swing the army upriver to the west. His subordinates held the plan in disdain, but the operation began on January 20. That night the troops became ensnared in a quagmire of mud and sludge as an unexpected nor'easter slashed the army. Rain poured down. Artillery pieces brought to the Rappahannock riverbank became caked in mud. Meanwhile, the Confederates on the other side of the river jeered at the Federals' misfortune. Holding up signs mocking the Union army—reportedly telling them where Richmond was—pickets laughed at the glum Yankees. With the river rising because of the rain, Burnside finally chose to cancel the crossing after three horrible days. Dejected and filthy troops began slogging back to their quarters on the twenty-third. Following what became known as the "Mud March," the Twentieth Maine and the Army of the Potomac as a whole settled into winter quarters. The men constructed wooden huts to protect themselves from the elements. For the rest of the winter, the regiment cleared roads and served as pickets. Most importantly, the men tried to stay warm and dry.[33]

Both sides waited with great anticipation—or dread—for spring to arrive. Ames wrote to his parents expressing optimism in his future and newfound pride in the Twentieth Maine. "My regiment has an excellent reputation," he noted. "I cannot ask for better success than what I have had." The colonel also felt confident that his long-desired advancement to brigadier general would arrive. "I consider my chances for a promotion very good," he told his parents. "Gens. Hooker, Howard, and Berry have given me strong letters. Gov. Washburn has written to the Secretary of War and aids me all he can."[34]

One of those staunch advocates received a promotion himself. Replacing Burnside, "Fighting Joe" Hooker assumed command of the Army of the Potomac on January 26. Hooker from the first displayed a level of bold aggressiveness that his predecessor had lacked. Yet while an assertive corps commander, his ability to lead the Army of the Potomac remained uncertain. Some officers favored him, but others loathed him. Hooker's closest allies after assuming leadership, Maj. Gen. Daniel Butterfield and Maj. Gen. Daniel Sickles, further fueled his critics. Some detractors thought Sickles emboldened Hooker's notorious hedonism while an equally immoral Butterfield manipulated the army's commander. Nevertheless, Hooker slowly molded the army into what he wanted. Emphasizing morale-boosting measures, he improved the army's furlough system, food, pay, and healthcare. All of those changes helped the general reinvigorate the army as he prepared a plan to unleash it to defeat Lee and the Army of Northern Virginia in the spring.[35]

The enlisted men in the Twentieth Maine profited at first from Hooker's reforms, as they notably received new uniforms. Inoculations against smallpox in April, however, proved disastrous. The regiment afterward became a health risk for the entire army. Deemed unfit for duty, the Twentieth Maine detached from its brigade and endured confinement to a new camp on "Quarantine Hill." During this period, "there were several cases of the disease [smallpox] in its most dreaded form," and three men died. The regiment's surgeon, N. P. Monroe, also thought that the Mainers were healing too slowly. As rumors circulated that the army would soon march against Lee, Monroe refused to clear the Twentieth for duty.[36]

The entire sorry saga infuriated Ames. He considered the treatment of his regiment as medical incompetence. "He [Monroe] and the Col. I hear are not very good friends," Private Long wrote, "in consequence as the Col. is very anxious to go with the army, and I hear says he will resign if the Regt. does not go, and the Doctor says if it does go he shall resign. So we shall be likely to lose one of them."[37] Ames had missed most of the battles during the Peninsula Campaign, while Second Bull Run, South Mountain, and Antietam had passed him by as well. He had no interest in staying on Quarantine Hill as another chance at glory came and went.

Ames contacted Butterfield, hoping to join an active unit. He told the general that while he genuinely cared for his command and preferred to fight alongside them, it was his duty to serve elsewhere if he was in good health. He had received the inoculation earlier in life, he added, and would not carry smallpox to any temporary assignment. "It seems unnecessary for all the field officers of the Regiment to remain in charge of a hospital camp," Ames added, "especially when it is earnestly recommended by the surgeon that as few officers as possible should be thus detained."[38]

While Ames contacted Butterfield, other generals wrote to Hooker asking if Ames could serve with them if the Twentieth Maine remained incapacitated. "I beg leave to call to your favorable attention Colonel Ames, 20th Maine," Brigadier General Griffin wrote, "to add to all he is able and ambitious and has that pride as a soldier which always brings successful results." In a letter dated April 19, Major General Howard further supported Griffin's claims. Describing Ames as "one of our most able and efficient officers," Howard suggested the army could benefit from the colonel serving elsewhere while his regiment remained quarantined. "If there is a Brigade for him in the Army I know of no officer who would command it better." Butterfield soon replied to Ames, telling him that he had talked with medical personal about issue. The regiment still could be healthy in time for the upcoming campaign, but "in the event of this not proving to be the case I will try and get you an opportunity to render service with the marching column."[39]

While Ames's men recuperated, Hooker prepared to launch his offensive against Lee. After consideration, he opted against crossing the Rappahannock south of Fredericksburg: not only had Lee strengthened fortifications along the river there, but Hooker also gradually accepted the fact that taking the entire army across the Rappahannock in that area was a mistake. The second iteration of Hooker's plan involved sending 10,000 Union cavalrymen under Maj. Gen. George Stoneman, across the Rappahannock to destroy Confederate supply lines, forcing Lee to leave his reinforced positions. If, or when, Lee moved, Hooker's army would pursue him. That plan stalled when heavy rains in April swelled the Rappahannock, preventing Stoneman's cavalry from fording the river. The third version of Hooker's spring campaign also required Stoneman's cavalry to raid behind Confederate lines. But as they did so, Hooker would mobilize 42,000 men and lead them across the smaller Rapidan River to the west at Germanna Ford and Ely's Ford. Maj. Gen. John Sedgwick would take a second wing of 40,000 Federal troops across the Rappahannock at Fredericksburg. If Hooker's plan worked, his and Sedgwick's wings would act as pincers, crushing Lee's army between them or forcing it to retreat from its entrenched position.[40]

As Hooker prepared to move the army, the Twentieth Maine remained quarantined. Honoring Ames's request, Butterfield finally transferred him to V Corps headquarters, where the colonel would serve as aide to the corps' new commander, Meade. Lieutenant Colonel Chamberlain, now acting commander of the Twentieth Maine, also petitioned Butterfield for a chance to serve in the upcoming battle. Denied, Chamberlain protested, even arguing bizarrely that the regiment having smallpox might work to the army's advantage, possibly infecting the Rebels smallpox. That idea went nowhere.[41]

On April 30 Hooker's plan looked promising. The wings of his army crossed the Rapidan and Rappahannock Rivers as Stoneman began his cavalry raid. The next day 70,000 Union soldiers had pushed Lee's men back toward Fredericksburg and reached the woods around the Chancellorsville Manor. The Army of the Potomac encamped in heavily wooded terrain, with the V Corps composing Hooker's left flank. The II, III, and XII Corps occupied the Union center, while Howard's XI Corps held the Union right.[42]

Facing daunting odds and a double envelopment, Lee divided his numerically inferior army—Longstreet and most of his corps were away in southeastern Virginia gathering food and forage. Leaving 20 percent of his diminished force to hold off Sedgwick's troops at Fredericksburg, Lee concentrated his primary attack on Hooker's wing at Chancellorsville. On May 2 he partitioned his army again, sending Stonewall Jackson's corps around the Union right flank early that morning. Around 5:30 P.M., Jackson's 28,000 men arrived in position in XI Corps' rear. Hooker warned Howard of a possible attack, and multiple generals in the corps drew up defensive positions, yet Jackson's attack proved crushingly successful. The Confederates tore through Union skirmish lines and turned the Federal right flank. Their attack stalled only because of darkness, troop exhaustion, and Jackson's accidental wounding at the hands of his own men. Nevertheless, the Rebels had crushed the Union army's right flank and inflicted 2,412 casualties on the XI Corps.[43]

Chancellorsville thus became a particularly dark time for two of Ames's prominent supporters. Howard and his XI Corps gained a tarnished reputation after Jackson's troops successfully turned their unprotected flank. The rest of the Union army already looked down on its German American troops with nativist contempt, and the stigma of cowardice first won in the Shenandoah Valley now latched on to Howard's command. Misfortune befell Major General Berry too. On May 3 Hooker ordered the III Corps to withdraw because Sickles's three divisions formed a bulge in the center of the reconfigured line. Lee capitalized on this and ordered another attack. Berry's division endured the heaviest fighting, his three brigades suffering 1,429 casualties, the most of any Union division at Chancellorsville. As the general approached his staff officers to discuss a withdrawal, North Carolinian sharpshooters opened fire, killing Berry. When Hooker heard that Berry had died, he reportedly sobbed.[44]

The Army of the Potomac did score some minor success repelling Confederate troops on the third. East of Fredericksburg, Sedgwick's troops managed to dislodge the smaller force Lee had left behind to guard his rear. That achievement came to naught the next day as outnumbered Confederates first delayed and then drove back the advancing corps. On May 5 Sedgwick retreated across the Rappahannock. Hooker then ordered a general retreat as well, and his army was across the river by the sixth. The Army of the Potomac lost 17,287 men in the Battle of Chancellorsville, while the Army of Northern Virginia incurred over 12,764 casualties; Jackson soon died of pneumonia as he dealt with the wounds he had received during the battle. The human toll aside, Lee had successfully repulsed a massive Federal force thanks to courageous conduct on the part of his rank-and-file soldiers and his bold military gambles. At the same time, Hooker and some of his highest-ranking subordinates suffered from miscommunication, tentativeness, and incompetence.[45]

Although the army withdrew in the wake of another loss, Major General Sickles applauded the efforts of his soldiers. "The most difficult and painful of duties remains to be performed, a tribute to the fallen and the just commendation of those most distinguished for good conduct." He went on to declare: "I shall fail in giving adequate expression to the obligations I feel toward division, brigade, regimental and battery commanders." Other, more reputable officers, such as XII Corps commander Maj. Gen. Henry W. Slocum, shared similar sentiments. "I cannot designate any particular regiment as worthy of special commendation without doing injustice to others. . . . Every one of the general officers [in the XII Corps] discharged his full duty."[46]

Ames drew praise too. During the battle, the colonel had assisted Meade as needed. Although it did not face the most ferocious fighting, the V Corps served with distinction during the engagement. Meade lauded the conduct and actions of his men, noting, "It is such a service as this that tries and makes the real soldier." In his official report the general also expressed his gratefulness for the gallantry of his staff officers, including Ames. "I desire to call particular attention to the intelligence and zeal exhibited by Lieutenant-Colonel Webb, assistant inspector-general, and Colonel Ames, Twentieth Maine, throughout the whole of the operations." One of Ames's later duties during the campaign was to command a guard that protected a vital telegraph line to Washington during the army's retreat across the Rappahannock.[47]

The defeat at Chancellorsville was another sour note for the Army of the Potomac. Aside from the thousands of casualties, the campaign's failure shocked Lincoln. Noah Brooks, a journalist and friend of the president, was with Lincoln when he heard that Hooker had retreated. "He could not have been more overwhelmed," Brooks remembered. "Never so long as I knew him did he seem to be so broken, so dispirited, and so ghostlike." The army was equally demoralized. A majority of the corps commanders wanted to continue to press Lee, but Hooker's refusal to do so dejected and angered them. Infighting within the officer corps of the army spiked (some vituperative claims of incompetence continuing even after the war). Above all else, the Army of the Potomac made no progress. Having started with 106,877 enlisted men at his disposal, Hooker was right back where he started after the battle, his massive army having suffered over 17,000 casualties while facing a numerically inferior foe. Despite all of this, Lincoln elected to retain Hooker, at least for the time being. The Army of the Potomac, meanwhile, had little time to convalesce—Lee's army was on the move.[48]

BOY GENERAL

After his success in consecutive battles, Lee took the Army of Northern Virginia northward in the summer of 1863, just as he had done after Second Bull Run in 1862. By June 3, the Army of Northern Virginia began shifting from the Chancellorsville-Fredericksburg region. Led by Longstreet's First Corps, the Confederate infantry marched to the northwest for five days before pausing in Culpepper County and reuniting with Maj. Gen. J. E. B. Stuart's cavalry. From there, Lee divided his infantry into three columns and moved toward the Shenandoah Valley. Stuart and his cavalry remained in Culpepper.[1]

As Hooker and the Army of the Potomac reacted to these movements, Ames received another promotion. Due to his gallant service at Fredericksburg and Chancellorsville, Ames accepted the rank of brigadier general in the US Volunteers on May 20, 1863. At the age of twenty-seven, Ames became one of the youngest generals in the entire Union army. One of the first in a distinctive group of young officers known as the "boy generals," Ames, along with Judson Kilpatrick, Wesley Merritt, Elon Farnsworth, and George Armstrong Custer, earned promotions after Chancellorsville, in part because of their zealousness and courage. While the other officers served in the cavalry, Ames's commission was particularly impressive, as he became the youngest infantry general in the Army of the Potomac.[2]

Despite his promotion and new brigade command, Ames kept a watchful eye on the men of the Twentieth Maine and his pupil Chamberlain, who finally managed to escape the confines of Quarantine Hill on May 3 as the Battle of Chancellorsville continued. On that day Butterfield asked the lieutenant

Brig. Gen. Adelbert Ames (Medford Historical Society and Museum)

colonel to lead the regiment to the Rappahannock River and guard the same telegraph line that Ames protected. Chamberlain "was in the saddle all night" and inspected the line continually "since the telegraph wire was broken and tampered with many times each night." He also participated in an advance the next day with Brigadier General Griffin, during which a second horse was shot from beneath the former professor.[3]

For his actions, Chamberlain likewise received promotion to colonel and commanding officer of the Twentieth Maine on May 20. Yet Ames's teaching and disciplinarian influence remained. Chamberlain enforced discipline as he had learned from Ames and drilled the men twice a day.[4] Hezekiah Long, likewise promoted (to sergeant), described the attitude of the regiment upon their original commander's departure. "Col. Ames has been appointed Brigadier General," he wrote, "and takes a command in the Eleventh [Corps], Gen. Howard's Corps. So we shall lose him. The soldiers are just beginning to find him out and like him, and the most of them are sorry to lose him."[5]

Reassigned to the XI Corps, Brigadier General Ames assumed command of the Second Brigade, First Division. Brig. Gen. Nathaniel C. McLean had commanded the brigade at Chancellorsville, but Howard "banished the former Cincinnati lawyer to a staff job" due to unsatisfactory leadership. The brigade comprised four valiant regiments. The Twenty-Fifth Ohio and Seventy-Fifth Ohio had enlisted in 1861, while the 107th Ohio followed in September 1862. The Seventeenth Connecticut, organized in Bridgeport, was the fourth regiment of his brigade. Col. Leopold von Gilsa commanded the other brigade in the division. A Prussian-trained officer, von Gilsa enlisted in the Union army in 1861, but his reputation plummeted after his New Yorkers and Pennsylvanians, most of them German immigrants, collapsed at Chancellorsville under Jackson's flank attack. Ames and von Gilsa in turn reported to twenty-nine-year-old division commander Brig. Gen. Francis Channing Barlow, another boy general. While young for their ranks, both officers had successful combat experience; Barlow had become a general after Antietam.[6]

Published three days after Ames's promotion, war correspondent L. L. Crounse's *New York Times* article discussed the Army of the Potomac, the XI Corps, and Ames's new rank. While he began by highlighting the officers in the XI Corps who had tried to distance themselves from the disaster at Chancellorsville, Crounse applauded the promotion of the corps' new brigadier general. "Col. Adelbert Ames, of the Twentieth Maine regiment, yesterday received his appointment as Brigadier-General," he wrote. "This is fitly bestowed. If all our appointments had as much merit as this, there would be fewer instances of incompetency and neglect of duty."[7]

After assuming command of his brigade, Ames received orders to join Brig. Gen. Alfred Pleasonton's Cavalry Corps as an infantry "attachment" on June 6. Butterfield gave Ames explicit orders to shield the cavalry's movements from the enemy and to keep his orders a secret. "Be careful that your column is concealed from the enemy"; he wrote, "that your own command is ignorant of their destination; that any guerrillas, spies, or wanderers through the country which you traverse are picked up, to prevent their communicating any information to the enemy."

Complicating matters, Ames's attached command was a composite five-regiment brigade. Instead of commanding a cohesive contingent of regiments from the XI Corps, he had units from the III, XI, and XII Corps. The Thirty-Third Massachusetts, led Col. Adin Ballou Underwood, was the lone regiment detached from the XI Corps, yet it hailed from a different division. Despite lacking familiarity with his men, Ames's temporary command dutifully marched with three days' rations and a mule train carrying an additional ninety rounds of ammunition per soldier.[8]

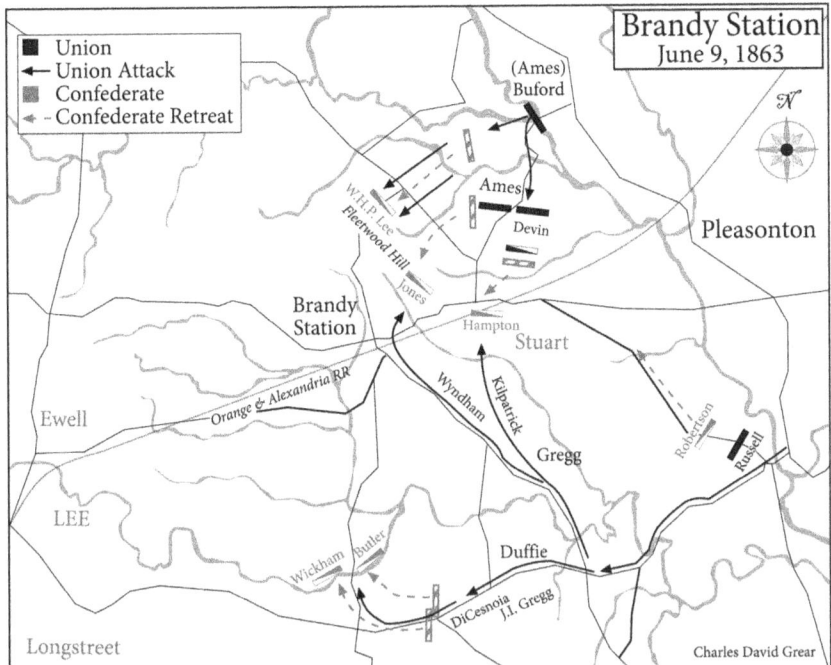

Brandy Station, June 9, 1863 (Charles David Grear)

Pleasonton's corps received instructions from Hooker to ascertain the whereabouts of Lee's army, and specifically Stuart's Confederate cavalry. Hooker feared that the Southern horse soldiers intended to stifle Union supply lines. On June 8 Stuart directed his troopers to bivouac near Brandy Station, roughly twenty miles northwest of Chancellorsville and three miles west of the frequently crossed Rappahannock. Unbeknown to the 9,500 Confederates, Pleasonton's force of 11,000 cavalry, infantry, and artillery arrived on the north bank of the river, from which the Union general hoped to surprise Stuart's men and thwart their crossing. Pleasonton divided his command into two wings. Both would cross the Rappahannock, one to the northeast and the other southeast of Brandy Station, with the intent to catch the Confederate cavalrymen in the dazed stupor of sleep. Supporting Brig. Gen. John Buford's right wing, Ames and his brigade participated in the northeastern crossing at Beverly's Ford.[9]

The Battle of Brandy Station started in the early morning hours of June 9. Before 5 A.M., Buford's wing crossed the river. Union forces shocked Confederate pickets and startled sleeping cavalrymen, but some of Stuart's troopers quickly assembled and charged Buford's columns. Other Confederates, disorganized from the surprise, rallied next to the light horse artillery and poured fire into Buford's regiments. Two-thirds of Ames's brigade managed to get across Beverly's Ford around 6 A.M. and took up a position near the edge of some trees on the south side of the crossing. Ames reported afterward, "Attacks were made by dismounted cavalry, but in each instance, he was repulsed, with considerable loss."[10]

Once his men repelled the first attack, Ames—now with his full brigade—moved south to a slight ridge once occupied by the Rebels. He claimed that "a very superior force of the enemy's infantry and cavalry was discovered" as they advanced. Buford's brigade commanders then requested his help to dislodge the dismounted Confederates. Ames sent elements from at least two of his regiments, the Second Massachusetts and the Third Wisconsin, to his right to expel the Rebel troopers. Simultaneously, the rest of his infantry engaged Confederate troops attacking their front. The more requests Ames received to help the cavalry, however, the more stress it put on his own flanks. Fortunately, his infantry did not yield until Pleasonton ordered his entire command back across the river at sunset. Ames's brigade suffered sixty-five casualties altogether—six dead, fifty-seven wounded, and two men missing or captured. The infantry had played a pivotal role in the largest cavalry engagement of the Civil War. Ames oversaw a river crossing without losing any men and dislodged enemy troops from a higher elevation. All the officers in the brigade worked well together and quickly solidified into a cohesive force. A testament to skilled leadership, Ames and his soldiers rose to the challenge.[11]

After the ten-hour battle concluded, both sides claimed victory. Pleasonton had successfully hindered Stuart's crossing, but Stuart argued that he won because he held the field at the end of the day. Neither commander, however, avoided criticism. Answering these complaints, the *New York Herald* asserted that Pleasonton had done his job, impeded Stuart's crossing, and was "justified" in returning to "this [north] side of the river." Confederate newspapers, however, chided Stuart for being caught off guard. The *North Carolina Weekly Standard* printed a scathing critique of the general's leadership: "It is a victory over which few will exult," and valor paid a high price because of "conceit and carelessness" on his behalf.[12]

Pleasonton was especially complimentary toward Ames and his men. He thought that Ames served admirably, especially considering he was leading an independent infantry unit alongside a cavalry attack.[13] In his official report

Pleasonton highlighted the new brigadier: "To Brigadier-Generals Russell and Ames, with their respective commands, I am under many obligations for the effective co-operation they gave at all times. The marked manner in which General Ames held and managed his troops under a galling fire of the enemy for several hours, is entitled to higher commendation than I can bestow."[14]

On June 12 Hooker wrote to Pleasonton, in part, to ask him to send Ames back to his brigade and his various regiments back to their respective corps. Headquarters also asked the cavalry general to keep an eye on Stuart and "be watchful, vigilant, and let nothing escape you." Even if Brandy Station had diminished the efficiency of the Confederate cavalry, both Hooker and Butterfield believed that Stuart would try something to reinvigorate his reputation. The Southern general did just that. He elected to lead some of his best brigades on an indirect gallop between the Army of the Potomac and Washington, inadvertently cutting off communications between himself and the northward-moving Army of Northern Virginia. Lee and his army, although safe for the moment from the Federal forces marching parallel to them farther east, could not rely on desperately needed intelligence as they invaded the Union states of Maryland and Pennsylvania.[15]

At the end of June, after days of bickering and working at cross-purposes, Hooker requested that Halleck and Lincoln remove him from command of the Army of the Potomac. Lincoln readily accepted Hooker's resignation, even with the army chasing Lee. with George Meade replaced Fighting Joe as commander on June 28. Meade, a career military man with a hot temper, did not desire the position but had ample experience for the command. Continuing the march northward to intercept Lee's force, the Army of the Potomac remained between the Rebel army and the cities of Baltimore and Washington, while the Confederates relished the profuse resources of Pennsylvania. By late June, some of Lee's men were near York, Pennsylvania, and the state capital, Harrisburg. Only then did Lee receive reports that the Federal army was in pursuit. Meade's forces, in fact, had crossed the Potomac River and were racing to get into striking distance of the scattered Confederate forces. Lee wanted to merge his dispersed army as soon as possible, even though rain had saturated the country roads, making reunification difficult.[16]

On June 30, Confederate forces approached the seminary town of Gettysburg in southern Pennsylvania. But Union cavalry, commanded by Brigadier General Buford, arrived there first. The following day Southern infantry approached the crossroads town as part of Lee's ordered concentration. In the early morning of July 1, both sides met along three ridges west of Gettysburg. Ironically, Meade's army approached the town from the south, while the Confederate soldiers throughout the day streamed in from the north and west.[17]

The fighting on July 1 started as a skirmish between dismounted Federal cavalrymen and infantry brigades from Maj. Gen. Henry Heth's Confederate division. The combat soon blossomed into a full-scale engagement once Union infantry from the I Corps, under the command of Maj. Gen. John F. Reynolds, arrived on the field. Troops from the XI Corps were on the way as well. Earlier that morning, at 3:30 A.M., Howard received orders to advance toward Gettysburg in support of Reynolds. He directed his entire corps to begin moving by 8:30. Later that morning Howard and the First Division arrived outside of Gettysburg. Around 11:30 A.M. the general received word that Reynolds had died, shot either by a Rebel infantryman or accidentally by his own men. As the senior officer on the field, Howard assumed command of all the Union forces engaged at Gettysburg. Realizing the scope of the developing battle, he knew that the situation could unravel quickly, with Reynolds dead and more Confederate troops on the way. Howard thus sent couriers to Major Generals Sickles and Slocum, asking them to bring up the III and XII Corps to Gettysburg as quickly as possible.[18]

Leaving one division of the XI Corps in reserve on elevated terrain south of town, Howard sent his other two divisions north of town to confront Confederate troops arriving from the Harrisburg area. Ames's brigade moved into Gettysburg between 1 P.M. and 2 P.M. and immediately ordered four companies of skirmishers to assemble. The rest of his brigade marched to the north and east at a brisk pace. In that portion of the field, Barlow positioned Ames's men south of a rise called Blocher's Knoll. The only troops farther to the right on the Federal line was a contingent of Union cavalry under Col. Thomas Devin. Positioning two of his regiments at the front and two immediately behind them in reserve, Ames anchored his position to the east on a north–south stream called Rock Creek and to his west on the Harrisburg Road, running from Gettysburg.

At 2:45 P.M. Confederate forces under Lt. Gen. Richard S. Ewell, commanding the Second Corps, arrived on the scene. Barlow ordered Ames's brigade forward, placing it to the left of Colonel von Gilsa's brigade on Blocher's Knoll. Maj. Gen. Jubal Early's Confederate division of Ewell's corps attacked Barlow's position. Ames and his men faced a numerically superior enemy who sent torrents of lead into the Union lines. Artillery pummeled the brigade's position, but Union troops later recalled especially the efficacy of Rebel infantry. "The regiment being exposed to a heavy fire of artillery and musketry," one of Ames's subordinates reported, "suffered heavily in killed and wounded." Every one of the young brigadier's regiments except the Seventy-Fifth Ohio had either their first or second in command killed or wounded. By nightfall, the Twenty-Fifth Ohio was on its third commanding officer after twenty-four hours.[19]

As the battle progressed, Barlow's decision to move both of his brigades to Blocher's Knoll proved disastrous. By doing so he formed a bulge in the Union line and exposed both Ames's and von Gilsa's flanks. Early's Division finally overwhelmed the salient and broke through von Gilsa's line. According to Ames, the Germans once again fled the line of battle, "running through [the] lines of the regiments of my brigade (the Second) and thereby creating considerable confusion." Barlow himself suffered a severe wound as his division began to break apart, leaving Ames in command. Ames immediately took charge, handing over his brigade to the capable Col. Andrew L. Harris of the Seventy-Fifth Ohio.[20]

"At this time," Ames noted in his official report, "General Barlow was wounded, and the command of the division devolved upon me. The whole division was falling back with little or no regularity, regimental organizations having become destroyed." He then received orders from Maj. Gen. Carl Schurz, temporarily commanding the XI Corps, to withdraw to the outskirts of Gettysburg. Shortly thereafter, Schurz told him to fall back south of town. Ames urged his officers to lead an orderly retreat and to dispute every inch of soil.[21]

On the Union left, division commanders in the I Corps sent urgent messages to Howard for reinforcements, but he replied there were no troops to spare. Around 4 P.M. the Union left broke down. Within ten minutes the entire line received word to fall back. Howard wanted the withdrawing brigades to rally around his reserve division on a geographic rise known as Cemetery Hill. In the meantime, Ames and his division almost failed to escape the pincers of Ewell's men. Union soldiers spilled into the streets of Gettysburg, streams of retreating Federals mixing with each other. Ames and his officers exhorted every ounce of effort to prevent such disorganization in their own ranks, even in the face of a "superior force of the enemy." When Confederate troops tried to cut off part of Ames's division before they could reach Gettysburg, the Federals evaded them. Once inside the town, companies of the Seventeenth Connecticut opened fire on pursuing Rebel troops, and the 107th Ohio regrouped on the southern side of Gettysburg to fight back. By evening, Ames had managed to get his division to Cemetery Hill, where Colonel Harris placed the Second Brigade on the eastern crest. Supported by artillery, and with some of

View from Cemetery Hill of area where the Louisiana Tigers attacked Ames's command on July 2, 1863 (Library of Congress)

his troops behind a stone wall, Ames held a strong defensive position parallel to a street called Brickyard Lane.[22]

From Cemetery Hill, Ames reported how many able men he had left: "The First Brigade numbers 650 muskets, and is in position, faced both to the right and front. The Second Brigade, about 500 muskets." A significant number of men from the division were now prisoners of the Confederate army. By nightfall, the II, III, and XII Corps of the Army of the Potomac arrived on the field, reinforcing and extending the Union line along the hills and ridges to the south and east of Gettysburg.[23]

The first day of the battle encapsulated the best aspects of Ames's character and leadership. In dire circumstances he remained cool and calm under mounting pressure. Although his lines eventually gave way through von Gilsa's collapse and Early's superior numbers, Ames managed the situation as best as possible. Col. Charles S. Wainwright, an artillery commander on Cemetery Hill who served meritoriously alongside Ames during the battle, described the Mainer as both a gentleman and the ideal soldier, "the best kind of man to be associated with, cool and clear in his own judgment."[24]

At the same time, the fight on July 1 highlights Ames's less attractive qualities too. He refused to take any blame for the retreat but gave himself all of the credit for saving the division. Even though his troops had fought their hardest on July 1, Ames minimized their role. He also downplayed the meritorious management exercised by his regimental commanders and, as historian Harry W. Pfanz observes, did them a disservice by not crediting them more in his reports.[25]

Confederate attacks continued the following day and featured assaults against both flanks of the Army of the Potomac. On July 2 Lee ordered two of Longstreet's divisions to strike the Union left flank. Although the attack did not start on time, Longstreet's men smashed the Federal line once it began that afternoon, driving back Sickles's III Corps. Fighting raged in that section while the Confederates prepared to strike the Union right. The troops on Cemetery Hill had a clear view of enemy positions and had seen Confederate officers amassing their forces all day. One solider from Ames's division reported, "As soon as it was light we could see the Johnnies moving along the fences in our front, keeping out of sight as much as possible." Ames's men only skirmished with Confederate sharpshooters up until around 4 P.M. Meanwhile, Early's Division probed the Federal defenses, ascertaining their weaknesses. Described as a "cat and mouse game," this skirmishing continued for hours. Ames's troops took cover behind rocks and trees to avoid Confederate fire.[26]

Once dusk fell, the fighting there intensified exponentially. A two-hour cannonade from Confederate artillery ensued, as Ewell tried to soften the Federal defenses. At 7 P.M. two of his brigades surged forward. Ames's and Early's men now tussled for the second consecutive day. Brig. Gen. Harry T. Hays's troops, the famous Louisiana Tigers, charged Ames's left flank. The Twenty-Fifth Ohio's and 107th Ohio's position formed a wedge behind a stone wall that the Fifth and Sixth Louisiana tried to crack. At this critical juncture Ames made a significant error, repositioning the Seventeenth Connecticut to fill a gap that did not exist in the center of his line. The men of that regiment and the Seventy-Fifth Ohio soon stared down their barrels at three Louisiana regiments.[27]

To the right of the Ohioans, Colonel von Gilsa's rallied regiments battled Col. Isaac E. Avery's North Carolinians. Outnumbered by roughly 400 men, von Gilsa's troops stretched from Brickyard Lane all the way to a meadow where the Forty-First New York and the Thirty-Third Massachusetts anchored his line. Multiple accounts again describe von Gilsa's men panicking and retreating behind entrenched batteries that soon were overrun. As Howard recalled, "Ames' men were assisting them [artillerymen] with their rifles, they were wielding hand spikes, abandoned muskets, sponge staffs, or anything they could seize."[28]

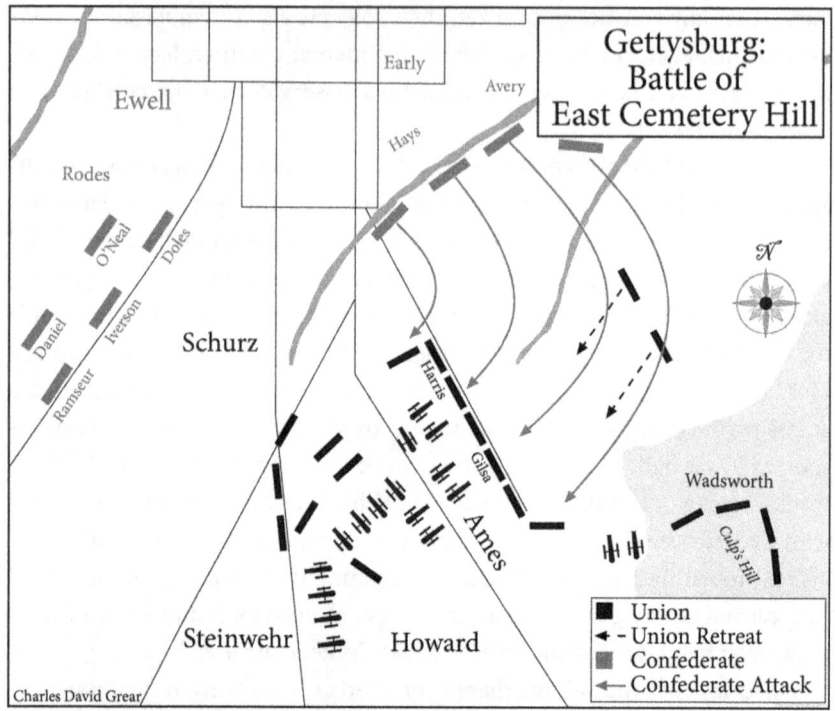

Gettysburg: Battle of East Cemetery Hill, July 2, 1863 (Charles David Grear)

Both sides detailed the viciousness of the fighting, which continued long after dark. Maj. Samuel Tate of the Sixth North Carolina described North Carolinians and Louisianans scaling the stone wall, pushing back both of Ames's brigades, and planting their colors among Union artillery pieces nearby. "The enemy stood with tenacity never before displayed by them," Tate reported, "but with bayonet, clubbed musket, sword, pistol and rocks from the wall we cleared the heights and silenced the guns." Their triumph was temporary, however. "The enemy made a desperate charge upon us, but without success," said the 107th Ohio's Capt. John M. Lutz. "They were repulsed with great loss. It was at this point the regiment captured a stand of colors from the 8th Louisiana Tigers." It was "by extraordinary exertions [that Ames] arrested a panic" at this moment, according to Howard, thus saving the guns and the position alike.[29]

As the night progressed, Cemetery Hill became the most vulnerable but important part of the entire Union line. With his division in bloody shambles and every regiment severely undermanned, Ames faced a calamitous situation. If Confederate troops stormed through the Cemetery Hill lines, the Army of the

Potomac would need to readjust its entire position. Fortunately, reinforcements from the XI and II Corps arrived. Brig. Gen. Włodzimierz Krzyżanowski sent the Fifty-Eighth New York and 119th New York to help protect the batteries behind Ames's troops. At roughly the same time, Col. Samuel S. Carroll's brigade from the II Corps passed by the gatehouse of the cemetery and charged the Confederate troops. Nicknamed the "Gibraltar Brigade" because of their tenacity, Carroll's men joined with Ames's Ohio regiments to shove back Hays's Southerners.[30]

Despite his successful charge, Carroll was unaware of his current position and whether the XI Corps had any organized regiments in the area. Principally, he wanted to know whether he could return to the II Corps or if he needed to stay where he was. When one of his couriers found Ames, the Mainer asked Carroll to remain, telling the staff officer that he had no faith in some of his men and could use the brigade's assistance. Carroll cursed Ames when the courier returned, declaring, "Damn a man who has no confidence in his troops." But Howard agreed with Ames; the division did not contain enough trustworthy and organized soldiers to allow Carroll to leave that night. The 107th Ohio, Seventeenth Connecticut, and reserve units from the Thirty-Third Massachusetts had fought superbly, but other units had shone less determination, and for the second day, the XI Corps suffered heavy losses. It needed help to maintain control of Cemetery Hill.[31]

The savage fighting finally subdued as both the defenders and attackers tried to reorganize their lines and gather stragglers. While the Confederates experienced some success on Cemetery Hill and captured half of the trenches on nearby Culp's Hill, the Union army still held the high ground. Thankfully for Ames, one of Ewell's divisions never attacked Cemetery Hill. Maj. Gen. Robert Rodes's troops had instructions to aid Early's attack, striking from the west as Early's men advanced from the north. Rodes reported that getting his men in position delayed his attack. By the time his division organized, the general declined to send his troops against Cemetery Hill and its many batteries.[32]

As Ames's men rested that night, the general worked with medical personal to collect all the wounded men on Cemetery Hill. He directed ambulances and orchestrated the care for the hundreds of wounded soldiers along the hillside. The Louisianans and North Carolinians suffered greater casualties on the second day of Gettysburg than the first, with Hays's Brigade losing more than twice as many men as they had the day before. Ames's division too paid a large butcher's bill to retain Cemetery Hill. After two days of fighting, the First Brigade's casualties numbered 527 men, with 211 casualties in von Gilsa's brigade

East Cemetery Hill, 1909 (Library of Congress)

coming from just one of his four regiments. The hard-fighting Second Brigade fared even worse. Ames's original command suffered 778 casualties. Total casualties for the division were 1,306 men killed, wounded, missing, or captured.[33]

As Ames oversaw his troops on Cemetery Hill that night, Howard and representatives from all of the Union corps met at Meade's headquarters, the Lydia Leister farmhouse on nearby Cemetery Ridge. This council of war debated whether to stay and continue the fight. Howard voted yes. Even though his corps had suffered severe casualties during two consecutive days of battle, he believed that its "partial successes" convinced him "to continue the assault next day." Howard was not alone; the consensus among the representative officers was to remain and fight. Meade concurred with this. As dawn broke the following morning, the commanding general wrote his wife: "All well and going on well with the Army. We had a great fight yesterday, the enemy attacking and we completely repulsing them; both armies shattered. . . . Army in fine sprits and every one determined to do or die."[34]

July 3 was a signal day in American history, but it was a less stressful one personally for Ames. From their defensive position that morning, his troops only skirmished with Ewell's divisions. Little came of this, and the Confederate lines eventually withdrew farther toward the town. During midday, Cemetery Hill received an artillery barrage as a precursor to the ill-fated charge against

Cemetery Ridge by Maj. Gen. George E. Pickett. Ames and his troops avoided taking any casualties, but other units in the XI Corps were not as fortunate. At day's end the Federals had repulsed every Confederate regiment that had moved against them, and the Army of the Potomac still held the coveted high ground after three days of fighting. The following morning, on a dismal, overcast Independence Day, Ames and his troops along the crest of Cemetery Hill noticed the lack of noise coming from enemy skirmishers. Sending soldiers to investigate, the general received word that the Confederates had retreated from the battlefield. Ames's troops were the first to reenter Gettysburg, where just three days prior many of them nearly became prisoners. Now they were the victors.[35]

Ames visited Gettysburg and other portions of the battlefield that day. He examined other portions of the Federal line, traveling primarily with Brig. Gen. Gouverneur Warren, chief of engineers for the Army of the Potomac. It was during this excursion that Ames came across his old regiment. In a letter home he described the surprise: "After three days' fighting I was riding over the field in front of our works with General Warren of Meade's staff. Passing some troops I found soon that cheering and swinging their hats in the air were being given for one of us. As General Warren [V Corps] was one of the heroes of the day, I thought it was for him—he told me it was for me. I found it was the 20th [Maine]. They gave me three times three."[36]

Like Ames, the Twentieth Maine endured vicious Confederate attacks on July 2. After pushing Sickles's III Corps back, Longstreet's men surged toward a hill at the southern tip of the Union line called Little Round Top. The Twentieth Maine and the rest of its brigade stalled a brigade of Texans and Alabamians under Brig. Gen. Evander M. Law. The Mainers, stationed at the extreme left of the Union line, faced two regiments from Alabama. Well disciplined, the Twentieth held its ground against multiple Confederate attacks. Finally outnumbered three-to-one, and with nearly no ammunition left, the Northerners faced yet another Confederate advance. In one of the most storied events of courage during the battle, if not the war, Colonel Chamberlain ordered his men to fix bayonets and charge down the slope. "Almost before he [Chamberlain] could yell 'charge!' the regiment leaped down the hill and closed in with the foe," a veteran remembered. The shock of the assault took the surging Fifteenth Alabama by surprise. The Mainers captured dozens and drove the remaining Alabamians down the hill. Casualties for the Twentieth Maine were steep, with 125 Mainers killed or wounded. As historian John Pullen writes: "It had not been a group of amateurs that had turned the Confederates back at Little Round Top, but a well-trained and highly effective regiment of infantry. And who could they thank most for that, if not General Ames?"[37]

After the battle's conclusion, Ames sent a warm and praise-laden letter to Chamberlain, applauding him and the entire regiment. "I am very proud of the 20th. Regt. and its present Colonel," he declared. "I did want to be with you and see your splendid conduct in the field. God bless you and the dear old regiment. My heart yearns for you; and more and more, now that these trying scenes convince me of your superiority. The pleasure I felt at the intelligence of your conduct yesterday is some recompense for all that I have suffered." In a letter home after the battle, Ames described a sort of reply, a gift from the officers of his former command. "The officers of the 20th have now in hand an elegant sword, sash and belt which they are awaiting for the opportunity to give me. The sword is very elegant."[38]

Less than a year earlier, Ames was a battery commander, Chamberlain a college professor, and the rest of the Twentieth Maine fishermen, farmers, or engaged in other civilian pursuits. After twelve months Ames had risen to the rank of brigadier general, Chamberlain had demonstrated poise and leadership as a regimental commander, and the regiment had become one of the finest in the army, displaying the discipline instilled in them by Ames.

The Army of the Potomac rested only briefly before it pursued Lee and his beaten invasion force south through driving rain and mud. Meade's men did not crush Lee's forces like some—especially Lincoln—hoped. Union cavalry under Brig. Gen. Judson Kilpatrick managed to capture over 1,000 Confederate troops and dozens of enemy pack mules and horses on July 4. But he failed to do anything else, according to Kilpatrick, because he needed to preserve his men, transfer prisoners, and protect the captured animals.[39]

Similarly, Union infantry eventually engaged the retreating Rebels. The VI Corps under Sedgwick attacked Ewell's rear guard on July 5, fighting until Meade ordered his army to stop. Meade feared that Lee and his army were plotting to instigate another battle on ground of their choosing and wanted to gather more definitive intelligence. Ames and his division pursued the Southerners with the rest of the XI Corps. Howard, who now commanded one of three designated wings of the Army of the Potomac, encouraged aggressiveness. Ames participated in one of the many skirmishes between the two armies after Gettysburg. On July 12 his First Brigade marched with Kilpatrick's cavalry to a crest outside of Hagerstown, Maryland. The two boy generals' units cooperated flawlessly. Kilpatrick wrote that they received orders to "drive the enemy out" and did so, capturing prisoners and controlling the town. While a successful endeavor, Hagerstown was not as important to Lee's army now as the town was earlier in the retreat. Confederate forces united a couple miles south of it, dug in, and prepared to receive an attack. In the meantime, Rebel engineers prepared for the army crossing the Potomac River. Meade hesitated to order an attack, and over the next two days, the Army of Northern Virginia made it across the Potomac and back to Virginia. Lee successfully escaped again.[40]

Ames never commented on the missed opportunity to prevent Lee's escape. Halleck wrote to Meade and told him, "You handled your troops in battle well," continuing, "I have lost none of the confidence which I felt in you when I recommended you for the command." But President Lincoln, among others, lamented the apparent shortcomings of the Federal army's pursuit. In an unsent letter to Meade on July 14, he made his opinion clear: "I do not believe you appreciate the magnitude of misfortune involved in Lee's escape. He was within your grasp. . . . As it is, the war will be prolonged indefinitely."[41]

Meade eventually followed Lee back to Virginia, where the two battered armies settled in to temporary camps. Then in August Ames left the Army of the Potomac, as the First Division received orders to report to the Department of the South and its commander, Maj. Gen. Quincy A. Gillmore. But it was not the same division that headed south. In command now was Brig. Gen. George H. Gordon, a West Point graduate who had not fought at Gettysburg. Ames, meanwhile, lost the 107th Ohio but gained three new regiments, the Fortieth

Maj. Gen. Quincey A. Gillmore (Library of Congress)

Massachusetts, the 144th New York, and the 157th New York, bolstering his brigade to six regiments. Before leaving Warrenton Junction for South Carolina on August 1, the division witnessed a sobering moment when a private in the 157th New York was executed by firing squad for desertion. A week later, Ames and the entire division was at Fort Monroe, Virginia. Two days later they sailed to Charleston, South Carolina, arriving there on August 13.[42]

The Union army and indeed the North as a whole saw Charleston as the epicenter of secessionist fervor and believed the city exuded arrogance and sedition. It was also a major port that allowed the Confederacy occasional access to the Atlantic when vessels broke the naval blockade outside Charleston harbor. Thus, the Union army desperately wanted to take the city for both strategic and morale purposes. The troops of the Department of the South had previously attempted to take nearby islands and put pressure on the city. In June 1862 Union forces attacked Confederate troops on James Island, but those efforts failed. In April 1863 a Union squadron under RAdm. Francis Du

Pont tried to pummel Fort Sumter. The Union navy lost a vessel, the defenders did not surrender, and Confederate forces used slave labor to reinforce the battered fortification.[43]

When Gordon's division arrived in August 1863, Gillmore immediately detached Ames's brigade and sent it to Morris Island, 840 acres in size and featuring the heavily defended Fort Wagner. A few weeks earlier Gillmore had approved an expedition to take the island, which rested on the cusp of Charleston's harbor. Federal officials thought that holding that position could help them finally take the besieged city. On July 10 Union forces took the southern end of Morris Island, then began an unsuccessful assault against Fort Wagner. Although troops managed to crack the position initially, the Confederate defenders soon repulsed them. On July 18 Gillmore ordered another attack, spearheaded by the famed Fifty-Fourth Massachusetts Infantry. This failed as well, with Federal forces suffering 1,854 casualties. In contrast, the Confederate defenders lost 513 men, 88 of them killed.[44]

Ames's brigade reached Morris Island on August 17 as much-needed reinforcements. None of his regiments incurred any casualties while there. Writing home, Ames described the close quarters they endured. "My camp is near where the lighthouse used to be on this [Morris] Island. In fact, all of the camps are crowded on this end of the island, the rebels hold the other end." The cramped conditions became doubly problematic when his men did not receive fresh supplies. Alone among the Federal force, they lacked knapsacks and enough tents. Lengthy exposure to the natural elements took a toll on the newly arrived troops. "In this destitute condition, unacclimated, exposed on the sand to the hot sun, rain and wind, many became sick and all suffered," Ames reported.[45]

The young general yearned for action. While on Morris Island, he boldly submitted a plan to take Fort Sumter. Capturing the fort would get his men off of the island, provide a morale boost for the army, and not incidentally put another feather in Ames's proverbial cap. But authorities there countermanded his proposal, pushing it aside for unknown reasons. Perhaps it was jealousy; perhaps Ames's ambitiousness irritated his superiors in South Carolina. More likely, as Harry King Benson notes, "there was little military reason for taking Fort Sumter by assault." Nevertheless, Gillmore created his own plan to do just that on September 8. The US Navy blasted the fort with powerful barrages, reducing its walls to rubble. The stubborn Confederate defenders, however, refused to surrender. Union sailors and marines tried to land and take the post, but most of their boats did not reach the fort. Over

The Union encampment on Morris Island, South Carolina (Library of Congress)

100 of the 400 men who participated in the amphibious attack ended up killed or captured. The Rebel garrison suffered no casualties during either the bombardment or the assault.[46]

Ames's brigade remained on Morris Island until August 29, when the men moved to nearby Folly Island. Although buggy and humid, it was not as intolerable as their previous siege duty. Other than digging trenches, Ames's troops did little there. On November 27 the army granted Ames a leave of absence. Col. William H. Noble of the Seventeenth Connecticut commanded the brigade while its young general visited Washington, DC, and New York City. In early January 1864 Ames returned to his brigade, still stationed on Folly Island, where they remained for several more weeks until transferred again.[47]

Around the end of 1863, Lincoln had envisioned a new military strategy. Instead of controlling captured Confederate cities on the coast, the president wanted to control the hinterland around occupied towns. The purpose was to make the presence of the Union army more apparent to the southern population, to elicit at least a modicum of support from sheepish pro-Union residents in the countryside, and to emancipate the enslaved. To Lincoln, Florida seemed like a good place to start. Devoid of a large Confederate military force, blessed with sizable herds of cattle, and easily accessible to the Union navy, a pro-Union Florida was an attractive endeavor to pursue. Lincoln thus instructed Major General Gillmore to dispatch as much military manpower and aid as possible to that state. Gillmore accordingly sent Brig. Gen. Truman Seymour to Jacksonville, Florida, on February 5, 1864. Roughly two weeks afterward, a ragged Confederate force soundly beat this Union expeditionary army at the Battle of Olustee. There, Seymour had assumed that he confronted only Florida militiamen. Instead, Confederate artillery bludgeoned his troops before veteran Confederate regiments, dispatched from Georgia and elsewhere in Florida, shattered the Union line. Seymour ordered a retreat. Although Confederate troops tried to attack the retreating Union column, the famed Fifty-Fourth Massachusetts and the Thirty-Fifth US Colored Troops stopped Rebel progress. The embarrassed Federals raced backed to Jacksonville, where the US Navy could protect them.[48]

Losing almost a third of its force in Florida as a result of the Olustee fiasco, Gillmore sent Ames's brigade south to support the beaten troops in Jacksonville and to keep alive the hope that Federal forces could wrest control of the state from Confederates in the region. Ames and his men arrived on February 28. Union forces afterward tried to disrupt Confederate supplies, encourage pro-Union citizens, and persuade enslaved persons nearby to join the Union army, but the effort soon collapsed.[49]

Ames remained in Jacksonville until April. While there, he assumed command of an entire division, consisting of three brigades, as he awaited action of some sort. His superiors, however, drug their feet. With a campaign unlikely, troops fashioned breastworks and defenses around the Union position, ensuring that any attack would certainly prove disastrous for the small Confederate forces in the area. Ames's overall experience during his two months in Florida was thus only moderately taxing. He had time enough to enjoy boating and even bought a carriage to ride around the city. Nevertheless, Ames believed that protecting Florida was a waste of his talents and time. In a letter home he told his father, "Florida is a place into which the rebels should be driven, not *out* of it."[50]

Others agreed. During the early spring, senior officers in the Union army sought to bring Ames back to Virginia and the Army of the Potomac to benefit from his experience and leadership. Initially, Meade and Pleasonton asked President Lincoln to transfer the young general to the cavalry to take charge of a division. Major General Halleck, now the army chief of staff with U. S. Grant's promotion to lieutenant general and the post of general in chief, balked at the idea. It was an abject waste, he concluded, to send such a fine infantry officer and expert engineer to the cavalry. Still, when the Department of the South consolidated into the X Corps in the spring of 1864, Ames received a new assignment. Ordered to report to Maj. Gen. Benjamin F. Butler, commander of the Army of the James, Ames left Florida on April 15. Disembarking from the transport vessel *Fulton*, he reported to headquarters at Gloucester Point, Virginia, on the twenty-seventh.[51]

Elated that he had left the muggy Florida backwater, Ames set to work priming his new division for the upcoming spring offensive. His new command consisted of troops he had never served with nor led. As the spring of 1864 began the final chapter of the war, Ames wished to show his worthiness and validate the praise he had received from his superiors, subordinates, and colleagues. Epitomizing the young officers who had risen through the ranks of the Union army since 1863, Ames also anticipated a chance to earn personal glory and further cement his status as a rising star in the army. In a letter home he appropriately predicted the imminent maneuvers: "Everything will be concentrated in Virginia for the final struggle."[52]

FUTILITY ALONG THE JAMES RIVER

When Ames arrived at Gloucester Point on April 27, 1864, the scene in Virginia bore an eerie resemblance to the Peninsula Campaign two years earlier. An army of over 165,000 men stood ready for action that spring. The intention was similar—ending the war in a decisive fashion—and the subsequent campaign would take place in terrain that largely featured the familiar tributaries and landmarks of northern Virginia.

There were, however, major differences. The most notable was in the dynamic of the war itself. After three years of bloody fighting, the attitude of the Union army in the eastern theater had shifted. In 1862 McClellan's official policy emphasized reconciliation while capturing Richmond. The Union now advocated a "harsh war" approach that had originated in the West. The new goal was to use as many soldiers as possible to pound Lee and his army to pieces, forcing them to surrender instead of coercing capitulation by taking Richmond. The Peninsula Campaign of 1862 had ended in futility. The architects of the Overland Campaign, led by U. S. Grant, sought to avoid earlier pitfalls.[1]

The Army of the Potomac also had a radically different officer corps in command compared to when Ames was a lieutenant commanding a battery in 1862. McClellan, Burnside, and Hooker were long gone. Not one corps commander from the Peninsula Campaign still retained his position. Maj. Gen. Edwin Sumner had died in 1863. Both Maj. Gen. Fitz John Porter and Maj. Gen. Erasmus Keyes had been relieved, with Keyes soon following Porter into civilian life. Maj. Gen. Irvin McDowell sat idly, awaiting a new assignment. Maj. Gen. Samuel Heintzelman, deemed too old to serve in the field, commanded the Washington defenses. And finally, Maj. Gen. William B. Franklin was in Louisiana. Apart from Major General Sedgwick, most of the new corps and division commanders with the army in 1864 had led only brigades or regiments—or in Ames's case, batteries—in 1862. The army's commander since just before Gettysburg, Major General Meade, was in charge of a brigade during the Seven Days.[2]

The army also featured a few new officers from the western theater, among them Maj. Gen. Philip Sheridan, who did not fear the Army of Northern Virginia. The most important of the westerners stood at the top. On March 12, 1864, President Lincoln promoted Grant to the rank of lieutenant general and awarded him command over all Federal armies. The cigar-gnawing Ohioan soon proposed that Union forces across the nation work together and coordinate their offensives. While trusted subordinates led Union forces elsewhere, Grant remained in the East at Lincoln's request. There he could wield the brute force of Federals arms to apply unyielding pressure against Lee. Establishing his headquarters with Meade and the Army of the Potomac, Grant's presence slowly changed the demeanor of the army.[3]

Beside Meade's command, Grant had two other Federal armies at his disposal in Virginia to destroy Lee. The men of Maj. Gen. Franz Sigel's Department of West Virginia were tasked to destroy valuable resources and railroads in the Shenandoah Valley to deprive Lee's men of sustenance. The brand-new Army of the James, created from troops already in Virginia and North Carolina as well as Gillmore's X Corps coming up from the Deep South, would apply pressure against the Richmond defenses. Initially stationed on the peninsula at Fort Monroe, it was commanded by Maj. Gen. Benjamin Butler, a textbook model of the political general. A Massachusetts attorney and Democratic politician, Butler's connections had garnered him favor from Lincoln and helped preserve his notoriously provocative military record. Whether it was occupying Baltimore in 1861, establishing "contraband" policies at Fort Monroe later that year, or serving as the hated military governor of New Orleans in 1862, Butler attracted controversy by being harsh, confrontational, and self-interested. He had fewer critics when it came to his military leadership at this time, but that was only because he had never led large bodies of troops in the field.[4]

Grant met with Butler on April 1 at Fort Monroe to discuss operations. When poor weather forced the general in chief to stay another day, Butler approached him with an idea. His 40,000-man army would sail from Fort Monroe up the James River and, protected by Union gunboats, would disembark near the convergence of the James and Appomattox Rivers at a small

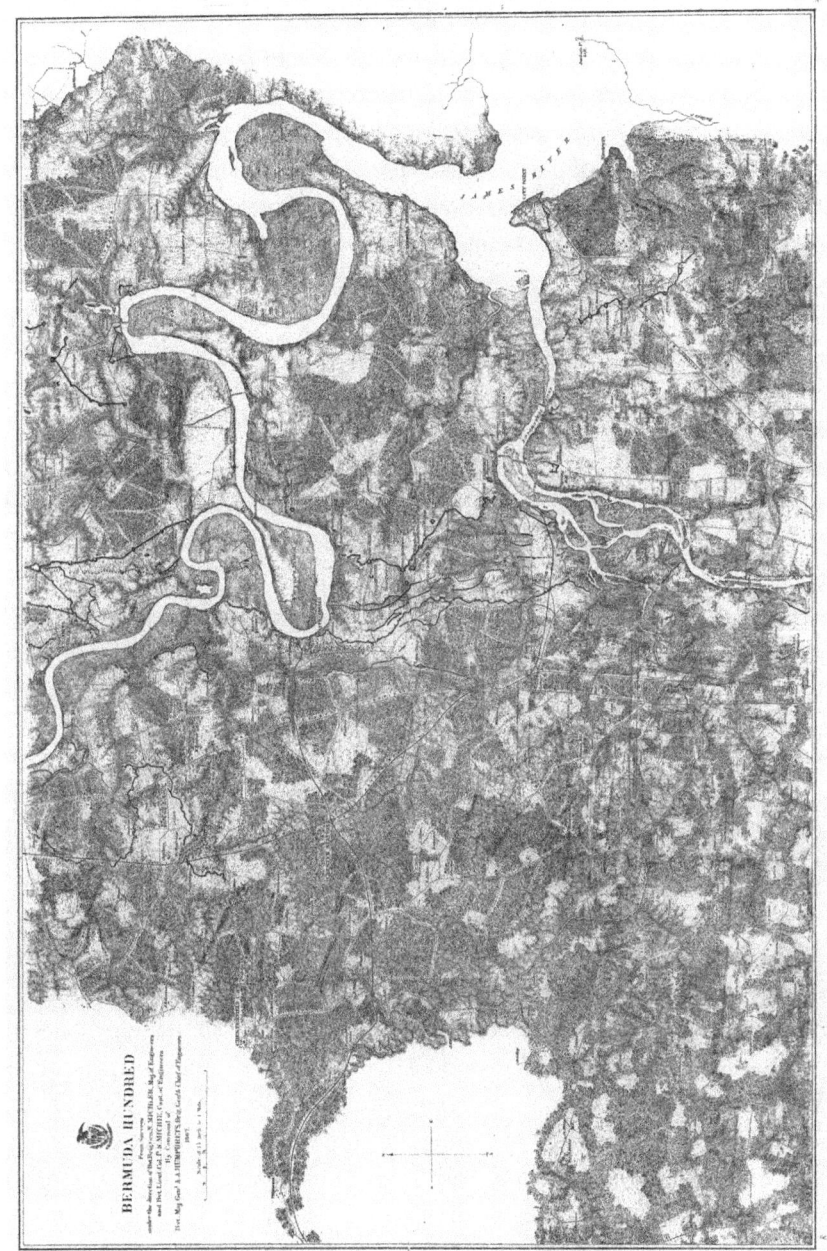

Map of the James River and Bermuda Hundred region (Library of Congress)

peninsula village known as Bermuda Hundred. From there, his army could march quickly to Richmond or farther south to the valuable city of Petersburg and its railroad junctions.[5]

Grant approved of Butler's overall idea but suggested some alterations over the next few weeks. The Army of the James should sever the Richmond and Petersburg Railroad and prevent valuable supplies from reaching Lee from the south and west. He also wanted Butler to prioritize holding the vital communications and supply port of City Point while remaining flexible enough to coordinate with the Army of the Potomac if necessary. Although Grant wanted the Army of the James to operate separately, causing diversion and havoc, he told Butler on April 18 to delay his campaign until the Army of the Potomac moved against Lee. Timing mattered; Grant wanted cooperation across the front. He added that if the Army of the Potomac began to besiege Richmond, the Army of the James would then link up with it and help.[6]

Grant's guidelines and suggestions nonetheless remained vague enough for Butler to interpret them as he saw fit. And interpret he did. Grant notably gave him too much leeway to make choices about how to proceed once his troops landed at Bermuda Hundred. Furthermore, the message of April 18 convinced Butler that his movements needed to correspond more closely with Meade's than Grant actually wanted. That left Butler with the responsibility to determine when and where to attack Confederate forces, how to coordinate with the Army of the Potomac, and whether to move against Richmond or Petersburg.[7]

The new Army of the James consisted of veteran soldiers and corps, division, and brigade commanders. Both of its corps commanders had extensive experience but persnickety personalities as well. Maj. Gen. William F. "Baldy" Smith commanded the XVIII Corps. An intelligent man and a skilled engineer, he unfortunately considered himself smarter than most of his colleagues, especially Ambrose Burnside. Smith had lost his field command after Burnside's ouster as chief of the Army of the Potomac. He then only commanded militia during the Gettysburg Campaign before going west. Grant grew to respect Smith, however, during the Siege of Chattanooga in 1863, where he masterminded the "Cracker Line" operation. He supported Smith's long-delayed promotion and expected him to do well during the 1864 campaigns. The other corps commander was Ames's superior officer in the Department of the South, Major General Gillmore. He had grown frustrated and thin-skinned following his inability to take Charleston. Furthermore, his X Corps consisted of men with low morale who thoroughly disliked him. Nevertheless, he had extensive engineering experience and was a highly regarded artillerist.[8]

Butler, Smith, and Gillmore each had noteworthy weaknesses, but the Army of the James benefited from excellent midlevel commanders, especially in the X Corps. Ames, Brig. Gen. Alfred H. Terry, and Brig. Gen. John W. Turner all had reputations as dependable officers. This trio also served as important breakers against both their superior officers' hubris and untrustworthy subordinates, specifically those in Turner's division. Ames's division consisted of two brigades made up of men from New England, New York, and Pennsylvania along with a stray Indiana regiment. Col. Richard White from Pennsylvania commanded the First Brigade, having risen from regimental command. Col. Jeremiah C. Drake, a former Baptist minister from New York, commanded the Second Brigade. Both brigades contained Maine regiments, making it the first time Ames commanded Mainers since 1862.[9]

Waiting for Grant to set a date for the campaign to start—rainy weather and mud made him reconsider more than once—Butler worked diligently to supply and organize his army. He opened Fort Monroe to workers from the US Sanitary Commission and US Christian Commission. Butler strove to improve the condition of local military hospitals and had subordinates prepare field hospitals for deployment in the upcoming campaign. He also removed supervisors and surgeons who seemed incompetent while working closely with his chief nurse, Clara Barton, to safeguard the well-being of his men. When the campaign began, the army would not lack supplies or resources.[10]

Grant finally wrote to Butler and suggested that he leave Fort Monroe on May 4. A day later the Army of the James steamed into Hampton Roads and entered the James River. Ames was full of optimism. "We are all in hopes this campaign will put Richmond in our hands and virtually end the war," he told his parents. "Grant is confident—so are we all." Ames, however, realized the importance of Grant and the Army of the Potomac to his own army's success. On May 7 he described what would happen if the general in chief faltered. "Everything will depend on Grant," the young division commander believed. "That is, if he is beaten we shall have to fall back and re-embark. If he beats [Lee] we shall here render much assistance in the capture of Richmond."[11]

As Ames worried, Grant indeed found progress tough. Meade's men struggled to break through Lee's lines during the gruesome Battle of the Wilderness, May 5–7. Butler and his army, meanwhile, managed to make better progress at the onset of their campaign. With naval assistance, the army arrived at Bermuda Hundred on May 5. Butler dropped Brig. Gen. Edward W. Hincks's division to secure City Point, roughly ten miles north of Petersburg, per Grant's request. After establishing his base and expanding earthworks and rifle pits on the peninsula, Butler ordered the army to move west the following day, seize nearby Port Walthall Junction, and start destroying railroad track. Smith tarried, however, and Gillmore did not move at all. At 4 P.M. Brig. Gen. Charles A. Heckman's brigade from Smith's Second Division marched toward a rail junction, but when the men arrived, they saw Confederate soldiers from the Twenty-First and Twenty-Fifth South Carolina, under Col. Robert Graham, dug in roughly 300 yards in front of the Richmond and Petersburg Railroad. Although outnumbered three to one, the Confederates turned back the Federal attack. Heckman became one of the casualties that afternoon when his wounded horse bucked him from the saddle.[12]

Fighting at Port Walthall Junction continued on May 7. This time 8,000 Union troops—four brigades drawn from both corps—took part in the attack. Graham's defenders received reinforcements from their brigade commander, Brig. Gen. Johnson Hagood. The Federals managed to push Hagood's men back, but they could not destroy the railroad track for lack of levers or claw crowbars to effectively tear it up once they drove the Confederates from the junction. Two days later some of Ames's men began to move to destroy track at Chester Station, four miles north of Port Walthall Junction. Ames marched with Colonel White's First Brigade, which led a column of four brigades siphoned from every division in Gillmore's corps. The soldiers arrived in the early morning and by 8 A.M. began to destroy railroad track.[13]

The destruction at Chester Station ceased after Union and Confederate forces tussled again along Swift Creek, two miles south of Port Walthall Junction. Smith asked Gillmore to pause his demolition efforts and march south to help shore up his left flank. Some men from Terry's division remained behind to continue the work, but Ames ordered his First Brigade to go help Smith. The men promptly dropped their tools, shouldered their firearms, and raced toward the fighting. The heat and humidity became brutal as the troops moved southward, led by brigades from Turner's division. By midafternoon, Union forces launched an unsuccessful attack against Hagood's South Carolinians. Ames's men stayed on the left flank and did not participate in the heated combat. Both sides launched unsuccessful attacks, and the battle ended without any significant progress for either side. Butler began to think that any chance of quickly moving to Richmond was evaporating.[14]

After Swift Creek, Butler proposed that his force create its own diverting movement. He suggested that the Army of the James try to simultaneously threaten Petersburg, via City Point, along with Richmond. While the bulk of his army would move north to take the capital city, Hincks's division, consisting of US Colored Troops, at City Point would demonstrate to convince Rebel defenders in Petersburg that Butler could move against them. He discussed the plan with his two corps commanders, but neither Smith nor Gillmore favored the idea. When they proposed a more cautious alternative that did not involve any diversions, Butler condemned them and cited his authority as commander. He then ordered his men back to the Bermuda Hundred fortifications to resupply for another foray.[15]

As Butler reequipped, Confederate hero Gen. P. G. T. Beauregard and roughly 18,000 men faced the task to stymie the Army of the James. Recently returned from service in the Carolinas, Beauregard quickly asserted himself when he arrived in Virginia on May 10. His forces did not waste any time before engaging Federal troops. That same day elements of the two armies clashed east of Chester Station. The remnants of Terry's division remaining in the area faced the brunt of the Confederate assault. The fighting began at 5:15 A.M. on a battleground that featured dense woods and thick foliage. Confederate regiments from two brigades broke through Terry's lines and captured a lone artillery piece. Union reinforcements from the south, consisting of the rest of the division, helped strengthen Terry's line and then counterattacked. Lagging behind, Ames's Second Brigade under Drake rushed to the battlefield as quickly as possible and, although its ranks were depleted because of sunstroke victims, bolstered Federal defenses but did not see any action. Personally leading White's First Brigade, Ames moved to Port Walthall Junction to guard that crossroads. The Battle of Chester Station ended in a stalemate. Both sides withdrew after requesting a flag of truce to rescue wounded from burning woods where the fighting had started. Butler's troops suffered 280 casualties and once again retreated to Bermuda Hundred.[16]

The Federals rested on May 11 while Beauregard discussed countermeasures with his superiors. Around 4 A.M. on May 12, the Army of the James set out to engage the Confederates again. The objective was to take the entrenchments at Drewry's Bluff, which rose ninety feet above the James River and featured the imposing Fort Darling. The site was within marching distance of Richmond, so taking it could open up the James farther west and turn the tide of the campaign. With Turner's division from the X Corps, Butler personally led it along with the XVIII Corps toward Drewry's Bluff; Ames's division again served as the reserve. During a brutal downpour, the roads turned to sludge. The advance slowed, and by the evening of May 12, Butler had halted and formed a defensive position in front of Drewry's Bluff. As he and Smith discussed how to take the fort, Ames's division held near Port

Walthall Junction, three miles to the east. Unexpectedly, Butler syphoned soldiers from both of Ames's brigades to support Smith's upcoming assault against Fort Darling, leaving the young general with a little over a brigade to guard the army's rear and destroy more railroad track.[17]

May 13 featured heavy rain and additional sporadic fighting against the Confederate right flank. Miles away from the front, Ames reported, "Everything is quiet, and [there is] no indications of the enemy at any point on my front." The rain continued the next day as Smith and Gillmore's troops successfully took lightly defended entrenchments at the front of the fort. The Federals paused, however, when they saw more extensive and imposing redans and earthworks higher up on the bluff. They then used whatever tools they could to modify the trenches they captured earlier that day and awaited further orders.[18]

Butler and his subordinates continued to debate the merits of their attacks throughout the evening. Gillmore wanted Ames to leave Port Walthall Junction and bring forward his remaining troops, suggesting that they needed them to help turn the Confederate defenses. Butler instead chose to keep Ames at Port Walthall Junction but left the Eighth Maine from his First Division to support Smith's line. By May 15, more of Ames's division had been called forward to help the efforts against Drewry's Bluff. That evening Ames had only the Thirteenth Indiana, the 169th New York, a single battery of artillery, and some horsemen from the First US Colored Cavalry at the junction. Butler, further delaying his attack and gathering reinforcements, planned for Gillmore and the X Corps to move against the Confederate right the next day. But this only gave Beauregard time to consolidate his position and prepare his own strike against Butler's right flank.[19]

On May 16, Confederate forces under Maj. Gen. Robert Ransom emerged from the morning mist and struck the XVIII Corps on Butler's right flank. His brigades managed to turn the Union flank as the defending regiments fired aimlessly into the fog. In the rear Ames received word that Butler and Smith needed reinforcements and sent the 112th New York to help. The intensity of the battle skyrocketed after another Confederate assault smashed into the Union center. Although the Federal line held, confusing communications, timid leadership, and the persistent fog all led Smith to think his situation dire. When his XVIII Corps retreated, the X Corps fell back as well. Butler's chief of staff, Col. J. W. Shaeffer, told Gillmore to hurry his troops to Port Walthall Junction, where Confederate troops were pressing Ames's undermanned division.[20]

Ames indeed was in dire straits. Beauregard had ordered Maj. Gen. William H. C. Whiting's troops to leave their defenses in Petersburg and move north toward Drewry's Bluff the previous day. Whiting led 5,300 infantrymen, several artillery batteries, and cavalry to participate in Beauregard's attack planned for the following morning. By 8:30 A.M. on May 16, these troops neared Port Walthall Junction and Ames's threadbare command. The young general had not expected to see any combat that day, having the unpleasant assignment of commanding the attacking army's rear guard. Now, Whiting unlimbered two batteries and shelled the Federals at the junction. Ames responded by slowly moving his men out of range. Butler sent the 97th Pennsylvania to help, but Ames still faced daunting odds even after they arrived. He sent a message to army headquarters to say that a Rebel line had formed and seemed poised to strike his division.[21]

Thankfully for the Union troops at Port Walthall Junction, Whiting tarried. He first sent out a scout to review Ames's line. Maj. Gen. D. H. Hill scouted the Federal line as well and, seeing it was only a minor force, advocated for an immediate attack. Whiting instead chose to believe erroneous reports that enemy reinforcements immediately threatened his position.

Ames, meanwhile, decided to place his scant artillery into a good position to make a threatening display and further deter Whiting. At 1:30 P.M. Ames reported to Butler: "I have pressed the enemy back to the hills beyond the crossing of the pike and the railroad. There he has taken a position and is now shelling my advance. The size of my force and the long front I cover do not justify, in my opinion, an effort to attempt to force the enemy from his position." Instead, he sent skirmishers to press Whiting's men when he saw them beginning to move back. These movements confused Whiting, who convinced himself that Ames had more men than he did and was luring him into a trap. In response, Confederate artillery again opened fire on Federals.[22]

After delaying his attack throughout the day, Whiting eventually decided that a full engagement was too risky. He later told Beauregard that he did not know where the rest of the Army of the James was and protecting Petersburg was his primary responsibility; taking out Ames at Port Walthall Junction or helping the attack at Drewry's Bluff were only secondary considerations. In hindsight, it was the wrong decision. Whiting's numerical advantage could have overwhelmed Ames's men. Alternatively, he could have marched to Drewry's Bluff without any obstacle and struck Butler's main force unexpectedly. Instead, the Confederates missed an opportunity. Ames's bold gambit and Whiting's hesitation likely helped save Butler's main force from a crushing surprise attack.

Ames's troops, and the rest of Butler's command, retreated that night to the defenses at Bermuda Hundred. Beauregard told his superiors that he was "pursuing the enemy, and still driving him nearer and nearer to his base." He also assumed that the soldiers of the Army of the James were distraught. In this, he was correct. The Federals staunchly believed that horrendous leadership and disunity between the XVIII and X Corps had doomed their prospects. During the night, Union soldiers, probably still damp from rain, constructed more earthworks, and Butler's self-imposed isolation at Bermuda Hundred became quasi-permanent.[23]

The fighting on May 16 resulted in heavy casualties. Tragically, 3,000 Union soldiers were either killed, wounded, or captured. Most of the dead remained where they fell, caked in mud just like the survivors who returned to Bermuda Hundred. Adding insult to injury, the Army of the James lost five regimental colors during their five-day excursion to Drewry's Bluff. Butler thoroughly misunderstood the situation, reporting to Secretary of War Edwin Stanton that he thought his force was outnumbered and in a dire quandary.[24]

Confederate skirmishers prodded the Federal line on May 20, then Beauregard's army attacked in force. Butler warned Gillmore that he thought the weakest part of his line was just to the left of Ames's division. He was right. For the first time in the campaign, Ames's men faced the brunt of the main Rebel force. Beauregard moved against the X Corps and broke through Ames's pickets near Ware Bottom Church. Union skirmishers suffered heavy losses as Confederates took both Ames's picket line and their rifle pits. A courageous counterattack from the Ninety-Seventh Pennsylvania and Thirteenth Indiana did not dislodge the Rebels. It was not until later in the day that troops from Terry's division reclaimed the lost ground.[25]

Butler decided to hold his line without attempting another advance. Ames received orders from Terry, now acting commander of the X Corps, to modify his entrenchments and dig in, just as the men had done in South Carolina and Florida. His woebegone troops felled most of the trees within their line of sight so that Union artillerymen had a clear line of fire. On May 21 Ames reported that his pickets warned of Confederate troops massing in front of their position, but no attack followed. Writing to his parents, he described the failures of Bermuda Hundred. "We have made advances towards Petersburg and Richmond," Ames reported. "The first resulted in a little fighting, in which we had the advantage. But the latter was wholly against us."[26]

The Confederates constructed new earthworks as well. Known as the Howlett Line, these defenses stretched roughly three miles across the neck of the peninsula. The line started at the James River to the north and proceeded southward to the banks of the Appomattox River. Once constructed, the manned works prevented Butler's men from escaping Bermuda Hundred over-

Federal earthworks during the Bermuda Hundred Campaign (Library of Congress)

land. Unless naval transports carried them across the James River, the Army of the James could not move without engaging the enemy. Meanwhile, sporadic fighting continued. May 22 saw another skirmish, but little came of it.

Butler now focused exclusively on reinforcing his defensive works. The Army of the James floundered as its campaign under "Bottled-up Butler" proved an abject failure. His corps commanders received chastisement from both the press and comrades for timidity, and the operation became one of missed opportunities. While Butler received the greatest scorn, officers such as Ames and the enlisted men, according to historian Edward G. Longacre, "encountered more than their fair share of adversity and had few victories to sustain them. Still, most served gamely and effectively to the last, refusing to quit short of that final triumph to which their fortitude and fidelity entitled them."[27]

In later years Grant regretted Butler's inability to accomplish anything of consequence, blaming him, Smith, and Gillmore. He thought that if the army had possessed two corps commanders with more skill and aptitude, perhaps the campaign would have been successful. Different subordinates could have prevented Butler from dictating foolish plans and might have acted aggressively and boldly. A general who Grant thought would have made an ideal corps commander was Ames. "If I had given him [Butler] two corps commanders like Ames, [Brig. Gen. Ranald S.] Mackenzie, [Brig. Gen. Godfrey] Weitzel, or Terry," Grant reckoned after the war, "he would have made a fine campaign on the James and help[ed] materially in my plans."[28]

Ames and his division remained at Bermuda Hundred until later that month, when Grant ordered the Army of the James to supply Meade with reinforcements. With the general in chief increasingly making the major decisions, the Army of the Potomac had fought its way south from the Wilderness, engaged in a long and bloody confrontation at Spotsylvania Court House, and escaped a well-laid trap on the North Anna River. Most recently, Ames's old V Corps, now under Gouverneur Warren, had engaged Rebel troops along Totopotomoy Creek, northeast of Richmond. Refusing to accept another stalemate like Spotsylvania, Grant again tried to flank south of Lee's right and force the Confederate commander to shift his army. At the same time, he ordered Butler to release Smith and the XVIII Corps to him. Two additional divisions from the X Corps, including Ames's, would temporarily join Smith's detachment to Grant's army.[29]

Gillmore objected to losing these men: "The reorganization of Ames' and Turner's Division, Tenth Corps, under strange commanders, will materially diminish the efficiency of those divisions. On this ground, and this only, I earnestly request that no steps of the kind be taken or allowed. General Ames and Turner are educated, accomplished, and efficient soldiers, and have the entire confidence and the most zealous and enthusiastic cooperation of the officers and men of their commands at all times."[30] Butler denied Gillmore's request. Keeping Ames at Bermuda Hundred was pointless, he believed. The Army of the James was stagnant, the Army of the Potomac needed reinforcements, and Smith needed veteran midlevel commanders to join him. After the reorganization, Ames assumed command of a single brigade in the XVIII Corps while becoming second in command to Brig. Gen. Charles Devens Jr., commanding the Third Division. Smith wrote to Grant, promising that his troops would arrive as quickly as possible. Boarding ships, the XVIII Corps sailed back down the James River, around Fort Monroe, and up the York River. The transports then steered northeast into the marshy, winding Pamunkey River. On May 30 the troops disembarked at White House and happily walked on land again. Ames

Maj. Gen. Benjamin Franklin Butler (Library of Congress)

and his fellow officers met with the corps commander for instructions. Grant hoped that Smith could get his troops to him by the following day, marching them up the banks of the Pamunkey as soon as possible. Smith tasked Ames with the rear guard as he had during most of the Bermuda Hundred Campaign. Numbering roughly 2,500 men, his force guarded White House and the Pamunkey River while standing ready to reinforce Smith.[31]

Roughly three miles south of Totopotomoy Creek, both Grant and Lee turned their attention to a crossroads at Old Cold Harbor. This feature had meant little to either side earlier in the campaign, but now it became exceedingly important. Grant saw Cold Harbor as a location to link with Smith's XVIII Corps and then put pressure on Richmond, roughly ten miles away. Lee in turn feared that reinforcements from Bermuda Hundred would allow Grant to extend the Union line farther than he could extend his own. Both sides rushed to move manpower to Cold Harbor and secure the crossroads.[32]

After the XVIII Corps left Ames at White House on May 31, Grant sent instructions to Smith to follow Pamunkey Creek northward to New Castle Ferry, placing them next to the V and VI Corps. Leaving so early that the men did not eat breakfast, the corps reached the ferry but found it devoid of any soldiers. The problem was that the orders Grant sent were wrong and, instead of New Castle Ferry, should have specified Cold Harbor.[33]

Because of this delay, the XVIII Corps did not arrive at Cold Harbor until the afternoon of June 1. Fortunately for Grant, US cavalry held off Confederate forces under Lt. Gen. Richard Anderson until the VI Corps and the redirected XVIII Corps arrived at Cold Harbor. There Smith placed his troops to the right of the VI Corps and prepared to attack Anderson per Meade's orders. At 6:30 P.M. the infantry moved against Anderson's Corps but failed to dislodge it from its position. For their efforts, the VI and XVIII Corps suffered over two thousand casualties, while the Confederates lost almost as many. Both Grant and Meade advocated another attack the following day, but it did not occur until June 3. This assault comprised the VI, XVIII, and newly arrived II Corps. A signal gun would fire to commence the attack at 4:30 A.M.[34]

The three Union corps slowly began their advance at the signal. The volume of fire that the XVIII Corps encountered during its assault across the field was blistering. Passing through cover provided by foliage and two ravines, the men came under a heavy crossfire as they entered open terrain and marched toward the fortified Confederate position. The Federals experienced torrents of musket fire that surpassed what any had endured at Fredericksburg. When Meade ordered the XVIII Corps to make another assault, Smith obstinately refused, later saying, "An assault under such conditions I looked on as involving a wanton waste of life."[35] In their massive volume on Abraham Lincoln and the Civil War, the president's aides John Nicolay and John Hay later noted, "Smith, with the Eighteenth Corps, also did all that brave men could do; his divisions were torn to rags in their assault."[36]

Devens fell ill on June 3, so Smith hastily summoned Ames to assume command of the division at Cold Harbor at this critical moment. As Ames and his rearguard troops approached Cold Harbor, they saw ambulances carrying wounded to the rear. After leading the men on a seventeen-mile march in sweltering heat, Ames reached the XVIII Corps at 1 A.M. the next morning. Neither side made an assault the following day, but sharpshooters continuously peppered the line, sometimes finding and slaying their target. Two years prior Ames had commanded his artillery battery as a lieutenant during the Seven Days' Battles at nearly the exact same spot. Now, as a brigadier general commanding a division, he had to make sure his infantry was safe from Confederate rifles and field guns. On June 5 and 7, Ames's men helped turn back Confederate counterattacks. The division suffering 592 casualties while at Cold Harbor, accounting for 20 percent of the total losses the XVIII Corps reported. Smith's men fought admirably, and Ames himself would receive a battlefield promotion for his service during the battle, to captain in the regular army.[37]

From May to mid-June 1864, beginning at the Wilderness and continuing to the Chickahominy River, the Army of the Potomac suffered staggering losses. None of the previous battles, however, brought the same level of disappointment and bitterness as did Cold Harbor. "It never should have been fought," argued one survivor. "There was no military reasons to justify it." Even Ames, who usually refrained from criticizing superiors, began to question the general in chief: "I hope he [Grant] will prove equal to the emergency." Grant himself later admitted, "Cold Harbor is, I think, the only battle I ever fought that I would not fight over again under the circumstances."[38]

Maj. Gen. Adelbert Ames (Library of Congress)

Unwilling to spend the summer besieging Lee north of the James, Grant began moving the Army of the Potomac toward that river, planning to cross it and move against Petersburg rather than Richmond. On June 6 he informed Butler of his intentions. Butler wanted to take Petersburg before Grant, Meade, and the Army of the Potomac arrived, but ineptitude reigned once again when Gillmore botched an attack that could have taken the city on the ninth.[39] The two Union armies finally linked up on June 15, and Ames reassumed command of his old division in the X Corps. Initially, his men helped tear apart two miles of the Richmond and Petersburg rail line. While they severed that railroad, other XVIII Corps troops moved against Beauregard at Petersburg. From June 15 through June 18, the Federals wasted their chances to take the underdefended city while incurring over 10,000 casualties. Lee and his army eventually arrived in Petersburg on the eighteenth, bolstering the Confederate fortifications and expanding their lines. Although Lee saved Petersburg, the risk of his army becoming ensnared in a siege grew significantly.[40]

Federal forces in front of Petersburg began building rifle pits and other semipermanent positions, which exasperated Ames. His mood oscillated through the rest of June and into July. "Here we are all hopeful and confident," he wrote on July 10. "We are justified in gathering hope from the fact that the rebels are putting every man, young and old, into the ranks. Their losses cannot

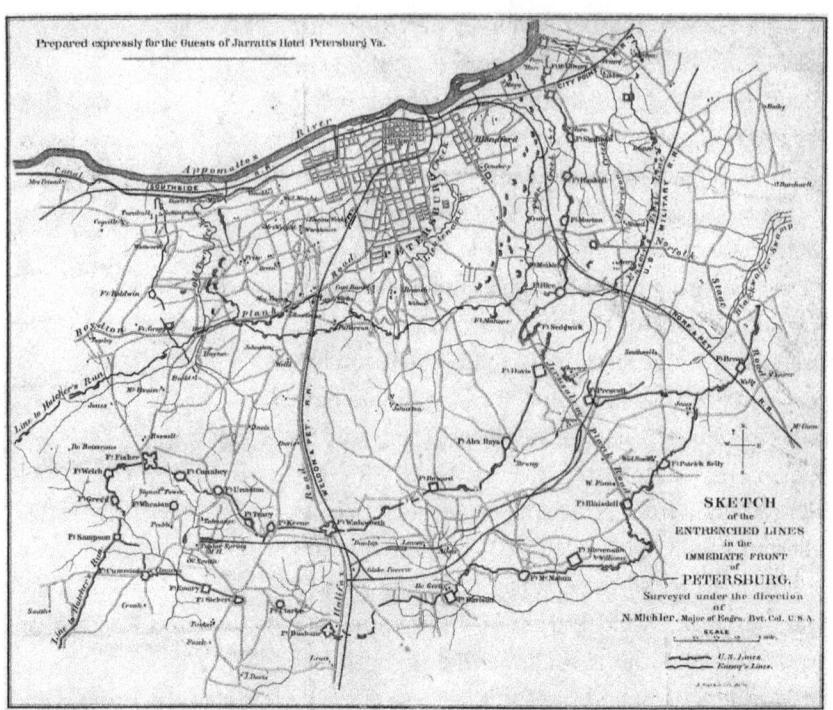

Sketch of the entrenched lines at Petersburg, 1864–65 (Library of Congress)

be replaced." This letter was perhaps his most joyful of the entire month. In it he also discussed sending a photograph to a Miss Lowell and expressed his joy at the sinking of "the pirate ship CSS *Alabama*." Yet his impatience could also prompt pessimism. Ames told his parents on July 21 that he "was well, though a little discontented at the inactivity of our forces." Soon his feelings turned toward misery. Historian Harry King Benson notes, "Nothing could be more illustrative of the young soldier's aggressive temperament and impatience with siege type warfare than the tone of despair which had crept into his letters by the end of the month."[41]

Indeed, Ames finally admitted that he felt dejected at Petersburg. Inactivity contributed to his noxious mood, but so did the state of the nation. The Union, exhausted by war, disgusted by the loss of life, and amid an election year, was rife with raw emotions. In a tirade-laden dispatch to his father dated July 30, Ames expressed his bleakness. "I cannot tell you," he complained, "how depressed and sad I feel in the consequence of my belief that the Northern people are to show themselves unworthy the liberty won them by their fathers."[42] Yet the staunch young Republican also denounced the president, as did many Radical Republicans that summer. Some even worked to remove Lincoln from the ticket, replacing him with someone such as John C. Frémont. One of only two letters during his entire service to reference Lincoln, here he thrashes the president: "Lincoln is not a fit person for the Head of this nation in its hour of trouble and grief. He evidently has not the *nerve* or brain needed by one in his high and responsible station. If I had the opportunity to vote I should vote for some other candidate, not Fremont, who would insist upon a vigorous prosecution of the war. We, here, think Mr. Lincoln has prostituted his authority and responsibility to the vile purpose of self-aggrandizement—his re-election."[43]

Regardless, the war went on at Petersburg. East of the city, Brig. Gen. Robert Potter's division of the IX Corps faced Rebel works that included a position known as Pegram's Salient. Lt. Col. Henry Pleasants of the Forty-Eighth Pennsylvania proposed a scheme to Potter to crack the Confederate line. A mining engineer before the war, Pleasants wanted to dig a massive mine shaft under Pegram's Salient, fill it with explosives, detonate them. The explosion ideally would kill all the defenders in the area and wreck the fortifications. If Union troops could rush through the gap, they would crack Lee's line. Pleasants and Potter approached their corps commander, Major General Burnside, who had returned east and joined Grant with his IX Corps in May. Burnside favored the idea. He told Pleasants that he would ask Meade for permission to implement it. Wanting to avoid costly frontal assaults, the army commander gave Burnside his approval, although he believed that Pegram's Salient was not the best target. Grant, who yearned for another offensive against Lee, thought the mine might help. He had used a similar tactic at Vicksburg against the Third Louisiana Redan on June 25, 1863. The immense blast there created a massive crater in the Confederate line. Although the attempt ultimately failed to break the Rebel defenses at Vicksburg, Grant approved digging a mine at Petersburg.[44]

A year to the day of the redan's detonation in Vicksburg, the Pennsylvanians began digging on June 25. The enemy line was only 100 yards away, and the Confederates managed to observe a great deal. According to historian Earl J. Hess, Rebel deserters reported that their officers knew that the Federals were digging a mine and had prepared countermeasures. On July 27 Maj. Gen. Winfield S. Hancock's II Corps moved against the northern end of the Confederate line to divert Lee's attention from Pegram's Salient. Known as the First Battle of Deep Bottom, Rebel defenders repulsed Hancock's larger force, although the Federals killed or wounded 471 men and captured 208. Ames could hear that battle, writing, "I heard the cannonading this afternoon, but as no word has been received in relation to the matter, I think our efforts were unsuccessful."[45]

The II Corps did not break through the Confederate defenses, but their mission to misdirect worked. Grant officially authorized Burnside to execute his plan on July 28. Divisions under Brig. Gen. Edward Ferrero and Brig. Gen. James H. Ledlie would take part in the assault following the detonation. Burnside wanted Ferrero's division of Black soldiers to spearhead the attack, but Meade overruled him and ordered Ledlie's division to take the lead. Ames's division and Turner' division from the X Corps would serve as reserves. If Ferrero and Ledlie's men got through, Ames and Turner were to support them at once and move toward Petersburg.[46]

In the early morning hours of July 30, Union engineers lit the fuse. Due to faulty splicing, the mine packed with powder did not detonate on time. After a delay, the flame finally reached the explosives, and at 4:44 A.M. a massive eruption took place. But this created a crater in the earth rather than the anticipated gap in the line. Debris that soared into the air rained down, striking the first wave of Union attackers with sod and other items. Rather than charging around its rim, the troops surged into the crater, where chaos and disorganization ensued. According to a Confederate general on the scene, "our troops on both flanks and in the rear had caused many of the enemy to run the gauntlet of our cross-fires in front of the breach, but a large number still remained unable to advance, and perhaps afraid to retreat." As fighting in the manmade depression intensified, Ames received orders to move his division toward the fray. Due to the congestion and chaos, however, he found it "impossible to advance my men, the way being blocked by other troops." That may have saved his life and the lives of many in his veteran division, which never participated in the battle; indeed, later Ames marched his troops off the field.[47]

Ames did not receive criticism for holding back his men from the battle; Grant and Meade were certainly relieved that he had the sense to not risk a fine division in a useless and foolish endeavor that Grant would later call "the saddest affair I have witnessed in this war." In his official testimony at a military inquiry investigating the fiasco, Ames explained why the Battle of the Crater became the disaster that it was. "I think the trouble was no one person at the front was responsible," he testified. "In consequence of which there was no unity of action," he continued. "It took a long time for commanders in the front to communicate with those in the vicinity of the 14-gun battery in the rear." Ames argued that rifle pits or breastworks to the left of the crater could have helped shield reinforcements, while the first wave should not have run into the pit but rather around it as planned. In the end, the general told the committee that the attack as it unfolded could never have worked. He pointed a finger at Ledlie, who was rumored to have been drinking during the assault. "I don't see how ordinary troops, with good commanders and one head to direct, could have possibly failed, under the circumstances," Ames observed. "It was necessary that some one person should be present to direct the various movements and make them one operation."[48]

After the Battle of the Crater, Ames assumed command of the Second Division, XVIII Corps. He established picket lines and widened his trenches, after which the division covered a line between the Appomattox and James Rivers on the Union right flank. The most compelling development during this time was when the XVIII Corps' new commander, Maj. Gen. Edward O. C. Ord, who relieved Smith in July, warned Ames of the possibility of Confederates constructing a mine themselves. Ames and his men braced for a retaliatory, earth-shredding explosion when, on August 5, the Rebel mine erupted. It made "a great dust only," going off forty yards in front of the Union line. Ames and his division still looked for a Confederate assault, but it never occurred. By the end of August, his men were on the move again. Ord instructed them to cross the Appomattox River to the north of Petersburg on August 25. They remained in this new position as Ord shuffled divisions and brigades along the Union right flank. Soon, however, the men got sick. "Here we have little to do," Ames complained. "No firing is going on this front. We come here to recuperate."[49]

As autumn arrived in Petersburg, Grant sought other avenues through which the Union army could conduct aggressive attacks against the Rebel defenses. On September 28 both the X and the XVIII Corps crossed over from the south bank to the north side of the James River. The following day the troops assaulted Fort Harrison and Fort Gilmer during the Battle of Chaffin's Farm. Finding themselves near the familiar terrain of Bermuda Hundred, the X Corps fought admirably.[50] The combat was ferocious, but the Union troops finally overwhelmed the Confederate defenders at Fort Harrison, taking the salient as well as over a dozen pieces of artillery. Brig. Gen. R. S. Foster's report, written later that year, discussed the courage of the X Corps. Foster took the time to highlight the conduct of all the combatants, including Ames, writing, "I am glad to be able to congratulate you upon the fact that my successor to the command of the Second Division is that gallant young soldier and able officer, Brigadier-General Ames, of whose brilliant reputation you are already aware."[51]

Ames's boredom subsided for a time after Chaffin's Farm, but it quickly reasserted itself. Rather than languish, he applied for a leave of absence for the second half of September and early October. The army granted his request, and Ames traveled all the way to Minnesota, where he hoped to settle down after the war with his parents and siblings. His father's new flour mill was growing, and the prospect of helping his family intrigued the young veteran officer.[52]

Shortly after Ames returned in October, his division fought at the Battle of Darbytown Road on October 13. Confederate troops under Anderson tried to regain ground they had lost earlier in the campaign, but their attack faltered. In response, Ord instructed Ames to move his division against Anderson, whose men held newly constructed earthworks extending from Petersburg to Richmond. "General Ames' division will move out to and across the Darbytown road, forming in the open ground," his orders read, "attack the enemy and endeavor to find and turn the left of their entrenchments." Ord also cautioned him to keep his men together and not let a gap form between his division and Brig. Gen. William Birney's division, advancing on his left flank. Like many engagements during the siege, it had the possibility of being a decisive battle. Darbytown Road, however, ended in another stalemate, depriving

Bvt. Maj. Gen. Adelbert Ames and staff during the Petersburg Siege, November 1864 (Library of Congress)

the Union of victory and Ames and his men of glory. The division suffered 315 casualties among its three brigades, although Ames's men inflicted 500 casualties that Anderson and Lee could ill afford.[53]

Two weeks later Ames's troops participated in another battle. The Second Battle of Fair Oaks had a promising start. In coordination with Union efforts to destroy the South Side Railroad, an invaluable supply line for Lee's army, Butler ordered his two corps to attack Confederate entrenchments along Darbytown Road again. The Union advance stalled, and a Rebel counterattack ended the fighting. Between the X and XVIII Corps and their artillery and cavalry support, Butler lost 1,603 men total; the Confederate defenders lost only 64 men. Although Ames's command suffered only 14 casualties, the troops achieved far less than the ambitious brigadier general had hoped they would.[54]

Ames assumed command of the X Corps on November 4, when Terry, now a brevet major general, temporarily took control of the Army of the James. Ames immediately told his subordinates to look out for a possible attack. "Brigade commanders," he instructed, "will have their commands in readiness to be placed under arms at a moments notice during the next twenty-four hours." Terry believed an assault was likely as well. "General Ames," he wrote, "please get ready 2,000 men, with their arms, to make rifle-pits on the line which it is proposed to fight on if the enemy attempts to turn our right. Collect every shovel that is to be found." While Confederate cavalry harassed some Union pickets, no infantry movement or full-scale assault manifested.[55]

The expectation of action, with nothing coming of it, created a dreary atmosphere in the X Corps. In November a photographer took a picture of Ames and his staff. Although posed daguerreotypes and images from the Civil War rarely show gaiety, Ames's complexion truly looks drab. Sitting outside in a field chair in front of winter quarters, the general has his feet crossed, his hands in his lap. Along with a double-breasted general's coat, Ames wears a slouch hat, slightly crooked and bent. His face, particularly his eyes, look sunken, and his mouth is obscured by his mustache. By his feet is a sleeping dog, while to his left are four staff members and to his right two others. All of the officers are facing the camera, but only Ames is clearly starting at it. His piercing eyes had seen three years of war by that time, and he looks as if wondering what he would be doing next.[56]

And so, Ames and his men manned their posts, drilled, and bided their time. In December units from the X and XVIII Corps were consolidated to form the XXIV Corps, under the command of Ord. Ames's men became the First Division, while the Black troops from the Army of the James became

Inspection of the 2nd Pennsylvania Artillery by Gen Ames, by William Waud, 1878; the inspection occurred at Petersburg in 1864 (Library of Congress)

the XXV Corps on December 3. Other than the reorganization of the corps, nothing of major consequence happened on the multiple fronts of Petersburg. Grant and his army chose to besiege the city though the winter, refrain from attacking Lee, and slowly strangle the Army of Northern Virginia. For Ames, an ambitious, proud, and increasingly frustrated officer, 1864 ended in an anticlimactic, disappointing fashion.[57]

6

THE FINAL STRUGGLE FOR VICTORY

As winter deepened, Ames and his division remained encamped outside of Petersburg; Grant turned his attention elsewhere. Fort Fisher, a Confederate stronghold that protected Wilmington, North Carolina, rested at the southern tip of the slim Federal Point peninsula, bracketed by the Atlantic Ocean to the east and the Cape Fear River to the west. By the end of 1864, Wilmington was the Confederacy's last connection to the outside world other than the porous border between Texas and Mexico. Fort Fisher allowed valuable information and supplies to enter the port, nestled twenty-one miles upstream. The city imported both vital resources and luxury items while exporting tobacco and cotton abroad. Blockade runners from Canada and the Caribbean frequented Wilmington without significant Federal interference. Fort Fisher kept it safe, and Grant believed that capturing the stronghold would accelerate the Confederacy's demise.[1]

Structurally, Fort Fisher was a giant earthen fort that anchored an extensive series of batteries and coastal fortifications along the Cape Fear. The absorbency of the sandy earth helped neutralize the kinetic power of large-caliber projectiles against the fort's walls. Hundreds of Confederate soldiers and impressed slaves had made its traverses and ramparts even more impenetrable and expansive. Fort Fisher housed a bomb-resistant telegraph office, a hospital, and quarters for an entire regiment within its confines. By 1863, it was the largest fortification the Confederacy could boast. President Davis visited the site to admire its progress later that year.[2]

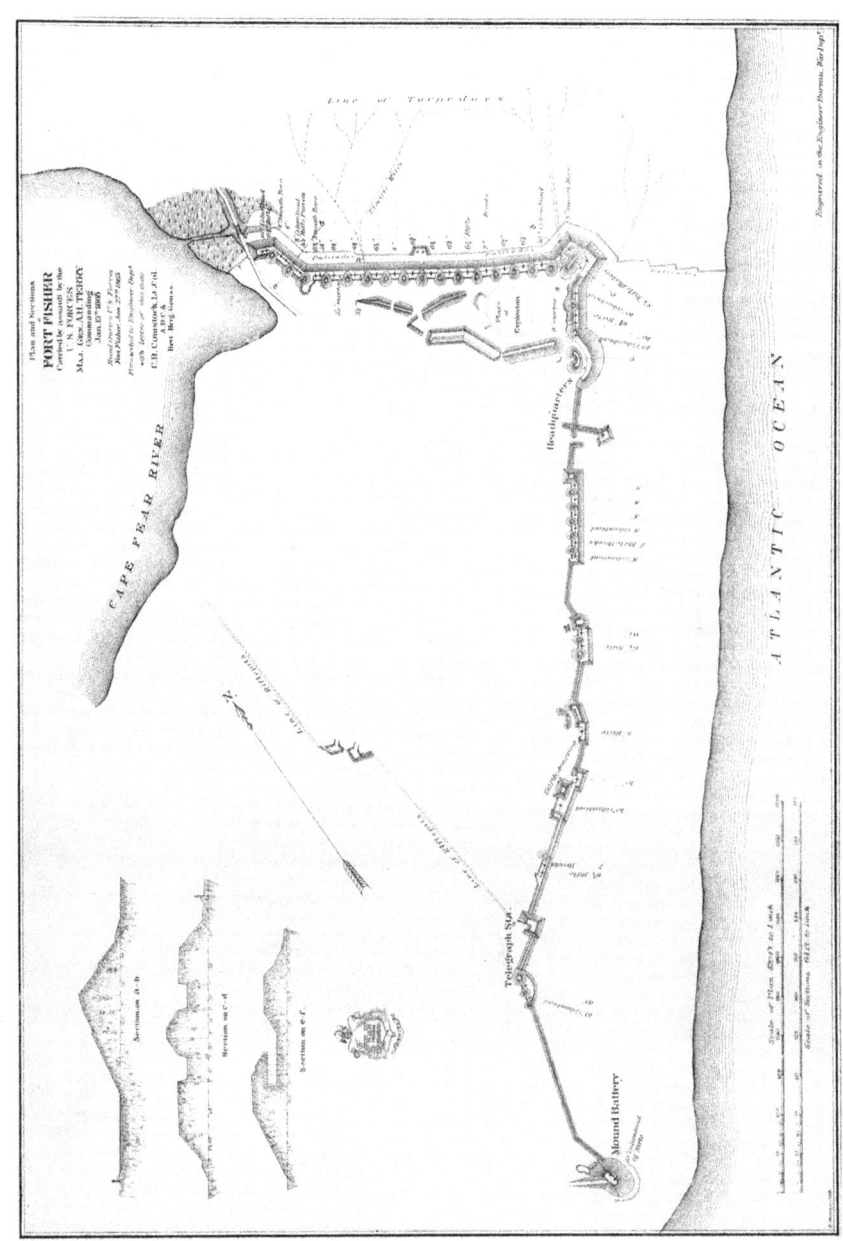

Defenses at Fort Fisher, North Carolina (Library of Congress)

Fort Fisher was also well designed. Its commander, a self-taught engineer from Virginia named William Lamb, studied and adapted Crimean War designs for his stronghold once he arrived in 1862. The fort as modified by Colonel Lamb had two faces, one landward (north) and the other seaward (east). Since its mission was to keep enemy ships out of the Cape Fear River, the fort did not need four sides. The sea face extended from the north face to the end of the peninsula, culminating with the imposing Mound Battery, sixty feet high and mounting two long-range guns. The two faces combined held sixteen traverses and intersected at the Northeast Bastion, a thirty-foot-tall parapet. Instead of walls covering the south and west, a strategically placed fortification called Battery Buchanan guarded the very tip of the peninsula next to Cape Fear's New Inlet.[3]

Innovative weaponry, including a 150-pound rifled Armstrong gun, further bolstered the peninsula's defenses. 4.2-inch Parrott rifles, Coehorn mortars, and 12-pound Napoleons stood ready in the fort and in its works along the peninsula. Lamb placed his guns above sea level to easily maul any Union ship that dared sail into the mouth of the river. In addition, his Confederates littered the channel with wreckage, debris, and aquatic mines, or "torpedoes," to inhibit enemy movement even more. All in all, any assault on Fort Fisher would prove to be a deadly undertaking.[4]

In early December 1864 Grant read about a potential weakness at Fort Fisher in Confederate newspapers. Gen. Braxton Bragg, commanding the nearby Wilmington defenses since October, at that time left with 8,000 men to defend Savannah, Georgia, as Sherman's Union forces marched to the sea. Fort Fisher remained a formidable target, but the reported absence of these 8,000 soldiers, in Grant's estimation, offered the best chance yet to take it and then Wilmington. "For these reasons," he later wrote, "I determined, with the concurrence of the Navy Department, in December, to send an expedition against Fort Fisher for the purpose of capturing it."[5]

The general in chief accordingly ordered troops from the Army of the James to make the expedition to Fort Fisher and tapped Maj. Gen. Godfrey Weitzel, a corps commander in the army and a gifted solider with copious engineering knowledge, to lead the effort. Grant believed that Weitzel could take the fort with only a fraction of the Army of the James, roughly 7,000 soldiers. RAdm David D. Porter received supporting orders to escort the transports carrying the troops to Fort Fisher and then assist in the military operation. Ames and his division of 3,300 men, soldiers from Indiana, New Hampshire, New York, and Pennsylvania, formed the most important contingent of Weitzel's force.[6]

Backed by expert leaders who were skilled engineers, the expeditionary army officially received orders on December 6 to embark for the North Carolina coast. Grant urged Porter and Weitzel to move quickly. While Ames and his men left their entrenchments outside of Petersburg to board transports on December 7, Major General Butler stepped in to complicate the mission. He commanded the Department of Virginia and North Carolina as well as the Army of the James and had the right to assume command of the operation. Grant wanted Weitzel to lead, however, and cautiously tried to manage the situation. Nonetheless, Butler maneuvered his way into taking charge of the expedition. In the end, Grant did not—or could not—stop him. Butler later claimed that the general in chief assented because Weitzel was a younger commander. Butler argued, "I think I had better go with the expedition so as to take the responsibility off of General Weitzel, as I am the older officer." In fact, he wanted to take on Fort Fisher to improve the negative trajectory of his military reputation after Bermuda Hundred. Porter, who had despised Butler since working with him in New Orleans in 1862, fumed at the prospect of having to serve with him again. Sherman was equally skeptical of both the mission and its commander. Writing to Grant from his headquarters in Georgia, he confided to his friend, "I take it for granted" that the undertaking would have no chance to succeed.[7]

Although Porter tried to work with Butler for the sake of the mission, the operation radically changed once the Massachusetts general had more direct oversight. Since August Butler had considered the efficacy of exploding powder-laden vessels to destroy Confederate coastal defenses. Now, he envisioned such a ship running aground roughly 400 yards from Fort Fisher and exploding, damaging the outer defenses of the fort and stunning its defenders. Both Butler and Porter approved of the idea, with the admiral thinking it was worth a try. Porter thought the explosion would "be simply very severe. Stunning men at a distance of three to four hundred yards, demoralizing them completely." He added, "I think that the concussion will tumble magazines that are built on framework. . . . [T]he famous Mound will be among the things that were, and the guns buried beneath the ruins."[8]

Grant was wary but had little choice once Lincoln endorsed the scheme. He remained doubtful. "It is at least foolish to think," the general declared, "that the effect of the explosion could be transmitted to such a distance with enough force to weaken the fort." Engineers and demolition experts likewise encouraged Butler to reconsider due to logistical issues. US Army chief engineer Brig. Gen. Richard Delafield openly lambasted the futility of such a measure. In November he conducted research and could not find suitable evidence to support Butler's plan. Citing the unknown distance between the water and Fort Fisher, Delafield concluded that the fort would avoid serious damage. He also cited instances of foreign militaries doing the same thing against enemy forts and cities. Not once, Delafield noted, had earlier schemes succeeded as expected.⁹

The powder-ship plan, however, surged ahead. The vessel selected for the suicide mission was the *Louisiana*, an iron-hulled, propeller-driven steamship. Built in 1860 and commissioned in 1861, it had helped the naval em-

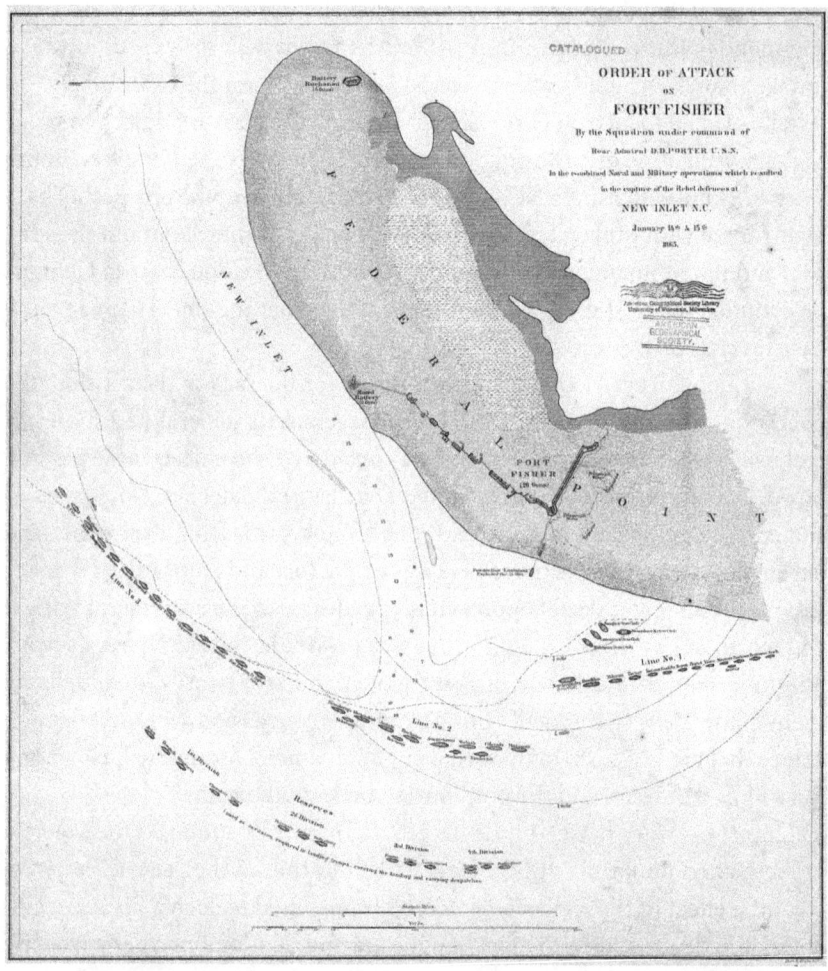

Order of attack for the US Navy during the First Battle of Fort Fisher, December 1864 (Library of Congress)

bargo of the South by preventing numerous Confederate blockade runners from making berth. Its captain and crew had captured Confederate schooners and burned multiple enemy vessels during its dignified wartime career. Yet while the *Louisiana* served the navy admirably, its final act of service was as a glorified powder keg. Built in Wilmington, Delaware, its demise could lead to the capture of Wilmington, North Carolina—at least that was the hope. On December 10 Admiral Porter gave directions to have the ship towed from Hampton Roads, Virginia, to the North Carolina shoreline.[10]

That same day a massive weather system out of the Midwest struck the Atlantic Coast, immediately delaying the operation for four stormy days. After taking an elongated route to confuse potential spies on the shoreline, Porter's transports finally sailed into the Atlantic on December 14. Ames's division required seven steam-powered transports to move its 3,000 men: the *Baltic, C. Thomas, Haze, Idaho, Perrit L. Moore, Starlight,* and *Wybasset.* "Our transports reached the rendezvous off New Inlet, N. C. Thursday, the 15th. Friday," Ames later wrote. "Saturday, and Sunday, we awaited the coming of the Navy." Porter arrived with his gunboats on December 18, but another fierce storm struck as he reached the location. On twentieth he directed most of the division's transports to Union-held Beaufort, North Carolina, near Cape Lookout, to avoid the storm and to resupply. Ames recalled that the ships needed both "coal and water" and their "ten days' supply had run short" while waiting for Porter's flotilla to arrive and the gale to end. The ship carrying Ames and 1,200 men, the *Baltic,* was the only one that did not need significant aid. The captains of the other transports considered making a harrowing landing on the Carolina coastline and sending men ashore to get much needed resources for thirsty soldiers and sputtering engines.[11]

As the transports moved back to their rendezvous point, Butler informed Ames that his division would spearhead the assault, landing three miles north of Fort Fisher on the narrow peninsula. On December 23 the gunboats bombarded Fort Fisher but did little damage. Concurrently, the wooden-hulled *Wilderness* towed the explosive-laden *Louisiana* toward the Rebel stronghold. Crewmembers lit fuses and abandoned ship, rowing back to the *Wilderness.* The fuses failed to ignite the explosives, but the crew had set a fire on the deck as a failsafe. Once the flames reached the power, the ship detonated, sometime between 1:40 A.M. and 2 A.M. on Christmas Eve. Butler's notorious scheme caused only minimal damage to the Confederate works, making the explosion anticlimactic if not innocuous. A naval officer who witnessed the event wrote, "We all believed in it from the Admiral down, but when it proved so laughable a failure we, of the navy, laid its paternity upon Butler." Porter immediately distanced himself from the scheme, reiterating to Grant and his own naval colleagues that it was attempted as a last resort. Ames, writing years later, thought the notorious *Louisiana* experiment "a failure" but considered both Butler and Porter culpable of the mortification.[12]

On Christmas morning at least seventeen ships in Porter's flotilla opened fire on Fort Fisher to cover Ames's landing. The *Brooklyn* moved closer to the shoreline than any other ship and sent Rebel defenders looking for cover with its barrages. Shortly before 2 P.M. Ames's men boarded their surfboats and set out for Federal Point. Ames wanted his Third Brigade to establish a beachhead, but Weitzel altered the plan without conferring with him, tasking the First Brigade, under Bvt. Brig. Gen. Newton M. Curtis, to land first. The division commander was unaware of the new plan until the operation was in motion, and he bristled at Weitzel for it.[13]

Curtis, standing six feet, seven inches tall and weighing close to 300 pounds, had landed at Federal Point by 2:10 P.M., planting a signal flag on a nearby dune to show where the rest of the division should land. He then took a reconnaissance force of 500 men and, per Weitzel's orders, pushed southward as far as he could go. About a half mile in, Curtis's men approached a small sand redoubt north of Fort Fisher called Battery Anderson. Without putting up a fight, its seventy-two defenders raised a white flag and surrendered. To the chagrin of Curtis, Ames, Weitzel, and the army as a whole, Union sailors saw the banner over Anderson and briskly rowed ashore to accept the garrison's surrender.[14]

Although the navy laid claim to Battery Anderson, the First Brigade now had to defend it, as a detachment of the Seventeenth North Carolina soon moved to retake the post. While the Rebels managed to drive in Curtis's pickets, the main body of Federal troops turned back the North Carolinians with ease. Meanwhile, Porter's warships resumed their barrage of Fort Fisher, targeting the Mound Battery. The fleet lobbed an estimated 10,000 shells against the Confederate positions.[15]

Ames oversaw the landing of his Second and Third Brigades while Curtis's men approached the Northeast Bastion. Weitzel, who by then was ashore with his staff, joined Curtis and examined Fort Fisher. He did not like the look of the place, thought it imposing, and overestimated its strength. Relying on inaccurate cartography, he also thought the installation had four walls and was taller than in actuality. Fort Fisher was formidable, Curtis agreed, but he believed that an assault could succeed. But Weitzel decided to leave the scene and report his findings to Butler, telling Curtis to stay in position and not to engage the enemy except to deploy skirmishers.[16]

Once Weitzel left, Ames—roughly two miles north of Curtis—became the ranking general on Federal Point but remained unaware of what was happening near the bastion. He got his other two brigades ashore and then ordered them to move south toward the fort. As this happened, Curtis and his men grew more emboldened. Soldiers from the 142nd New York slithered to within seventy-five yards of the north face. Federals also occupied rifle pits outside of the fortification near its wooden bridge and gate. The 142nd New York also managed to accomplish three surreptitious feats. The New Yorkers shot down a mounted Confederate courier carrying a dispatch to Wilmington, sneaked up to a gap between the north wall and the palisade fence to capture a Confederate battle flag, and cut Fort Fisher's telegraph line to the city. These actions further convinced Curtis that an assault would work. With the other brigades presumably in route, he soon could confer with his division commander, who generally favored aggressive action.[17]

Meanwhile, at 4 P.M. Weitzel told Butler quite a different story, saying that it "would be murder to order an attack on that work with that force." He instead proposed that the navy continue its bombardment for the time being. The infantry could consider making an attack after the fort was pounded sufficiently. Weitzel did not have to apply much effort to convince Butler. The *Louisiana*'s detonation had not worked, and Butler laid the blame squarely on Porter's shoulders; the political general did not think the navy was doing a good job reducing the fort since naval gunfire seemingly did little damage. Weitzel then compared Fort Fisher's defenses to those of Fort Monroe, which Butler impregnable and further pushed him to call off the infantry attack.[18]

Butler's apprehension grew even more after hearing from interrogated Confederate prisoners Curtis's men had captured. One soldier declared that the entirety of Maj. Gen. Robert Hoke's division from the Army of Northern Virginia was nearing the fort. Curtis had already fought troops from Hoke's Division, the Seventeenth North Carolina, at Battery Anderson, which corroborated the prisoner's story. With 2,500 troops on shore, Butler did not like the prospect of Ames's men fighting a veteran infantry division in the shadow of Fort Fisher.[19]

Yet another factor that compelled the general to stop the attack was the fear of an oncoming storm. The water grew increasingly choppy and rough that day. Brig. Gen. Charles Graham, a midshipman in the navy during peacetime, oversaw loading of the landing boats and noted that Ames's men needed reinforcements and supplies or should be called back. Butler needed to make a decision soon. The confluence of Weitzel's report, prisoner testimony, and Graham's emphatic ultimatum convinced Butler to recall Ames's division.[20]

When the order to withdraw reached Curtis, he was shocked. He sent an immediate and obstinate reply to his commander, telling Butler that his men could take the fort. Curtis secretly thought he needed more soldiers to do it, but still liked his chances. While waiting for a reply, he withdrew his men to Battery Holland, an empty Confederate position facing the north wall. Minutes after Curtis sent his message, another courier from Butler arrived and again told him to withdraw. Curtis optimistically assumed that the general had not yet received his reply and elected to wait. The storm, meanwhile, began to intensify as dusk fell. At the same time, Ames and his Third Brigade arrived at Battery Holland. Ames reportedly knew nothing about Butler's orders to retire, and the news astounded him when Curtis told him everything. The division commander also seethed because, for the second time that day, his superiors had bypassed him in the chain of command—first Weitzel and now Butler. Instead of communicating with Ames about attacking Fort Fisher or withdrawing to the boats, Butler had broken protocol and communicated directly with his subordinate.[21]

Quelling his rage, Ames discussed the present situation with Curtis. Although only able to make out the silhouette of the fort now that dusk had fallen, he was pleased nevertheless to finally see it for himself. Butler had yet to send a response, which encouraged Ames to entertain Curtis's bullish desire to attack. He then stated that "if an attack was made on the fort, the responsibility would rest with the officer in immediate command."[22] Yet this wording prompted confusion. Ames was assuming responsibility, but Curtis initially thought that Ames was referring to him as "the officer in immediate command" so that he could pass off the blame if something went awry. Nevertheless, both men thought the attack was still possible, especially since Curtis did not believe the fort was heavily manned.

Ames finally told him, "Go ahead and make it." Curtis deployed skirmishers backed by the Third New York, 117th New York, and 142nd New York of his brigade. The 117th New York, led by Col. Rufus Daggett, pushed forward and snatched up 200 Confederate prisoners from the North Carolina Junior Reserves, boy volunteers in their middle-to-late teens. Union skirmishers then opened fire, blindly shooting at the fort's parapets in front of them, now concealed in darkness. Curtis's regiments neared Fort Fisher, but a full assault never manifested; his overconfident veneer began to shed. The prospects of a nighttime assault looked less promising to him, especially when Colonel Lamb ordered troops along the parapets to open fire.[23]

For the first time in his military career, Ames displayed genuine uncertainty and hesitancy. He noticed that the volume of fire coming from Fort Fisher did not resemble a position lacking manpower. He began to worry that perhaps Weitzel, who had his maps, storied engineering prowess, and the experience of scouting the fort, was correct. Lt. Col. Cyrus Comstock, an engineer on loan from Grant's staff, had supported Ames's decision to take Fort Fisher at first, but now he also grew apprehensive. Weitzel, Ames, and Comstock all had garnered acclaim for their engineering abilities—all were West Point graduates. Then there was Curtis, a lawyer and farmer before the war, convinced he could take the fort regardless of what his superiors said. After consideration, Ames put an end to the attack, and Curtis recalled his skirmishers.[24]

Ames, Comstock, and other officers returned to the landing site north of Fort Fisher. "An order reached me at this time to return and re-embark," the general recalled. "All returned to the transports, except for part of the first brigade, which owing to the surf was forced to remain on shore until the 27th when the sea had sufficiently subsided."[25] Ames's annoyance with the entire operation spiked. Unable to get hundreds of men off the beach because of rough water, he had no choice but to pause reembarking. A total of 600 Union soldiers, along with roughly 200 prisoners, remained stranded on the peninsula overnight. Butler and his colleagues feared that those troops might end up prisoners themselves, but all of Ames's men avoided capture, which was never actually imminent.

The landing force had suffered only fifteen men wounded, one captured, and one drowned. Yet Wilmington remained open; ironically, two blockade runners reached the Cape Fear River within a day of the assault to bring valuable supplies to help the Confederate cause. Multiple factors had inhibited the operation. The Union forces lacked accurate intelligence about the current state of Fort Fisher. Their maps were unreliable, and they had a poor idea about the effectiveness of the navy's bombardments. Most of the Confederate guns remained operable even after the barrage, and the defenders, while outnumbered, were more than prepared with canister to shred any oncoming infantrymen. The cooperation between the Federal navy and army was miserable, with both sides accusing each other for not doing their job. Most of the blame for the failure nonetheless fell on Butler. Some officers theorized that the only reason the general managed to lead the expedition was because he somehow could blackmail Grant. Rumors spread that Butler had

Maj. Gen. Alfred H. Terry (Library of Congress)

witnessed the general in chief intoxicated while on duty, using that to finagle his way into commanding the Fort Fisher expedition.[26]

Regardless, Ames and his troops afterward sailed back to Hampton Roads, dejected and annoyed. He wrote home about not only his humiliation after Fort Fisher but also how responsibility for the fiasco was not on his shoulders. "I feel disappointed and mortified at our failure," he asserted, "but have the consolation that the fault was not attributable to me in the least." Grant was as upset as Ames. At first he accepted Butler's explanations for the debacle but later confessed to leaders in the administration, including President Lincoln, that he had yet to determine who deserved most of the blame for the abject failure. Everyone, from Butler down to Weitzel and from Ames to Curtis, thought they acted commendably. Grant's old friend Porter argued that the navy had done its part; any failure rested on the shoulders of the army. In the end, Grant sided with Porter and finally persuaded Lincoln that Butler had to go. With the elections of 1864 safely behind them, orders directly from the White House relieved Butler of departmental command and ordered him back to Massachusetts. But he fought back, defended his withdrawal, and defiantly told the Joint Committee on the Conduct of the War that Fort Fisher could not be taken.[27]

After the first expedition failed, and even as Butler railed in Washington, Grant began assembling another force to take Fort Fisher. He tasked Bvt. Maj. Gen. Alfred H. Terry to lead the troops for this second attempt. Called "Terry's Provisional Corps," the force consisted of essentially the same personnel as before, minus Butler and Weitzel. Terry had over 9,000 infantrymen and fifty-eight ships at his disposal. If he felt it necessary to lay siege to Fort Fisher, he also had thirty-six siege guns, with three companies of the First Connecticut Heavy Artillery and seven companies of the Sixteenth New York Heavy Artillery to man them. In addition, Grant told his trusted subordinate, Maj. Gen. Philip Sheridan, to be prepared to send a division of troops to Terry's force if needed. In the end, the general in chief instructed Maj. Gen. John A. Schofield to transfer his XXIII Army Corps from Tennessee to Annapolis, Maryland, to stand by in reserve. This time Fort Fisher would fall.[28]

On December 30 Ames's men had returned to their camps near the James River after having lived on transport ships for nearly a month. Four days later the division received new orders to march to Bermuda Hundred to embark on transports once more. From the evening of January 4, 1865, into the morning of the fifth, Terry's Provisional Corps boarded vessels and then sailed to Hampton Roads.

The flotilla left Hampton Roads on January 6, but Ames did not. Left behind, the general boarded the hospital tender *Blackstone* and caught up with his men only two days later. He blamed Curtis for his missing the boat for the second time in his career. The First Battle of Fort Fisher already had strained their relationship. Ames had sided with Butler and Weitzel to call off the attack, while Curtis agreed with Porter's opinion that the navy had softened up Fort Fisher enough for a successful infantry assault. Dissention between them continued the following month. Now, the Mainer fumed that Curtis had told Ames's ship, the *Atlantic*, to leave without him. The brigade commander denied it, but Ames furiously pressed his point. Although he later tried to apologize to Curtis for his outburst, the damage was done. Furthermore, by this time, Curtis apparently envied the division commander's position and had no tolerance for the perfectionistic general. As Ames now suspected Curtis of foul play, they avoided each other whenever possible.[29]

The second expedition to Fort Fisher, much like the previous one, endured a grueling gale that greatly affected the flotilla on its way south. Off Cape

Hatteras the ships could barely move ahead, as waves rolled twenty feet high. They managed to wait out the storm by anchoring near Beaufort and set out again on January 12. Eighty ships reached their anchorage five miles east of New Inlet that evening, much to the surprise of Colonel Lamb. General Bragg, recently returned from Savannah, had positioned scouts and coastal guards north of Fort Fisher to report on any Federal ships moving southward. They were to alert Bragg, who would relay the information to Lamb. But the system failed.[30]

As the Confederate defenders equipped themselves for an imminent assault, Ames's division prepared to make a landing. The Third Brigade, under Col. Louis Bell of New Hampshire, disembarked by 8 A.M. on January 13. The rough surf capsized several boats, sending blue-clad soldiers into frigid water. The rest of Terry's men followed, and by 3 P.M. his entire corps had landed on Federal Point peninsula. The only opposition they faced came from coastal swells and chilly saltwater. With 9,600 men ashore, Terry kept a brigade under Col. Joseph C. Abbott at the beachhead to dig in and keep an eye on Confederate troops stationed to the north on a fifty-foot rise called Sugar Loaf. Ames's division, as well as that of Brig. Gen. Charles Paine, marched southward to the eastern bank of the Cape Fear River. By 8 A.M. on the fourteenth, Paine's men had incorporated unoccupied Battery Anderson into an extended series of breastworks facing Fort Fisher. All the while, Porter's ironclads and wooden warships pummeled the Rebels with incessant barrages.[31]

As Terry's men landed and built earthworks, Colonel Lamb and his garrison troops prepared for an imminent attack. Maj. Gen. William H. C. Whiting, Ames's "sparring partner" at Port Walthall Junction the previous year, commanded the Cape Fear District. On January 13 he pleaded with Bragg to use Hoke's Division and attack Terry's men before they assaulted Fort Fisher. He sent another message at 8 P.M. that day before deciding to sail down the Cape Fear himself and join Lamb. Bragg considered moving against Terry but changed his mind, instead allocating 1,000 additional men to reinforce Fort Fisher—only about 350 made it in time. The fort's 1,500 men would have to hold with further aid.[32]

As was often the case, Bragg continued to waffle. At one point he favored an attack and ordered Hoke's men forward, but then he became convinced that attacking was the wrong choice. Hoke's men held defensible ground along Sugar Loaf and bottled up the peninsula. If they attacked Terry and failed, Union troops could march northward straight into Wilmington. Moreover, Confederate reconnaissance confirmed that the Federals had constructed their own defenses. If Hoke attacked, his men would have to deal with entrenched infantrymen as well as Porter's gunboats. Hoke and his brigade commanders did not think their men could succeed against such odds. Bragg concurred, believing that Terry's men outnumbered them by a two-to-one margin. In his mind the best course of action was to keep the enemy contained on Federal Point and hope that Fort Fisher and bad weather again would force them to abandon the operation. Meanwhile, Porter's flotilla continued barraging Fort Fisher on January 14, killing or injuring at least 200 of Lamb's men.[33]

While Bragg, Hoke, Lamb, and Whiting waited on opposite ends of Federal Point, Terry left Ames in charge and met with Porter on the flagship *Malvern*. He told the admiral that the two-day bombardment had done a solid job and proposed an attack for the following day. Porter would continue to shell Fort Fisher until the afternoon, when Ames's division, with Curtis's experienced brigade in the lead, would attack the fort and hopefully take it before dark. Terry notably wanted Curtis to operate as a quasi-independent force because of the feud with Ames. Porter supported the general's idea but suggested an addendum: he wanted sailors and marines to participate in the assault. Terry agreed. Ames's men would attack overland against the land face of the Fort Fisher after sailors and marines came ashore and targeted the Northeast Bastion.[34]

January 15 was clear and chilly. The oystercatchers and pelicans that frequented the isle conducted their daily business, unaware of what was to come. Porter's flotilla, formed in three curved lines offshore, soon opened fire on the fort. By midday, the warships had silenced most of the Confederate guns. But while the navy excelled in its bombardment, the 1,600 sailors and 350 marines sent ashore failed miserably in their amphibious attack against the sea face at 1:30 P.M. Armed only with cutlasses and pistols, the seamen and leathernecks charged in a discombobulated mass. Officers and sailors did not know whom to follow or where to report. Surging toward Fort Fisher, they were easy targets while crossing open and sandy terrain. Unaccustomed to combat on the land, Porter's personnel suffered 20 percent casualties. Still, their ill-fated assault succeeded as an unintended diversion, drawing the Confederates' attention away from the area Ames's division was to attack.[35]

The defenders cheered when they repulsed the first surge of Union attackers, but their demeanor changed when the primary assault moved forward. While Terry remained over 800 yards away on the shoreline, Ames exercised complete authority over the details of the ensuing engagement. Capt. Henry C. Lockwood later related a conversation, overheard by Capt. Charles

The Bombardment and Capture of Fort Fisher, N.C. Jany. 15th 1865, by Currier and Ives, c. 1865–72 (Library of Congress)

A. Carlton, between the two generals prior to the battle. After Terry agreed that the assault should begin, Ames asked if he had any specific orders. "No," Terry replied, "you understand the situation and what it is desired to accomplish. I leave everything to your discretion."[36]

Once everything was in order, Ames commenced his attack. "Gentlemen," the young general told his staff, "we will now go forward." Curtis's brigade set off first at 3:25 P.M. Lockwood, Ames's aide-de-camp, wrote a detailed account of what followed. "It was half past three when the steam-whistles shrieked out the signal for the attack," he recalled. "The Confederate officers had scarcely ceased cheering at the repulse of the sailors when they were surprised to see Federal battle-flags on the left of their work. The ground over which the right of our column passed was marshy and difficult; sometimes the men sank waist-deep into the mire, and some of the wounded perished here."[37]

Curtis's brigade advanced, followed closely by Col. Galusha Pennypacker's Second Brigade. A 12-pound Napoleon and a 3.2-inch Parrot rifle opened up on the Federals, enfilading them as they worked their way forward. Curtis's regiments became a rabble of disorganized blue coats as soldiers tried to evade the fire from Confederate artillery and infantrymen. The gunners could not reload quickly enough to fully break up the assault, however, nor could marksmen stop the advance once the Federal troops made it to the fort's earthen wall.

Curtis's men soon flooded the traverses of Shepherd's Battery, anchoring the land face near the Cape Fear River. Ames joined the Second Brigade as they swarmed the ramparts and Lamb tried to turn his guns on his own walls.[38]

As Union troops poured over the parapets, the hand-to-hand fighting became some of the most vicious of the war. "It was a charge of my brigades, one

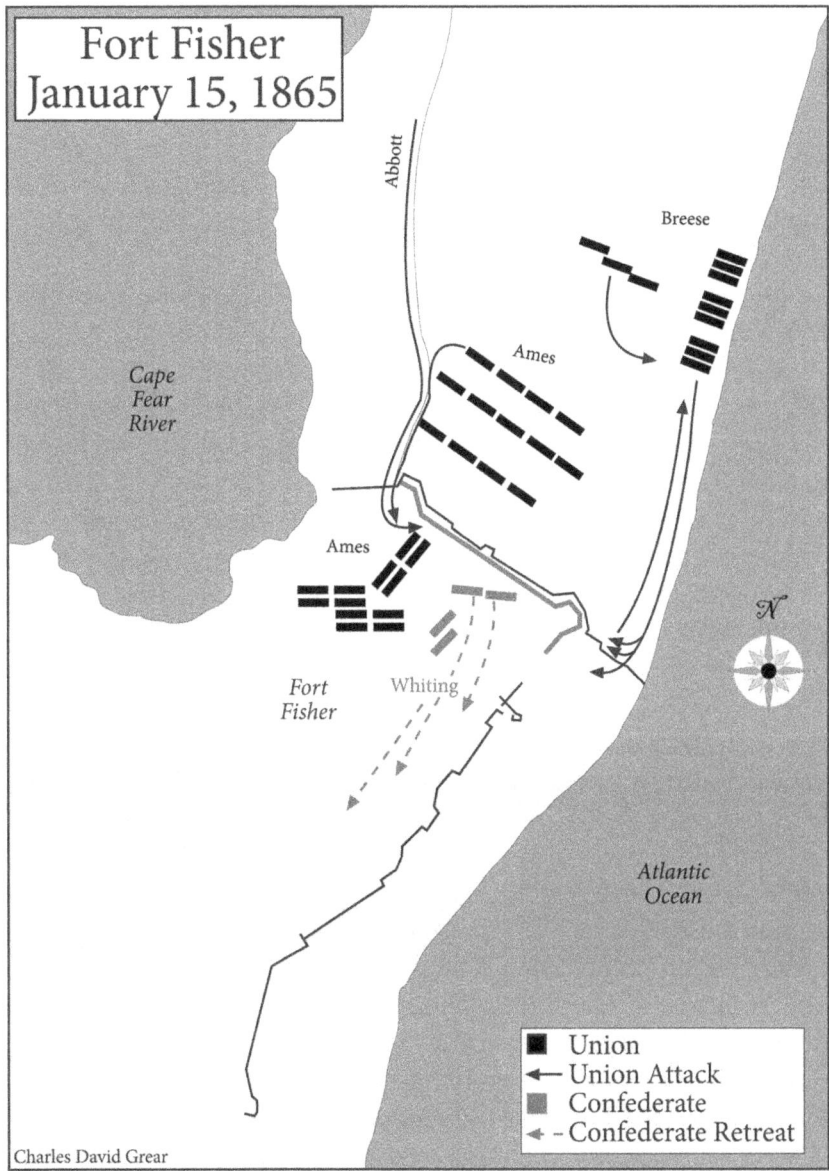

Fort Fisher, January 15, 1865 (Charles David Grear)

after the other," Ames recalled, "followed by desperate fighting at close quarters over the parapet and traverses and in and through the covered ways. All the time we were exposed to the musketry and artillery of the enemy, while our own Navy was thundering away, occasionally making us victims of its fire."[39]

Ames's brigades managed to gain a foothold in the fort, but bullets and shells continued to tear through his men. The Union soldiers met staunch resistance every time they reached a new traverse along the land and sea faces. Lockwood commented that the ability to hold the captured traverses while pressing onward was a difficult problem, but one effectively managed by Ames and his officers. Giving ample credit to the veteran troops and their immediate officers, Lockwood focused a great deal of his praise toward Ames, describing him as a commander in the thick of the fighting.[40]

Ames sent word for Colonel Bell and his Third Brigade to assault the land face. A Confederate rifleman mortally wounded Bell before his men reached the breach at Shepherd's Battery. With Bell down, Ames assumed direct command of the brigade and deployed its four regiments against the Northeast Bastion. Once they took the position, he ordered the men to turn the captured Napoleon there on the Confederate defenders. At the same time, Lamb had finished directing two smoothbore Columbiads and two more pieces on Mound Battery to begin firing upon the land face. "It is difficult to understand how Ames went unscathed at this time," Lockwood wrote, "while exposing himself, as he did, for he wore a brigadier-general's dress-coat." In a letter home Ames expressed his own surprise that he evaded injury or death. "My escape unhurt was quite miraculous," he admitted. "Of the six staff officers whom I took into the fight with me, only two escaped unhurt. The fighting was of the most desperate character and reflects the highest honor upon all concerned." As his troops pushed through each traverse and parapet, the fighting only escalated in ferocity. Soldiers discharged their muskets at point-blank range, while officers wielded their swords and sometimes muskets, fighting fiercely alongside their men. Maj. Leonard R. Thomas of the Ninety-Seventh Pennsylvania, recalled Second Brigade commander Curtis, "with blood streaming down his face," yielding a musket. Likewise, Ames "used a musket with effect. Every man was engaged."[41]

In such conditions regiments, already disorganized from the charge, broke down into informal groups of soldiers from different commands. While Ames was unable to keep units intact during the assault, he did keep it going, although at one point he considered digging in and waiting for reinforcements. Officers, with voices hoarse from giving orders over the cacophonous inferno, directed their men to use the cold steel of swords and bayonets to rush the defenders of each traverse until they themselves fell. The Mound Battery continued to pour shells into the fray, however, "killing and wounding them [Federals] by the score." As Ames's aide-de-camp recalled, "The enemy still kept up an impetuous resistance, and would not permit darkness to put an end to hostilities."[42]

Captain Lockwood described the zenith of the battle: "At last Ames stood within this circuit of fire amid the fragments of his division; every brigade and almost all of the regimental commanders had fallen, as well as most of his personal staff, so that for necessary duty substitutes for the latter had to be taken temporarily from the most available officers at hand. Ames, who had entered the fort at the head of the Second Brigade, remained there fighting with his men until the close of the action."[43] As dusk approached, the defenders stiffened their resolve as Ames ordered his men to take the fort's parade grounds. The Confederates fought hard, but their zeal decreased when Lamb and Whiting both went down with painful wounds. By 4:45 P.M., Ames, Pennypacker, and Curtis had claimed seven of the fort's traverses. Forty-five minutes later, the small-arms fire in Fort Fisher finally died down.[44]

Terry himself arrived on the scene at that moment and demanded that Ames and his exhausted men not entrench but rather keep the fight going. He summoned Colonel Abbot's brigade to Fort Fisher and, with these reinforcements, pushed through the fort as weary Confederate soldiers retreated. The fighting at last concluded with Ames's men in sole possession of the prized Fort Fisher. Any Confederates who evaded death or capture retreated two miles away to Battery Buchannan on the tip of the peninsula. Terry, joining a contingent of Abbot's brigade, pursued them. According to Abbot, Whiting tendered the surrender of his despondent and depleted command to Terry. Ames, in contrast, contended that Lockwood had already accepted the surrender of the troops who retreated to Battery Buchannan. Nevertheless, by 10 P.M., the Union army finally had taken the last great Confederate bastion, captured 1,200 men, and landed a crushing blow to the morale and logistics of a flagging foe. But the victory came at a heavy cost: Ames's division suffered 110 dead, 536 wounded, and 13 missing.[45]

Terry sent a telegram announcing the news, giving Ames and his men ample credit for the victory: "I have the honor to report that Fort Fisher was carried by assault this afternoon and evening by General Ames' Division (the second) and the 2nd Brigade of the First Division of the 24th Corps." He applauded Ames in one of his official reports, recommended him for a promotion, and praised the operation as a whole. People in the North were ecstatic about the fall of Fort Fisher. Secretary of War Stanton soon left Washington to conduct a personal interview with Terry and discuss the details of the successful operation.[46]

Yet as was so often the case, Ames soon had reason to complain about a personal slight. A second report from Terry, which highlighted himself as the primary decision maker, became the one that journalists relied upon to chronicle the events of January 15, 1865. The result was that in most cases, whether it was in the *Portland Daily Press*, the *Daily Davenport Democrat*, or the *New York Herald*, papers printed succinct articles that praised Terry while frequently excluding Ames from the narrative entirely.[47] Ames's omission in the northern press exasperated him and confused loyal soldiers such as Lockwood, who called it a "great injustice to a gallant officer."[48] In a later report Terry admitted, "On reflection, I feel that I have not done full justice to General Ames' merits." Regardless of such postbattle reflections, Ames failed to receive credit or widespread praise for his efforts to capture Fort Fisher. And while he did receive a promotion after the victory, it was only to brevet brigadier general in the regular army. Only a few individuals knew of Ames's central role in taking Fort Fisher, which dampened even that the promotion. And as a final blow, Curtis received the Medal of Honor.[49]

The snub in the press and the limited promotion both rankled Ames. He wrote to his parents: "I believe he [Terry] gives me the credit of my services in his report, but the newspapers do not. I was in hopes I should be made a Major General, but think it doubtful for the present."[50] Ultimately, most of the participants in the taking of Fort Fisher wanted their just accolades and adoration for their part in one of the final, and most impressive, assaults during the war. Ames never got over it. He still felt slighted thirty-two years afterward, prompting him to write his own account. Ames's work, while backed by solid research, once again angered his former rival on the field. Curtis, in response, offered a well-investigated rebuttal to Ames's account. While Ames described Terry as a spectator and minimized Curtis's s role—he actually calls into question the worthiness of his Medal of Honor—Curtis maintained that Terry deserved primary credit and added that Ames would have rather dug in around Fort Fisher than scale the ramparts. He did not question his division commander's intelligence or coolness under pressure, and likewise Ames applauded the brigade leader for his bravery and judgment. Yet both men took their quarrel to the grave, each refusing to concede that they exaggerated their own part in the battle. In the court of public opinion, Curtis's account initially gained a more supportive following. To men like Lockwood, however, both

Ames and Curtis deserved acclaim for their feat. Regarding Ames, he believed, "The nation should be thankful that we had the right man in the right place."[51]

In 1865, although frustrated with the press, Ames praised his troops for their efforts. "The conduct of the officers and men of this division was most gallant," he reported. In a later account of the battle, he applauded each of his brigade commanders, including Curtis, citing their bravery and fervor. Ames's service and theirs, throughout the war but particularly at Fort Fisher, displayed the type of invaluable leadership young generals and midlevel commanders had in producing military success for the Union.[52]

With Fort Fisher in Federal hands, Wilmington faced inevitable occupation. Ames rested his division, now numbering 111 officers and 2,623 enlisted men, as long as he could before leaving Federal Point. On February 17 the troops crossed the Cape Fear River. This flanking movement forced the evacuation of Fort Anderson, an installation that faced Fort Fisher. Two days later Ames's division returned to the east bank of the Cape Fear. Rebel deserters soon afterward reported that Confederate forces had abandoned Sugar Loaf, and the path to Wilmington was open.[53]

At 8 A.M. on February 22, Ames's division advanced with swords drawn and bayonets fixed toward earthworks outside of the port city. They surged over the Confederate defenses, but the only obstacles they encountered consisted of spiked cannons and discarded ammunition boxes. Met by the chief of police bearing a white flag, Terry received word that the mayor of Wilmington had authorized the surrender of the city. At 9:30 A.M. Terry and the leading columns entered the city, the Yankee bands blaring "Yankee Doodle" as they marched.[54]

The day after Wilmington fell, Ames wrote to his parents: "The rebels now have only Richmond, and I do not believe they can remain there long on account of the difficulty of procuring subsistence.... The Confederacy is going with a crash." That seemed to be the case in North Carolina. Following the capture of Wilmington, the Federals went in pursuit of Bragg's forces, which had withdrawn from the city. Ames marched with his division north, pausing nightly to rest the men. The opposing forces did not clash again in a full-scale engagement, but they did skirmish. Terry's troops also played a supportive role in replenishing Sherman's army, which had entered North Carolina in March after torching Georgia and South Carolina. As Grant's army wore down Confederate resolve in Virginia, Terry joined Sherman on March 21, making Sherman's command 88,000-men strong. Ames and Sherman had both served at First Bull Run in the summer of 1861. Now, nearly four years later, they were

Adelbert Ames, 1865
(Library of Congress)

again in the same army, and this time Ames could see that the end of the war was realistically in sight.⁵⁵

Ames's division did not participate in the final skirmishes in the Carolinas—supporting Sherman's troops was its role—but futile Confederate attacks dogged the men. "Our forces were attacked by the rebels," Ames wrote home, "and it is thought they intended to fight Sherman at a disadvantage and improve the only opportunity they probably will have to do anything positive to retrieve their waning cause." In the meantime, another personal change had occurred. When Ames dated his letter on March 26, 1865, he did so as a major general in the US Volunteers, having finally received his coveted promotion.⁵⁶

Ames's service during the Civil War began with the peril and excitement of First Bull Run, but it ended quietly. Following three days of deliberation, Gen. Joseph E. Johnson surrendered his forces to Sherman, as well as all active Confederate military from North Carolina to Florida, at Durham Station, North Carolina, on April 17. In the aftermath of the Lincoln's assassination, authorities in Washington found Sherman's terms so generous that they forced the signing of a revised surrender agreement between Sherman and Johnston on April 26.⁵⁷

Historian Harry King Benson observes: "For Ames, a Major General at twenty-nine years of age, the long, bitter conflict had been a springboard to almost instant military success. Vigorous, able and dedicated, the young West

Pointer had all of the prerequisites for military leadership." Although positive recommendations from senior officers and former commanders aware of or having witnessed his actions advanced his career, Ames had earned his promotions. "Wherever circumstances placed him," Benson continues, "he earned the encomiums of superiors. If he frequently aroused animosity among subordinates by his strict military discipline, it was turned, often as not, into respect and loyalty by his courage and willingness to endure the same hardships as his men."[58]

For hundreds of thousands of soldiers, their military service was about to be over. Ames, on the other hand, elected to remain a commissioned officer in the US Army, which meant relinquishing his generalship in the volunteers. On May 12 he assumed command of X Corps, with his headquarters in Raleigh, North Carolina. Ames paused a few days later to describe his comfortable situation there. "I am living in a fine house," he told his mother, "have an elegantly furnished room and take my meals with the [host] family. So long as I have to remain away from home at the North, nothing could be more desirable than my present situation."[59]

To supervise the readmission of the rebellious southern states and reestablish federal authority over them, Congress established five military divisions immediately after the large Confederate armies surrendered. Meade commanded the Atlantic District, formed on June 27, 1865. Ames's initial Reconstruction duties placed him in this district, alongside familiar officers such as Quincy Gillmore. He attended to military affairs in Person, Orange, Chatham, and Moore Counties, North Carolina, as the US government debated the readmission of former Confederate states. President Lincoln's plan for reconstructing rebellious states had traced its lineage back to 1863. Republicans in Congress, however, found his propositions for general amnesty and readmission preposterous and lenient in 1865. The debate over Lincoln's plan continued until his shocking assassination on April 14. Vice Pres. Andrew Johnson then assumed the presidency. Lacking the political and personal tact of his predecessor, Johnson proposed a similar plan that summer while Congress was in adjournment. He also took steps to prevent successful enactment of land reform in the South under the Freedman's Bureau, established in March 1865 to aid the former slaves. This created wedges between the administration and Congress.[60]

Later in the summer of 1865, the army sent Ames from Raleigh to Hilton Head, South Carolina, and then on to the state capital of Columbia. He had assumed that his destination was Charleston and believed the disadvantages of living there during the summer would have been "counterbalanced by advantages" he had, like his superior state of health.[61] Instead, Ames's new assignment was to oversee burned-out Columbia and the regions west and north of the capital. He spent any spare time studying law and contemplating the possibility of falling back on a legal career if he grew tired of the army with the war now over. In September he wrote his parents that South Carolinians "treat us [soldiers] like gentlemen" but still passionately loathed the presence of federal troops and extended no superfluous civilities toward men donning blue uniforms.[62]

Other observations of the postwar South included the condition of freedpeople who had endured slavery. Sickened, Ames witnessed repeated acts of violence against them. He informed his parents in Minnesota that his duties primarily involved aiding agents from the Treasury Department and the Freedman's Bureau in prosecuting white men accused of killing Black residents in the surrounding area. Noting that the guardhouse was full of such killers, Ames told his mother and father, "they think about as much of taking the life of a Freedman as I would that of a dog." He added with disgust, "I am in hopes that in course of time the pious people of this State will be convinced that according to our law it is, if not a sin, at least a crime to kill what they term a— nigger." Never as staunch an abolitionist as his parents, Ames's experiences in the Carolinas steadily began to persuade him of the necessity for the protection of the civil liberties of freedmen and their families. "When we [the army] go there will be no security for them and they will be in a much worse condition than when slaves," he remarked.[63]

Ames stayed in Columbia throughout the winter of 1865–66 and into the spring. He turned thirty years old during that period and oversaw the gradual rebuilding of the city's infrastructure. Severely damaged by Sherman's punitive forces in February 1865, Columbia had worn-torn streets and a manufacturing center that now consisted of dilapidated buildings and ashes. Much like Sherman's men at the time, Ames was not brokenhearted about it. Since this was the region where secession first ignited, he reasoned, the charred city was a just punishment for instigating the war. Although the literal embers ceased to burn, "fire still burns in the hearts of the people here; and our star-spangled banner or our country's uniform are only needed to fan the flame into wrath."[64]

Aware of that potential wrath, Ames wanted a successful, peaceful resolution to regional strife. In 1866 he believed that Johnson acted more reasonably compared to the Radical Republicans in Congress. Writing home, he confessed that he actually thought that Johnson was "nearer right than the majority in the two branches of Congress, in this present issue." Balancing his critique, Ames added: "Yet I fear he will go too far in his reconstruction and too soon relive the

South from the debt its actions during the past four years had brought upon itself. Most truly, the politics of the day is deeply interesting."⁶⁵

Not surprisingly, Ames imagined a life for himself far from the defeated Confederacy. In his letters home he again asked about the family's business ventures in Minnesota, wanting to be a part of their growing mill operations in Northfield. Encouraging his father to be at peace with purchases he had made, Ames encouraged the former sea captain to hold fast and not sell the mill if things went awry. He even suggested loaning his father half of his savings to fund any necessary repairs. Offering a dose of stoic optimism in one letter to him, Ames declared, "I think we should act by the best light we have or can command; and even should we sometimes make mistakes we should not permit them to make us unhappy."⁶⁶

Ames finally sought a leave of absence and a much-needed furlough. He desperately wanted to see his family, but he also hoped that he might receive a year's leave so he could tour Europe too. But the work of Reconstruction continued. The army sent Ames from Columbia to Charleston in April 1866. Major General Devens, with whom he had served at Cold Harbor, had mustered out of the service, and Ames was designated as his replacement. Devens's departure delayed any reprieve. The continual cycle of officers leaving the service left fewer and fewer veteran and competent men to run military departments in the South. Desiring a break for military monotony, Ames awaited his furlough in the city where the first shots of the war were fired five years earlier.⁶⁷

7

TRAVELS ABROAD

After months of delays, the army finally approved Ames's leave of absence in July 1866. His furlough was to last twelve months, as he did not have to report back until August 1867. Ames promptly left South Carolina and traveled northward on the first leg of his long-planned trip to Europe. The officer hoped that a tour of the continent would give him a mental reprieve from his duties. He was still in New York City, preparing for his excursion, when the army endorsed his latest promotion; Ames became a lieutenant colonel in the US regulars. With that commission, he also became the commander of the Twenty-Fourth Infantry Regiment.[1]

The presence of American tourists traveling overseas increased following the Civil War. Ames, like many of his countrymen, sought to broaden his horizons and return to the continent of his ancestors. Americans had frequented Europe since the 1780s, but in the nineteenth century this tide of US visitors "became a torrent and the American tourist in Europe became a commonplace." Between 1860 and 1870, American travelers increased from 28,700 annually to 35,800—many going to Europe as a part of the "great tourist invasion" of the continent. Historian William W. Stowe has noted that economic, social, and cultural intrigue led to more Americans venturing across the Atlantic Ocean at this time. The increasing modernization of transatlantic travel, along with blossoming hotel, banking, and tourist-centered periodicals, made touring Europe easier and more economically feasible.[2]

Americans sought new experiences abroad. Some historians posit that it was liberating for some travelers. Women could experience lavish, even scandalous, social atmospheres that were alien to their everyday domestic life. Like flies to honey, young people, lured to Europe by glamour and new experiences, sought adventure in both the cities and the countryside. Clergymen, artists, and writers flocked to London, Paris, and Madrid now that they could afford robust tourist experiences once confined only to the very wealthy. A thirty-three-year-old bachelor-officer, such as Ames, could on army pay traverse the continent.[3]

Ames was keen on enjoying his much-deserved holiday, and he was not content with lackadaisically touring Europe. He vowed to dutifully record his activities and strengthen himself philosophically: "Henceforth I pledge myself to make herein, as regularly as possible, entries of whatever I may see and hear which I may think will, at some future day, tend to recall this year of my sojourn in Europe . . . with one design which takes precedence overall others—it is, that I may be improved thereby. . . . [T]o write with greater facility . . . and to improve myself is the object of my travels."[4]

In this he was not exceptional. Many Americans who flocked to Europe also kept a record of their journeys, as Ames documented his entire trip in three journals. Most travelogues, however, produced accounts of identical experiences; instead of being unique they were repetitive. But some accounts still garnered more acclaim than others. Noteworthy travelers such as Henry James, Frederick Douglass, and Mark Twain published popular books about their time in Europe, yet even their adventures bore similarities with other Americans overseas. In short, Ames going to Europe and recording his escapades was not unique. At the same time, the idiosyncrasies of Ames's journey chronicle the experiences an American might have as he or she sought to bask in the glamourous, invigorating, and cosmopolitan atmosphere of Europe.[5]

The steamship *City of Cork* left New York on July 18, 1866. After two weeks, on August 2, the ship arrived at Liverpool, England. There Ames disembarked on the island nation that his ancestor Anthony Eames had left over 200 years earlier. He traveled first to London and remained in the British capital until August 15. There he briefly fed his intellectual fascination with English culture, but as a soldier he had decided to visit central Europe and prioritize German and Austrian cities first. Seeing the armies of Austria and Prussia intrigued him, although he lamented, perhaps with a hint of dark humor, that he could only see Austria and Prussia during times of peace.[6]

Both powers had just ended what in many ways was a German civil war that had started earlier that year. Austria and Prussia had jointly agreed to control the German-speaking Schleswig-Holstein region of southern Denmark after defeating the Danes in 1864. In January 1866 Prussian prime minister Otto von Bismarck claimed that Austria had broken their pact, although this was primarily an excuse to go to war, firmly establish Prussian hegemony among the other German states, and eventually engineer a united Germany under Prussian (not Austrian) dominance. Both sides mobilized their armies and those of their allies in March, and the Austro-Prussian War—also known as the Seven Weeks' War—began. By late July, Prussia held the upper hand, and the last significant engagement took place on July 24 in the Duchy of Baden, in modern-day southwestern Germany. The peace treaty of August 22, 1866, greatly strengthened Prussia's influence over the other German states and opened its path to German unification. Ames thus arrived in a newly peaceful Prussia and could not see its modernizing army operating in pitched battle.[7]

Nevertheless, he desperately wanted to see that army even in peacetime. Watching 10,000 Prussian troops during a military review in Berlin on August 24, Ames became convinced that the victorious Prussians were second to none, although their marching reminded him of the "Dutchmen" in the XI Corps he served alongside at Gettysburg, writing, "The motions, figures and bearing of both were the same." The Mainer also was impressed with the cavalrymen and artillerymen he saw. He critiqued the quality of the Prussian horses, however, and also thought that the lancers, albeit impressive, "would be worse than useless in our country." He was even less impressed by King Wilhelm I when he cast his eyes upon him. The nearly seventy-year-old monarch, the American wrote, looked aged and did not appear very kinglike as he stood near the Brandenburg Gate. Ames was more impressed by the marble royal residence, which he saw the following day in Potsdam.[8]

The real holder of political power in Prussia had impressed him more than its king. Watching a session of the Abgeordnetenhaus, the lower chamber of the Prussian government, Ames witnessed a short speech given by Bismarck at a pivotal moment in German history. "I did not understand what he said," he confessed. "Yet I was glad to see the man who now appears to have no superior in Europe."[9]

Ames's frustration with Bismarck's speech nonetheless pointed to a serious handicap. In addition to learning about the military culture of central Europe, he urgently desired to learn the German language while immersed in Prussian culture. During his early travels, Ames admitted in his journal that German overwhelmed him. "Chaos reigns supreme," he declared. "What I knew with certainty at first has been confusedly mixed with what I have since but imperfectly caught and to extricate myself is beyond my power. On the contrary new sounds, new words and new combinations are crowding the already overcrowded brain."[10] Ames's lack of proficiency hindered him in many ways. He went to a castle, but his ignorance of German delayed his ticket purchase. Although he eventually succeeded and enjoyed the staterooms, galleries, and chapel he visited, he knew his language skills had to improve. Typically, he immediately dedicated hours to study and actively searched for tutors to aid in his endeavor.

Still in Berlin, Ames dined with John Van Buren and his daughter on August 26. Van Buren, son and advisor to former president Martin Van Buren, had traveled extensively through Europe, and his peers heralded him as a shrewd political mind. Ames delighted in spending the evening with him and his daughter, discovering that he had crossed paths with a cousin of theirs while serving in South Carolina. The next day Ames traveled toward Dresden. He commented that he passed the vicinity of Wittenberg, which excited him, as he was near where "Martin Luther first began his battle against popery and the iniquities of the Romanish Church." That excitement, however, declined sharply. On August 28 he wrote, "Tonight I feel that I am not strong as I used to be—it is a sad feeling—I have hardly strength to write." Ames's health remained strong for the remainder of the journey, but he had to overcome travel fatigue as he prepared to leave Saxony.[11]

He left Dresden the following day and traveled six hours by train to Prague. Again exhausted, Ames found it impossible to sleep. Worse, a large party of Prussian officers kept him awake, and the smoke from their tobacco hung heavily in the car like a coastal fog. Along the way, a Syrian tried to converse with him "in his imperfect English." Ames found the man intriguing, and their conversation kept his interest. When a luggage officer examined the American's items at one point, Ames again struggled to converse in German when the Prussian began to interrogate him. But the man soon stamped Ames's portmanteau, and he continued on his journey without any more encumbrance.[12]

When Ames arrived in Prague, he toured the city as he awaited the next train to Vienna. He especially explored the Jewish quarter of the city and was both impressed and intrigued by the old and weathered synagogues. He was less charmed by Prague's many Roman Catholic cathedrals, which were more prevalent in Austria than in Lutheran Prussia. Protestant Ames took particular grievance with the popular images of Jesus Christ in the cathedrals. "The favorite picture and status is Our Savior"; he complained, "but caricatured as he is—dead and ghostly at one time; bloody and malformed at another—it has in its various forms become absolutely repulsive to me." Ames more enjoyed

Facade of Wallenstein Palace, Prague (Library of Congress)

touring Wallenstein Palace, the home of Albrecht von Wallenstein, a famed Bohemian military leader and statesmen who had commanded the Hapsburg armies during the Thirty Years' War (1618–48). He noted that the palace "was of greater interest to me than any object seen today."[13] It notably featured a taxidermical marvel that absorbed Ames's interest, a massive warhorse that had participated in the seventeenth-century war.

The stuffed warhorse aside, Ames was happy to leave Prague. The city was rife with Catholic imagery he did not care for and grimy streets he did not appreciate. Furthermore, according to the American consul in Prague, Ames risked contracting cholera, which at this time was rampant in the city as a major epidemic. During his travel to Vienna, he made note of lovely castles along the route but inevitably viewed them through the eyes of a modern soldier. "I noticed at long intervals castles upon the summit of hills," he wrote, "where they were quite secure against any such attacks as they might have been subject to years ago when they were built. But new, modern firearms would soon subdue them." Upon seeing the ruins of another castle, Ames observed, "Railroads and gunpowder have so changed the nature of warfare that a glance at the ruins here is enough to convince one that their days of usefulness have long since been passed."[14]

He enjoyed Vienna, but the city reaffirmed his belief that he did not care for Catholicism. Ames groused that everything in the churches was visual and ornate when the most important earthly presence to him, the Holy Spirit, was paradoxically invisible. He did not care for the adoration of idols either, commenting, "Although the Church of the Pope has wrought great deeds and done everything for Christianity in the past, it seems not fitted for the work of the future."[15]

Ames kept moving quickly, taking a train into Switzerland and visiting Zurich and then Bern, where he stayed through September 20. While in Bern, he happily encountered former general Charles Paine on September 9 during a church service. He enjoyed the surprise meeting, and the colleagues who fought together at Fort Fisher "chatted the afternoon away." Paine was just the first of many fellow travelers Ames met whom he had known from the States. He dined with the American diplomats in Bern and accompanied the US ambassador's daughter to church.[16]

The United States, in fact, was never far from Ames's mind. He was grateful to keep in touch with Americans both at home and abroad, and he also kept track of political developments at home. While in Heidelberg on September 25, Ames devoted his entire entry for that day to commenting on the sparring in Washington between President Johnson and Congress. Radicals by then decried Johnson's policies and thought he was too lenient on the former Confederate states. The president had already tried to stop the 1866 Civil Rights Act with a veto in March 1866 that Congress overrode. Making matters worse, Johnson's national speaking tour from August 27 through September 15 thoroughly alienated Republicans. He tried to court moderates in both parties by thrashing the Radicals during his "Swing Round the Circle" stump speech campaign to Chicago, during which he called them "blood suckers and cormorants." Every one of his speeches took place in the Midwest, where Radical Republicans who believed in abolition now unwaveringly supported civil rights and Congressional Reconstruction. Angering them further, Johnson voiced support for moderate candidates during the 1866 midterms, while more Republicans and northern citizens turned against him.[17]

Startled by the infighting, Ames hoped that Johnson, even if he sullied his own reputation and standing, would not end up "trailing his presidential mantel in the mud" and that "coolness and calculation" would prevail. Ames still was no Radical himself, however. Interested in protecting the safety and livelihood of freedmen, he—like many Republicans in 1866—did not support extending them suffrage and indeed worried that the Republican Party's demand for Black suffrage would jeopardize its overall platform in future elections.

The 1866 Civil Rights Act and Johnson's stump speeches severed the rocky marriage between the executive and legislative branches. Republicans passed legislation including a voting bill for the District of Columbia and bringing Nebraska into the Union. Johnson vetoed both, with Republicans overriding both vetoes.[18]

Ames noted that most Americans he met in Europe more strongly supported the Republicans and their mission to overrule Johnson's policies than he did. He wrote, "I find nearly every American I meet here a supporter of the congressional party, or radicals, as they are called."[19] Discussing American politics with non-Americans was not an alien pursuit during his trip. As Ames ate dinner with two English women on a train, they asked the officer about the state of American politics. He obliged, commenting in his journal, "like all Englishmen—or nearly all," the English ladies sympathized with the American South and Jefferson Davis. "I quietly gave them a chapter of American history," he continued. "They acknowledged they knew nothing of American politics. Mine was a regular stump speech without the American Eagle." In another interaction with a British subject, Ames bluntly suggested that the royal family did not possess any particular intellectual prowess over the common people. He further argued that every man in England should have the right to vote. Both statements angered the British gentlemen with whom he talked, which amused Ames greatly.[20]

Ames returned to Prussia in September and fully immersed himself in studying German, even proposing his abandonment of using English altogether. He worked tirelessly to acquire the language, sought lodgings with German families, and at least abstained from speaking English whenever he could. He did attend dinner parties in Hamburg, however, where he conversed in his native tongue often. Another enjoyable instance came when he had a long ride in the country discussing military history with a noted Scottish veteran, Brig. Gen. Sir Charles Shaw, who had served under the Duke of Wellington, fought in both the Portuguese and Spanish civil wars, and later became a pioneering police commissioner. Shaw and Ames both loathed inactivity or fruitlessness during their military careers. At Waterloo, Shaw recalled, he was put on baggage-guard duty and missed the combat. "I did all I could, to 'share in the triumph,' but was unsuccessful," he said.[21]

During another foray through the countryside, Ames bristled at a comment that an American woman made that the river scenery in Prussia was more beautiful than in the United States. He fumed that she had "no love for her country" to suggest such a thing and wrote, "I am of the opinion that if Americans would but travel as carefully and observingly over their own country as they do here they would see more to admire and be proud of than they have as yet succeeded in doing."[22]

After dedicating weeks to his German, Ames made a strategic change to work on his French as he entered Paris on October 18. He was not ashamed that he struggled with what he did not know, noting, "It is an ignoramus who cannot be convinced of his ignorance, who ever remains the same." As he did with German, he spent hours working on his French, without immediate progress. On October 25 Ames wrote, "I spent five hours with my instructor and at the end of the time was able to perceive I had made no little improvement."[23]

Such intensive study was important to him nonetheless because Ames did not want to tour Paris until he felt comfortable with the language. So he remained at work in his hotel room. His diligence in his study of French despite the lures of Paris reveals how obsessive Ames could be when he wanted to accomplish something. He was a war hero, highly educated, and a handsome bachelor in one of the most hedonistic cities in the world, but he remained dedicated to his language study first and foremost. On October 31, as he toiled, Ames turned thirty-one but did little to celebrate other than venturing out to see a vaudeville show. He had a bad time, not because of the content of the play, but because he did not understand as many words as he hoped. Ames also went to a famous ballroom, "le bal Valentino." Located on Saint-Honoré Street, it was one of the grandest in Paris. Ames did not appreciate that men had to pay entry but women did not. He added that it turned out to be a place where "no honest woman goes" and did not visit it again.[24]

Once Ames began to feel better about his linguistic progress, however, he started to enjoy Paris. Always the soldier, on November 5 he attended a review of French troops in the Bois de Boulogne, a large public park created by Emperor Napoleon III in 1852. But the day became a frustrating one. Ames asked a young female acquaintance of his to accompany him. In a humorous turn of events, the young lady's sister assumed Ames's invitation extended to her as well, so she tagged along with them and also brought along her two children. Ames thus became the "commander" of a gaggle of people in a large crowd of Parisians assembled to watch the soldiers. It was a challenging task. "So, with one eye on the ladies and both on the children," he wrote, "my attention

Panoramic view of Paris, 1865 (Library of Congress)

was somewhat diverted from the review." He even had to protect the children from wandering in front of carriages or away from adult supervision during the entire affair. He lamented at the end of that day, "Conclusion—avoid if possible taking a very large family of small children to a review in the *Bois-de-Boulogne*. Advantage—if it does not irritate and make unhappy, it will convince one that he is something of a philosopher." Yet he was at least able to see the troops as they left the area and concluded prophetically" "While willing to admit that the French is a military nation, I am forced to confess I saw that in the Prussian soldier which nothing here appears to equal—a solidity and intelligence whish [which] *should* have weight in battle."[25]

Five days later Ames saw the heads of the French state during a large royal procession through Paris. Although seeing the royals was exciting—raising his hat, Napoleon III's wife, Eugénie, bowed in return—Ames was more pleased to meet another old friend the following day. Joseph Foxcroft Cole was a childhood companion from Maine whom he had not seen in eight years. He had traveled to France to study with Émile Lambinet and Charles Jacque, both livestock and landscape artists, and had become a struggling artist living in Paris with his wife. But his fortunes turned about this time, when he managed to have his work exhibited publicly at the Salon. Ames thoroughly enjoyed the time he spent with Cole and his wife. Yet like so many elements of his trip in Europe, Ames found himself wrestling with his preconceived perceptions, his philosophies, and his life itself because of his encounters with Cole. "Instead of having that which gives peace and contentment," he lamented, "I am adrift, seeking for what God only knows. I do not. Thus far, life has been with me one severe struggle and now that a time of rest is upon me, I am lost to find my position."[26] Ames resolved to look forward to what life brought and committed himself to the future, although he professed to his journal that he still struggled with deep, conflicting thoughts.

The American tourist continued visiting with friends and seeing sights. One excursion of particular interest that dominated Ames's journal was a tour of the sewers of Paris on November 21. Their size and scope impressed him, and the odor was not nearly as abhorrent as he had predicted. In a less malodorous environment, Ames visited the Louvre with his expatriate friend. He enjoyed the paintings, gaining a deeper appreciation for the medium from Cole. Indeed, Ames so loved the museum that he returned at least three times while in Paris. He also saw Notre Dame Cathedral and was impressed by its storied history and its gothic architecture. He did not think highly of the religious tokens—relics of saints—passed as being original, however, and was skeptical of their validity.[27]

On November 24 Ames left Paris and arrived in London after a ten-and-a-half-hour journey. In his journal he praised England as a much better land than France. He felt calmer hearing English, he admitted, and walking through London's streets left him satisfied and comfortable: "I felt a home-like feeling in treading English soil and in being where I could understand and make myself understood." He also defended England as more liberal and freer than France, even if the English people themselves were more reserved. Unlike many Americans, he praised the Anglo-American relationship, celebrated the similarities between Great Britain and the United States, and found the British government "stands forth like gold" compared to the governments on the European mainland. He further noted the civility and fortitude of the British people. "The Frenchman of the present day is without virtue," he wrote, "without love for his home, without principle, without soul. His one god is his passions and to it everything else is sacrificed."[28] He had grown tired of French profligacy, he declared, and joyously studied the homeland of his ancestry.

Ames did not remain in London for long. Indeed, he quickly ventured back to hedonistic Paris, his critique of the city and its people aside, where he remained through Christmas. He observed that lengthy feasting was a prerequisite in Paris to celebrate Christ's birth. Far from lonely during this winter season abroad, Ames attended multiple parties, received invitations for outings, and visited the Louvre again with American expatriates. And his social circles continued to grow. He accompanied American minister John Adams Dix, a former Union general and briefly James Buchanan's secretary of the Treasury, during the minister's many duties. Much of early January 1867 consisted of Ames eagerly awaiting an invitation from Dix to meet Napoleon III at a royal ball. On January 17 he at last had his chance. The ball took place at the royal home at Tuileries Palace along the River Seine. Built in 1564, the Tuileries was adjacent to the Louvre. Napoleon III specifically favored this residence and oversaw renovations that made the pristine locale even more opulent. As a young, dashing war hero, Ames received pleas from six Americans, mostly women, to accompany them to the ball. "I had no desire to have any ladies under my charge on such an occasion," he admitted, "but the young lady in question [the daughter of a Mrs. Coyle] so expressed her wish that someone would take her and her mother in charge that I could not well decline."[29]

The invited throng entered and assembled themselves in a long line to await the French ruler. The order of guests irked Ames because the Americans were the last in line, with English, Austrian, and Portuguese dignitaries all ahead of them. "After we had waited too long," he recalled, "the Emperor came into the room, attended by high officers of the court. Beginning at the end of the line, almost a circle, he stopped a few seconds before each person, giving the ambassador or minister, as the case might be, of the nation to which the person belonged an opportunity to present her or him." The young man from Rockland, Maine, soon met the French emperor. They spoke for a moment and then, according to Ames, the emperor and the empress advanced to their throne room. There hundreds of additional guests swarmed the monarchs and enveloped Ames and the other dignitaries. Dancing and celebrations continued into the evening. The royals supplied dinner at midnight, and the crowds began to disperse at two in the morning. Exhausted, Ames did not reach his bed until 3 A.M.[30]

Meeting Napoleon III was a highlight of his journey, but Ames soon made plans to leave Paris and take his sightseeing to Italy. He traveled by rail to Nice and Marseilles en route to the Italian peninsula. He felt anxious, but the trip turned out to be a decompressing venture. On February 3 Ames arrived in Genoa; two days later he was in Milan. Shaking off his earlier Roman Catholic criticism, he frequently attended church services and visited cathedrals. The basilicas in Italy loomed over any he had seen previously on the continent. He climbed to the top of towers and marveled at the view over the city. In Verona he visited the house where the fictional Juliet, the well-known Shakespearean heroine, was born, and he reveled in seeing the archaic fortifications of the town. He quickly moved on to Venice, to Florence, and then sped across the peninsula. All the while he shook off the pessimism that had developed in France, and his mood grew bright.[31]

Ames toured Naples and then was impressed with Rome, although he admitted it was smaller than anticipated. He especially noted the impressive papal basilica of Saint Maria Degli Angeli and the unique yet "ghostly decorations" of a nearby friars' cemetery, where the dried bones of disinterred friars decorated the vaults. Ames saw the Coliseum too, but the American Protestant turned down an opportunity to be presented before Pope Pius IX. He did witness the pope pray in Saint Peter's and noted the attention the bishop of Rome paid to bronze statues, which reinforced Ames's denunciations of Catholicism.[32]

Boarding the steamer *Thabor* on March 8, Ames cruised across the Mediterranean Sea, into the Atlantic Ocean, and north to Dorset, England. After spending a week in Dorset, the home of his ancestors, the American returned to London. Ames visited the Tower of London and marveled at the extensive armory. Although centuries old, the British Royal Army Ordnance Corps still used the installation. On March 24, in the Newington district of South London, he attended a sermon given in a massive agricultural hall by the famed Baptist preacher Charles Spurgeon of Essex. The number of Christian pilgrims in attendance numbered ten to twelve thousand, Ames guessed. Like most people he met, Spurgeon did not impress him physically. The portly, heavily bearded minister did not strike Ames as a physically fit man. His intellect was another matter. Spurgeon encouraged those in attendance to ask themselves: "Am I on the Lord's side? Am I for Christ, or for his enemies? Do I gather with him, or do I scatter abroad?" He further questioned if they were nominal followers inclined to consciously sin or committed to the word of God both intellectually and spiritually. "Yet I came not here to tell you only of your sins," Spurgeon went on, "but to help you escape from them." He concluded his sermon by imploring his audience to trust in God, accept their sinfulness and the free gift of salvation, and put their past deeds behind them. The message left a notable impression on the visiting American.[33]

Two days later Ames heard another intellectual giant of the age. Along with some friends, he went to Saint James Hall to hear Charles Dickens. The famed author read extracts from his works, including *The Pickwick Papers*. Ames was disappointed: "He read well—he certainly knows better than anyone how to render his own works—but to my thinking and that of my friends, he did not do as well as others have." He also found Dickens to be a "fat fellow" who could not say or do anything on stage, whatever his objective, "without appearing ludicrous and provoking mirth."[34]

Continuing a streak of encountering famous figures, Ames attended a concert at Saint James's Hall that featured an array of renowned musicians. He listened to beautiful violin concertos by the renowned Hungarian violinist Joseph Joachim, the renowned pianist Charles Hallé, and the Italian cellist Carlo Alfredo Piatti. The music he heard overwhelmed him, although confessing in his journal: "I have long since made up my mind that I am naturally incapable of understanding the highest order of music. It is a strange language to me which never so much study will make clear."[35]

The arts aside, Ames the soldier continued trying to learn and see as much as he could of the military infrastructure of Europe. In April he visited the British Army's massive military arsenal at Woolwich in southeastern London. The Royal Arsenal manufactured small arms, artillery pieces, and gun carriages for naval vessels but also featured the Storekeeper's Department, which oversaw the storage of the items produced there. He described the arsenal as a labyrinth and noted that it employed 12,000 men.[36]

In continuing his desire to see the hallowed halls and homes of rulers in Europe, he went to see Windsor Castle. Prince Albert had died there in 1861, and since that moment Queen Victoria had kept the castle in a state of mourning. Becoming more reclusive, she elected to use Windsor instead of Buckingham Palace as her primary residence. With the help of a servant during his visit, Ames even toured the royal stables and saw the carriages used by the royal family. After visiting Windsor, he covered adjacent tracts of land in Berkshire and Surrey Counties. He toured the home of William Penn, the Quaker founder of Pennsylvania, in Ruscombe, near Twyford. And in nearby Runnymeade in Surrey, Ames saw the site where King John signed and sealed the Magna Carta in June 1215.[37]

Ames began a third journal, which he devoted to his final two feverish months in Europe. From April through the first week of June 1867, he raced across western Europe. At the same time, he dedicated himself to studying mnemonics, a subject he found invigorating. As during most of his European excursion, Ames also balanced study with leisure. Back in London he took a female friend to see a musical concert featuring popular songs he recognized from his time in the Union army, including "John Brown's Body." The following day Ames toured the Crystal Palace—the site of Queen Victoria's 1851 imperial exhibition—with the US consul, former Maine congressman Freeman Harlow Morse. The impressive 990,000-square-foot structure still hosted a variety of events. Leaving London, Ames delayed his travels to watch Oxford and Cambridge University's rowing teams race each other. He enjoyed the event, writing, "It is almost as important an event as the Derby race which moves all England much as one of our elections arouse our people. As they rowed by me, Cambridge was ahead by a half a length, but in the end, the Oxford [crew] beat [them] by about the same distance."[38] Ames also traveled to see the Marston Moor battlefield in North Yorkshire, site of a First English Civil War engagement on July 2, 1644.

After visiting the archaic city of York, the American boarded a train and set off for Scotland. At the border Ames commented on the soil, terrain, and the iron mills and coal mines that dominated the local economy.[39] His first visit was to Edinburgh. "I then walked to Holyrood Castle," he wrote, "the ancient palace of the kings of Scotland. Many are the histories given of this place." He observed bloodstains on the floor from victims purportedly killed before the presence of Mary I of Scotland. Another home he visited in the city belonged to Scottish reformer John Knox. "Every step was made interesting by the histories of past years," Ames ruminated.[40]

Ames left Edinburgh and traveled west Glasgow and then the village of Perth on April 18. He visited the Robert Burns sites in Alloway, South Ayrshire, where he saw the writer's adult home and found Burns's miniscule, thatched boyhood home two miles away just as intriguing. Admitting that he had time to only "catch a glimpse" of the country, Ames quickly bade Scotland goodbye and left that evening to sail for Ireland.[41]

By April 21, he was in Dublin and immediately prepared to go to Belfast. Ames did not travel through Ireland comfortably. He clutched a document from US minister to Great Britain Charles Quincy Adams, son of President John Quincy Adams and grandson of founding father John Adams, that gave him safe passage through the island. Irish officials had previously arrested Americans, viewing them as suspicious. Ames, as a military man, might stand out and even cause anti-British Fenian patriots to detain him as an infiltrator with sympathies for the royal government. The weather also annoyed him. Noting the city's bleak weather, he concluded the pelting rain and jaunting car contributed to "the most unpleasant spring which man ever rode on." Water saturated his shoes and trousers, his umbrella failed him, and he thought the ride forced him to study "how not to go to the ground." Perhaps not surprisingly, he saw little to like in Ireland. Outside of Dublin, he noted the sad economic state of the people: "The almost total absence of decent houses I saw in the country and small villages; and constantly recurring low, dirty hovel of the lower dirtier peasantry." Ames described their lack of wealth in comparison to the Scots and the English and observed that the Irish were in a similar predicament as the former slaves in the United States. He further noted how British landlords had forcibly removed Irish families from their homes and sent them to America.[42]

Ames went on to Killarney and Cork, left Ireland without encumbrance, and sailed to Wales. He noted that when he arrived, that country still featured impoverished people but added that their communities were far less dirty than those in Ireland and he saw not a single beggar. Returning to England, Ames visited the home of William Shakespeare in Stratford-upon-Avon. "This very valuable and interesting relic of that greatest genius of the pen, we know, still exists as it was when he lived," he gushed. He also visited a castle in "Warick" that had armor worn by Edward II, the Black Prince, and Oliver Cromwell. These relics impressed Ames, but he did not describe the castle in any detail. He spent more time in his journal describing a beggar who spoke to him with a "gin-flavored throat" and demanded money.[43]

On April 30 Ames bid England farewell and went to France one final time. Spending several days with the friends he had made in Paris, he dedicated his time there to shopping and procured gifts for his family, including paintings, scarves, and gold watches. "I am quite satiated with sightseeing," admitted Ames. Notably, he met the Duke of Edinburgh at an art gallery but made little mention of it. Fatigued from travel and meeting new people, Ames received surprising word that American dignitaries in Europe wanted him to remain longer and had even written home to ask if the army could extend his leave. A military board, organized for an exhibition, would examine and report on different kinds of ordnance on display and feature the leading military minds in Europe. The inducements to join the board were strong, but Ames was not interested in remaining in Europe any longer. "I do not think I would be more influenced than I am at the present time, which is not at all," he commented. On the first day of June, the American officer left Paris and arrived in London. He packed his valuables, ensured everything was in order, and then traveled to Liverpool. By 1:00 P.M. on June 5, Ames and his fellow passengers boarded a "steam tug" that took them to the *City of Antwerp*, captained by John Mirehouse. "This accomplished," Ames wrote in the final sentence of his journals, "the brig cast off and we went on our way."[44]

When the *City of Antwerp* arrived in New York on June 17, Ames was tired from his travels but a different man because of his journey. From Germany to France, from Great Britain to Italy, Ames saw nations that were about to embark on profound trajectories, revolutionizing themselves economically, politically, militarily, and hegemonically. More importantly, his journals offered unprecedented insight into Ames's state of mind as he transitioned to a new chapter in his life. Instead of seeing the world as a young cabin boy on his father's ships, he had now traveled the European continent by himself as a mature man. On his own he taught himself foreign languages and had the honor of dining and accompanying heads of state and dignitaries. In his mind he had reached a new plateau of life marked by cosmopolitanism. Ames was not just a soldier anymore, but a well-traveled man who could boast of European tourism that Americans lusted after in the late nineteenth century.

Additionally, his European travels forced him to encounter experiences that made him wrestle with how he viewed the world. He had to process the presence of Christianity interpreted differently from his Protestant upbringing in Rockland. He was reminded that being a Christian was having a personal relationship with Christ, not just following a set of religious customs. On multiple occasions he witnessed the cultural and political dynamics of European politics and militarism. These experiences brought him into contact with the forthcoming change the continent would witness. Ames grappled with his personal future as well, now at a crossroads. His journals chronicle the struggle he had over his career and life choices. His time with Joseph Cole, which showed what gratifications a simple life with a family could provide, forced Ames to contemplate if his military acclaim and his trip was enough to satisfy his soul. Ultimately, he returned to America ready to reassume his place as an officer in the US Army.

A MILITARY MAN WEARING POLITICAL HATS

The political climate in the United States was fierce when Ames returned to his homeland in the summer of 1867. The relationship between Congress and President Johnson had deteriorated further. Johnson had vetoed acts to dissolve and reconstruct southern governments and prevent the president from removing certain officeholders without congressional approval. The Republican-dominated Congress overruled Johnson with ease. In the shadow of political sparring, Ames arrived in the States and promptly reported to his regiment. In August he and the Twenty-Fourth Infantry Regiment headed to unruly Mississippi.

Ames had never been to Mississippi before 1867, and he arrived to find it still reeling from the war. After the Confederacy collapsed in 1865, the state fell into chaos. There were several causes for this—primarily the war's rampant destruction. Union military excursions had destroyed the state's railroad system and the buildings in many towns. In Okolona, a town in agriculturally abundant northeastern Mississippi, only a handful of homes remained intact. In Meridian, located in the state's east-central hill region, Sherman's troops had burned every single building in the business district in February 1864 except for two hotels.[1] In more urban areas, the damage was even worse. In the capital of Jackson, Sherman's troops had looted and pillaged the city on May 15, 1863. Then in July Sherman's men returned and laid siege to the Confederate-held city after Vicksburg fell to Grant's forces. Rebel troops escaped the city, which Sherman's men then torched. Before the war, Jackson boasted 140 businesses

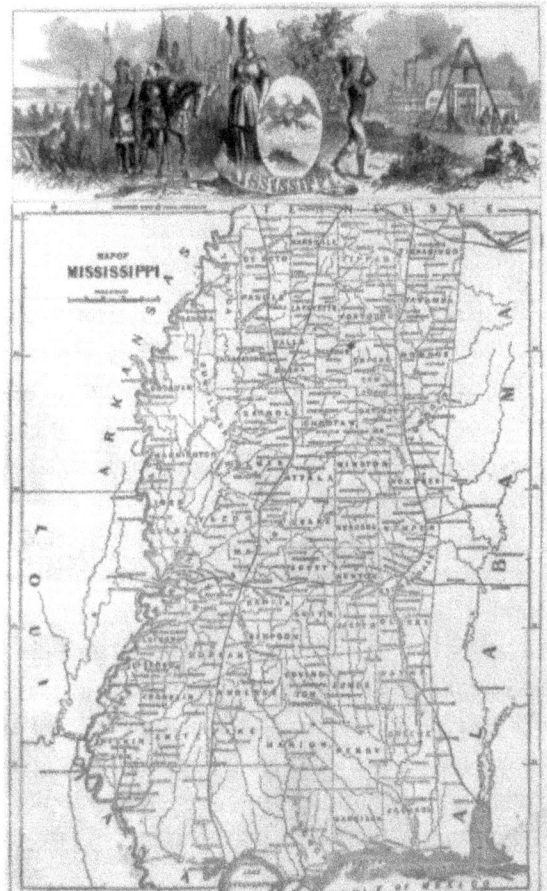

Woodcut map of
Mississippi, 1866
(Library of Congress)

and establishments. After the war only 40 businesses remained, among them two hotels rather than the ten present before the conflict.[2]

Vicksburg and Greenville had fared poorly too. Situated 200 feet above the Mississippi River, the high bluffs could not protect Vicksburg from besieging Federal forces inland. Union shells tore into homes and gashed streets. The bombardment wrecked the interior of the Warren County Courthouse, the most imposing building in town. While Vicksburg was under siege, Union troops burned every building in nearby Greenville to the ground. The degree of the damage forced residents to relocate their city.[3]

Counties in Mississippi had suffered from guerrilla warfare as well during the conflict, and widespread disorder persisted afterward. During the war,

Confederate soldiers had deserted their units with regularity and received warm welcomes from their kin when they returned home. Their families shielded them from any governmental attempts to punish them as they stole from local people. Sympathetic locals encouraged bands of deserters to hide from Confederate authorities.[4] Many of the deserters kept committing crimes after the war ended and continued to evade the law in battered postwar communities. State authorities could not impede lawbreakers, and outlawry remained a serious issue.

The preeminent issue in Mississippi, however—it caused occupation forces the biggest headaches—was a keen determination among white residents to retain the racial hierarchy that existed before the war. Under Johnson's Reconstruction plans and led by Confederate sympathizers, Mississippians had forged a new constitution, elected a governor—former Confederate brigadier general Benjamin G. Humphrey—and convened a legislature in 1865 that requested readmission to the Union.

The legislature also crafted a series of harsh legal codes specifically for Black Mississippians. Ironically entitled "An Act to Confer Civil Rights on Freedmen" by legislators on November 25, 1865, the new laws implemented mobility-restricting "Black Codes" that essentially relegated African Americans to quasi-enslavement in agricultural jobs. The codes, both the first and the strictest in the former Confederacy, prevented freedmen from exercising most civil rights and privileges such as assembly. Underneath the veneer of legal protection, they limited employment opportunities and enacted punishments if a freedman "deserted" his employer. If incarcerated, local law enforcement could loan the prisoner back to his former employer to work. Additional addendums included the broad charge of "vagrancy," which would lead to imprisonment and then unpaid manual labor. The codes also restricted Second Amendment rights for freedmen. Less than a month later, the legislature rejected the Thirteenth Amendment, and Congress refused to readmit the state into the Union.[5]

The result was a new round of military occupation. Intending to implement Radical Republican policies in recalcitrant states such as Mississippi, Congress set to work at the end of 1865 to replace Johnson's leniency. The Republican majority rejected the validity of southern elections, launched investigations into conditions there, crafted the Civil Rights Act of 1866 to undermine the Black Codes, and attempted to make that new law constitutional by approving the Fourteenth Amendment. In 1867 Congress passed three measures that became known as the Reconstruction Acts. Together they stipulated that all former Confederate states except Tennessee, which had ratified the Fourteenth Amendment, had to abide by a strict new set of rules before readmittance. Congress created five southern districts governed by the US military. Unruly Mississippi, along with its western neighbor Arkansas, composed the Fourth Military District. The inaugural commander was Maj. Gen. Edward O. C. Ord, with whom Ames had served with during the war. Col. Alvan C. Gillem, a Union officer originally from Tennessee and one more friendly to ex-Confederates, commanded the subdistrict of Mississippi. In December Gillem replaced Ord as district commander, as the military would supervise a new round of constitutional conventions and elections that would produce loyal governments.[6]

This was the Mississippi that awaited Ames. On his way there in 1867, he stopped in Washington and met with the postwar commander of the US Army, Ulysses S. Grant. The general told Ames that his duty was to aid the civil authorities, enforce order, and help the Freedman's Bureau and its agents assist former slaves. Founded in 1865 and extended over Johnson's veto, the Freedman's Bureau was tasked to oversee "such issues of provisions, clothing, and fuel ... for the immediate and temporary shelter and supply of destitute and suffering refugee freedmen and their wives and children."[7]

While working frequently with bureau agents, Ames would witness firsthand just how laborious and dangerous a task it was. Crimes against African Americans in Mississippi remained frequent, and the intense acceleration of Ku Klux Klan activity led to a new spike in violence. Founded in Tennessee as a fraternal club for resentful Confederate veterans, the Klan grew rapidly, expanded across the South, and operated as an extralegal paramilitary force designed to intimidate Black voters and other Republicans while reasserting white supremacy in their communities. Its first Grand Wizard, Nathan Bedford Forrest, had been a fearless cavalry leader in the western theater during the war, and his prominence within the organized helped intensify its growth before he stepped away from the group. Ames's former commander, Benjamin Butler, knew that the Klan would use "force, fraud, and murder" to circumvent federal authority, defy constitutional amendments, and subvert the Civil Rights Act. Butler was correct; violence against communities in Mississippi necessitated the creation of a local commission to handle the trials and punishments of white citizens who killed African Americans or committed arson. Ames, appointed president of this body, used his legal knowledge to manage the prosecution of civil rights offenses.[8]

Butler was about to play yet another major role in Ames's life. In February 1868 Ames was in Washington at the same time as the impeachment trial of

Sketch of young Blanche Butler Ames (From Butler, *Butler's Book*)

Andrew Johnson took place. Representative Butler was the chief prosecutor, joined as an impeachment manger by notable political figures such as Rep. Thaddeus Stevens and Rep. George Boutwell. The managers produced eleven articles of impeachment before the Senate. Arguably, the most serious charge was that Johnson had violated the new Tenure of Office Act when he jettisoned Edwin Stanton from the position of secretary of war. Ames was in the Senate gallery during the testimony, as were many of the prominent figures in the nation's capital. Many highly regarded women, as interested in political developments as men, also frequented the seats overlooking the Senate. Blanche Butler, Benjamin Butler's twenty-year-old daughter, was one of them. She one of the most well-known young women in Washington, with accounts of her beauty and intellect preceding her. Ames and Butler met and sat by each other for most of the proceedings. He found her a captivating and intelligent young woman. Ames had to swiftly return to Mississippi after the trial, but Blanche Butler left enough of an impression that he would court her through letters for the next two years.[9]

One of the army's major duties under the Reconstruction Acts was to oversee and protect those creating new state constitutions from the interference of groups such as the Klan. Before Gillem replaced him, Ord set a date for the state to accept or reject a constitutional convention in Jackson. On November 5, 1867, an election was held in which 69,739 voters cast ballots to support a convention, while only 6,277 opposed the measure. Many voters were conservatives and Democratic loyalists who saw the convention as a chance to establish a quasi-antebellum government and limit the political power of newly freed African Americans seeking to exercise their rights.[10]

In January 1868 the convention met under the watchful eye of the federal occupation force. Eighty-five delegates assembled, and accounts suggest that as many as seventeen were African American. One of Ames's notable acquaintances in the convention was Beroth B. Eggleston. Having enlisted as a private in an Ohio regiment, Eggleston ended the war as a general and relocated his family to Mississippi afterward. A so-called carpetbagger, he acquired a large plantation and tried to earn the nomination for governor of Mississippi. Eggleston and other Union veterans like him composed the backbone of the state's Republican Party, but partisan divisiveness rent their ranks. In addition to divisions between white and Black members, Republicans ranged ideologically from conservative to radical, so internal factions materialized.[11]

Republican and Democratic delegates to the constitutional convention discussed topics such as education and interracial marriage, with both white and Black members advocating fines and penalties for cohabitation. The most important topic, however, was voting rights. In 1866 Congress had passed the Fourteenth Amendment, which, once ratified, would grant citizenship to all persons born or naturalized in the states, solidifying the argument that African Americans were citizens without specifically mentioning suffrage. Ratification was on the horizon, and Mississippi would need to ratify the amendment to return to the Union. In the face of such a contentious topic, the convention produced a constitution on May 18, 1868. Democratic operatives aggressively opposed it, telling the citizenry that it was a segue to Black control of the state. Residents voted on the constitution on June 22. The numbers were 56,231 in favor of the constitution but 63,860 opposed. Intimidation at the polls frightened away droves of Black voters and pro-Republican southern-born whites, called "scalawags," contributing to the constitution's demise. Voters also cast ballots for state officials. Democratic candidates did well, and Benjamin G. Humphreys won reelection as governor.[12]

The media cheered the constitution's implosion. The *American Citizen* of Clanton praised what the editors considered a remarkable victory, writing: "The white race of Mississippi are of the truest and most resolute courage. Federal bayonets failed to cow them both before and after the election.... Is it surprising, then, that such a people, such a race, would refuse to surrender their State to the control of negros and bummers?" The editors of Jackson's *Daily Clarion* asserted: "The scallywags and carpet-baggers are in sore tribulation and discomfiture. To have the cup of bliss dashed to earth, at the very moment of anticipated fruition, is terrible indeed!" They denied that there was any violence or intimidation at polling booths, claiming, "The truth is, our great victory was won by reason and argument, fairly addressed to the minds of colored men."[13]

Failure to ratify a constitution for the second time necessitated greater federal intervention as far as Republican leaders were concerned. Grant, deeply interested by the summer of 1868 in running for president himself, decided to remove Humphreys and install a provisional governor. A constituency that had not cooperated with Reconstruction policies had elected him, the general reasoned on June 5, and so Humphreys "should not control the state." He conferred with Maj. Gen. Irvin McDowell, Ames's commander at First Bull Run and who had briefly assumed authority over the Fourth Military District. Grant was adamant that "the appointment of a politician be avoided" and suggested Bvt. Maj. Gen. August Kautz. A cavalry officer well known to Grant, Kautz had experience in the postwar army and the Deep South. The sudden death of Kautz's wife, however, made him unavailable. Ord was a reasonable second choice for provisional governor since he had experience in Mississippi, but he was about to transfer to California. Gillem was another obvious option, but he clashed too frequently with Radical Republicans and was seen as too lenient with Confederate veterans as well as civil leaders in Mississippi like Humphreys. Both McDowell and Grant wanted someone with experience and fortitude who would uphold the law and stand up to Humphreys if he tried to impede a new constitution.[14]

In the end, Ames was only other viable option on the scene. Grant knew his character and competency, had met with him recently, and so approved the appointment. Ames also had some experience in Mississippi, so the turmoil there would not surprise him. McDowell agreed, and he telegraphed President Johnson and told him the news. Despite his young age—he was only thirty-three years old—Ames became provisional governor of Mississippi on June 15, 1868.[15]

Ames brimmed with idealism and already had developed a robust interest in Mississippi's improvement. Both common citizens and political figureheads alike, however, declined to work with him after his appointment. Governor Humphreys curtly refused to comply with his own removal, arguing that the army and the new governor were usurping the civil government of Mississippi. His obdurate and disrespectful tone likely angered Ames, who nevertheless kept his composure and did not reward Humphreys's slight.

What followed was a seemingly miniscule affair regarding the governor's mansion that in fact displayed the trouble Ames would face as provisional governor. White Mississippians fought him over everything—even where he slept. Ames initially decided Humphreys and his family could remain in the governor's mansion, a massive home built in the 1830s with a Greek temple portico featuring four pillars attached to the front. But at some point Ames changed his mind. Perhaps it was because he needed a residence in Jackson himself and considered the governor's mansion as the appropriate place; or maybe Ames's anger spiked, and he wanted to put Humphreys in his place.

Either way, on July 6 Ames sent a curt message to the former governor: "Sir: Soon after my arrival here as Provisional Governor, I notified you that you might continue to occupy the Governor's mansion. Since then I have had cause to change my mind in the matter. You will oblige me by vacating the mansion at as early a day as convenient."[16]

Humphreys parried Ames's "blow" by replying that his family was inclined to remain. The home was paid for by Mississippians, he went on, and the person elected by the people of the state should legally live there, not an outside-appointed provisional governor. Ames countered that he would occupy only a portion of the mansion; it was probably difficult for Humphreys to find a new home quickly, and he was sure that they could live together comfortably if not amicably. Humphreys balked. It might "disagreeable" to share the home with other "permanent tenants." Ames, his patience worn thin by this point, fired a message back saying that the authority of the Reconstruction Acts superseded the unconstitutional defiance of the state. Humphreys had no real power, and now courteous conversation was over. "The feeling entertained not only by me, but by others, not to cause you any personal inconvenience, has, through your own action, ceased to exist," said the provisional governor. With that final salvo, Ames had Capt. James Biddle of the Ninth US Infantry tell Humphreys that half of the mansion was now set aside for use by the provisional governor and that military force was going to enforce the arrangement. The press decried Ames for being a tyrant. The *Oxford Falcon* printed all the correspondence between Humphreys and Ames, its front page elaborating on the unconstitutionality of these federal activities.[17]

Problems persisted and then increased. Mississippi Democrats, with the support of Humphreys, next issued a prerogative writ of quo warranto. It demanded that Ames appear before the Circuit Court of Jackson in November 1868 to produce proof showing by what authority he could take on the duties of governor. It was a desperate attempt to impede Ames. The nationally published Reconstruction Acts were all the proof he needed, and the writ went nowhere. Ames did not entertain such Democratic antics but continued to govern the state as he saw fit, including the removal of Mississippi attorney general C. E. Hooker, a former fire-eater and Confederate officer who had lived in the state since the 1840s. Ames replaced Hooker with Capt. Jasper Myers, an Indianan who graduated West Point in 1862.[18]

Other notable political changes were in the offing as Ames attempted to solidify his footing as provisional governor. In July three-quarters of the states ratified the Fourteenth Amendment and granted African Americans the rights of US citizens—except the vote—across the nation. No longer would the states determine citizenship. In addition, no one could deny a citizen equal protection under the law. Congress would enforce the amendment, which also prohibited anyone who had participated in rebellion to the United States from holding office. It marked an emphatic change to fundamental law. It also complicated the tiresome situation in Mississippi because readmission now required a state constitution to acknowledge both the Thirteenth and Fourteenth Amendments. In addition, thousands of Mississippians, unpardoned civil or military veterans of the Confederacy, could not hold office or vote.[19]

The baton of executive power returned to the Republicans later that year when Grant became the eighteenth president of the United States, defeating New York Democrat Horatio Seymour. The Republican ticket benefited greatly from the votes of freedmen. The only "reconstructed" states to not vote for Grant were Louisiana and Georgia; in fact, some parishes in Louisiana did not record a single Republican vote. Mississippi, still a wayward child, could not cast a vote at all in the election. Grant took office on March 4, 1869, and within days of his inauguration, addressed Ames and his work in rowdy Mississippi. Approving of Ames's governorship so far, Grant not only extended his term but also appointed him to serve as military commander of the Fourth Military District. Fortunately for Ames, reconstructed Arkansas was no longer a part of that district.[20]

Although he had ample support from a Republican president and Congress working in unison, his challenges amplified as well. The difficulty of managing military as well as political operations in Mississippi prompted Ames to institute significant changes. District headquarters was stationed in Vicksburg, the city along the Mississippi River that five year earlier witnessed a siege that devastated the Confederate war effort. But Ames needed to be in the state capital to facilitate his gubernatorial duties, and Jackson was over forty miles east of Vicksburg. To remedy this, he expeditiously consolidated his offices in Jackson before the end of March. Once military and governmental operations both stemmed from the capital, Ames reorganized the military units under his control. Compared to the thousands of soldiers who once occupied Mississippi in 1865, Ames now had only hundreds. At one point Union troops occupied nearly forty posts in Mississippi; now they had ten. This reduction in troops and their presence hampered Ames's agenda.[21]

The standard functions of soldiers consisted of routine guard duty and escorting officials. Historian Gregory Downs has described postwar soldiers as simply police and prison guards. In his own reports Ames explained that he sometimes had to send soldiers on peacekeeping expeditions "into the country for the purpose of arresting lawless characters who had been guilty of murder or other serious offenses, by which were endangered the safety of persons and the quiet of communities."[22]

Troops nonetheless played a vital role in Mississippi. Ames valued them greatly and frequently thought that he needed more of them to protect civil rights, bring violators of the law to justice, and ensure safety for everyone. Civil officers were either inept or unwilling to do so, while public opinion, as Ames noted, did not view him or the soldiers favorably. Mississippians managed to break the law and perpetrate brutal acts even under the vigilance of Ames and his men. "The cases are not numerous where violence has been offered [against] the regular constituted authorities," he declared, "and in those instances the acts were committed generally by individuals, who nevertheless were secreted and shielded by the people."[23]

One such atrocity was the murder of Bvt. Maj. Joseph G. Crane, the acting military mayor of Jackson, killed on a city street in June 1869 over a tax dispute. The assailant, Edward M. Yerger, a querulous Jackson newspaper editor, former Confederate colonel, and notorious drunk, attacked Crane with a large knife, saying "go you damned dog" and slew the officer on the spot. Ames put Yerger in army custody and prepared to try him before a military commission. Grant congratulated Ames and the prosecution, writing, "I am delighted that you put the wretch in irons." Yerger's lawyer-uncle, however, denied the army's jurisdiction and appealed for a writ of habeas corpus. Eventually, the case went to the US Supreme Court, putting Chief Justice Salmon P. Chase and Congress on a collision course over the court's powers during Military Reconstruction. In *Ex Parte Yerger,* Chase granted the defendant a writ. US Attorney General Henry Stanberry, a Johnson loyalist, turned the editor over to a state court, which granted him bail. Yerger never stood trial for murder. It was a signal defeat for the governor and district commander.[24]

Ames soon recognized the obvious reasons behind the continuing violence—an unwillingness to recognize the rights of freed slaves and the loss of voting rights for veterans. These two facets drove the unrest in Mississippi. As noted previously, Ames had not fervently supported universal equal rights for freedmen before he arrived in the state. A journal entry on September 15, 1866, for example, notes that "the negro ought not to be allowed to vote." Upon seeing the plight of African Americans in Mississippi, however, Ames rethought his positions. Noticing the unchecked violence of some whites, he came to believe that legal protection for all could only be provided if the laws of the state recognized Black equality and the legislature produced civil rights bills. To do that, Ames surmised, freedmen needed to vote. Without their vote, there would be a Democrat-dominated legislature, especially if disenfranchised Confederate veterans regained their voting privilege. Democratic control would cement the status quo of legal inequality in Mississippi, with the state and local governments looking the other way when bloodshed occurred. In an October letter to James B. Fry of the Military Division of the South, Ames observed how Democratic forces within the state drove away any white citizens "who entertain political sentiments different from the community" and advocated that "blacks should be, if not deprived of rights undeniably theirs by law, at least seriously curtailed in the exercise of them."[25]

Ames soon morphed into an aggressive defender of civil rights. One way in which he quickly asserted himself was the publication of General Orders No. 33. This authorized anyone to serve as a juror in the state, not just white citizens. It significantly helped curb the overt racial prejudice a freedman would face in a trial before an all-white jury and created a more accurate cross-section of the state's residents in the jury box. Like most of Ames's policy decisions during his tenure in Mississippi, he did not rewrite law but merely administered rights already embedded into the nation's constitution.[26]

Regular communications allowed Ames to discuss matters in Mississippi with Grant and his staff in Washington. One of the chief issues he faced as governor was trying to fill offices forcibly vacated because the holder could not take the "test oath," or "ironclad oath," of past and present loyalty to the United States. Ames had to find suitable replacements, which was not easy to do. Grant nonetheless told a Mississippi delegation visiting Washington on March 25, 1869, that he had faith in the governor. Ames, the president continued, had the authority to "appoint his class of men in Mississippi, and he had no doubt he would do so as rapidly as possible." Yet some appointments took time. In one case Ames asked if he could remove the political disabilities for John Duncan, whom he wanted to make the state treasurer in 1869. "Mr. Duncan is a thoroughly upright and honest man and in full sympathy with the present administration," he assured Grant. After a delay, the president agreed, commenting that Duncan had apparently been a Union man before the war and "so far as such a position could be maintained . . . throughout the rebellion." He could serve.[27]

Some of Ames's other appointments required explanation, however, and Mississippians took umbrage with his decisions. Sometimes they contacted his superiors to grumble. In one instance Samuel G. French, a West Point classmate of Grant's and a former major general in the Confederate army, complained to the president that Ames had suspended the Mississippi Board of Levee Commissioners just at the moment when the river was reaching dangerous levels of flooding. French had liked Gillem, the former military district commander, but he did not care for Ames. When the latter disbanded the commissioners and transferred responsibility to one of his own men, French boiled over with rage. In his memoirs he recalled going to Jackson to confront Ames. He saw Jackson as a place where "the carpetbagger was generally holding the arm of his colored brother" and the statehouse was "a travesty on intelligence and decorum." French's report worried Grant enough that he had his longtime aide Horace Porter write from Washington to ask Ames about it. He sent an immediate telegram in response: "Successors to the old board of Levee Commissioners have been appointed and qualified, river has fallen, no danger whatsoever. Fear misrepresentations have been made to you."[28]

Although he faced numerous other tasks as provisional governor, Ames's primary responsibility was to ensure that the state held a fall election and drafted a constitution that accepted the Thirteenth and Fourteenth Amendments, although the legislature had approved neither. Congress passed and the president signed a series of rules in April 1869 that dictated how Mississippi, along with Virginia and Texas, were to reenter the Union. Congress had the final say on whether a state could be readmitted, while only men who had sworn loyalty and had not been Confederate agents could keep civil offices.[29]

The general election scheduled for November 30, 1869, would produce a legislature that bore the responsibility of ending Military Reconstruction in Mississippi and also determine the identities of the next governor, lieutenant governor, secretary of state, treasurer, attorney general, public auditor, and superintendent of public schools. It needed to be above reproach. Congress by then had passed the Fifteenth Amendment, granting freedmen the right to vote. Ames realized that this might intensify intimidation at the polls and acts of violence and thus had to take many precautions to ensure a fair election. He appointed a state voting committee, comprising two white and two black men from different parties, to detect any duplicity. Ames replaced old state-election officers and declared "that a new election would be ordered if there should be fraud at any polls." He ensured that ballot boxes would stay locked when the polls closed and made certain that the four-member board served responsibly.[30]

At the Mississippi Republican Party convention held on July 2, the attendees passed a resolution praising Ames and stating that loyal constitutionalists in the state "owe him a debt of gratitude which they can never repay, save by a life of like devotion to the principles he represents." Delegates then turned to choose their party's candidates. The gubernatorial election was the most important of the statewide elections. For their candidate, Republicans selected James L. Alcorn. A scalawag leader who had moved to Mississippi as an adult in 1844, Alcorn supported both Black suffrage and the Fourteenth Amendment, still unapproved in the state. Most of his support came from freedmen, now able to vote with more confidence than in 1868. He garnered Ames's backing as well, and Republicans nationally accepted him. Democrats, meanwhile, sponsored their own candidate under the National Union Republican Party (NURP) label, a carryover from the Johnson years that Mississippi members hoped would confuse freedmen and scalawags. For similar reasons, Democrats allied with conservative white Republicans to nominate Judge Louis Dent as the NURP candidate for governor. Dent was Grant's estranged brother-in-law, although hardly a supporter of the president or his policies. The Democratic Party itself did not choose a formal candidate but supported Dent.[31]

The political stakes intensified as the election approached. Conservative Mississippi newspapers attacked the Republicans. Among the many ills that editors highlighted was the disenfranchisement of some whites in the state while Republicans professed to "favor universal suffrage." Fearing that they would not have enough votes to defeat the Republican candidates, the NURP encouraged voter registration and a flurry of measures to get people out to the polls regardless of their political awareness. Fueling dread, the editor of the *Weekly Clarion* in Jackson opined: "The opportunity, and the last they will have, of delivering the State from the rule of the carpet-bag Radical adventurers, is now afforded. Let no patriot fail to improve."[32]

Even though their rancorous newspapers did their part, Democrats and the NURP faced several noteworthy problems in 1869. They expected freedmen to vote universally for the Republicans and some white voters to do so as well. Although Alcorn supported the Fourteenth and Fifteenth Amendments, he also had fought for the Confederacy as a brigadier general, suffered as a prisoner, and exhausted much of his fortune in hopes of Confederate victory, thus possibly drawing some support from moderate Democrats.[33]

In contrast, Democrats knew the top of the NURP ticket was as weak as it was deceptive. Judge Dent was not a particularly strong candidate and did little to inspire confidence. His famous family had owned slaves, but they did not support the same policies as he did and offered no support. Grant himself had long had a problematic relationship with his in-laws, held Judge Dent in contempt, and outwardly expressed his displeasure with his candidacy. Ames wrote to him in October that Republican victory looked promising, which made Grant beam. The president replied, "Brother Dent we think will go under, and be handsomely tomahawked right through the centre of the head." Dent's only hopes were chicanery and violent voter suppression, but Ames's policies worked to counter Democratic voter intimidation.[34]

On November 30, Mississippians voted. Alcorn proved victorious as the alliance of freedmen and scalawags triumphed over Judge Dent and his conservative coalition with a vote of 76,186 to 38,097. "Alcorn shakes the rod of his boasted black majority over the heads of white people of the state," a Democratic newspaper lamented. The only development that Democrats relished was the impending conclusion of military oversight. Alcorn's victory did not sit well with many white Mississippians, but they viewed Ames as a greater villain still. Newspapers editorials called upon state Democrats to give Alcorn a chance; he was a Confederate general and former Democrat after all. "We have considered it a good symptom in Gen. Alcorn," a column in the *Macon Beacon* in Noxubee County suggested, "that though he was boasting of 'having the negroes at his back' he was yet solicitous of the support of intelligent white men. He is now in a position to win their good opinion by deserving it." Their real problem was Ames. The *Weekly Clarion* pronounced that Ames and his "minions" were responsible for orchestrating Alcorn's nomination and victory. The *Vicksburg Weekly Herald* positively looked forward to his departure, with Alcorn and Mississippi welcomed back by Congress into the Union. Alcorn would at least be a duly elected governor unlike the "lordly Ames."[35]

The political fighting aside, Mississippi now had a newly elected legislative body that went to work getting the state back into the Union. Essentially, the legislature resurrected the dormant new state constitution that had laid unratified since May 1868. Representatives made few changes, apart from addressing the new amendments to the US Constitution. Article I emphasized the abolition of slavery, and the addition of Section 19 also made it clear that freedmen were citizens. Article VIII addressed the enfranchisement of Black men. Thus, the convention easily embraced the two amendments. The legislature then turned the vote over to the electorate for ratification. On December 1, 1869, Mississippi voters adopted the new constitution.[36]

With its passage, Ames oversaw the first assembly of the new Reconstruction legislature on January 1, 1870. With the Fourteenth and Fifteenth Amendments finally passed later that month, Mississippi petitioned the United States for readmittance and representation in both congressional chambers. On February 23 Congress welcomed Mississippi back. "Mississippi has at last gained admission to the union under circumstances that must gladden the hearts of all the truly loyal," wrote the editor of the *Weekly Clarion*. "Legislative and Executive departments of the government," he continued more morosely, "are in the hands of the Bitter-Enders, and the power which they possess under the new constitution is almost supreme. Our people can expect nothing but evil."[37]

For Ames, the most obvious developments of early 1870 were that the offices of provisional governor and military district commander now disappeared, and he found himself without a position. This predicament did not last long. After a decisive victory for Republicans, the legislature bore the responsibility of selecting two US senators to represent the state. They would fill unexpired terms left vacant since secession, with one left absent by former Confederate president Jefferson Davis. The legislature first selected Dr. Hiram R. Revels. A well-traveled minister of the African Methodist Episcopal Church, Revels had served as a chaplain and recruiter for the Union army during the war. He would fill the remaining year of former senator Albert G. Brown's term. Although Revels was born free and had both African and European ancestry, prejudice toward him was severe. In January he endured weeks of political underhandedness when Democratic senators in Washington tried to prevent him from taking his seat. But in February Revels, with unanimous support from the Republican Party—and universal opposition from Democrats—officially joined the Senate.[38]

The other senator elected to Congress, filling the seat vacated by Davis, was Ames. Friends and colleagues had encouraged Ames to run, but at first, he was reluctant. Although becoming a senator was enticing, it meant that he would have to walk away from his military career. Ames ultimately chose to become a candidate for personal advancement and a commitment to civic duty. He had strong connections too with several members of Congress as well as the leading figures managing the Freedman's Bureau. His prominence and favor among African Americans and the Republican voting base in Mississippi would help ensure political influence too. Ames was no saint, but he was keenly concerned about the civil rights of Black Mississippians and convinced that his record as provisional governor provided him the experience to help lead freedmen through this transitional period. A senate seat also could protect the suffrage of all Black Americans, prevent destabilizing forces from toppling Reconstruction, and help the "pacification of the country." In the end, he agreed to serve.

Ames quickly garnered unanimous support from the Mississippi Senate, which elected him in February 1870. His family reacted gleefully to the news. "We congratulate you on this great event," his mother, Martha, wrote, "and hope you will be able to do your country good. Before you are great responsibilities. May God ever direct you in the right." Jesse Ames wrote his son as well. The former sea captain spoke on behalf of the family when stating, "I assure [you] we most heartily congratulate you in your success in obtaining your seat in the United States Senate."³⁹

Ames left Mississippi in a better condition in 1870 than when he arrived in 1867. The state was more stable and less violent, although the threat of instability and violence still hovered like a malevolent specter, and Ames hoped his time in the Senate would help protect reforms for a modernizing Mississippi. Ames and Revels presented themselves and the newly minted Mississippi Constitution before the Senate in February, as Blanche and her mother watched from the Senate gallery. That evening Representative Butler invited Ames to his home for dinner with his family and a few friends. Blanche's intellect and glowing charm mesmerized Ames. When not committed to senatorial activities, he escorted her to museum exhibits and art galleries, his interest in art having peaked since his time in Europe. They also took pleasant carriage rides through the streets of Washington.⁴⁰

Politics provided rockier progress. The Senate Judiciary Committee initially barred Ames from taking his seat due to reservations about his election. The central problem pertained to his residence, with an investigation held to determine whether Ames was an inhabitant of Mississippi. Senators who opposed his candidacy logically underscored the fact that Ames had lived in Mississippi only because of his military assignment. His residence there was nothing more than a byproduct of orders from the army, they complained. Democrats on the committee also expressed concern about his motives for being in the state and wondered about his intentions. The most serious assertion, however, was that Ames had oiled the political machine in Mississippi as provisional governor to become a senator once the state was readmitted. One piece of evidence that highlighted this peculiar dynamic was a letter in which Ames the governor and district commander certified that Ames the senator-elect had legally won the seat. As Sen. Roscoe Conkling, a Republican ally of Grant yet disapproving of Ames, argued: "The sound is strange.... Brigadier Gen'l Adelbert Ames certifies that Brig.-Gen'l Adelbert Ames is entitled to a seat in the U.S. Senate."⁴¹

For twenty-three days the Judiciary Committee held up Ames's future in the Senate before they presented their report before the upper chamber on March 18. The committee's report confirmed that the election "seemed to have been regular and waiving any criticism," members would not pursue that angle further. Instead, the committee focused most of its attention on Ames's residency. The report described his personal history and related where he lived, from Maine to West Point, and stated that he owned no land. The bulk of his personal possessions now resided in Minnesota with his parents. The report concluded, "The committee therefore recommend the adoption of the following resolution: That Adelbert Ames is not eligible to the seat in the Senate of the United States to which he has been appointed." Senator Conkling did the lion's share of the talking after the findings were read before the Senate. Refusing to deride the "personal worth of General Ames" and "his distinction and bravery as a soldier," Conkling nonetheless declared that Ames could serve elsewhere but not in the US Senate.[42]

Ames's statement defending himself was emphatic yet composed. "I was repeatedly approached to become a candidate for the United States Senate," he wrote. "For a long time I declined. I wrote letters declining. I hesitated because it would necessitate the abandonment of my whole military life. Finally, for personal and public reasons, I decided to become a candidate and leave the army." Ames avowed that his intentions were to remain a resident in Mississippi. "I even made arrangements, almost final and permanent, with a person to manage property I intended to buy," he noted.[43]

As the debate intensified on the Senate floor, the minutia of what constituted residency and the definition of residency received copious deliberation. Sen. Jacob H. Howard of Michigan, one of the founders of the Republican Party, interrupted Conkling's soliloquy to disagree with his reasoning. Incensed, Conkling shifted his focus to show that Ames did not have legal precedent on his side by citing the case of John Bailey of Massachusetts. In 1824 Congress declared Bailey could not take his seat because he failed residency requirements. Conkling also raised questions about Ames to further cement his point. Could he file taxes in Mississippi? Was he subject to jury duty in Mississippi? Had he been a married man, could his wife claim residency in Mississippi? If the answers were no, Conkling declared, then Ames had no right to represent the state.[44]

Other senators spoke on Ames's behalf. Arkansas senator Benjamin F. Rice, a Union veteran and minority dissenter on the Judiciary Committee, firmly expressed his disagreement. He argued that a military man on assignment could change his residence. Those who supported removing Ames, like Conkling, did not deny that such a course of action was possible, they just did not think it was true in this case. "They are citizens as well as soldiers," Rice maintained. He added that the Senate had sworn affidavits from residents in Mississippi affirming that Ames considered himself a resident. Conkling parried that military service and obeying an order to relocate did not establish residency.[45]

Before long, more senators jumped into the discussion. Ames tried to remain composed while watching the back and forth. Howard referenced Ames's statement and argued that he absolutely intended to remain in Mississippi. Sen. John Milton Thayer of Nebraska joined Howard in defending Ames: "They [Mississippians] regarded him [Ames] as an inhabitant of the State. What reason have we to dispute it?"[46]

The Senate tabled the debate until March 23. More members of the Judiciary Committee spoke when the chamber revisited the topic. Wisconsin senator Matthew H. Carpenter viewed Ames as a noble man worthy of the "the highest respect and admiration" but nonetheless wanted to bar Ames from the Senate.[47] But Oliver P. Morton, Republican senator from Indiana and that state's wartime governor, and Conkling carried much of the back and forth that day. The incessant debate over residency, and what constituted it, produced ludicrous hypotheticals. One, for example, analyzed whether Ames could have assumed residency in Mississippi if kidnappers had smuggled him there. More and more senators joined the discussion. Republican Aaron Cragin of New Hampshire did not contest Ames's admission, while Garrett Davis, a Democrat from Kentucky, declared: "I am utterly opposed to the admission of General Ames. . . . I think that every rule and every principle that applies to this case ought to be applied with the most rigid strictness." As the issue dragged on through the end of March, Ames discussed his options with Representative Butler and spent relaxing moments with Blanche to mitigate his annoyance with the Judiciary Committee.[48]

The turning point in the Senate's elongated debate over Ames's future occurred on March 31. Republican senator Lot M. Morrill of Maine presented a document from the Mississippi legislature that affirmed Ames's legitimacy in their eyes. It read, in part: "The immediate admission of Adelbert Ames to his seat in the Senate of the United States, to which he was elected as aforesaid, is earnestly desired by this legislature. Approved March 23, 1870." The document rattled senators who sought to dismiss Ames. When famed senators Charles Sumner and John Sherman, the latter the brother of Gen. William T. Sherman, both entered the debate on Ames's behalf, the issue neared its end. Sherman concluded that he did not consider the issue of residency remotely important. Ames using his influence to alter the election or force himself into a position of power would have been worthy of preventing him being seated, but that did not occur. He thus had every right to assume his place in the Senate.[49]

On April 1 a vote finally took place. The resolution of Ames being eligible to serve in the Senate passed 40–12, ending a two-month saga. Six Republicans joined six Democrats in voting against Ames's eligibility. Republicans like Conkling seemingly opposed seating a Republican elected questionably. Democrats seemed opposed to seating any Republican senator from a southern state. On that same day, Ames approached the president of the Senate, took his oath of office, and assumed his Senate seat, escorted there by his ally Senator Morrill. His first foray into politics had been burdensome, yet it was a moment of triumph for Ames and the Republican Party in Mississippi. James H. Pierce, a Republican who would work with Ames as an employee for the US Marshals Service, wrote the new senator, "I assure you that all good republicans in Miss. greet the news with joy; and the Senate has placed us under renewed obligations."[50]

SENATOR FROM MISSISSIPPI

In the spring of 1870, Ames basked in the glow of both his political victory and his blossoming relationship with Blanche Butler and her family. Blanche adored Adelbert, tenderly calling him "Del." She also was impressed with his record as a soldier and enjoyed his stories about his time abroad. Her mother and the other members of the Butler household similarly liked Ames's wit. They often discussed Shakespeare, the arts, and languages with the young senator. General Butler for his part had long respected and admired his former subordinate's poise and aspirations. Ames's ambitions made him not just a bright political prospect but also a worthy adversary at the elder man's billiards table. Ames, in return, respected Butler. Their relationship was never rocky, and Ames genuinely idolized the man despite what had happened at Fort Fisher. The opulent Butler mansion in Washington, south of the Capitol, soon became a second home for the senator, yet it also elicited fears in him about being able to provide for Blanche. Rarely an anxious man before, Ames now worried that he would never be able to offer his prospective bride the luxurious lifestyle he thought she expected and deserved.[1]

Del was a rising political figure, Blanche was a heralded young woman in Washingtonian society, and it did not take long for news of their courtship to circulate. Gossip about the impending match reached Ames's parents in Minnesota even before he proposed marriage. Annoyed, Martha Ames gently chided her son on April 5: "The papers say you are engaged to Miss Butler. ... We suppose it is all a hoax, as had it been true, you would have informed your parents before you had the public."[2]

News reports were premature, but when Ames did propose in late April, Blanche accepted, then almost immediately left his side for a trip to New York with her mother. Writing to him from the city, Blanche admitted she was so overcome with bridal giddiness that her mother and aunt asked her if she was all right, worried that she was shaking because she was ill. Excited by the prospect of becoming a senator's wife, she was particularly thankful that her fiancé possessed other sterling qualities. "How happy I am," she exclaimed, "that you are so noble, so handsome, so young, and so good."[3]

While Blanche was away, loneliness and illness afflicted Ames. He wished that they could have spent time together after announcing their engagement, and he regretted that she would be away from him for some time. He went to the trouble of mailing the engagement ring to her, but Blanche refused to wear it during the trip, preferring to wait until he could place it on her hand in person. On top of this lamentable separation, Ames suffered an attack of malaria that summer. Writing to Blanche on May 24, he complained that he could neither make himself comfortable nor alleviate his pain. The illness soon subsided, and the couple began to discuss their wedding plans.[4]

In their first exchange of letters to each other that spring, the two young lovers also revealed their expectations about married life. Blanche made it clear that she did not wish to follow some traditional wedding customs, such as promising to "obey" Ames in her marital vows. She did not care for the word, even though she expressed an interest in serving her future husband. Her request did not bother him. "Do you think people love, honor, and obey because they promise to do so at the altar," Ames asked her rhetorically. "If there be love an[d] honor what need of the obey. . . . When a wife ceases to find her love strong enough to be a motive power, no promise will control her to the good and happiness of her husband." Honesty, transparency, and commitment were better than tradition, he assured Blanche: "We are the architects of our own happiness. If we only determine and hold to our determination to make each other happy—be charitable, careful, considerate towards each other—we shall find the days passed were far less happy and bright than those we live in." Finding their marital philosophy compatible, the couple set their wedding date for late July. They also decided to take their vows in Massachusetts rather than in muggy Washington.[5]

Saint Anne's Episcopal Church in Lowell, Massachusetts, hosted the ceremony on July 21. Ten thousand people reportedly cheered outside, while 600 invited guests—among them President Grant and his wife, Julia—observed the service within. The esteemed Revered Dr. Theodore Edson, who had led

Bridal party of Adelbert and Blanche Butler Ames, Butler home, Lowell, Massachusetts, July 21, 1870 (Ames Family and Smith College)

the congregation since the 1820s, officiated. Groomsmen, all of them veterans, flanked Ames. Lawyers' and senators' daughters served as Blanche's bridesmaids. He said "I do" with the firm voice of a military officer, while her "I do" was soft and mellow. A reception followed at the Butler house. Ames finally had shed his bachelorhood at the age of thirty-four while also cementing his place in American political circles. He was a war hero, a new senator, and now married into a prestigious and wealthy family with connections throughout the halls of Congress and the White House.[6]

The couple decided to forgo an immediate honeymoon, delaying their travel for several months in order to spend some time with the Butlers. When September arrived, the Ameses finally left Massachusetts, heading south. Passing through New York, they paid a brief visit to West Point—the first time Ames had seen his alma mater since graduation—but recorded nothing of their time there. Boarding a train, the couple traveled west to Northfield, Minnesota, to spend a few weeks with his parents. Blanche was as pleased with her more rustic in-laws as they were with her. "They [Ameses] all seem very glad to see me," she informed her mother, "and I think [they] are gentle, kindly, independent people." The newlyweds enjoyed their time in Minnesota, hunting, fishing, and sampling the delicious honey from the bees that Ames's mother kept. He also inspected his family's flour mill for the first time. Just a few years before, as a soldier fighting in a brutal war, he had sent money to the family to help them fund their mill. Now he was a civilian, married, and able to take time off to see his loved ones, explore the mill he helped acquire, and enjoy a lengthy respite from work for the first time since his European tour.[7]

Remaining in Minnesota through October, the couple then journeyed to Mississippi, arriving on November 1, the day after Ames's thirty-fifth birthday. It was Blanche's first experience of life in the Magnolia State, and a decidedly mixed one at that. On the one hand, she found Natchez a charming town suitable for settling down, as her husband was keen on buying a home there. They enjoyed gatherings and dinner parties in nearby Holly Springs, where there was a small community of Yankees who made her feel at home. On the other hand, she could not help noticing the ostracism that "carpetbaggers" and other northern-born residents often faced in the postbellum Deep South. Writing to her mother, Blanche recounted the hardships of the Gills, a northern family then living in Holly Springs. Mrs. Gill's only misconduct, she explained, was that she wanted to educate Black children, which infuriated the locals. Mr. Gill, by virtue of serving as postmaster, had endured even greater hostility, for he had "been very much abused by the Southern people, his life threatened, and every possible obstacle put in his way."[8] It was a disquieting end to the Ameses' honeymoon.

What Ames witnessed upon returning to Mississippi, meanwhile, confirmed all of his previous suspicions about southern-white loyalties. The state had become dangerously unstable since he left in February 1870, he concluded. Democrats, although a minority in the legislature, were relentless in their attempts to subvert Republican power and eviscerate civil rights for African Americans. Their "secret" weapon was a revived Ku Klux Klan. After consulting with local Republican leaders, Ames became convinced that the greatest determent to a bright future for Mississippi, and even for Reconstruction more generally, was the Klan. He feared that its brutality would dissuade Black Republicans from voting or otherwise participating in civil soci-

Sen. Adelbert Ames of Mississippi (Library of Congress)

ety, thereby nullifying the Republicans' majority and costing them control of the state government. If Mississippi jettisoned Republicans, could it motivate other states to do the same and undercut postwar progress? Determined to save the state from the partnership of the Democratic Party and the Klan, a motivated Ames returned to Washington with his wife in late November. The young couple moved into the Butler mansion, as his father-in-law had an extension built so the couple could have some privacy.[9]

When the US Senate reassembled on December 5, Ames the war hero earned a seat on the seven-member Military Committee, which had legislative supervision over the army. At once the junior senator introduced Senate Bill No. 794, "The Removal of Political Disabilities," meant to relieve the legal and political disabilities against former Confederate soldiers. Eighteen Mississippians were included in the lengthy list of people who would benefit from this measure, including former Confederate brigadier general Peter Burwell Stark and lieutenant colonel Cadmus H. Alley, whose Seventeenth Mississippi fought opposite Ames's Twentieth Maine at Fredericksburg. Perhaps alleviating these political disabilities could temper some of the hostilities in Mississippi and across the South, Ames reasoned, and draw voters into the Republican Party to help in the 1872 election.

While the bill languished in committee, Ames moved on to his chief concern—exposing the Klan and, hopefully, hounding it out of existence. He could count on a good deal of support in this effort because other senators were equally concerned about the group's revival, which they saw as symptomatic of a more general southern-white rebelliousness and lawlessness. Ames, albeit a relative greenhorn, held a unique and important position in the upcoming session. He was not concerned about hiding his agenda or offending colleagues with harsh realities. Furthermore, he was by now a loyal Radical Republican who could rely on his own personal experience to argue why Black civil liberties needed defending and how volatile the Deep South really was.[10]

Ames rose to give his first Senate speech on March 21, 1871. He outlined the numerous problems in his state and traced their sources at least as far back as the war years. "We have upon us there [in Mississippi]," Ames declared, "the natural consequences of slavery and rebellion.... The ideas which were contesting for the supremacy from 1861 to 1865 are now in antagonism and are leading to more dangerous results than many of us are ready to believe." Despite federal demobilization, the Civil War was not yet over. An internal conflict over Reconstruction now tore Mississippi asunder. Chaos ruled, and Ames had no doubt about what was responsible, and who. Illegal activities by white-supremacist groups, condoned or downplayed by Democrats, were at the root of Mississippi's troubles. Ames was too politically astute to come right out and accuse the Democrats of wielding the weapons of insurrection themselves, saying, "I am not prepared to assert, nor do I assert, that these murderers are recognized auxiliaries of that party which is opposed to the Republican Party." Nevertheless, he declared, "it is a fact that their deeds result to the advantage of that party."[11]

His Democratic counterparts in the Senate, Ames continued, would never admit to any of this publicly. They wanted to focus public attention on the wild claims that countless white Mississippians had been robbed of the right to vote or harassed by federal agents. Yet only freedmen had been turned aside at the polling booths, Ames countered, and, moreover, he and his fellow Mississippi Republicans were willing to reenfranchise former Confederates in exchange for promises of good behavior. What had Republican generosity earned from white southerners thus far, Ames asked. "I am sorry to say that [my party's] conduct, magnanimous in the highest degree, has met with no return; hardly that of empty words of approval," he proclaimed. Instead, "outrage upon outrage is being committed, and the Republican members of this same Legislature which adopted those resolutions have petitioned Congress for protection...."

This question of justice, of humanity, and of freedom, as understood in our country, which should be dispassionately considered by all, is opposed, it appears, by one party being made subordinate to party schemes and purposes."[12]

Ames thrashed the Democratic Party, but he lambasted some Republicans too. Although devoted to his party, he was unwilling to exonerate his fellow partisans from all blame for the situation in Mississippi. He noted that Governor Alcorn had spent $40,000 on a special police force to round up Klan members but had not secured a single prosecution. Even if a man was arrested, his peers on the jury would find a way to acquit the accused.[13] African Americans and other Republican allies could not be expected to keep supporting the party of emancipation when they saw their persecutors consistently evade justice. As far as the soldier-turned-senator was concerned, Republican leaders from northern states now bore the responsibility to help ensure that justice prevailed. Castigating his colleagues, Ames pointedly asked, "What would honorable Senators from the North say if their own constituency were the victims?"[14]

First Colored Senators and Representatives, in the 41st and 42nd Congress of the United States, by Currier and Ives, 1872 (Library of Congress)

According to Ames, it was the duty of the federal government to correct the evils afoot, once and for all. "Were there ever the necessity for such an intercession," he declared, "it now exists." What was happening in the Deep South was more than a political battle—it was a titanic moral struggle as important as the war. Ames told the Senate that he was willing to fight against the nefarious forces still at work, but it seemed as if other senators were ambivalent. He concluded by reaffirming the legacy of the founding fathers and the Declaration of Independence for each and every citizen:

> It is believed that the revolutionary war of our forefathers gave us one and all what they were entitled to in the Declaration of Independence; namely "that we hold these truths to be self-evident that all men are created equal." . . . But such is not the fact. When millions are suffering as are our friends at the South, . . . I believe the Constitution does authorize protection to our citizens; that not only authorizes but imperatively commands the General Government to give the needed protection where all other power fails.[15]

Public debates over Ames's speech began almost at once. Newspapers across the nation highlighted the senator's prose, and as might be expected, their responses were partisan. Many Republican editors, believing that the Democrats were deliberately overlooking native southern-white resistance to Reconstruction, considered the speech a capable piece of oratory. The *New York Tribune*, for instance, noted that Ames had thrown down the verbal equivalent of a gauntlet while making a definitive statement about the state of the South: "Mr. Ames gave a graphic account of the conditions of affairs in Mississippi, submitting letters from prominent Republicans of that State. . . . [He] left a very clear impression that he and the leading Republicans of Mississippi were not satisfied that the course of Governor Alcorn had been altogether right and proper."[16]

Democratic editors in response mocked Ames and called anti–Ku Klux legislation tyrannical. The senator was a demagogue like his nefarious father-in-law. An editor in northern Louisiana wrote that Ames's speech made him more of a "beast" than "Beast" Butler: "Our opinion then is this, that Ames approached nearer than any person mentioned in history or fiction, whether man or devil, to the idea of consummate and universal depravity."[17] On Missouri editor called Ames "a sap-headed New England pimp," while an upcountry South Carolina editor proclaimed that he was "a coward, a liar, a poltroon, and a puppy," loaded words that had provoked duels in the antebellum South.[18]

Another significant side effect of Ames's speech, whether intended or not, was the beginning of a feud with Alcorn. The governor was responsible for overseeing a state wrenched by severe economic and social dislocations. He favored economic modernization and supported public education for all children, regardless of race. Yet Alcorn never garnered much sympathy within his party, much less complete support, for the challenges he faced. One charge that stuck to him better than others concerned an unwavering loyalty to old cronies. He reportedly rewarded longstanding Whig and Democratic friends with positions of prominence. One example was Hiram Revels, the Black former senator who gained the presidency of a new Mississippi college exclusively for African Americans—Alcorn State University—in 1871. Many observers shared Ames's judgment that although well meaning, Governor Alcorn was fundamentally incapable of instilling order in his state.[19]

Beyond patronage, the two men represented contending wings of the Republican Party. Both supported the restored Union, but they differed on the best method to promote and protect civil rights in the state and modernize Mississippi's economy. Alcorn was more moderate, not surprising given that he had fought for the Confederacy and was little inclined to radically alter the state's antebellum social fabric. Moreover, he had no problem adjusting his policies to fit the whims of the unreconstructed white populace. That enraged the Radical wing of the party that Ames represented. His own former moderation in the past, the senator preferred more unflinchingly aggressive solutions. Ames wanted Mississippi's antebellum history left buried in the past and never resurrected again. He could not tolerate the moderate and flimsy policies that Alcorn proposed and would certainly never consider himself ethically bound to obey those strategies. There was as yet no overt hostility between Ames and Alcorn over Mississippi's path through Reconstruction, but the political erosion between them was starting.[20]

Inevitably, Ames's speech prompted counterattacks within the halls of Congress. Democrat Thomas F. Bayard of Delaware, who had voted against Ames being seated, declared that any congressional intervention in Mississippi against alleged disturbers of the peace would be unfounded and overreaching. Another Democrat, Allen Thurman of Ohio, argued that the unruliness Ames had seen and spoken of came from corrupt and flawed civil governments. Who dominated these governing bodies—Republicans and African Americans, of course.[21]

The hardest Democratic blows against Ames, however, came from Francis P. Blair Jr. of Missouri, a former Union general, ex-Republican, Democratic vice presidential candidate in 1868, and brother to Lincoln's first postmaster general. On April 3 Blair came after Ames and his allies with a four-hour speech. As was his wont, the Missourian contended that the people of the Deep South were suffering unduly under Radical military governments. Reconstruction made a mockery of popular sovereignty because "the governments of the people were superseded on this pretext and governments of major-generals substituted, in order that the political power of these states might be appropriated, the people plundered, and enormous debts contracted." Blair's reference to "governments of major generals" struck a raw nerve in Ames, according to family lore. His daughter, named Blanche after her mother, later claimed that the Missouri senator had meant to publicly charge the violent mess in Mississippi to her father's account.[22] Given that Blair was a brother major general in blue himself, it was a severe insult.

Blair also chided his colleague, a fresh and inexperienced senator, for having the audacity to disagree with his own well-rounded and lengthy statements. He pointedly asked Ames whether he thought that Governor Alcorn had pocketed the money used to combat the Klan. Of course not, Ames replied, but even with $400,000 Alcorn would not accomplish anything in "seeking after the Ku Klux." Blair wittily retorted, "Seeking what was not to be found, I suppose." This joke amused the assembly. As laughter echoed through the chamber, Ames countered, "he [Alcorn] acknowledges it [the Klan]" in public addresses. The skirmish soon devolved into Blair dredging up of Ames's disputed selection to the Senate, which Ames allowed to pass unacknowledged, possibly because of embarrassment or annoyance. Sensing he would make little headway on this occasion, the freshman senator yielded his time to bring the duel to a close.

Ames refused to let this somewhat embarrassing encounter stand, however, and spent the next week preparing for a rematch. By Tuesday, April 11, he was ready to take on Blair again.[23] Ames opened with a biblically inspired insult. Blair, he remarked, could "Out-Herod" King Herod, the child-butchering Jewish puppet king of the New Testament. From there, Ames pivoted to an expose of Blair's admitted prosouthern stances, acts befitting a traitor. "What a remarkable spectacle," he mused. "He who wore the blue in the days of rebellion now leading the rebel gray!" As an example, Ames, with dripping sarcasm matching that of his opponent, pointed to Blair's newfound political affiliation with the former vice president of the Confederacy. "We have been told by the Senator from Missouri that he and his friend Mr. [Alexander] Stephens of Georgia are willing to give 'negro suffrage' a fair trial! How grateful should this troubled country be to the Senator and his friend!"²⁴ All this was, of course, part of the standard Republican tactic of "waving the bloody shirt," but it was nonetheless effective.²⁵ Ames had challenged Blair's loyalty, hitting him in a sensitive spot.

The Mississippi senator continued his barrage. He reminded his colleagues that it had been a Republican president, a Republican-controlled Congress, and thoroughly Republican Union army that helped liberate the slaves. Against these now stood Blair, siding with people who had gone to war to maintain slavery and who were now oppressing southern freedmen. Taking aim at the Missourian's tepid support for the Civil Rights Act of 1871 and the Fourteenth Amendment, Ames snidely counseled his listeners, "We should sincerely thank the honorable Senator for informing us how he and his new allies will treat the colored people of the South should they ever have the opportunity to consummate their desires." Blair had blamed him and the Republicans for corruption and violence in Mississippi, but the real culprits, Ames insisted, were pro-Confederate sympathizers in legislatures. At best, Blair was criminally, if not deliberately, ignorant about conditions in the South. "With a generality he sweeps over [these] State[s] with a 'so far as I know' she [the state] is squandering her money," Ames mocked. "He ought to have known just the reverse to be true. . . . His argument was formed to show that the deeds of blood at the South find, if not justification, at least some palliation because of corrupt legislatures. He fails to show the cause in Mississippi. Her legislature has not squandered the people's money nor refused to pay her just debts."²⁶

Yet Ames was not done. He now brought out an older Blair speech lamenting the "shameless disenfranchisement" of "loyal" ex-Confederates in order to sneer at it. Ames noted that just recently Blair had called Reconstruction despotic, expressed sympathy for the Confederate cause, and purported that the postbellum amendments were only passed by fraud. Blair not only had himself gone south after the war "with a carpet-bag" but also had gone on record in the past encouraging veterans to do the same, even once suggesting that that government should grant them southern homesteads. How were the Missourian's constituents supposed to square these contradictory sentiments? Was he a hypocrite who slandered Reconstruction policy only when it suited his political ambitions to do so? Was the senator only capable at casting unfounded aspersions to mask his clumsiness in debates? "As [Blair's] professional weapon is his tongue," Ames slyly noted, "I [am] surprised to perceive that his vituperative powers have not perceptibly improved." That particular remark was so shocking that it drew Ames a rebuke from Vice Pres. Schuyler Colfax, presiding as president pro tempore, for unparliamentary behavior.²⁷

The novice senator apologized for his transgression, however, he immediately returned to the offensive by contrasting the reality of violence in Mississippi with the unfounded nature of the attacks against himself. Sharing excerpts from the letters of Henry R. Pease, Mississippi's state superintendent of education, Ames tallied sixty-three political and racial homicides and thirty incidents of church and school burnings in the first three months of 1871 alone. Not a single Democrat in Mississippi, he complained, had been willing to second his efforts as provisional governor to stop this madness, protect the citizenry, and ensure peace. Instead, Ames's opponents could find nothing better to do than harass him. He then insisted that he had never been, and was not now, a military interloper in Mississippi's politics. The state legislature had rightfully elected him, a loyal citizen "previously little versed in matters civil, with ideas of equality and liberty formed in a New England village," to represent Mississippi before the nation.[28]

Ames concluded his speech with an appeal to his colleagues:

> I regret, Mr. President, the necessity which compelled me to occupy the time of the Senate with matters more or less personal. But when the Republicans at the South, white and black, personal and political friends, are vilified and the President and Congress denounced for their acts in behalf of an oppressed and a long-suffering people, I am constrained to give facts showing in one State the baselessness of such denunciations and to bear testimony that the effect of your laws has been to sustain justice and protect humanity.[29]

Ames skewering his fellow Republican might not have increased his popularity in the Senate, but it gained at least one admirer. Dr. Nathan Hughes, a northern-born doctor residing in Hico, Arkansas, applauded the senator for his speech in defense of the Fourteenth Amendment and northerners who now lived in the South. "I improve the opportunity to thank you," wrote Hughes, "with a heart full of gratitude, for your defense of those, who, like myself, are often denounced as Carpet-baggers." Indeed, so impressed was Hughes that he and his wife had named their newborn son Adelbert. "We have adopted your name as one to honor a little one recently born to us," he informed the senator, "and pray God that should his life be spared, he may grow to love his Country and be just towards men."[30]

Four months later Ames finally found the time to respond. "I am sensible of the honor you have conferred upon me," he assured Hughes, "and am highly gratified to know that you, a stranger to me, view my efforts in so favorable a light." Ames confessed that he was "not professionally a speechmaker, the one you refer to being the second I ever made," but he would labor to "protect the inoffensive colored men" and those "who for four years had fought by my side." Unconcerned by the "false and senseless howls" of the press or partisan foes, he knew that he was "laboring in the cause of truth and the right."[31]

Ames's sparring with noted political personalities does not seem to have negatively affected his social calendar. He and Blanche still regularly attended parties in the capital, including several receptions held by Julia Grant and other wealthy Washingtonians. Still a newlywed at heart, Ames hated to be apart from his wife when he had to leave her in Washington to visit his parents in Minnesota. "Though I am among my own family, there is a great void which nothing fills," he lamented to her from Northfield. Blanche equally missed her husband's absence at the Butler family dinner table. He filled "a great space there if one may judge of it by the void now you are away. I felt just a little sad to have you go off without me and refreshed myself with a tear or two."[32]

The distance between them grew greater when Blanche and the Butler family decamped to Lowell for the summer in order to escape the Washington heat. She was pregnant and clearly showing it. After working on some family business in Minnesota, Ames made a flying visit to his wife and in-laws before returning to Washington. Upon arrival in the capital, the senator found a stack of letters awaiting reply. "Many were very complimentary," he informed Blanche. But, he added, "I naturally doubt such. I do not think flattery or praise, even when more or less deserved, a wholesome kind of food."[33]

Ames did not like being away from his pregnant wife, but he kept to his work. One important matter he attended to was the special Senate deliberations regarding the wide-ranging Treaty of Washington between Prime Minister William Gladstone's British government and the Grant administration. Signed on May 8, 1871, it promised to prove beneficial for the United States, which would receive sizable payments for damages to American shipping at the hands of English-built Confederate commerce raiders such as the *Alabama*, stop illegal fishing off the North American coast, and deal with British civilian losses during the Civil War. The treaty also would codify international law pertaining to neutral powers in wartime. Most importantly, it would thaw relations between the two countries that had been raw since the Civil War, deescalate tensions on the Canadian border, and begin a process of détente that led to the "Great Rapprochement" between the two powers on the eve of the twentieth century.[34]

Ames and his fellow senators debated the treaty from May 10 to May 27. Writing to Blanche on the twenty-third, Ames expressed hope that the sessions would end soon. "We have just adjourned to meet at ten o'clock tomorrow," he told her, "and it is the decision of almost all of us to force a continuous session till the matter shall be settled." This done, he predicted, "I think we will avoid all side issues and scatter." Yet Ames somehow had not anticipated his colleagues' verbosity. Republican Henry Corbett of Oregon, he later complained, tended to make "prosy and pointless" speeches. Charles Sumner of Massachusetts, who apparently loved to hear himself talk, was continually digressing about the values of fisheries, among other topics. Patience—never a strong virtue for Ames—gave way to annoyance as the deliberations continued with no clear end in sight. Then there was the press. Initially, journalists were excluded from the proceedings, save a few called to testify about printing full copies of the treaty. Fearful of inspiring too much negative commentary, however, the Senate reversed itself and invited in reporters. "The newspaper correspondents gallery is [now] crowded with the gentlemen of the 'Fourth Estate,'" Ames observed, "who with the shadow of their pens frighten a few of our number. At least such is my opinion." By the end of the month, the Senate finally ratified the treaty, and with that Ames quickly left Washington.[35]

Following another brief visit to Lowell, Ames returned to the Midwest, crisscrossing Wisconsin and Iowa throughout the summer on family business ventures. Blanche, pregnant and lonely, remained stoic in the face of her husband's prolonged absences. Only once, in late July, did she take him to task: "You know that I was expecting you here last Friday by every train," she complained, "and my disappointment took away a little from the pleasant thoughts I ought to have had on such a day." To her relief, Ames returned to her side within four days. Less than a month later, on August 22, 1871, the couple welcomed their first child into the world, a son named Butler after his mother's family.[36]

Only days after the birth of his firstborn, however, Ames left his family to go back to Mississippi, once again prioritizing the responsibilities of his job. He was pleased to discover while in Jackson that Republican donors frequently called on him. To Ames, this was evidence that the party was turning on Alcorn, who increasingly was becoming a personal political foe. Indeed, his letters to Blanche consisted of frequent stories of the citizenry decrying the governor. "Alcorn is exceed-

James Lusk Alcorn (Library of Congress)

ingly obnoxious and the true Republican spirit prevails on all hands," Ames wrote in one. "He is dishonest and everybody knows it. Therefore, his influence is on the wane." While the governor's popularity dwindled, the senator's popularity rose. Ames gave more speeches than he ever had before, he told Blanche, although he worried that he was too stiff and did not possess the common touch necessary for appealing to southern voters: "Stories and jokes please them much, and of such material I have but little. I do pretty well. . . . I am getting at the simple parts of the art of holding an audience." Although preoccupied with matters at hand, including Republican in-fighting, yellow fever raging from Natchez to Jackson, and violence throughout the state, he took time to ask how little Butler was faring. "You will not know the baby, Del," Blanche replied. "He is changing from hour to hour. Already he seems most grown up."[37]

As much as Ames wanted to be with his family, he had work to accomplish, which increasingly involved combating the rising tide of violence at the hands of the Klan. Both Black and white citizens were unnerved about the spike of brutality in Mississippi. The *Macon Beacon* reported that in just the first week of October, parties unknown had burned a Black church to the ground, administered a severe whipping to a kidnapped freedman, and killed a Black man in cold blood on his own doorstep. In an attempt to strike at the source of the troubles, squads of soldiers had "re-arrested" supposed Klan members in the fall of 1871. The only immediate effect of this measure was to anger Democrats.[38]

Amid the unrest, Ames learned that Alcorn intended to replace Revels himself at the end of the senator's term. This made him suspect that the governor's naming of Revels to the Alcorn State presidency had been merely a bribe. Ames also believed that the next governor, a former Democrat and Union veteran from Ohio named Ridgley Powers, would serve as "his [Alcorn's] tool." Whether or not Ames's suspicions were correct, he accurately foresaw that he was going to have to fight Alcorn—who became a senator on December 1—in Washington. As he explained to Blanche, "Now he [Alcorn] is to go to Washington [where] he and I will have a 'row.' The warfare he began on carpet-baggers when he became Governor is raging more fiercely today than ever, and now comes the question, shall he whip me or I him?"[39] If Alcorn did indeed "whip" him, Ames worried, it might undercut the narrative of a hostile and supremacist Mississippi the senator had spent two years promoting.

Ames returned to Washington and the next congressional session in early 1872. In February a committee assigned to investigate Klan activities presented its findings. This mammoth report consisted of fourteen volumes covering investigations in six states: North Carolina, South Carolina, Georgia, Alabama, Florida, and Mississippi—the last state covering two volumes of 1,266 total pages. Subcommittee members had visited each of the six states to assess evidence. Their interviews included accounts of Black men flogged and killed, teachers of Black students threatened, schools torched, and white scalawags murdered for voting against the Democratic Party.[40]

The committee's majority made three recommendations. The Enforcement Acts of 1870 and 1871 should be extended, not only to protect freedmen's suffrage rights but also to make electoral coercion a federal offence. A stronger federal judicial presence in the South was an absolute necessity. Finally, there should be a general amnesty for ex-Confederates, excepting certain high-ranking leaders of the rebellion. Ames's recent opponent, Senator Blair, stood for the committee's minority opinion that sympathized with white-supremacist southerners.[41]

Senators offered rebuttals to the committee's findings. On May 20 Alcorn gave his first speech on the Senate floor. Challenging the committee, he sought to deflect blame for the unrest from white southerners; the federal government and carpetbaggers were the problem, he said. Congress, he contended, should not impose further upon the southern states than it already had. Any bill that gave the federal government more oversight in Mississippi would be ineffective, unwise, and unwelcome. Ames's portrait of the state, Alcorn added, was farcical. The people did not need additional federal intervention. Overall, his statements echoed the debate between federal and states' rights that had contributed to the war eleven years prior.[42]

Like Blair, Alcorn did not demean Ames's personal character, but he did classify him as "a representative of the class of men who occupy positions under the abnormal condition of things incident to revolution. No one present supposes that he could by any possibility become clothed with the honor of representing Mississippi in this Chamber." Alcorn also reopened the issue of legal residence, calling Ames an outsider and an unwelcome firebrand to Mississippi. Like many before him, he attacked his fellow senator's Yankee nativity. Ames might legally be considered a resident of Mississippi, Alcorn joked, but he had not been in the state long enough to wash his shirts there. Ames was "not connected with my state by any of the ties which make up the genuineness, the reality of representation," Alcorn declared. Simply put, Ames the Mainer was "not a citizen of Mississippi" and did not represent its interests or people.[43]

Historian Harry King Benson has described this speech as a subpar attempt to blame Radical Republicans for everything while presenting Alcorn as "someone standing before the Senate representing all political factions in the state of Mississippi." Alcorn's oratorical victim knew better, and no sooner had the new senator delivered his "dirty" laundry than Ames interrupted him. Clearly weary of being called an alien in the Deep South time and again, he affirmed that he had every right to live in Mississippi and serve in Congress. Certainly Alcorn, of all people, had no grounds to challenge him on this point, for "these very carpet-baggers whom he now abuse[s] and the freedmen in that State elected him and me at the same time. If I am not entitled to my position, he certainly is not his." Truth be told, Ames regarded himself as the only rightful representative of Mississippi in the Senate, given that he was committed to protecting the state's citizens through civil rights legislation, whereas Alcorn continually quashed such measures. In consequence, Mississippians had "lost confidence in my colleague; he had played one trick too many with the Democracy." Alcorn's portrait of Reconstruction efforts not functioning properly was correct, although the fault was with his do-nothing policies as governor, not with Ames and his ilk.[44]

After addressing Alcorn's unwillingness to fight the Klan or support civil rights, Ames enunciated his own support for the anti-Klan legislation. Alcorn had described the bill as "a menace to the people of Mississippi," and Ames actually agreed:

Of course it [Ku Klux bill] is a menace. These Ku Klux are cowards. They go out at night and commit these murders. They go in large numbers and attack a single person. The only way to keep a coward in subjection is through fear. You cannot reach him in any other way, and it is the fear, it is the menace that these people respect and nothing else. The very passage of the Ku Klux law itself carrie[s] menace with it, and [will] result in great good. . . . I can speak for the Republican party of the State of Mississippi, and I do assert they desire a continuation of this law. They have been at all time in favor of the Ku Klux law; they have been [and] are now in favor of the civil rights bill, whatever my colleague may say to the contrary.[45]

From the moment Ames concluded his speech and sat down, the break between himself and Alcorn was irreparable. Yet both men voted in accord on the Amnesty Act of 1872 two days later, thereby removing all political disabilities for thousands of previously disfranchised Confederate soldiers.

Butler had helped craft the bill in the House of Representatives, and he and Ames worked together in private to formulate its final draft.⁴⁶

Ames's summer passed languidly, with tobacco-tax and tariff discussions, billiards matches against his father-in-law, and longings for his wife and his son, who remained in Lowell. He was overjoyed when both houses of Congress agreed to adjourn the second week of June, freeing him to go to Blanche. As so often before, this was a brief visit, and he was soon off again to Northfield, then Fort Atkinson in Iowa—investigating yet another company mill—and finally to Pittsburgh in September for a veterans reunion. It was probably well for Ames that, as an army officer, he had become inured to the discomforts of living on the road. His current responsibilities as an officeholder and his far-flung network of family and business interests left him little time to stay in any one place. Although he often regretted being away from his wife, Ames told himself that she was happier awaiting his return in high style on the East Coast than she would have been at his side in a succession of midwestern lodgings. Nonetheless, when the senator returned to Mississippi in late September to stump for the Republicans, he spent some time house shopping so that his wife and growing family could be comfortable when they inevitably joined him there.⁴⁷

But more serious duties beckoned. Ames had his work cut out for him during the 1872 election campaign. To help his party, the senator decided to traverse the state to rally support for local and national Republican candidates. "I shall start soon on a stumping tour," he told Blanche, "[and believe] that I shall do much better [than before]."⁴⁸ For three weeks, Ames visited Mississippi's largest towns and cities. Although no longer in the army, Ames the former soldier viewed the 1872 election as a military campaign weighted with unusual gravitas, pitting the Republican legions of Grant against the Democratic battalions of famed New York City newspaperman Horace Greely. He considered Reconstruction Democrats as villainous now as they had been before the war. Once staunch secessionists, they were now Black Code enforcers, Klan nightriders, and red-shirted insurrectionists. Against these forces, Ames proudly informed Blanche that he was stumping for the party of progress—the Republicans were a political force that was helping African Americans enjoy the rights of the ballot box, jury box, public office, and self-defense. It could, should, and must prevail, he informed his wife.⁴⁹

Some Mississippians apparently thought that only Ames could win that victory. While touring the state, he increasingly heard calls from supporters to run for governor. He was confident that he "could get the nomination" but believed he would need a Black running mate. Ames added that "weak-kneed Southern Republicans" would balk, but he knew "the Lieutenant Governor must [if possible] be a colored man" to win Black support. His motivation was equal parts political and noble. Politically, Ames was uncertain he could again win his senator seat. He did not elaborate on his reasons for this, but one possibility was that he feared that Republicans could lose control of the state legislature, which would drastically hurt his reelection chances. In contrast, he thought that he could harness the political power of the party if he became governor, solidifying his influence and Republican control of the legislature. "They [white Republicans] would not care to have a colored man as governor," so he would have to take the reins himself since no other white man, he believed, had enough clout. At the same time, Ames began to warm to a gubernatorial candidacy because he feared reprisal against the Black citizens should Democrats win. He strongly believed that together under his leadership, he and the state's freedmen could stave off the erosion of their rights and liberties.[50]

Willing to give up a tenuous Senate seat in Washington, Ames allowed the party bosses to put forth his name as a candidate in the 1873 gubernatorial election. His platform would be everlasting hostility to the Klan and distrust of Democrats. Ames also made a firm pledge to "try to show the colored men that they should hold together come what may, for they are yet far from being out of the wilderness." He permanently attached his political legacy to fighting for civil rights and enforcing the Constitution, his star rising or crashing depending on the outcome.[51]

Democrats quite naturally saw it the other way around. Ames was not a hero fighting for legal equality and a better future. In their reading *they* were the virtuous heroes, battling against the harebrained scheme of giving social equality to nonwhite men and altering the socioeconomic environment to which they were accustomed. Lest any of its readers forget, the *Weekly Clarion* reminded, "the Radicals are a party of Proscription as well as Plunder, and of Strife . . . attested by their acts from the close of the war to the present time." A Canton newspaper warned that "the re-election of Grant will continue, to the disgrace and injury of the country, the revels or 'the hideous offspring' of anarchy 'masquerading in the stolen robes of peace.'"[52]

On November 5 Grant clinched a second term as president, winning twenty-nine states and 286 electoral votes to Horace Greeley's six states and 66 votes. Ames's stumping may have helped Grant somewhat in Mississippi, but there the Republican triumph probably was owed to a large, already-loyal Black voting base. In the Magnolia State Grant won 63.4 percent of the vote and eclipsed Greely in the popular vote by nearly 35,000. Democrats were crestfallen, full of "apprehension" and "despair," according to the *Weekly Clarion*.[53] The *American Citizen* simply noted, "The Radicals have swept the country."[54] Ames, by contrast, was pleased: "The telegraphic returns indicate a most humiliating defeat for Horace Greeley—whereat we rejoice, I do, most sincerely and thankfully, away down in the depths of my heart." Flushed with victory, he bought a house in Natchez "for six thousand and one hundred dollars. . . . It is a very good locality," he informed Blanche, "and a fair bargain as all say whom I have consulted."[55] By May, his young family—augmented by the arrival of daughter Edith on March 4, 1873—was again reunited in Mississippi.[56]

Blanche enjoyed Natchez, but as a carpetbagger's wife, she was never truly at ease there. Once she related a story to her parents about the locals' inhospitality toward Yankees. At first, Natchez residents thought Edith an adorable child and beamed when they saw Blanche taking her for strolls around town. Their opinion—and facial expressions—changed when they discovered that mother and child were part of the family of the "Black Republican" Senator Ames. Even nature seemed hostile to the family. Almost as soon as they settled down, a cholera epidemic broke out. Rather than tempt fate with the "blue death," Ames sent his brood back to Lowell.[57]

Ames could do little to cleanse the humid air or win over hearts and minds already inclined to hate him. Instead, he put all his energy into his gubernatorial campaign. Powers, the current governor, seemed ripe for displacement. This was due in large part to a lackluster record with few accomplishments. Powers had remained a loyalist to Alcorn and his moderate faction after succeeding him, but his efforts to play Radical and conservative factions against each other only earned him enemies in both camps. Worse, he did not offer any solutions to fix Mississippi's economic doldrums and was lukewarm on civil rights. Much like Alcorn before him, Powers also succeeded in angering the state's Republican base. Ames thought little of Powers, and guests at social functions repeatedly told him that the governor was doomed. According to Ames, even Alcorn and Powers were "convinced at heart that they cannot beat me."[58]

Such bombast and boasting had some merit, because his opponents were reeling. Conservative Republicans were so desperate to defeat Ames that they went so far as to one-up him, putting forth their own Black candidate. They supported Senator Bruce, who had held several county offices such as registrar, sheriff, and tax assessor before becoming sergeant-at-arms in the Mississippi senate. But their last-minute machination did not work. Ames won 187 of 226 delegates at the party's August convention, including several in Alcorn's stomping ground, Coahoma County. The rest of the slate was, fittingly, multiracial. African Americans Alexander K. Davis and James Hill won the nominations for lieutenant governor and secretary of state respectively. Thomas Cardozo, who had interracial parents, won the nomination for superintendent of education.[59]

But moderates were not willing to let Ames win the governorship without a fight. Within days of Ames's nomination, Alcorn announced his own candidacy as an "Independent Republican," with Henry Musgrove, a former Union officer and Mississippi secretary of state, as his running mate. Ames professed indifference at this turn of events. "Alcorn has announced himself a candidate for Gov.," he noted to Blanche offhandedly, "and made a violent speech against me and others of our party. Blind with rage, he only does himself harm [and] ... makes himself the laughingstock of the state. We will defeat every scheme of his by the 4th of November."[60]

In truth, Ames stood to lose more than Alcorn if his campaign was unsuccessful. As a Radical closely identified with Black Mississippians and the US military, his political career might not survive a trouncing, whereas Alcorn, even if defeated, would still enjoy solid support among native whites. Nevertheless, Ames had a lock on the votes not only of the freedmen and carpetbaggers but even some Democrats in Vicksburg and Tupelo. These residents preferred economic vitality and good schools over maintaining rigid racial boundaries. Critically, Ames's rallies were better attended than Alcorn's, thereby making him appear to be the "people's" candidate of choice. At one appearance in Holly Springs, Ames reported to have addressed 2,000 people. At the same time across town, Alcorn's stump speech attracted only sixty attendees.[61]

The rival tickets frequently addressed crowds in the same locations at the same time. In some cases the candidates spoke next to each other on the same stages throughout October. At such times, the initiative seesawed between Ames and Alcorn. Once, Ames claimed that he "whipped [Musgrave] completely," yet the next day in Vicksburg, the tables turned on him. Alcorn spoke first and took "the lion's share of the time, forcing Ames to reply in the evening."[62] Ames inaccurately reported to his wife that he had outperformed Alcorn, but he barely had time to mount a rebuttal. A week later in Greenville, he cunningly made sure that he got the chance to speak first and, declining to yield at the halfway point as was customary, carried on for four and a half hours, rendering Alcorn effectively mute and superfluous.[63]

Ames also managed to overcome the hostile press. Mississippi newspapers routinely described his oratorical skills as juvenile or even mentally handicapped. Furthermore, being the son-in-law of the pompous and loathed Benjamin Butler was an albatross around his neck. The *Weekly Clarion* alleged that Ames's real goal was to turn "Mississippi into Massachusetts." Editors thought he would tax the state's citizens into impoverished, pliant serfs in a northeastern-style industrialist system—an allegation that Alcorn had echoed.[64]

None of it worked. With Ames's campaign surging, Governor Powers contemplated postponing the election until the following year despite any viable reason for doing so. The state had no logistical issues or statewide turbulence that might justify the move. Simply put, Powers wanted to cripple Ames's faction to help Alcorn, who otherwise seemed destined to lose. Although the Mississippi House of Representatives actually agreed to Powers's suggestion to postpone the vote, the Senate held back, and by the last day of October—Ames's thirty-eighth birthday—the matter was permanently tabled. Ames now had no doubts that he would win. "The long struggle in the [Mississippi] senate, which began on the 20th has ended today with a victory for us," he informed Blanche. "There will be an election, for [which] we have been fighting. . . . I am willing to leave my fate to the will of the people at the ballot boxes on Tuesday next." Blanche agreed; her husband had experienced "a hard battle" but had "gained the day, and with it more credit than you would have had in a little contest."[65]

On November 4, 1873, Mississippians voted for their new governor. Ames purportedly campaigned through Election Day. During a downpour, he had to ride forty miles from his last stump speech to Natchez to cast his ballot before the polling booth closed. The Republicans won 58 percent of the popular vote to 41.9 percent for Alcorn's Independent ticket. Writing to his wife, Ames pronounced himself "satisfied" with the result, although he had wanted to win by a larger margin. For all of Alcorn's and Powers's attempts to scuttle his campaign, Ames received 19,000 more votes than his closest opponent. Most importantly, the Radical Republicans gained majorities in both chambers of the legislature.[66]

Ames's father-in-law was no less delighted by his accomplishments than Blanche was. Three days after the election, while young Butler was running through the family house in Lowell to tell his grandfather that dinner was ready, he slipped and fell. The young boy hit his head and started to bawl. Grandfather Butler scooped up the toddler and comforted him, saying, "Never mind, my boy, your father is Governor of Mississippi."[67]

THE HEIGHT OF THE PARTY AND THE HEIGHT OF PREJUDICE

Governor-elect Ames could hardly wait until the next year to take up his new responsibilities. He submitted his resignation from the US Senate on January 10, 1874, and left immediately for Jackson. Up until the eleventh hour, Ames's predecessor attempted to obstruct his path to office. Powers appealed to the Mississippi Supreme Court to throw out the electoral results and schedule another gubernatorial contest for the following November. If Ames was concerned about Powers's machinations, he did not show it. For her part, Blanche was confident. "Political affairs, although unsettled, of course look promising," she told her mother, "and I think there will be no trouble about Gen'l. Ames taking his seat, in spite of Mr. Powers. I have hope we shall get settled next week." Three days before the turnover, the state court ruled that the election had been valid and Ames's inauguration could proceed as scheduled.[1]

Once Powers had vacated the governor's mansion, the Ames family moved into the residence. Blanche quickly assumed control of household operations in the manner of a captain calling all hands on deck. The resemblance was more than metaphorical, for as she told Martha Ames, her "great barn of a house," like some old sea vessel, was gargantuan and ill kept. Governor Powers had apparently left the mansion dilapidated and dirty, and although it was well furnished, the outside walkways had "a weedy appearance." Blanche also changed the food the house staff served and felt compelled to admonish the cook that "lard is not the staff of life." It took multiple weeks' worth of work to put the mansion in suitable condition for visitors.[2]

The Mississippi governor's mansion in Jackson, 1936 (Library of Congress)

On the evening of January 22, Ames became the twenty-seventh governor of Mississippi. His inaugural address stressed the need for unity—in other words, Democrats accepting their defeat and falling in line. He praised Mississippians as courageous people "with high hopes to meet disasters," such as Confederate defeat and the end of slavery. They must once more steel themselves to overcome longstanding racial prejudices and bitterness over their lost antebellum society. "The continuation of the struggle [between North and South] can but result in evil," Ames reasoned. It was best to let some things go, particularly the old belief that African Americans were not, and could never be, a part of the body politic. Freedmen's rights were not going away, for they had been model citizens "[who have] never attempted to secure an advantage over their opponents by fraud or violence." The Republican Party would not countenance any further contentiousness over race and would look unkindly on those who kept stirring the pot. As far as Ames could see, the supposedly insuperable differences between white and Black Mississippians were merely artifices. "In all things save politics," he declared, "the two races are as closely united as are people of the same surroundings elsewhere." It was up to both to realize this and work together to effect their own happiness.[3]

Ames promised to do all he could to bring about reconciliation. His first policy goal—furthering literacy and education—would naturally appeal to everyone. He envisioned "a [future] happy day for the State when no child can grow up without the means of receiving the elements of a good education," but unless "our most persistent efforts should be directed" to that end, it would be a vision unfulfilled. The governor proposed to create a free public school system for all children age five to fifteen, with attendance mandatory for at least three months out of the year.[4]

Schools cost money, but Ames informed his listeners that he would not ask them for a penny more. He was well aware of his party's less-than-stellar track record in making good use of state finances since the war ended. Criticizing Alcorn without mentioning him by name, Ames voiced his displeasure that the state debt and interest had expanded by leaps and bounds under Republican leadership. He, however, was committed to a "retrench[ment] in expenditures" and a "rigid economy" using available revenue only. As one example of this program, he suggested that the legislature switch to biannual elections to keep down expenses.[5]

The new governor also wanted to take the state's economy in a different direction. Cotton might still be the primary cash crop, but its value was ever subject to market fluctuations. Ames urged Mississippi planters to diversify, saving the better part of their acreage for grain and cattle. As a byproduct of this change, smaller farmers could be protected from the vicious postbellum credit-lien system, which often ate up their savings, increased their debts, and dropped them into the ever-growing ranks of poor sharecroppers. Beyond the tangible benefits it would accrue to Mississippi, Ames's call for diversification reflected his disdain for the manorialism of the Old South. A free-soil Yankee, he championed the independent American agricultural producer emancipated from bosses and landlords and able to supply his own wants. He feared that unless the antiquated, aristocratic southern labor structures changed, "a system of peasantry and tenantry might so readily and naturally result." With judicious planning, Mississippi might become a manufacturing center as well as a refurbished agrarian state, one offering jobs and business opportunities aplenty to immigrants from elsewhere in the Union.[6]

Carrying out Ames's platform, however, would depend on the "honesty, capacity, and fidelity" of Mississippians and their public servants. Dishonesty, he declared, ought to bring contempt and scorn as well as removal from office. Ames could not say what others might do, but as for himself, "I shall endeavor fearlessly and conscientiously to administer the affairs of state. I shall strive to secure to every citizen, however humble and poor, his rights, and see that none, however rich and powerful, override the laws."[7]

The young governor would need all the confidence, enthusiasm, and integrity he could muster. He would also need a good economic game plan, for Mississippi was in the direst fiscal straits. Dicey finances were nothing new but had been hurting it for thirteen years. Like some other slave states, Mississippi had gone into the war with negligible liquid capital, limited infrastructure, and a top-heavy monoculture in King Cotton. Confederate recruitment had swiftly drained off the few cash reserves left, forcing Gov. John J. Pettus to rely on cotton sales and general taxes to make up for the budgetary shortfalls. This had been a policy of dubious wisdom, given cotton's market volatility and the public's inability to pay more than a pittance in depreciated currency. Further stresses had followed and mounted as the war continued. The 1861–62 harvest was mostly a failure, and the government was forced to relocate in haste after Sherman's occupation of Jackson in 1863.[8]

Former Confederate brigadier general Charles Clark, succeeding Pettus in November 1863, instituted additional taxes. He also encouraged Mississippi farmers to grow rice, sugarcane, and potatoes instead of cotton. Clark's plans had been of little avail, however, for the most profitable counties were by then under occupation and thus inaccessible to his revenue agents. In addition, thanks to Union control of the principal waterways and rail lines, vegetable transportation never became viable. At the close of the war, the state government was $4,979,324 in debt, and most Mississippians were destitute.[9]

Despite Republicans' promises of economic revival, Mississippi had not blossomed under Alcorn and Powers. Railroad companies and plantations, the principal antebellum moneymakers, were skeletal in the state at best. The Mississippi Railroad, for example, had been left with only one operative locomotive after the war and had neither the resources nor the manpower to repair damaged or worn-out tracks. Many of the largest planters, meanwhile, had sold out in despair, with the few that remained dead set against negotiating contracts with their formerly enslaved workers. The use of convict labor had eased but not resolved the state's desperate shortage of agricultural labor.[10]

Worse overall, the national economy was sputtering like a faulty steam engine. The principal stressor was runaway railroad construction. Although regularly undercapitalized and heavily indebted, American railroad companies built lines with reckless abandon through the 1860s and early 1870s. Quite a few of the new routes led from nowhere to nowhere and helped none but a couple of investors. With miles of track thus unused, there was little money made on shipping or transportation. Rather than tighten their belts, these companies and steel mills simply ramped up production.[11]

Executives blithely assumed that bond sales to Europeans would more than cover outlays. Unfortunately, lingering uneasiness from the recent Franco-Prussian War (1870–71) made investors cautious. By May 1873, the bills were due, and in August the market began to wobble. On September 17 the house of cards had collapsed. Stocks shrank by 25 percent in a single week, and before December, even financially hearty cities like Pittsburgh were feeling the economic sting. One railroad company after another went bankrupt, dragging their parent states' credit with them. Mississippi and its railroad companies were left reeling from the fallout.[12]

Reasonably confident that he could reform the state and alter its trajectory, Ames submitted a special letter to the state legislature detailing his plan of action. Obviously, expenditures must be reduced, receipts maximized, and credit restored. Because he was unequivocally opposed to raising taxes, there were only two courses of action available to the government: either economize and fix the current financial system, or "retrench under a new and different system." Ames favored the latter. One way to accomplish this was to recall all of Mississippi's depreciating state bank notes and only use US currency, or "greenbacks." In addition, the government would need to tweak several minor areas of outflow, such as juror compensation, legislators' pay rates, and county school superintendent salaries. Everyone would have to make do with a little less for the time being.[13]

The state's railroad companies, Ames warned, needed to straighten out too. In an address to the legislature on March 14, the new governor deplored the regular misappropriation of funds and improper management of railroad contracts of prior years. Under Powers, the state had approved an act giving the Vicksburg and Nashville Railroad Company $320,000 to build track. Yet "the railroad company to which this fund is proposed to be surrendered has not completed a single mile of road." In the face of a stock market crash caused by railroad swindling, Ames would not tolerate any more fraudulent deals; after all, it was the taxpayers who were always left holding the bag. Mississippi's legislators, the governor believed, were duty bound to be "if possible, more cautious and circumspect in the disposition of the funds of the State than with our own. Are we prepared as individuals, to invest our own funds in this enterprise?" Ames asked pointedly. If the answer was no, then neither ought they make questionable investments with someone else's money.[14]

Continuing his campaign against bad railroad deals, Ames attacked a measure that Powers had signed in January 1872. This law, providing complete tax exemption for the Grenada, Houston, and Eastern Railroad Company, at a minimum had sealed off 10 percent of the state's taxable property from government assessment. That was far too much beneficence for one company; was it any wonder that the state was now in financial ruin? More disturbingly, the exemptions were unconstitutional, for as Mississippi's constitution clearly states, "The property of all corporations for pecuniary profits shall be subject to taxation, the same as that of individuals." Ames reminded legislators: "The people who adopted the constitution, and bear the burden of supporting the government, will never consent to such a flagrant violation of it. . . . If any are to be [exempted], let it be the poor rather than the rich and powerful." State investment in internal improvements was good and desirable, but not so when "unwise and unconstitutional laws shall find place in our statue books for that or any other purpose. No true friend of the State, or progress," Ames concluded, "can ask [for] that."[15]

At the onset of Ames's gubernatorial term, his egalitarian, fair-tax vision appealed to freedmen and even garnered support from a few Democrats. One Democratic paper, the *Weekly Clarion,* called his economic plan a practical and salient one and reprinted an article from the *Hinds County Gazette* declaring that "the people would support him [Ames] in every good and wholesome act" to help the state. The once-frightening spectacle of a Radical Republican Yankee governor looked less menacing to some conservatives now. Ames sounded more polished and professional than his predecessors and enemies claimed. According to one report, leading Mississippians "informally called upon Ames" during his first few months of office "and assured him of their willing[ness] to be fair and cooperative."[16]

On the home front, Blanche had made a good impression by organizing gatherings and trying to instill New England customs in Jackson. She held popular croquet parties for prominent Yankees in the community and invited influential Black leaders to dine with her family. Although missing Massachusetts's comforts, she took pride in hosting receptions and claimed that her guests enjoyed themselves. The Ames family, particularly young Butler and Edith, came across well to most Republicans.[17]

During the start of the gubernatorial term, Ames's forthrightness also won the grudging admiration of bitter enemies. Canton's *American Citizen* pointed to glaring errors in his inaugural address about who was to blame for racial violence (not white Democrats, it insisted) but conceded that his tone was at least sincere and patriotic. Democrats in northeastern Lee County, according to one Republican informer, were vexed that they could find no flaws with the governor's financial plans, which made it harder, they complained, to hate him.[18]

Nevertheless, Ames was already under pressure to return to Washington. His father-in-law proposed that he run for senator again in 1876, leaving the Mississippi legislature in the hands of his allies. At the same time, Representative Butler would run for governor of Massachusetts. Beyond the purely political machinations of Butler, it is possible that the Ames-Butler women were pressuring their husbands toward this end. In the event of dual victories, the two men could spend most of their time in Lowell or Washington while their families could be together and secluded from the Deep South for most of the year. Sarah Butler, informed of the violence attending Reconstruction and the antagonistic environment that carpetbaggers faced, frequently fretted about the safety of her son-in-law, daughter, and grandchildren. Blanche's letters offered little cause for hope; "with the exceptions of a few white families," she told her mother, "every white person in the city is inclined to be prejudiced against us."[19]

As Blanche suggested, the veneer of civility in Mississippi wore down. Ames's platform of decreasing debt, promoting good education, and keeping the peace had never been in the interests of certain Mississippians. The state's elites, a coalition of planters and political insiders known as the "Bourbons," remained cool at best toward the upstart Republican reformer and what they considered his egalitarian flights of fancy. Private land ownership, universal literacy, and civil rights for freedpeople did not square at all with the hierarchical antebellum social structures that had once benefited them and, quite naturally, wanted to restore. Despite Confederate defeat and federal occupation, the Bourbons, thanks to the affable indolence of Alcorn and Powers, had managed to have most things their way in Mississippi. If Ames dared to cross them, they vowed to stop him.[20]

There was also an upswell in Republican opposition. The more conservative scalawags, increasingly identifying with Alcorn, slowly withdrew their support. In consequence, and especially after the 1873 election, the party's voting base became majority Freedmen and thus utterly alien to most white residents. Reflecting that growing faction, Ames's own lieutenant governor, Black attorney Andrew K. Davis, regularly took power whenever Ames left Jackson's city limits.

Had Davis possessed any political tact, or had the state enjoyed stability, his attempts at playing king for a day might have been inoffensive. He was, after all, an important political figure who was instrumental in getting Black candidates elected to the state legislature as well as ensuring that Cardozo and Hill won their statewide offices. If he wanted to help give freedmen pride in holding sway over state politics, he did a superb job. But his actions also further divided the party and the administration along racial lines. One notable occurrence happened in May 1874, when Ames traveled to New Orleans intending to visit some the state's southern counties along the way. Although he neglected to inform Davis that he had left, the lieutenant governor soon learned of it and began to implement his own ideas about railroad reform and make judicial appointments that the governor would not have opposed. Fearing that Davis would disembowel the railroad-reform agenda, Republicans in Ames's camp rushed to track down their absent chief. Jackson was "thrown into quite a state of excitement," Blanche later noted, "and Gen'l Ames was telegraphed to return at once" before Davis could draw from the state treasury. Ames quickly crossed the state line and reassumed control.[21]

After this episode, some of Ames's supporters begged him to remain in Jackson throughout the summer months. Someone, they insisted, needed to keep an eye on Davis. Ames, however, did not want to remain tethered to the state capital "as a watch dog," especially with the legislature adjourned and his in-laws waiting impatiently up north. Disregarding advice, Ames and his family left Mississippi in June to visit the Butlers and vacation at Bay View. While claiming that his young children's health required a cooler climate, he also probably wanted to give his lonely wife and mother-in-law a chance to see each other.[22]

In leaving Mississippi, Ames maintained that there were sufficient provisions to keep the lieutenant governor in check during his absence. With no legislative meetings scheduled, all that Davis could do was fill some minor offices, such as civil-court justiceships and state-government chancellorships. Ames had, he thought, already circumvented the possibility of such mischief by submitting his own recommendations to the Mississippi Senate just before its recess.

Unfortunately, Ames had not reckoned on the restless Davis. No sooner had the governor departed than Davis swung into action, canceling many of Ames's nominations in favor of his own, giving unsanctioned pardons, and making divisive appointments in Sumner County; he even replaced the night watchman in Jackson. When Ames returned in July, he found his nominees disgruntled and his party seething with dissention. Forced in haste to nullify all that Davis had done, he counseled the party faithful in Sumner to "settle among yourselves your differences."[23]

Eventually, the trouble in Sumner County subsided, yet Ames had upset more than a few constituents by overruling his unruly lieutenant. Several commentators professed a preference for the lieutenant governor's choice of chancellors and credited Davis, a native of Tennessee but less alien to Mississippi than Ames, with making the right choices. One paper labeled the governor a "peaked-nose Puritan," implying that his attempts to rein in Davis were not in the interest of party or state but more to satisfy a cold, intolerant, personal rectitude. Ames ought to have stayed in New England with his hated father-in-law, the editor griped, where such rigid self-righteousness was customary.[24]

Democrats readily seized on this Ames-Davis feud aiming to divide and conquer the opposition. Ignoring the responsibilities of governorship, they claimed that Ames was monopolizing the right of appointment to advance his own interests. According to them, he should have waited until the Senate reconvened to fill the contested offices instead of announcing them far in advance. Soon, scores of Republican detractors were saying the same thing. Such divisions posed an existential threat not only to Ames's administration but also to Reconstruction in general. Without unity and harmony among the state's Republicans, Mississippi might well lapse back into a rebellious posture.[25]

As if a portent to this possibility, that same troubled summer the peace and order that Ames craved was violently shattered. Republicans in Vicksburg, including many African Americans, gathered to peacefully celebrate Independence Day. White Democratic residents in the river city immediately took offense to this, for to them the birthday of the United States was a foul holiday evoking bitter wartime memories. Eleven years earlier they had endured siege, starvation, and surrender, followed by military occupation and forced emancipation. The sight of joyous freedpeople commemorating the anniversary of their humiliation with speeches, songs, and barbecues left them boiling with rage. Vicksburg's county sheriff, Black veteran Peter Crosby, had earlier warned Ames that the city was teetering on the edge of a racial volcano. The governor ignored him.

Crosby's warning proved prophetic. In the middle of the festivities, a mob of white men suddenly produced firearms and fired into the holiday crowds, scattering men, women, and children. "Several has been killed upon the streets of Vicksburg today and several wounded also," Crosby informed Lieutenant Governor Davis, as Ames was again out of state. Bloody as it was, the Fourth of July massacre threatened to be merely a precursor of worse to come during the city's fall elections the following month. White supremacist "White Line" leagues organized in the aftermath of the massacre began to harass and oppress Black voters. The city fathers begged for help from Davis, who, to his credit, swiftly telegraphed the news to Washington, requesting that the US Army send two infantry companies to watch over the polls.[26]

When Ames learned about what had happened, he raced back to Mississippi, reaching Jackson a little more than three weeks later. From the accounts of Republican "refugees" who had escaped the massacre, Vicksburg was now a lawless place. More alarming, the army reinforcements had not yet arrived. Ames sought to spur Washington to action with a lengthy telegram. "Of the causes of this lamentable state of affairs," the governor notified President Grant, "it is now useless to speak. I only seek peace & protection for all. Can there be any serious objection why troops can not be sent there? ... Will it not be the ... (least?) of evils to have troops there for any emergency?" Impatient for an answer, Ames telegraphed the president again three days later.[27]

Lethargy within Grant's cabinet and a counternarrative disseminated by Vicksburg Democrats delayed the help. Secretary of War William W. Belknap, who received the telegrams, was not inclined to haste. An indifferent public official and late Republican convert dogged by scandal, Belknap had few troops at hand anyway, given the volunteer army's rapid postbellum demobilization. Additionally, the city's White Liners had preempted Ames with a notification of their own, blaming the violence on Crosby. They claimed that the sheriff had tried forcibly to keep eligible white voters from registering; the massacre had, therefore, actually been a case of self-defense.[28]

Rather than send the infantry companies requested, Belknap detached an officer from Holly Springs to investigate conditions in Vicksburg. The officer's subsequent report was terse, lackluster, and dismissive of the possibility of another riot, which was enough to satisfy the War Department and the president. A few days later Grant notified Ames that no troops would be necessary to keep the peace in Vicksburg. Furthermore, he declared that the US military had no jurisdiction in the city—an excuse that, according to historian William Gillette, Grant frequently employed as a graceful way out of intervention.[29]

Ames was enraged and disappointed by Grant's response. It seemed to him that the president, desirous of reelection, wanted to court votes from the other party. The cost of Democratic support, unfortunately, would be federal noninterference in the southern states. The nation's greatest war hero, who had once smashed a rebellion through the force of his perseverance, was now, in Ames's view, making a terrible moral compromise for selfish reasons. "I have tried to get troops," he lamented, "but the President refuses. It is thought he wants the support of Southern Democrats for a third term. Most true it is that they are generally for him in this state." Electoral horse trading had become important than Black civil rights and justice before the law. Never mind, Ames mused bitterly, that "they in Vicksburg who . . . laud him to the skies . . . are rioting [and] ready for murder and frauds."[30]

Ames might have wished, if only for a moment, that the massacre had happened when he was still military governor, with hundreds of soldiers at his disposal. Yet those days were gone, along with his martial power and authority. There was no way now to stop unsanctioned militia forces from taking control of any Mississippi municipality whenever they wished.[31]

Vicksburg was the first to fall. In elections there on August 5, Democrats swept the boards. Although the city was majority African American, most Black voters, afraid of falling victim to another massacre, had stayed away from the polls. The victory marked a permanent change in Mississippi's Reconstruction politics. The opponents of Reconstruction had won through intimidation, plain and simple. They knew they need not hesitate in the face of a state government paralyzed by infighting and orphaned by the federal government—moreover, they knew they could go further still. "Redeeming" larger Warren County from carpetbagger control now seemed entirely possible.[32]

Meanwhile, the violence spread. A few days after Democrats reclaimed Vicksburg, white and Black residents came to blows in the Tunica County hamlet of Austin, just south of Memphis. The trouble began when a white doctor shot and killed two Black men for singing too loudly late at night. Although arrested by local Black law enforcement, the doctor did not remain in jail for long, as white neighbors took up arms, assaulted the jail, and freed him. Simultaneously, Black residents grabbed weapons and took station in the local municipal building, which white residents in turn invested with a cordon of armed men. Thankfully, the climatic shootout everyone expected fizzled out, and Ames was able to report, "The cloud which hung over Tunica Co. portending a storm has passed." Even so, at least eight people had died—the state government had been shown powerless yet again.[33]

For the first time, Ames began to seriously question the idealism that drove him to run for governor. After only eight months in office, with little more to show for his efforts than bloody chaos, he contemplated leaving the state for good. Perhaps he would never be accepted by Mississippians. Perhaps they were incapable of change, improvement, or growth. Perhaps the crushing weight of their past was too heavy to cast off and start again. "Slavery blighted this people." he reminded Blanche, "then the war—then reconstruction—all piled upon such a basis destroyed [their] minds—[or] at least impaired their judgement [sic] and consciousness to that extent that we cannot live among them." He then admitted: "I do not know how recent my convictions have settled upon me, but they are here in full force. . . . Mississippi, which has commanded my thoughts and time for the last six years, has lost its power over me forever. . . . I have no cause to grieve over any fate, however adverse, to my political preferment this state may have in store for me."[34]

To add to Ames's disappointments with white Mississippians, some Black Republicans in the state turned out to be fallible. In Vicksburg the district attorney and a mostly Black grand jury indicted several county officials, including State Superintendent of Education Thomas W. Cardozo, for forging documents and pinching from the public coffers. They charged Cardozo with allegedly pocketing $5,000 while serving as the circuit clerk of Warren County one year earlier. In the end, he and the other defendants managed to evade jail time when records relevant to their cases disappeared. Nonetheless, the trial had been damning for the Republican Party, which now seemed on the surface to be as corrupt as its opponents had claimed.[35] Mississippi's young governor must have been embarrassed and distraught, but he did not describe the particulars in his letters to his parents, the Butlers, or his wife.

Blanche tried to be supportive amid the disarray. She encouraged her husband to banish "state affairs, that is, the annoying part of them, from your mind." His third child, she informed him, was soon to be born—reason enough for him stay strong and take care of himself during Mississippi's "sickly [summer] season of the year." Ames took the hint, went on a vacation in Bay Saint Louis to "get fat" on oysters and shrimp, and then again left Mississippi, seeking the bosom of his loving family in Massachusetts, where he stayed until early October. More practically, Blanche sent him his wartime pistol just in case. "I do not imagine it will be of any use," Ames replied when he received it. "However I will carry it as of old."[36]

The greatest headache Ames wrestled with during these months was the rise of a dauntless political adversary. Hailing from Oxford, Lucius Quintus Cincinnatus Lamar had become the US representative for the First District of Mississippi when Ames became governor. Born in 1825, Lamar was physically and intellectually unprepossessing in his formative years, but in time he became a lawyer, antebellum congressman, and draftsman for Mississippi's ordinance of secession before raising the Nineteenth Mississippi Infantry Regiment.[37]

While Ames embodied the stereotypical uncompromising, courageous Yankee, Lamar was the beau-ideal of the charismatic, loyal Bourbon. Like others of his mold, Lamar feared that outsiders such as Ames and freedmen would upend Mississippi's social institutions and dominate its politics forever. "On one side of which you see property, intelligence, virtue, religion, self-respect, enlightened public opinion, and exclusion from all political control," he wrote. "On the other the absolute unchecked political supremacy of brute numbers, and there you will behold not one attribute of free government, but the saddest & blackest tyranny that ever cursed this earth." Noble whites, he believed, had to put a stop to this. It was the destiny of "the white people of this state, the men in whose veins flows the blood of the ruling races of the world," to act.[38]

The Bourbons would need to craft a plan for dethroning Ames. Lamar considered the governor a capable leader, neither incompetent nor corruptible. Waiting for him to err or overstep the bounds of his power would mean waiting indefinitely. It was better, he decided, to encourage Ames's Republican opponents to wear themselves out fighting each other. The Mississippi representative would start that process in Washington.

Lamar's chance came in March 1874, when Ames's Republican ally Sen. Charles Sumner died. The Ames-Butler family was well aware of a growing political fracas within Massachusetts, and the party, to replace the statesman. So was Lamar, who cast his first congressional speech as a eulogy for the departed, even though he had never met Sumner. In a skillful oration he came across as a sincere, reformed Confederate reaching across the aisle to bring order to the Deep South. The *Chicago Daily Tribune* praised him: "Mr. Lamar's eulogy on Sumner is one of the most hopeful signs we have had from the South during these weary years of misrule."[39] By carefully disguising his hatred for Reconstruction and racial equality, Lamar positioned himself as a more moderate option to Ames and the Radicals.[40] Conservative Mississippians now had a legitimate standard bearer to rally behind. "Lucius Q. C. Lamar, of Mississippi, is the strongest mind among the Democrats."[41]

Republicans, on the other hand, could not agree on the next step. The party's autumn convention in Chattanooga fell far short of presenting a united front. Conservatives dominated the meeting and swept all progressive suggestions from the table. Radicals, in turn, angrily washed their hands of the whole mess. "Our delegates . . . are loud in denouncing the cowardice of the convention," Ames noted. "It failed to endorse the civil rights bill! Instead of building up respect for Southern Republicanism they have drawn down upon it." While his party fractured, the opposition was gaining strength. Even former Confederate president Davis seemed to Ames to be actively and openly courting voters at the state fair in October. Caught up in his emotions and stuck in a large, empty house, the governor professed now to desire only a quiet life. "I find little I care for outside of the house and my own thoughts," he confided to Blanche, and "am more and more inclined to abandon these surroundings and all they proffer and seek a new life in a different atmosphere."[42]

Election Day, 1874, saw the Republicans convulsed by midterm defeats across the Upper South and Midwest. Democrats gained seats in both houses—170 in the lower chamber alone. Even up north the news from the hustings was bad. To the dismay of Ames and Blanche, Benjamin Butler lost both his bid for governor of Massachusetts and his congressional seat. Ames wrote with resignation: "The Democracy [Democrats] have triumphed in every quarter. Surely it is startling news. . . . [T]he old rebel spirit will not only revive, but it will make itself felt."[43]

Not surprisingly, it made itself felt first in Vicksburg through the "taxpayers' leagues." Less radical than the White Liners, the leagues, as their name suggested, sought to clamp down on corruption and the high taxes associated with carpetbag governments. Local leaguers in Vicksburg wanted to go further still by removing all Republicans from power in Warren County. Tensions escalated when Sheriff Crosby, who also acted as the county tax collector, prepared to gather due taxes on December 2. Calling a meeting the same day, the city league produced a resolution demanding that Crosby resign. When the sheriff refused to comply, 500 white men marched to the courthouse to "convince" him. Crosby fled to Jackson and relayed the story to the governor.[44]

To Ames, Crosby's ousting had been a blatantly illegal coup d'état. It was not a random insurrection, but one clearly brewing in Vicksburg. If the city fathers had a legitimate complaint about the sheriff, they ought to have filed suit, not muscled him out with the threat of violence. Ames quickly called a meeting to consider next steps. No one kept official minutes, but according to later sources, Ames's advisors, most notably Attorney General A. G. Packer, agreed that the sheriff's resignation had been made "under duress," making it "invalid and void." Ames suggested that Crosby grasp the nettle by assembling a freedmen militia, marching into Vicksburg, and reinstating himself. At first Crosby was hesitant for fear he would put himself and other local African Americans in danger. Ames reportedly replied that he had put his own life in jeopardy for freedmen, both as a soldier and now a public servant; surely Crosby could muster the courage to do the same. Encouraged, Crosby left to carry out the plan.[45]

Ames tried to make things easier for him by issuing a proclamation on December 5 commanding the citizens of Vicksburg to abandon their takeover. "Citizens," the governor asked plaintively, "shall we submit to violent

Warren County Courthouse, Vicksburg, Mississippi (Library of Congress)

and lawless infringements on our rights? No; let us with united strength oppose this common enemy, who, by all the base subterfuges known to political tricksters, and the audacious mendacity of heartless barbarians, are trying to ruin the prospects and tarnish the reputations of every republican, colored or white." In the end, Ames's declaration made a bad situation worse. Since the following day was a Sunday, Black preachers across Warren County read the governor's proclamation to their churches and encouraged their flock to join Crosby's militia. Unknown numbers did. The specter of wholesale Black mobilization played right into the league's hands, helping them portray the militia as an invading force. White officials warned Black residents to keep off the streets and threatened to kill any dissenters.[46] If neither side backed down, things would get ugly in Vicksburg.

Early in the morning of December 7, a lookout stationed in the courthouse cupola reported seeing a column of armed Black men approaching from the south. Democratic mayor Richard O'Leary declared martial law and placed Col. Horace Miller, a Confederate veteran, in charge of the city's defense. Miller found and arrested Crosby, who had already entered Vicksburg alone, then assembled 200 or 300 white residents five blocks east of the courthouse.

Meanwhile, he detailed white physician and fellow veteran James M. Hunt to ride out to the approaching freedmen and ascertain their intentions.

Leading the approaching men was Crosby's friend Andrew Owen. He and the Black militia were initially determined to enter Vicksburg come what may. "If you take these Negroes into town you are the biggest fool living," Hunt warned darkly, for "there will not be one of you left to tell the tale." Shrugging off the threat, Owen and several hundred men advanced into the city limits, pausing at a bridge spanning a deep ravine. Only then, with the two forces in sight of each other, did Miller and Owen agree to parley.[47]

Owen demanded to pass through the lines and visit Crosby in jail, which Miller permitted. It is uncertain what Owen and Crosby discussed; perhaps Owen only sought assurance that his friend was still alive. In any case, after seeing Crosby behind bars, Owen decided that nothing more could be done. He rode back to the Black militiamen and told them to disperse. Angered and confused by this sudden change, they refused to comply. In short order, Owen began to lose control over them.[48]

Miller, sensing a chance to end the threat, pressed some of his men against the militia's flank, prompting them to retreat slowly. Suddenly someone, likely a white man, opened fire and missed. Although the shot incensed some of the militia, "not a one," according to freedman Dennis Bailey, returned fire. Nevertheless, more white men started shooting, and casualties mounted as the Black militiamen broke into a run. Later that day two other gunfights broke out around the city. In total, two white residents and at least twenty-nine Black citizens lay dead by day's end.[49]

A wave of paramilitary terror swept over Warren County in the aftermath. Gangs of armed white men roamed around exacting vengeance without let or hindrance. Two judges decamped to Jackson to avoid being lynched. Having reviewed the startling reports from Vicksburg, Ames called the state legislature into special session, although inclement weather delayed the opening until December 17.[50]

The governor declared to the assembly that the "Vicksburg Troubles," as they came to be known, were not over: "They [the white residents of Vicksburg] have organized companies and regiments, officered by men who pretend to by authority of the State, exercising all the function of an independent sovereignty, even so far as to search the homes of citizens of different political faith, to take from them their arms, incarcerate them in jail, compelling legally elected officials to resign their offices, and above all, putting citizens to death without even the formalities of law."[51]

The serious corruption in Warren County aside, there was no justification for the White Liners and taxpayers league taking the law into their own hands. In fact, Ames pointed out, they had not even tried to get redress by proper means. There were circuit judges, the state supreme court, and the legislature to appeal to, and of these, "no single . . . remedy had been exhausted. The cause of complaint in Warren County, if any there be, would, I have no doubt, have received full and favorable consideration by the [authorities]." The governor continued, "we are forced by the facts to the conclusion that a legal or legislative remedy has not been desired." Vicksburg's insurrectionists were determined to do things their way, and if they succeeded, they would return an entire people to abject servitude.[52] Ames elected to bring forth all the force he could muster to prevent this happening.

The legislature applauded the governor's speech and passed a resolution requesting that President Grant send US troops to Mississippi. They argued that under Article IV, Section 4 of the Constitution, guaranteeing the protection of democratic processes in the states, what had happened in Vicksburg required some federal response. The resolution also affixed some blame for the violence on outside parties, principally from Louisiana, crossing the state line to harass and hunt down African Americans in coordination with white Mississippians. State resources were insufficient to meet the emergency because "the Chief Executive . . . has no sufficient [militia] force at his command . . . nor other adequate power, to suppress such domestic violence." Ames added his own telegram to the president on December 19 asking for help. This time Grant proved receptive. In concurrent meetings at the White House, the president reportedly decided that Ames was the best man to govern and restore Mississippi and needed help in doing so. He replied to his former subordinate the same day: "Your dispatch of this date is received, and the proclamation called for by the law in such cases, will be forthwith promulgated." Grant gave the people of Vicksburg five days to stand down and notified Lt. Gen. Philip Sheridan of the trouble. Sheridan, in turn, telegraphed Ames on January 5, 1875, assuring him that as commander of the Department of the Gulf, he would send troops to Vicksburg immediately. Sheridan was as good as his word: within twenty-four hours a company of troops led by Maj. George Head entered the city, deposed the unlawful sheriff A. J. Flannagan, and reinstalled Crosby.[53]

Ames breathed a sigh of relief. He could afford to, for as Blanche told her mother, "this trouble in Vicksburg has united the [Republican] party, ended all [dissention] for the time being and made him the head and leader. His enemies," she added, "are quite disgusted" with their sudden setback. In an address to the legislature once the situation in Vicksburg was under control, Ames was his old confident self again. He reaffirmed his commitment to helping the economy and repealing railroad subsidies and talked about distributing aid for flood victims and reducing the number of tax collectors. The governor did not even address matters in Warren County until the end, where he noted in passing, "No act should be left undone to assert the authority and majesty of the law." While Ames spoke, his enemies held their own assembly in Jackson. The all-white "taxpayers convention" voiced their opposition to corruption with a resolution implying that they had only begun to fight. Democratic papers needed no convincing; the *Daily Clarion* opined "that as a formidable array of argument and figures against Radical misrule . . . the address of the tax-payers should be carefully studied."[54]

The search for culprits in the Vicksburg Troubles intensified after a congressional investigation produced a 607-page report late in February. The Republican majority opinion argued that the white Democratic narrative of "protecting" Vicksburg was a cover up to justify random acts of violence against African Americans. Naturally, the Democratic minority opinion suggested that by giving Mississippi freedmen rights in the first place, the Reconstruction government had deliberately endangered the peace. As a whole, the report identified two options for future policy: either use federal force to secure Black rights, or tell freedmen they must fight for themselves.[55]

Anti-Reconstruction forces paid little heed to the findings. White Liners, Bourbons, and former scalawags were already organizing a new coalition. These so-called Redeemers fully expected to undercut Ames's policies at the polls and in the streets of the state. For extra firepower in both venues, conservative white Mississippians formed the "Red Shirts," a paramilitary group operating as an enforcement wing of the Democratic Party. Donning bold red shirts, these men threatened or assaulted African Americans and berated or ostracized white holdouts who did not comply. Unless something was done about these organizations, Reconstruction would be a dead letter.[56]

Five years earlier, Senator Sumner and Representative Butler had proposed strict enforcement acts guaranteeing public accommodations to all persons regardless of race. Nothing came of it, as debates raged over the constitutionality of such bills. After the violence attending the 1874 midterm elections, Congress was ready to reevaluate their proposals. But with Sumner dead and Butler out of Congress, the enforcement bills' current advocates lacked the senior leadership necessary to get them passed with minimal amendments.

In consequence, an unholy alliance between Lamar and Republican Speaker of the House James G. Blaine undertook to whittle down the measure. Although signed into law on March 1, the Civil Rights Act of 1875 lacked provisions to enforce it. Concurrently, Lamar launched a new anti-Reconstruction campaign in Mississippi in the summer of 1875. Under the aegis of state party leader James Z. George, Democrats put forth the "Mississippi Plan," which would employ both legal and illegal means to topple Ames and the Republicans that summer and fall.[57]

The illegal side of the plan got under way first, with an eruption of violence in the west-central counties of Yazoo and Hinds. On September 1 Republicans held a public meeting on Main Street in Yazoo City, featuring Radical Republican sheriff Albert T. Morgan as the principal speaker. No sooner had Morgan commenced than a Black man allied with (or paid by) the Democrats rose to interrupt him. Morgan tried to shut down his challenger, but one of the sheriff's enemies, Henry Dixon, chastised him for suppressing free speech. Suspecting the whole affair was a trap to provoke an overreaction on his part, Morgan refused to acknowledge Dixon. Enraged, Dixon drew and discharged his pistol at the speaker. As if on cue, his armed compatriots swarmed into the building and opened fire. Miraculously, Morgan dodged the fusillade, escaped, and absconded to his plantation on the outskirts of town. An alarm sounded throughout the town, and dozens of white residents took up arms looking for the hated carpetbagger. Yazoo City had fallen into Democratic hands.[58]

Three days later a fight broke out at a public barbecue in nearby Clinton, where at least 2,000 Black residents had gathered. In a spirit of bipartisanship that they would later regret, the Republican organizers and hosts had extended invitations to white Democrats. Either the latter assumed that the party was to be racially exclusive or else they came intending to stir up trouble. Copious amounts of liquor probably stoked aggressive indiscretion among the attendees too. In any case, when a Black Republican attempted to give an address, many whites heckled him. The exchanges became angrier, and eventually shots rang out, and the screaming guests scattered. The final toll was three white men and seven Black men dead.[59]

For days afterward, Redeemers patrolled the countryside, murdering any Republican, white or Black, who got in their way. The Democratic *Weekly Clarion* justified the slaughter with rumors that Black attendees had sung songs about how they would "kill Clinton and kill Democracy that day." The *Greenville Times* gave a more balanced description of the events but nonetheless argued that the barbecue riot was "the natural and inevitable result of the theory of Radical Rule in the South. The tendency of the excitement produced by these affairs throughout the State during the campaign, is to create like occurrences."[60]

Based on reports that the perpetrators in both incidents had maneuvered and fired with military discipline, Ames suspected that white paramilitary organizations were to blame. On September 7 he ordered all illegal military companies to disband and the next day sent a telegram to Grant. Since "the legislature cannot be convened in time to meet the emergency," Ames wrote, "I, therefore, make this my application for such aid from the Federal government as may be necessary to restore peace to the State and protect its citizens." Already he had at hand admissions from multiple sheriffs that they could not hope to keep the peace in their counties.[61]

Although Ames expected Grant to lend assistance as he had done previously, the president took counsel of dissent within his cabinet. The new attorney general, former conservative Democrat and Reconstruction critic Edwards Pierrepont, discouraged giving military aid to the governor. After listening to Pierrepont, Grant waffled, first proposing to issue a proclamation in favor of intervention, then confessing that he did not know what to do about Mississippi. The crafty Pierrepont redacted the president's more displeasing statements (as he saw them), kept those opposing federal involvement, and sent the letter, appended to one of his own, to Ames. In short, Pierrepont suggested, it was up to the governor to get out of his scrape by his own efforts.[62]

The problem was that Ames had already tried to raise a militia only to fail for lack of support. Since March 1875 he had been authorized by the legislature to recruit two regiments of state troops. Unfortunately, these remained paper organizations only; by and large most white Mississippians refused to join them. Ames did receive some aid from a former comrade, Brig. Gen. C. C. Augur, who dispersed 500 soldiers to guard weapons stockpiles in three Mississippi towns; they were not enough.[63] Ames also requested 1,000 breach-loading rifles from out of state—none arrived—and courted white Republicans to enroll in the militia—none joined. For a time it seemed that Confederate-deserter-turned-Unionist Newton Knight might stimulate support for the militia among Mississippi's scalawags after Ames made him a colonel in the militia. In the end, however, Knight's prospective regiment folded for lack of recruits. It was all in vain, Ames realized, "owing to the universal protestations of all Republicans. . . . I have not been able to find even *one* [white] man to co-operate with me." With no other alternative, the governor sought to establish a Black state militia.[64]

Public response to Ames's decision can well be imagined. The idea of arming Black men horrified white residents and confirmed their fears of a Republican-fomented race war. Hostile newspapers charged the governor with harboring Napoleonic ambitions; why else was he allegedly acquiring massive quantities of arms and munitions from the US Army to enact martial law? In reality, Ames's militia was from the beginning understaffed, poorly armed, and poorly supplied. A mere $55,000 in outlays produced only two trained and outfitted companies. This paltry force could never match the numbers, firepower, or veteran leadership of the White Leagues and Red Shirts, most of whom had years of wartime experience in the Confederate army.[65]

Perhaps Ames realized this, for when anti-Reconstruction forces took up arms, he pulled back the militia. One aborted autumn supply mission highlights the militia's troubles. On October 9 a Black militia company commanded by Republican state senator Charles Caldwell set out from Jackson toward Edwards, a small town west of the capital. Caldwell's assignment was to deliver firearms to an unarmed militia company, a task that might have been done quicker and easier by rail except that Ames feared that white paramilitary organizations would hold up the trains. By prioritizing the safety of the cargo, however, he put the safety of Caldwell's men in jeopardy; their cross-country trek was deliberately provocative in the eyes of white residents in Hinds County. Local Democrats vowed to kidnap and lynch Ames if Caldwell's men passed through; even Lamar issued a few threats against the governor. Over a thousand white men prepared to annihilate Caldwell's company. Realizing the seriousness of the situation, Ames hastily recalled the men. "A revolution has taken place," he told Blanche bitterly, "by force of arms—and a race are disfranchised. . . . [I]t is too late." It appeared as if Ames's quest for equal rights and a new age in Mississippi had died.[66]

If there was a silver lining to this dark cloud, it was that the recall preserved a tentative peace, opening the way for talks between Ames and his opponents. Pierrepont's friend George K. Chase arrived in Jackson as an informal mediator, although he insulted Ames by regarding the rebellious Redeemers as a legitimate party in opposition.[67] After some consultation, Chase called a meeting at the executive mansion for the middle of October with Ames and inviting James Z. George and Ethelbert Barksdale, editor of the pro-Redeemer *Daily Clarion*.[68]

The governor went into the meeting with crushed spirits. He had been noticeably despondent since the summer and especially once Blanche and the children returned to New England to avoid the heat. Now Grant had abandoned him. Seeking to distract himself, Ames went into a shell. He read memoirs and law books, thought about inventions and patents (such as one for a clothes cleaner designed by Blanche), and considered various ways to improve the family business in Minnesota. He increasingly ignored politics and was not even willing to arbitrate disputes between Republican factions. More alarmingly to Blanche, he told her he would not run for the Senate again. She was still willing to fight on and tried to stimulate her husband's latent ambitions. Ames must not, she counseled, "allow your present unpleasant life to so far influence your decision that there may be danger that in the future when you have forgotten the discomforts you may regret it."[69] Increasingly, however, her advice on this matter had little effect. Ames had had enough.

Depression might explain why Ames did little more than show up to meet Chase, George, and Barksdale. According to one attendee, the ordinarily talkative governor said little while his opponents spoke at great length. With an amazing level of decorum purposefully on display, both sides came to an agreement. Ames would send his militiamen home without disbanding their units and keep their weapons locked away at the local army post. George and the Democrats guaranteed that freedmen would be allowed to vote without molestation on November 3. Ames left the meeting convinced that he had gotten the best deal possible under the circumstances. He also believed—or somehow convinced himself that he believed—in the sincerity of the Democrats. Grant's refusal to send help left him no choice anyway. "But be that as it may," he later wrote, "all of my means to protect had been exhausted," for "the U. S. had substantially refused to aid us."[70]

Ironically, a fortnight later the federal government assured Ames that it would do its part after all to ensure fair elections. This was likely Chase's doing. Having remained behind in Mississippi after the "peace" meeting, he had seen the chaos in the state firsthand. Every day refugees flooded into Jackson seeking shelter from bands of white men threatening to kill them. Those citizens who did not flee their homes wrote numerous letters about the violence the witnessed. Slowly the scales fell from Chase's conservative eyes, and he not only befriended Ames but also frankly informed Pierrepont that unless the Redeemers were forcibly constrained, there would never be fair elections in Mississippi. With the attorney general now lukewarmly supportive of intervention, the Grant administration shifted course and permitted Augur to place his troops at Ames's disposal. Yet now despondent, Ames turned down the offer. A Republican defeat the following month was inevitable, in his view; all that was left was the crying. "The election ceases to have any interest for us," Ames wrote Blanche. "It is lost. Gone forever."[71]

On the surface, at least, the elections proceeded peacefully as Ames's opponents had sworn. Democratic coordination kept overt violence down to a dull roar. Other than an incident in Lowndes County on November 1, in which White Liners killed four and wounded three, white Mississippians did their best to avert outright bloodshed. Yet behind the scenes, there was plenty of electoral skullduggery. Sometimes Democrats verbally intimidated Black voters to keep them at home and away from the polls. At other times party operatives might bribe a Black man not only to vote Democratic but also to convince dozens of others to do likewise. Refusing to leave anything to chance, masked riders had aroused Black men from their beds on the evening of November 2, threatening to kill them if they dared voted Republican.[72]

The next day, while plenty of white voters cast ballots, few freedmen did. White Liner sentries, placed near roads and river fords, turned most of them back. To the desperate appeals of Black sheriffs, Ames had no good reply. With unchallenged control of the polling booths, Democrats won both houses in the Mississippi legislature and scored 30,000 more votes than Republicans statewide. Ames's sad postmortem to Blanche only stated the obvious. "So complete and thorough was the intimidation of Republican voters that we have yet to hear of the first county which has gone Republican. . . . The legislature will be nearly unanimous in both branches and will be able to do anything it may incline to do. The election has been a farce—worse than a farce."[73]

A GOVERNOR AND RECONSTRUCTION ON TRIAL

Redeemers argued that Mississippi's 1875 election was above reproach. "The election passed off very peaceably," the editor of the *Star of Pascagoula* in Jackson County claimed, "no disturbance reported at any point." The *Greenville Times* concurred, adding, "And we find that not one planter, or merchant failed to attend the polls and do his whole duty! It was this spirit, this resolution to win which has enlisted all the energies of our people during the past month that has achieved this signal victory." The *Times* also declared, "there was no intimidation practiced on election day." The *Weekly Clarion*, meanwhile, thanked Ames for keeping his end of the bargain with James Z. George. The paper's editors hoped that the governor would join Democratic Redeemers "in achieving the reforms to which the triumphant party in the last contest stands pledged."[1]

In contrast to the efficacious Redeemers in the Democratic Party, Ames and his administration faced stormy prospects after a pessimistic 1875. The governor himself received scathing criticism within his own party after the defeat. Former senator Revels and other Mississippi Republicans of both races scourged him. Revels wrote a letter to President Grant on November 6 that leaked to the press and was printed across the nation. He claimed that Ames had not adhered to Republican principles, so the defeat rested on his shoulders. Republican Henry R. Pease, the Connecticut-born former superintendent of education who took Ames's place in the US Senate in 1874, agreed that the governor and his backers were at fault. He did not dismiss Democratic voter intimidation as a factor, noting "armed bands" marching through communities and "frightening the negros," but he still argued that Ames had bungled the entire situation by demanding federal interference and not working with moderates to mollify angry Mississippians.[2]

Ames mulled resignation after the devastating 1875 results and the firestorm of criticism that followed, but he received a boost when his wife and children returned to Jackson on December 8. Blanche was pleased to find the house in good condition and her husband looking healthy. She was, however, keenly aware that the governor's political future seemed grim. "The Democrats are determined to get rid of Gen'l Ames and if they should not succeed in impeaching him, they would not hesitate to assassinate," she justifiably feared.[3] Not only had the Redeemers openly discussed hanging Ames, but someone also had fired a shot at the mansion the past summer, leaving bullet holes on the outside. On election night a servant reportedly claimed hearing men outside of the mansion discussing whether to storm the house and kill the governor.[4]

Physical harm, however, seemed less probable than political harm. The media fanned impeachment rumors, which intensified weekly. President Johnson was impeached for "upholding the constitution and laws," the *Weekly Clarion* proclaimed in December. "If Ames is impeached, it will be for trampling them underfoot." A few weeks later Ethelbert Barksdale, a Democrat, former Confederate congressman, and brother of a Confederate general killed at Gettysburg, openly advocated removing Ames. His Jackson newspaper announced on January 4, 1876, that the "Legislature should rigidly investigate the charges [of abuse of power and malfeasance] against Ames and if guilty of the crimes charged against him, and we believe he is, he should be indicted, tried, convicted, and removed from the high place he now disgraces."[5]

Republican newspapers countered that the scheme was entirely political. The *New Orleans Republican* observed, "no sooner does the Mississippi Democracy find itself in power than it threatens to impeach Ames." The paper added that Republicans abhorred Democratic governor Samuel J. Tilden in New York, but the Republican-controlled legislature would never advocate removing a properly elected official only because they did not like him. "Such is the difference between a party which is sustained by principle and one whose sole object is salary grabbing."[6]

By January 1876, the probability of impeachment had increased, but an unexpected side effect of all this talk was a rejuvenated Ames. For the first time in months, his competitive and obdurate personality resurfaced. The speculation of impeachment made him more resolute and more willing to confront Redeemers and prove that their charges against him had no merit.

His pride was hurt, his legacy was spiraling, and he was not going to give in harmoniously. According to Blanche, the governor told her he would not "mince matters" and would not cower in the face of a hostile political fracas.[7]

Ames was thus combative when he addressed the new state legislature on January 5, 1876. He boldly declared the assembly illegitimate and chided the representatives. "A free people should resort to every *legitimate* means to maintain, for their government, peace and order; and for themselves, personal security and liberty," he declared to an elected body full of political adversaries. "Unless every class of citizens be thoroughly protected in the exercise of all their rights and privileges," Ames warned, "our government proves unequal to its pretensions."[8] He lauded Mississippi's improving financial condition and showed no interest in acquiescing to a legislature elected through fraud and violence.[9]

While the governor railed against his foes in Jackson, Butler met with Grant in Washington to discuss the possibility of impeachment. The president told him that he would support Butler's son-in-law no matter what happened. In a letter to Ames, Butler reiterated that "he [Grant] has faith in you and in your attempt to do the best you can." Simultaneously, a former colleague in the Senate, wartime Indiana governor Oliver P. Morton, introduced a bill proposing a federal investigation into Democratic organizers in Mississippi during the 1875 election. He hoped that the inquiry could bring to light what was happening in the state. Although Democrats genuinely wanted to remove Ames from office, they now had to do so with careful calculation, since Ames had powerful national allies and was not willing to go quietly. L. Q. C. Lamar proved invaluable for Redeemers' efforts at this juncture. He openly lied to Butler and Republican leaders that he was doing his utmost to stop Ames's impeachment, going so far as to recommend lawyers who could help the governor. In reality, however, he wanted him gone. Lamar's brilliantly duplicitous political interference gave Democrats in the legislature more time and latitude to find fraud and corruption in Ames's administration.[10]

Violence continued throughout the state in the meantime, heightening the political stakes. Some Republican officials went into hiding for fear of reprisal, while others were even less fortunate. Just before the new year, Charles Caldwell, a formerly enslaved blacksmith who had commanded militia troops for Ames and served in the state senate, was drinking with a white friend in the basement of a store in Clinton. A white assailant fired one shot into the back of Caldwell, who died later that day. When his brother Sam rode into town to discover what happened, a gunman killed him too. Small acts of violence

Lucius Q. C. Lamar
(Library of Congress)

such as these later blossomed into community quarrels across the state in the winter of 1876–77. In the town of Rolling Fork, white riders forced six Black men from their homes and killed them in a cotton field.[11]

Back in Jackson in January 1876, a five-person impeachment committee, consisting of four Democrats and one Republican, began to question witnesses. In the wake of postelection unrest and violence, the panel managed to engineer twenty-one articles of impeachment by February 22. The investigation took a total of thirty-eight days and involved forty-five witnesses—twenty-six were Republicans. With loquacious prose, the *Canton Mail* observed, "The mills of God's grind slow, but they grind exceeding fine." The potential impeachment of the "deceitful" Ames, the editors continued, was evidence of the widespread corruption and dishonesty that proliferated in the Republican Party. The *Weekly Clarion* similarly published a snippet from the *Chickasaw Messenger* anticipating the governor's impeachment. "Ames expects [it] and knows he deserves it," they said, "to which we say, amen."[12]

Governor Ames did indeed expect it, but he was not willing to go down without a fight. Forever convinced that Mississippi Democrats were devious and fraudulent, he concluded that they would "not hesitate to vote themselves into the possession" of the governorship by passing the impeachment proposal. It was, however, not as easy a task as some Redeemers—and even Republicans—initially thought. The inquiry was tedious and took longer than projected because evidence was difficult to come by. Nevertheless, the committee managers, led by Tennessee-born representative and "chief manager" Winfield S. Featherston, presented their resolution and recommended impeachment in a succinct six pages.[13]

The charges leveled against Ames spread across a wide spectrum of alleged malfeasance. Of the twenty-one items, nine of them related to his questionable judicial appointments. Ames's connection to Reconstruction judicial activities angered Democrats immensely, and the articles expressed that rage. Three subsequent charges pertained to alleged corruption within the state treasurer's office that Democrats alleged was the governor's doing. Two additional articles contended that Ames had defrauded state finances for political gain. The most inflammatory charges, however, pertained to his culpability in the violence that had afflicted the state during the previous two years. Multiple articles stated that Ames bore responsibility for the bloodshed between white and Black citizens and purposefully intended to "stir up strife" for the sake of partisan and personal gain.[14]

The lone Republican on the five-member committee, Frederick Parsons, disagreed with the Democratic majority. He argued in a lengthy minority report that "the Governor did not do anything except what the Constitution and the laws of the State, and his own oath of office, required him to do." Parsons added that for at least three hours a day for six weeks, he and his fellow committee members had investigated Ames's record. Insinuating that his Democratic colleagues were desperate to dig up dirt, Parsons stated that they resorted to investigating Ames's conduct before he was even governor to try to find transgression. Even with Ames's entire public career in Mississippi under scrutiny, Parsons contended that no actual evidence for criminal action was apparent. "Much of this [evidence] will be found to be irrelevant—nearly all of it hearsay—and none of it proof of guilt of any treason, bribery or high crimes or misdemeanors," he asserted. Ames and his advocates felt optimistic following Parsons's minority report. Blanche, writing to her mother, stated, "The indications now are that the Democrats are doubtful about impeaching." She was woefully incorrect. Seventy-one members of the House of Representatives voted "yea" on the measure to begin proceedings, with only eight in the negative and thirty-seven absent and not voting. The impeachment trial of Adelbert Ames would begin on March 16, 1876.[15]

Local newspapers dedicated immense swaths of each issue to the story, but the *Daily Clarion* did the lion's share of the work. It published articles from northern newspapers, highlighting what outsiders said about the Ames impeachment. More often than not, the only snippets offered came from Democratic newspapers. According to the *New York World*, which was a leading voice for the national Democratic Party, "the evidence is amply sufficient to warrant his [Ames's] impeachment." That article went on to put the blame of the violence on Ames's shoulders, insisting that the bloodshed that took place in Vicksburg in 1874 was worthy enough "to send him to the jail or the gallows." It continued, "The jig appears to be up with Mr. Ames, of Mississippi, and it will take all the eloquence of his distinguished father-in-law, General Butler, to save him from the something that to his kind is more terrible than disgrace."[16]

Not all papers in Mississippi printed anti-Ames editorials, however. The *Jackson Times*, a conservative Republican newspaper that often opposed the governor's policies, nonetheless defended him:

> The charges are trivial in the extreme. The political leaders who make themselves responsible for this foolishness, would, in any Northern State be hooted from public life. It is gravely proposed that Governor Ames shall be impeached for not appointing certain men to office, and for appointing others and for sustaining the legal authority of Warren county [Vicksburg] in a crisis that called for all the help every good citizen could afford. These are what the White Leaguers of Mississippi call "high crimes." Could anything be more preposterous.[17]

With the press already primed and enemies in both parties ready to pounce, the impeachment trial commenced at noon on Thursday, March 16. All other legislative and executive business ceased "for the purpose of proceeding to business connected with the impeachment of the Governor."[18] Chief Justice of the Mississippi Supreme Court E. G. Peyton could not preside over the proceedings as planned, however, due to poor health. Replacing him was Associate Justice Horatio F. Simrall, formerly a Kentucky Confederate. The associate justice took oaths from the senators, then the secretary called roll. The trial began.

Simrall promptly ordered Sergeant-at-Arms James W. Langley to issue a "writ of summons" and call forth Ames, but the governor was not in attendance. In his place was a legal team that would try to stop what seemed an almost guaranteed conviction. For his defense team, Ames—assisted by and with the recommendation of Ben Butler—had hired two prominent attorneys, Thomas J. Durant and Roger Atkinson Pryor, Butler's law partner.[19] Durant, a distinguished lawyer originally from Philadelphia, had once been the president of the New Orleans bar. Pryor was a southerner, former Confederate general, and loyal Democrat who had moved to New York City after the Civil War; Ames and Pryor had served in the same theater of conflict during the war. Pryor and Durant were experienced and knew the daunting odds they faced. In a March letter, Blanche noted that Durant thought that the result of the trial would almost inevitably be Governor Ames's removal from office. Still, Durant and Pryor as well as Durant's assistant, Michael A. Clancey, tried to stifle the Redeemers' efforts.[20]

During that first morning in the Mississippi Senate Chamber, Durant addressed the senators and Justice Simrall, informing them that the governor would not be attending. "I am here as counsel of his Excellency, the Governor," said Durant, "and have his authority to enter his appearance in answer to the summons to him from this Court."[21] In addition to producing a signed document from Ames stating that his attorneys had his permission to represent the respondent, Durant also requested that the court provide more time for Ames to file his answer to the Articles of Impeachment.[22] The senate put a substitute order to a vote, which provided Ames's legal team until Wednesday, March 22, to reappear before them. It barely passed. Sixteen senators supported the measure, but thirteen voted nay, while eight senators were absent and not voting.

While the legislature waited for Ames's answers, it turned to ridding itself of other Republicans. The governor's impeachment was the most important legal proceedings taking place in Mississippi—if not the nation—in the spring of 1876, but he was not the only public figure on trial. Lieutenant Governor Davis and Superintendent of Public Education Cardozo, both African Americans, also faced removal from office. In contrast to Ames, there was less of a partisan defense for either man. The Mississippi House of Representatives adopted five impeachment articles against Davis on February 17. Each charge contended that he "unlawfully, corruptly, and feloniously" received bribes on multiple occasions in June and July 1874.[23] One of the bribes came after he issued a pardon for Thomas H. Barrentine, a man who murdered a woman on August 25, 1874. The evidence of Davis exchanging pardons for money was damning. After taking testimony for eleven days, the Senate voted 25 to 4 to impeach Davis and remove him from office on March 23, 1876. Ironically, in doing so they drove away one of Ames's leading critics within his own party.[24]

Cardozo, meanwhile, faced twelve impeachment articles because of well-documented illicit activities. The legislature charged him with embezzlement, misappropriating money, and taking government funds and investing them into private business ventures.[25] Democrats and Republicans both thought he was corrupt. Five days into his trial, Cardozo addressed the state house of representatives. He asked permission to "resign from office of State Superintendent of Public Education of Mississippi and that the said proceedings against me be dismissed with the consent of the senate."[26] The legislature accepted his resignation on March 22, 1876. The greatest sin of both Davis and Cardozo was the color of their skin, but their alleged malfeasance offered the veneer of legitimacy to a kangaroo court wanting to sweep away the Republican administration.

Ames's defense team returned to the Senate Chamber the same day that Cardozo resigned and a day before Davis would leave office. The abdication of Cardozo and the conviction of Davis gave added traction to the case against Ames. Although the charges he faced drew scrutiny due to their legal fragility, the legislature had shown that corruption within his administration existed. Democrats also had the numbers in the senate to easily impeach the governor, but now they could frame their efforts as being concerned about fixing statewide corruption rather than removing Republicans from power, stopping Reconstruction, and maintaining the racial hierarchy they sought to protect.

On March 22 the proceedings resumed. Five senators previously absent were sworn in and then the floor was given to Durant to address the impeachment articles. For every charge, he argued that Ames did not do anything with malicious intent or abuse the power of his office. Most importantly, the accusations merely emphasized that Reconstruction angered Redeemers and they wanted to stop it.[27]

Article I charged Ames with not fulfilling his duties by not removing the supposedly corrupt sheriff and tax collector of Noxubee County, W. M. Conner. It alleged that Conner did not file monthly reports or make payments from his collection of local taxes. Included was a letter from Noxubee County treasurer Joshua Stevens dated August 3, 1875, in which he alerted Ames of Conner's wrongdoing. Stevens wrote, "I, therefore, do hereby make known the said default to your Excellency for such action as to your Excellency may seem meet and right, and in accordance with the law ought to be done."[28]

The article stressed that Ames was guilty of refusing to suspend Conner, which was a violation of his oath of office. Yet as documented in the minority report from Parsons, Ames was innocent. Parsons noted that Conner and the Board of Supervisors of Noxubee Country were embroiled in a heated dispute. The supervisors, he noted, disregarded "certain claims" that Conner made regarding his accounts, which led to divisiveness.[29] Parsons further revealed that this political infighting encouraged Stevens to write his letter to Ames, which the senate was now using to try to paint the governor as irresponsible. Ames had supposedly directed the letter to the state auditor, who told Stevens that the governor would "take action" if the corruption was in fact real. A grand jury, with a majority of Democrats, then failed to indict Conner, who was a Republican. If Ames had in fact removed the tax-collecting sheriff, he would have harmed an innocent man. Considering an attempt was also made to unseat Conner's position as sheriff, this was clearly political jockeying at the local level and not a corrupt governor trying to keep another dishonest Republican in power.[30]

As he addressed the Senate, Durant concluded that Ames had done nothing wrong and acted "to the best of his knowledge and ability." The charge involving Sheriff Conner was innocuous compared to the later ones Durant addressed, however. This was, at most, a misdemeanor offense if one had been committed. Nevertheless, the greatest inference from Article I was that it revealed the extent to which the Mississippi legislature was willing to go to find wrongdoing.[31]

Ames's lawyers easily debunked the second article as well. The committee claimed that in January and February 1876, Ames made partisan appointments of two justices and two constables. The charge asserted that the governor made these choices for the purpose of degrading the sovereignty of the state. Durant showed, however, that Governor Ames had proper authority "existing in the Constitution and the Code of Mississippi" and did not break any laws of the state, thus this charge of "degrading the sovereignty of the state" was too nebulous to be substantive.[32]

The next two articles alleged that Ames had defrauded the state treasury. The house managers claimed that the governor knowingly permitted an $80,000 bond on February 19, 1875, even though its sureties were questionable. The charge further contended that he approved the bond only because of corrupt and partisan reasons. Ames remained resolute in the fact that he was told that "sureties on said bond were good," the Treasury Department had resolved the issue for the state, and the bond did not suffer any defalcation or loss of capital.[33]

The legislature included a letter form Attorney General G. E. Harris to Ames dated August 28, 1875. In it he claimed that "duty impels me" to inform the governor that the bond was insufficient and not "in due form of the law."[34] To the Democrats in the house, Ames had been negligent and prejudiced. Durant, however, quickly showed that the governor not only received the letter but also relayed the information to the Treasurer's Office, as was his duty. Secretary M. L. Holland was not there at the time, but the administration informed deputy John B. Raymond of the situation. Furthermore, Durant argued, the legislature failed to prove that the state had lost any money and that there was any unresolved financial matter regarding the bond.[35]

When Durant arrived at Article V, he had to address for the first time a charge regarding Ames's conduct during the Vicksburg Troubles in 1874. The accusations focused on the governor removing Warren County sheriff A. J. Flanagan using federal troops. Durant challenged the basis of the charge, asserting that Flanagan was not legally sheriff. Peter Crosby held that office, and the illegal voting and voter intimidation that took place in Warren County necessitated Flanagan's removal and Crosby's restoration. Ames was well within his right as governor to protect citizens and restore order by any means necessary, Durant argued.[36]

The managers claimed that the governor had conspired to take advantage of Mississippi's penal-labor program in Articles VI and VII. Ames, according to the charge, did "knowingly connive" to defraud the state of $33,750 when he leased convicts to Republican ally O. C. French without ensuring that the state would receive compensation for feeding or clothing the convicts as well as not allowing open bidding for the prisoners' labor.[37] Convict leasing began when the legislature passed a law in 1872 authorizing the practice. Ames did not deny that he had allowed low-cost leasing but maintained that the allegation he had defrauded the state was severely lacking in both evidence and testimony. Durant noted that inspectors of the local penitentiaries attested that French's contract was by far the best in terms of fiscal responsibility and the well-being of the incarcerated persons.[38] Ames gained no political or financial benefit from the convict-leasing system, which was the core of the Democratic charge.

When Ames's legal team worked their way through to Article VIII, they justified their credentials. The article alleged that the governor "connived" to have Hiram Cassidy Jr., the incumbent chancellor of the Nineteenth District of Mississippi, and J. B. Deason, the lawful incumbent district attorney of the Second Judicial District in Mississippi, swap their seats. This was portrayed in the article as reprehensible malfeasance. Durant noted that both men desired the other's position, were qualified to handle the opposite office, and that Ames had the power to accept resignations and make appointments. The Mississippi Senate, moreover, had unanimously backed this action in April 1875 and found no illegality. Primarily, this move did not garner Ames any political power or wealth, and there was no indication that he initiated the swap. His legal team powerfully argued that the Democratic Party was perfectly fine with Ames's actions at the time, but now they would exploit past deeds for political gain and warp the narrative to fit their agenda.[39]

Most of the articles that Durant addressed that day, however, related to Ames's handling of the judiciary. Articles IX through XV alleged that Ames made judicial and chancellorship nominations while the senate was on vacation and without their approval, "subverting the said constitution and laws, by defeating the selection of [an] enlightened, upright, and pure Judiciary."[40] Listing thirteen specific instances of the governor refusing to nominate justices during sessions of the senate, the charges depicted each appointment as an affront to the state. While the charge was lengthy, Durant noted that each justice was an incumbent, and Ames reappointed judges already approved by senators. Moreover, since the terms for these judges had expired after the senate had adjourned, he only reaffirmed them so the seats would not be vacant. Once again Durant argued that Ames's actions were not driven by partisanship or a thirst for power but were simply actions that any responsible governor would take. While they may not have been wise decisions, Ames had not broken any laws.[41]

Another particularly explosive charge involved Ames's removal from office of W. A. Drennan, chancellor of the Twelfth Chancery District. While the House Impeachment Committee claimed this again represented the governor wanting to exude control, Durant argued that Drennan was an incompetent chancellor and unable to lawfully oversee the responsibilities of his office, hence his removal.[42] Article XIII, which likewise specified the removal of Thomas Christian from office, followed a similar pattern. Christian became a justice when Lieutenant Governor Davis appointed him in Ames's absence. The charges implied that Ames removed Christian because he was not falling into line with the governor's intentions.[43] Thus, Ames had abused his power, the house argued. The governor had the legal authority to revoke Christian's selection, Durant countered.[44] The defense team reiterated the same argument for Article XIV, the last one pertaining to the judiciary. It asserted that Ames had appointed a total of six "notoriously incompetent, immoral, and dishonest" chancellors on June 6, 1874; February 5, 1875; and May 23, 1875.[45] Durant stated that the respondent not only possessed the authority to appoint anyone he wanted but also appointed these justices with the approval of practicing members of the Mississippi bar. No sound evidence was presented that showed the chancellors unable to make sound rulings or that they were corrupt.

Statistical data helped defeat the Democrats' claims that Ames was manipulating Mississippi's courts to get rulings he wanted. As noted in the minority report of Representative Parsons, the highest state courts under Ames reversed the decisions of 20 percent of appeals. In contrast, during Governor Alcorn's term, the courts reversed 33 percent of those appealed. Data provided under oath by Supreme Court clerk A. W. Little indicated that the judiciary before the Civil War had a reversal rate of 36 percent.[46] Using this data as a barometer, the records demonstrated that the courts during Ames's governorship actually were more willing to respect the initial verdicts of juries than previous administrations. Moreover, his defense showed that when Ames removed officials, it was well within the legal constraints of Mississippi law and that his actions did not weaken the state's courts or give himself extralegal influence over the judicial structure.

Articles XVI and XVII were particularly inflammatory—Ames purposely fueled racial tensions for political advantage—and shed light into the racial attitudes of the Democrats in the legislature. In short, the charges depicted Ames as a cruel manipulator sponsoring bloodletting. These two articles used potentially misleading quotes from the governor to prove that he was trying to bring forth the greatest fear of southerners—a race war. Claiming that Ames was abusing his power, the house in Article XVI insisted that he had tried to provoke "a conflict of arms between the two races of citizens of the state" on October 10, 1875, in Hinds County.[47] Durant, detailing Ames's version of events, noted that the militia—primarily comprising freedmen—were only called into service to escort a wagon of weapons to a depot, during which no bloodshed occurred.[48] It was never a ruse by Ames to intimidate whites with armed African Americans. The more egregious action, the house alleged in Article XVII, came when the governor intended to incite conflict between races in Vicksburg on December 3, 1875. Carnage did ensue then and resulted in casualties on both sides after several days of mob violence.[49] Trying to pin these deaths on Ames, the house alleged that provocative quotations from Ames—"that very likely fifteen or twenty Negroes may be killed, but that it would result to the benefit of the Republican party," and "what if it does cost blood, the blood of the martyr is the seed of the church," among others—impelled the killings. Durant replied that his client may well have uttered such statements before Black citizens and Warren County sheriff Peter Crosby, but they were taken out of context and during the course of lengthy discussion with multiple people.[50]

Three days later, on Saturday, March 25, the senate convened again. Unsurprisingly, Democrats rejected the legitimacy of each averment the lawyers produced. They reaffirmed their charges against Ames and refused to dismiss them. Not only did the representatives on the impeachment committee resolutely defend the validity of the charges, but they also informed senators "that it is expected that the House will, on Monday, next exhibit additional Articles of Impeachment against the Governor of the State."[51]

On the fifth day of the trial, March 27, at 10:30 A.M. the chambers opened, and the senate accepted two additional articles. Representative Featherston, along with four other members of the house, took their assigned seats in the senate to await the reading of the resolution that added two new articles of impeachment. Durant arrived in the chamber and introduced to the court Pryor, who had finally arrived in Mississippi to complete the governor's legal representation. Ames's father-in-law was slightly more optimistic now that Pryor had arrived. Butler believed that his law partner would complement Durant nicely and could, he suggested, offer the closing remarks. After the last session's proceedings were read and approved, "the following resolution, adopted by the Senate, was ordered to be read before the Court of Impeachment, to-wit," that both inflammatory articles delivered that day pertained to suspected malfeasance on the part of Ames that took place within the past thirty days.[52]

The new Articles XXII and XXIII stated that the governor feloniously pardoned Alexander Smith on March 11 after Smith had received a prison sentence for sexually assaulting a child under the age of ten.[53] They alleged that Ames abused his power to pardon criminals and that Smith had paid a bribe of $3,000 to gain his freedom. These new charges tried to capitalize on the shocking and repulsive nature of the supposed crime; Ames callously allowed a child molester to go free for money, ignoring the ruling of the Chickasaw County Circuit Court, thus demonstrating his disregard for law and decency. Unlike all of the proceeding articles of impeachment, the state house of representatives did not produce any witnesses, affidavits, or noncircumstantial evidence of any kind. Their introduction signified more so than any previous charge that the senate was going to remove Ames and crush his administration by any means necessary, regardless of how righteous the governor's legal team tried to depict their client. Although emotionally invested in the outcome of her husband's impeachment, Blanche Ames understood the inevitable outcome: "If they [the Mississippi senators] are determined to get rid of him [Ames], in spite of law and justice, of course they have the votes, and can do it."[54]

Faced with new allegations, Durant sought and received a postponement, gaining two days to address the added articles. With preparation for rebuttal under way, he and Pryor then received an unexpected official message from the executive mansion on March 28, a day before they would reappear in front of the Senate. Ames, who according to his wife was in poor health, had had enough. Referencing the disastrous 1875 election, he admitted being "embarrassed and baffled" as to how to govern the state and ensure its welfare with such a hostile, anti-Reconstruction legislature. Ames noted that he already had contemplated resignation after the election, but the impeachment articles that portrayed him as a corrupt tyrant had prevented him from doing so. "I could not, and would not retire from my position, under the imputation of any charge affecting my honor and integrity," he wrote Durant and Pryor.[55] Ames, however, informed his legal team that if the legislature dropped those charges now, he would be comfortable with resigning, which would give his adversaries what they wanted while also preserving his record and respectability. Blanche agreed and encouraged a compromise during her frequent audiences with her husband's legal team, since Durant, Pryor, and Clancey frequented their home for dinner; Durant was fond of the family's sponge cake recipe, and both he and Clancey offered homespun remedies for the head colds the children had that winter.[56]

In a less hospitable environment than the Ames's home, at 10:30 A.M. on Wednesday, March 29, Durant, Pryor, and Clancey faced the Mississippi Senate once more. The sixth day of the trial commenced with the adoption and approval of the previous session and minor parliamentary deliberation. When the court gave Durant the floor to address the two additional articles, he tersely rejected any alleged wrongdoing against his client and wasted little time reviewing their accusations. Reiterating that Ames was not guilty of taking a bribe to pardon a child rapist, the team concluded their concise defense by saying that the governor believed the senate should acquit him of these baseless, flimsy charges.

Afterward, senators, at the behest of the house of representatives, requested a recess until 3 P.M. to evaluate all twenty-three articles. With only one vote against the measure, "the motion was agreed to, and the Court thereupon took a recess till the time stated in said motion." During this time, Ames's defense team relayed the governor's wishes to leave office. When the senate reconvened, Associate Justice Simrall asked, "Have the Managers anything to present to the Senate?" Representative Featherstone addressed the body and stated that the managers of the impeachment committee were aware of Ames's interest to resign from office if the legislature dropped all charges. Guaranteed by his lawyers that the governor would uphold his intentions, Featherstone declared, "Be it resolved by the House of Representatives of the State of Mississippi, that the Managers on the part of the House, in the matter of the impeachment of Adelbert Ames, Governor of said State, be and they are hereby directed to dismiss the said Articles against the said Adelbert Ames." The house voted to dismiss the charges, and the senate subsequently concurred. That afternoon Ames submitted his brief resignation letter: "*To the People of the State of Mississippi*, I hereby respectfully resign my office of Governor of the State of Mississippi."[57]

The impeachment trial, with all its drama, thus ended abruptly. The Redeemers had won; Reconstruction in Mississippi was essentially over. Ames, the symbol of the Republican Party was out of office. The *Greenville Times* declared, "There can be no difference of opinion as to this event marking and constituting the successful, happy and glorious termination of our long struggle with Radicalism."[58]

Some people reacted with sadness. The freedmen of Mississippi, the Republican Party's prominent voting base, had lost an advocate who wanted to ensure the rule of law in the state and preserve African American voting rights. Ames's father-in-law voiced displeasure, although primarily because he saw the resignation as a deterrent to any future political opportunities for his impetuous son-in-law. "I will not conceal from you," Butler stated, "that the matter strikes the public mind unfavorably."[59]

Leaving office made others very happy. Local newspapers continued to print news of Ames's demise with joy after his resignation. "Under all existing circumstances this is the best termination of his infamous and tyrannical career," the *Greenville Times* declared.[60] Democrats had regained control in Mississippi. Moderate Republicans, some of them African Americans, hoped that they could pursue their own interests now that the Mainer was jettisoned. Arguably the most joyous person, however, was Ames's wife. Blanche was supremely relieved that her husband would not have to deal with any more turmoil in Mississippi and that their family could leave the hot and inhospitable state. "I have never been contented with this country, and I hail with pleasure anything which will shorten our sojourn here," she wrote.[61]

Two days after Ames resigned from office, the US Senate agreed to investigate the 1875 state elections in Mississippi. The purpose was to uncover "violence exercised toward the colored citizens of that state and the white citizens disposed to support their rights."[62] Republican senator George S. Boutwell of

Massachusetts chaired the five-man committee. The other members included two Republicans from the Midwest, Wisconsin senator Angus Cameron and Minnesota's Samuel J. R. McMillan, and two Democrats, Indianan Joseph E. McDonald and Thomas F. Bayard of Delaware.[63]

From April 27 through July 27, the committee met and took testimony thirty-six times. For the first eleven days, Boutwell's committee met in Washington. From June 9 to June 27, the committee took testimonies in Jackson and Aberdeen, Mississippi. They concluded their investigation back in Washington in July. The Democratic senators opposed the acquisition of personal telegraph correspondence for evidence, however, the Republican majority overruled their complaint. Other than that issue, the members cooperatively accumulated over 1,000 pages of testimony and evidence. The first person the committee summoned for testimony was Ames on April 27.[64]

Ames did not expect to go to Washington at all that spring, but the season had brought more than its share of unpleasant surprises. Sarah Butler's health had declined, and her throat bothered her greatly. Benjamin Butler worried as to what was the matter. Fearing that she had downplayed how ill she actually was, he hoped that Ames, Blanche, and the children could come and visit her soon. On April 6 Butler took his wife to Massachusetts General Hospital in Boston. Doctors discovered a malignant lump in her throat and performed a thyrotomy, which did not succeed. Two days later she died at the age of fifty-eight. Ames and his family went to Lowell to mourn, and from there he left for Washington to deliver his testimony.[65]

For three days the former governor supplied sworn testimony about his public career in Mississippi. He recounted that he had served in that state for nearly ten years as military governor, senator, and governor. The questions emphasized events in 1875–76, but each senator asked him questions about disputes that predated 1875. Most importantly, the committee questioned Ames about the environment that led to the downfall of his administration and Republicans generally in Mississippi. His testimony spanned forty-two pages and stressed that "there were anticipations of trouble" in 1875 that eventually proved warranted.[66]

On his first day of testimony, Ames discussed the numerous riots in 1875. He also fielded questions about voter intimidation and President Grant's response to the violence. When Boutwell asked him to talk about the disorder in Hinds County, he recalled how Republican stump speakers and assemblies could not meet without harassment. Both sides blamed each other, but "be that as it may," Ames told the committee, "the effect of it was to intimidate the Republicans."[67]

Senator Cameron asked him to describe what kind of intimidation white residents used. Ames replied that he received letters describing their hatred and could share them if desired. "They [the freedmen] were threatened to be driven off the plantations; they were threatened with harm, with danger, if they [were] persistent in voting the Republican ticket." Ames told the committee that the intimidation forced many to abandon their homes, causing homelessness to spike in the state: "In some counties since the election, or on the night of the election, Republicans were driven away and have not dared to return or did not dare to return for about a month. That was the case in one county [Amite County], particularly."[68]

On April 28 Ames continued fielding questions about white intimidation, noting how White Liners ably suppressed Black voters. In Republican strongholds, Ames testified, white intimidation was so severe that Black Republicans could not meet. In Monroe County, for example, the sheriff claimed that mounted white men, brandishing weapons, scattered hundreds of Republican voters on Election Day. "The county was generally estimated to have 1,500 Republican majority," Ames told the senators, but the votes at the end of the day gave Democrats a 1,100-vote edge. In Yazoo County, he further testified, Republicans received only 7 votes when the county had a Republican majority of 2,000. Democratic senator McDonald asked if Democrats simply cast more ballots in 1875 than 1873. Ames replied that it was possible, but that did not explain the massive disparity.[69]

Boutwell on April 28 also questioned him about taxation, since the common charge was that he financially plundered the state. Ames denied it. "The usual complaint in the South has been that the State has been plundered; but this shows, and the facts shows, that the financial condition of the State of Mississippi is flourishing." From 1873 to 1875, Ames told the senators, state expenses dropped from $953,000 to $618,000. Regardless of what Democrats and newspaper reported, the state's auditor confirmed that the numbers were correct. Ames's testimony was consistent: he denied wrongdoing, his motives were pure as snow, violence and voter suppression were real, and the Democrats had won a crooked election.[70]

When Senator Bayard began his line of questioning, he resurrected the issue that had followed Ames for years—his residency. Bayard asked him fifty-three questions about the history of his time in Mississippi, which clearly agitated Ames. The senator also brought up the smear that Ames had orchestrated his election to the Senate. "I believe it is a fact that you certified yourself into the Senate?" asked Bayard. "No, sir," Ames replied, "I believe I was voted it." He asked if Ames was going to return to Mississippi. Hoping to pacify the senator, he replied disingenuously that he was not sure, but that he would need to go where he could earn a salary, noting that he felt "as much unsettled as any man possibly could."[71]

Bayard's pressing questions on the twenty-eighth clearly annoyed the witness. Disgraced and defensive, Ames prepared a statement to read during his final day of testimony on April 29. "I wish to say, as of course the purpose of these questions has a political bearing," he observed, "that all my adult life has been passed in Mississippi once I left the army." Maine was not his home anymore. He could go wherever he could, and he freely chose "with the same purpose and determination that any citizen of the United States" enjoyed to live in Mississippi as a resident. His intensions had been noble.[72]

Bayard was not satisfied. The bulk of the day consisted of the senator hammering Ames's worthiness as an officeholder again. He referenced the frequency with which Ames traveled outside of the state and his questionable decisions. "I cannot assume what your motive is," Ames replied, "but of course it has a political bearing, and I desire to say that that question of residence has nothing whatsoever to do with the troubles in the State of Mississippi."[73]

Bayard then transitioned to asking about interparty turmoil, which also stoked Ames's defensiveness. He admitted that there were some who disapproved of his tenure as governor but asserted that they were few. Most such Republicans, Ames added, were carpetbaggers who had lost their seats in Congress, men such as Pease and George C. McKee. Others, he claimed, were corrupt county officials he had removed from office, opposing him ever since. When Bayard presented an interview Pease gave in October 1875 that criticized the state of Mississippi, Ames countered by testifying that Pease "stated a number of falsehoods in that which he has retracted," adding that he had a letter in Jackson that could prove Pease's recantation.[74]

The rest of the questioning on April 29 changed course. Boutwell, Bayard, and McMillan asked if Ames thought the reporting in Mississippi was accurate. He said he believed every report about violence and suppression were credible and trusted the official reports from county sheriffs. The senators then asked a variety of questions about his call for federal aid, the number of ballots cast in 1873 and 1875, and how many newspapers in the state were pro-Republican. Ames answered all of their inquiries. At day's end the senators thanked him, and he left.[75]

Ames remained busy while he waited for Boutwell's conclusions. He enjoyed spending time Butler, providing company for his mourning father-in-law and who was also dealing with a spring cold. He remained in the capital until May, when he left for Northfield to discuss expanding the family's mill business with his parents and brother. Ames by then was not thinking about returning to Mississippi. Minnesota beckoned now. "There is much money in this business if conducted properly. Can I conduct it properly?" he wrote Blanche. His father was looking to retire, and Ames wanted to buy Captain Ames's shares as he considered relocating to the Midwest for good.[76]

In August Boutwell finalized the committee's findings. The report asserted that the allegation that Ames was unfit for office was not true. "The committee finds from the evidence, as well as from general reports in Mississippi, that Governor Ames was not only not amenable to any just charge affecting his personal integrity . . . but that his fitness in all these particulars was sustained by testimony of those who were not in accord with him politically." The senators concluded that Mississippi suffered from corrupt officials at the state and local level, but "the conduct of these persons . . . was not approved by the governor nor by the masses of the Republican Party." Ames represented "brave men from the North" who were "entirely incorruptible."[77]

The financial allegations against Ames were false as well, according to the committee's investigation. Furthermore, taxation in Mississippi, while higher than it was before the war, was still lower than many other states in the Union. The senators also debunked the argument that Ames looked to start a race war in the state. Thrashing the Redeemers' narratives, they cited an official document dated September 7, 1875, from Mississippi's secretary of state James Hill that showed that Ames wanted both white and Black men to serve in his militia and did not intend to promote civil unrest.[78]

Ultimately, the committee placed all of the blame on Democrats for the violence and voter intimidation in Mississippi. "Democratic clubs were organized in all parts of the State," the report stated, "and the able-bodied members were also organized generally into military companies."[79] When Boutwell addressed the infamous events in Vicksburg and Clinton, he again pointed to the Redeemers. Democrats had instigated the riots to "break up meetings of Republicans, to destroy the leaders, and to inaugurate an era of terror, not only in those counties, but throughout the state, which would deter Republicans, and particularly negroes, from organizing . . . [and] especially to deter them from the free exercise of the right to vote."[80]

The Senate report vindicated Ames's tenure in his own eyes and in the mind of his colleagues, but white Mississippians did not care about what it said. They were too busy basking in the glow of having "redeemed" their state.

The *American Citizen* opined, "With the resignation of Governor Ames, every obstacle to the harmonious working of the various departments of the State government is removed and the Democratic and Conservative party will be left free to carry out in good faith the pledges of reform on which it has already won its way to power."[81] Democratic state senator John Marshall Stone assumed the role of acting governor. A staunch opponent of Ames, Stone's ascension made whites jubilant. The *Daily Clarion* reported that 1,000 people formed a procession and celebrated by firing a 100-gun salute in Corinth. Other celebrations took place across the state in towns like Enterprise and Iuka.[82] The Democratic-run legislature began to implement its own policy changes to the glee of white residents. They took advantage of the economic crisis four years earlier, the political scandals in the Grant administration, and weakening support for Reconstruction in northern states to strengthen their political grip on the state.[83]

Mississippi was not the only southern state that threw off the proverbial shackles of Republican-led governments in 1876. Georgians wrested control from Republicans and gave the governorship to Democrat Alfred H. Colquitt. Angry white residents in South Carolina mimicked the same violent strategies implemented in Mississippi. They sought to nullify Black voter turnout, and race riots raged across the state. One riot in Charleston became especially vicious, as Black police officers indiscriminately fired their weapons while hundreds of white paramilitaries rallied and fought back. South Carolina eventually ousted its Republican governor in 1876, as did Louisiana, Alabama, North Carolina, and Florida. By November 1876, every state that once composed the Confederacy had displaced Republicans from power.[84]

The twenty-third presidential election, pitting the Republican Rutherford B. Hayes against the Democratic governor of New York, Samuel J. Tilden, did nothing to calm the political environment. Tilden received 184 electoral votes, and Hayes was only 19 votes behind him, with 20 electoral votes from Florida, Louisiana, South Carolina, and Oregon unawarded. Hayes ultimately gained all the remaining votes from a partisan congressional committee, at which the Democratic Party cried corruption. With an extraordinary constitutional crisis looming, a fifteen-person congressional election committee formed in January 1877 to decide what to do. In short, a settlement was reached. The infamous Compromise of 1877 resulted in Democrats reluctantly agreeing to Hayes winning the presidential election in exchange for all US troops withdrawing from southern states as well as other favors. The agreement was more or less ceremonial—barely 1,600 soldiers were still deployed in the region.

Nevertheless, southern states, literally and ceremonially, had garnered the local control that they desired.[85]

Reconstruction, whether radical or conservative in form, officially ceased to exist. In post-Reconstruction Mississippi, the Republican Party withered away, and fewer Black officials held office. In the following years Democrats worked to impede African American enfranchisement, their right to bear arms, and essentially barred them from the political system. The Mississippi that Ames wanted, a state with robust economic growth and legal equality, never manifested as he had hoped during his lifetime, or even for decades beyond.[86]

LIFE REFUSING TO SLOW

After the Boutwell Committee's report, Ames committed himself to a new life out of the public eye. While most veterans of the Civil War had already completed the process of demobilization, for Ames it was just beginning. With the exception of the yearlong sabbatical in Europe, he had worked almost incessantly n a high-stress environment for fifteen years, training soldiers, leading men in combat, serving in the postwar army, and representing Mississippi as a senator and a governor during what some modern scholars term the "long Civil War." Now only forty years old, he had to find a home for his family and figure out what he was to do with the rest of his life.

Looking for something productive to do after his dismissal from politics, Ames decided to throw himself into the Ames family's milling business. He again left his own family with the Butlers in Lowell and headed to Minnesota. Spending hours reviewing the affairs of the Northfield mill, Ames took over the bookkeeping responsibilities. He envisioned the business changing with the times and wanted to find ways to export flour to Europe. His father and brother appreciated his presence. Both John Ames and his wife had health issues that increasingly hampered their involvement in the mill, while Captain Ames preferred growing grapes.

While the mill was profitable, it was not immune to the economic downturn that began in 1873 and needed strong oversight if it was to prosper.[1] The demand for flour mills already had decreased by the time Ames relocated to Northfield. The Homestead Act in 1862 initially had encouraged farmers in Minnesota to stay put and commit themselves to growing wheat. Northfield's surrounding Dakota County became a titanic wheat-producing area. During the later years of the war, however, drought and hard freezes repeatedly crippled Minnesota crops. After that, high water and flooding from melting snow and torrential rain caused havoc into 1867. In conjunction with the turbulent weather, the soil in southeastern Minnesota increasingly became nutrient deficient, and farmers had no cheap way to replace the minerals lost to massive grain harvests. Some farmers moved away from the region. Those who remained decided to diversify their crops or invest in livestock, neither of which helped the Ames's business. Minnesota was far different from Mississippi, but the same environmental and economic issues that plagued southern states in the 1870s affected northern states as well.[2]

As Ames worked at his family's business in Minnesota, the violence of the Civil War and Reconstruction in Mississippi seemed far away. Yet on September 7, 1876, Confederate sympathies and bloodshed found Ames on the northern prairie. Formerly Rebel bushwhackers from Missouri, the notorious James-Younger Gang sought a lucrative heist in, of all places, Minnesota. The gang included Jesse James, his older brother Frank, and Cole, Jim, and Bob Younger, all of whom had fought for the Confederacy along the Kansas-Missouri border.[3] The gang's disdain for carpetbaggers and Yankees spurred their motives for postwar robbery as much as the financial windfall. Cole and Bob Younger both later claimed that the gang finally selected the First National Bank in Northfield because of persistent rumors that both Ames and Benjamin Butler—two prominent and hated Yankees—were stockholders. According to historians, harming Ames, a man who dared promote Black equality, invigorated Jesse James in particular. In truth, Butler had no connection to the bank located on Division Street, but Ames's account composed fully 25 percent of its assets. With $10,000 in greenbacks, the depository was an alluring target for robbers of any ideology.[4]

The gang planned accordingly. Members had been in Saint Paul, Minnesota, since August, supposedly playing poker and "seeing the sights" while actually looking for the right bank to rob. By early September, Cole, Jim, and Bob Younger; the James brothers; and three additional associates—Bill Chadwell (also known as Stiles), Clell Miller, and Charlie Pitts—traveled south to Northfield. The party bought new horses and scouted their target more closely on September 6. Although Cole Younger held reservations about the robbery, Bob Younger and Jesse James reportedly were adamant about following through, so the outlaws agreed to assemble outside of Northfield the following day.[5]

Four of them entered the town that morning to scout the streets. Unfortunately for them, they drew the attention of people who saw their lean, athletic physiques and "reckless, bold swagger" as out of place in the tranquil principality. After eating lunch in town, the gang members regrouped outside of Northfield to finalize their plans. They decided that three outlaws would trot into town first, followed by two more to stand guard outside the bank. The last three would stay near a bridge leading to the town square. Just before 2 P.M., the gang trotted past the mill as planned. Ames's morning that day had passed uneventfully. That afternoon he arrived at the flour mill shortly before the James-Younger Gang rode past.[6]

Accounts of the robbery on September 7 vary. The first three men into town, Cole Younger later recalled, were the James brothers and Charlie Pitts. Other reports named Bob Younger, Pitts, and Frank James. Regardless, three men went into the bank while two others stood directly outside. The other three perched on their steeds at the edge of town. Joseph Lee Heywood, a Union veteran and the assistant cashier, refused to cooperate when the bandits demanded he open the safe. One of the outlaws—possibly Jesse James—slit Heywood's throat and then cracked his skull with a pistol. Of the two tellers present, one managed to escape in the confusion as the robbers brutalized Heywood. While the three bushwhackers were still inside the bank, residents up and down Division Street realized that it was being robbed. They grabbed weapons and opened fire.[7]

Ames heard the familiar sound of gunfire just as a townsperson raced to the mill to tell him about the robbery. Unarmed, he dropped what he was doing and crossed the same bridge into Northfield that the gang had traversed minutes before. "I walked over and made my way across the square to the corner of a stone building occupied by Mr. Schiver," Ames recalled. "As I went I saw quite a number of citizens hiding behind houses and a few firing up the street." The entire town was frenzied, and "citizens were making it so warm on the outside for those [outlaws] on guard that they called lustily for those in the bank to come out."[9]

Ames joined the throng of residents attacking the outlaws. He first approached Anselm Manning, a forty-three-year-old hardware-store proprietor who was crouching behind an outdoor staircase and some crates on Division Street. They peered toward the bank and saw the three members of the gang mounted on horses near the bank, firing their sidearms, shouting obscenities, and spurring their comrades inside to move quickly. The first bandit to fall dead was Clell Miller. Firing from the lobby of the nearby Dampier Hotel, Henry

Division Street, Northfield, Minnesota, 1877 (Minnesota Digital History)

Wheeler was credited with the kill. Miller was reportedly struck by Wheeler's rifle rounds, but buckshot also tore into him. Manning raised his rife, his hands severely trembling. Ames, like an officer in battle, told him to stay steady and reassured him, helping the shopkeeper zero in on his target. Calmer, Manning fired and hit outlaw Bill Chadwell in the heart, knocking him from the saddle. A second blast from Manning killed Bob Younger's steed. Bob recovered and raced toward Manning and Ames with a pistol gripped tightly in his hand. According to Cole Younger, a shot rang out from a second-story window of a nearby hotel, shattering Bob's elbow. Instead of continuing his charge, Bob switched his pistol to his left hand, retreated, and leapt onto Clell's mare.[9]

At that moment the rest of the gang exited the bank, the community now raking them with gunfire. "They went out, joined their friends, and rode away," Ames wrote Blanche the next day. "But they left two of their number dead in the street"; Miller and Chadwell lay on Division Street. Every other outlaw, apart from Jesse James, suffered wounds that day. Two residents died, the cashier Heywood (whom Charlie Pitts supposedly shot in the head) and Swedish immigrant Nicholas Gustafson. "Poor Mr. Heywood, the murdered cashier, was taken from the bank to his wife." Ames recorded. "They were married about a year ago."[10]

Once the smoke had cleared, Ames and his brother assumed leadership. John Ames raced to the telegraph office to notify the authorities and spark a manhunt. It did not take long for local law enforcement to alert the countryside and offer a $1,000 reward for each assailant, dead or alive. Adelbert Ames saw to the bank, finding the other two cashiers alive and discovering that the outlaws stole practically nothing. The bodies of Chadwell and Miller remained on the street, saturated in pools of blood, "to be looked at by all the world. Men, women and children had their fill."[11]

After sending his telegram, John panicked when rumors reached town that the outlaws had gone to his home. Ames told his brother to calm down. It was unreasonable for a wounded band of former Rebels to do anything but ride from Northfield as fast as they could, he explained, with a posse preparing to chase after the gang. Any pursuit would not catch the experienced robbers, Ames believed, and he needed more hands to help bring order to the town. Nonetheless, roughly a dozen men tried to pursue the bandits. One posse member, Frank Wyman, only had "a little pistol of no earthly use," Ames remarked.[12]

It unsurprisingly took time for the town to calm down after the gunfight. The surrounding countryside flocked to Northfield to see the aftermath. Onlookers purchased an estimated 50,000 photographs of the two dead outlaws, each photographed in a propped-up position with stains of dried blood on their torsos. Ames had remained composed during the fight and afterward, proudly writing Blanche about how stoic his father had been. The old sea captain, Ames told her, was "just the coolest man at such a scene of excitement I ever saw." Although he too remained outwardly unruffled, Ames admitted that the bloodshed reminded him of the killings in Mississippi. "Is it not strange that Mississippi should come up here to visit me," he wrote. "The killing of Republicans by a set of Mississippi K. K. produces a similar state of sensation as the murdering of a number of men by Missouri cut-throats who are after plunder."[13]

When life returned to normal in Northfield and the harvest was in, Ames went to see his family in Lowell. Pressing needs at the mill required him to return weeks later. This time he brought Blanche and the children with him, and they stayed with Ames's parents during the winter. The elderly Ameses were lovely hosts, but a diphtheria scare also made that winter a fearful one. All three children became ill with the disease. Edith and Sarah managed to recover quickly, but five-year-old Butler developed complications. His eyes crossed, and pain in his neck and spine increased until the boy's parents took him to Saint Paul to see a specialist. It took six weeks for their son to recover.[14]

Once the winter thawed, Ames's business with the mill preoccupied his time. While he devoted himself to the family business, however, Ames kept an eye on the political scene and current events. After Hayes won the 1876 presidential election, Ames deemed the new president's cabinet distasteful and his conciliatory policies both anti-Republican and anti–civil rights. "He pretends political virtue in selecting bolding Republicans—he who comes in as he does—and I doubt not he will try to ignore the states in the South by which he attained his place—leaving his supporters to the tender mercies of the Ku Klux murderers." In October 1877 Ames dined with his former commanding officer O. O. Howard in Fargo, Dakota Territory. The former commissioner of the Freedman's Bureau and the former governor of Mississippi did not discuss the current state of their party. Instead, Howard described the recent struggle with Chief Joseph's Nez Perce people. Ames envied him that he was still in the military, describing his colleague's exploits, albeit questionable, in more detail than some of his own wartime experiences.[15]

With one major exception, the birth of the couple's fourth child on February 18, 1878, the next year proved relatively uneventful. The parents named their newborn daughter Blanche. Ames, apparently, did not share the news of her birth quickly enough for Benjamin Butler, who jokingly chided him, "Think of it, you ungrateful fellow, keeping me four days without the knowledge that I had another grandchild." Now with four children, Ames began to reassess his commitment to the mill, which took him away from his family for long periods of time. He came to believe that a change was in order. By May 1878, he thought that the mill no longer required his presence. Its affairs were in order now, and John and Captain Ames could manage things on their own. In July Ames accordingly decided to relocate his family to New York City to pursue other opportunities. He could continue to help the family enterprise, he reasoned, by working in the "commission business" in New York and selling Northfield flour internationally.

House hunting before Blanche and the children arrived, Ames settled on a home at 76 East Sixty-First Street in Manhattan.[16] He enjoyed being with his family, and continuing business and financial turbulence in the stock market did not dampen their time together. The years the family spent living in New York and at their second home in Navesink Highlands, along the Atlantic shoreline in New Jersey, were some of the best of their lives. Blanche soon gave birth to two more children, a son in 1880 named Adelbert Jr. and a daughter in 1882 named Jessie. Adelbert and Blanche taught their younger children at home until they were ready for the best preparatory schools they could afford. Ames also spent his free time tinkering with inventions. Some focused on improving flour-mill machinery, while others included a pencil sharpener and special extension ladders for fire engines. He earned some patents, but they were never financially lucrative.[17]

Through the 1880s and 1890s, the family continued living on the East Coast, with Ames returning to the Midwest on occasion to see how the mill business was doing. While the economy of the United States went through cycles of economic prosperity and downturns, the Ames managed to evade any serious hardships, although the Minnesota mill nearly went bankrupt in 1886 after a three-year economic depression. Their children, meanwhile, excelled at their studies. Young Butler followed his father's footsteps to West Point. That excited Grandfather Butler, who reveled in another member of the family serving in the military: "God willing, one of the race will be the next to do honor to the blood of his father and the race of his mother." After graduating, however, Butler resigned from the army and attended the Massachusetts Institute of Technology on a scholarship. Adelbert Jr. attended Phillips Academy in Andover, Massachusetts, before enrolling in Harvard University to study law. Young Blanche graduated from Smith College in Northampton, Massachusetts, while Edith and Sarah went to Bryn Mawr College in Pennsylvania.[18]

While young Butler's military career was brief, the army continued to touch Ames. When he was fifty-nine, the former general was notified that at last he would receive the Medal of Honor by the direction of Democratic president Grover Cleveland. Issued on June 22, 1894, the distinction finally

Adelbert and Blanche (seated) with their children (standing, *left to right*): Butler, Edith, Sarah, Blanche, Adelbert Jr., and Jessie (Ames Family and Smith College)

honored his valiant conduct during First Bull Run. Ames earned the medal for "remaining on the field in command of a section of Griffin's battery, directing fire, after being severely wounded in the thigh, and refusing to leave the field until too weak to sit upon the caisson where he had been placed by men of his command."[19]

The 1890s also brought heartache. Benjamin Butler died on January 11, 1893, due to complications from a bronchial infection and was interred in the family cemetery in Lowell. The following year Jesse Ames's health deteriorated. The captain, revered by his son for his strength and fortitude, died on December 6, 1894. He was buried in Northfield on the ninth. Ames wrote to Blanche that he did not wish the girls to wear mourning clothes, not giving too much value to public sentiment. Butler Ames wrote to his father after Captain Ames died and encouraged him the best he could. "As you know," he told his grieving father, "when all is smooth and unruffled, we are undemonstrative in our affection and love for one another; but when trial and sorrows come then we stand by one another and offer what consolation we can, great or small, in the expression of our love." He asked him to not mourn too deeply: "Though his body be dead, his soul lives on. . . . [T]ime will soften the strangeness of God's call."[20]

Now the patriarch after the death of his father and of his father-in-law, Ames continued to manage the families' business dealings. Always impetuous, even as he neared sixty, Ames explored new business investments, ranging from buying land in Buchanan County, Virginia, to managing ranchland near Fort Union, New Mexico, that his father-in-law had acquired.[21] The most important thing to happen during these years, however, was the arrival of Ames's first grandchild. His daughter Edith had married in 1896 and gave birth to a son a year later. Blanche gleefully wrote a letter to her husband, signing it as "Grandmother Blanche Butler Ames"; the Ameses reveled in this new addition to the family.[22]

Since his testimony before the Boutwell Committee over twenty years before, Ames had tried to remain far from the public eye. He had committed himself to family and business and had ignored any prospect of another public office, allowing him a comfortable if rather unspectacular life. But in the spring of 1898, Ames entered the spotlight again. Named after his home state, the battleship *Maine* had received orders to sail to Cuba and lay anchor in Havana harbor. The ship was meant to represent US interest in the Cuban War for Independence, fought between Cuban revolutionaries and the Spanish government. On February 15, 1898, the *Maine* exploded, sank to the bottom of the harbor, and took 261 American sailors with it. While the explosion did not result in the United States immediately declaring war, the event fueled fervent anti-Spanish public sentiment. Newspaper tycoons printed lurid stories about the disaster. Pres. William McKinley signed a congressional resolution after the *Maine*'s explosion, demanding that Spain withdraw from Cuba, after which the United States would help Cuba obtain its independence. On April 21 Spain severed all diplomatic ties with the United States. In response, the US Navy established a blockade off the Cuban coast, and both sides declared war.[23]

Ames was sixty-three years old in 1898, yet he wanted to join the army again. He was not alone. Shortly before the United States declared war, Ames attended a function at the Waldorf-Astoria Hotel in New York City. Those in attendance included Civil War veterans such as Howard, Andrew McDowell McCook, and Joshua Lawrence Chamberlain. These men vowed to volunteer as members of the National Volunteer Reserve, an enlistment bank that agreed to fight in foreign wars. Ames was elected vice chairman.[24]

Once war was imminent, Ames soon after reached out for a commission. He contacted his former colleague and Senate defender George Boutwell, now governor of Massachusetts. "Will you write to President McKinley recommending me for appointment as a General?" he requested. "I see a number of generals are to be appointed. I have no doubt as to my capacity to render service equal to the best named." Ames immodestly flaunted his own credentials and reminded Boutwell that he had commanded the division that took Fort Fisher. "I can do the same thing on the Cuban coast," he asserted. Ames was confident that the United States could promptly win a war against Spain. He believed that after successfully landing in Cuba, the army could drive Spanish troops into the cities, surround them, and force their capitulation. With the help of Cubans "armed with rifles and artillery as an auxiliary," the United States would claim an expedient victory. Boutwell fully agreed with Ames and sent a recommendation to McKinley, who assented. On June 21 the Senate approved Ames's nomination for a position in the US Volunteers as a brigadier general.[25]

Secretary of War Russell A. Alger ordered Ames to board the steamer *St. Paul* in New York City. From there, the vessel would depart on July 5 for Santiago de Cuba, where Ames would report to Maj. Gen. William R. Shafter, V Corps commander. Shafter, then age sixty-three, was a veteran of the Civil War and a longtime Indian fighter. Ames would not head to Cuba alone, as Adelbert Jr. accompanied him. Ames's other son, Butler, rejoined the army, became acting engineer of the II Corps, and would depart for the Caribbean as well. Blanche wrote to her husband on July 6 from her family home in Lowell and expressed her concern about her sons going to war. She also hoped Butler would somehow end up under her husband's command and begged General Ames to make sure that he and Adelbert did not drink anything other than tea or coffee for sanitary reasons. A few days later she wrote: "My thoughts are always with my three absent love ones. . . . I have been praying that Santiago would capitulate before the arrival of the *St. Paul,* although I know you are very anxious to be in the fray."[26]

Ames was indeed anxious to get into action. Like a fresh West Point graduate, he felt confident and full of braggadocio. From the ship he shared more thoughts with Governor Boutwell about the war and what he prognosticated from the Spanish. Ames did not expect much trouble from his new foes: "Spain is in the last stages of decay. We [the United States] are in the early stages of vigorous manhood."[27]

The *St. Paul* sailed along the Eastern Seaboard without any issue. Ames noted in his diary that the ship was "in command of Captain Sigsbee, Capt. of the *Maine* when destroyed by the Spaniards in Havana." During the four-day cruise, Ames commiserated with former West Point colleague Guy V. Henry, who had won the Medal of Honor for his valorous conduct at Cold Harbor. He mused that Henry was his junior during the Civil War but was now his senior, a circumstance that would occur often during Ames's Spanish-American War service. He also remarked privately that Henry held military leadership in contempt: "I find he is severe on [Nelson A.] Miles, Shafter, [Henry W.] Lawton, and [Joseph] Wheeler who are held responsible apparently by the authorities in Washington for the failures at Santiago de Cuba, failure in the sense that many lives were lost without equivalent gains."[28]

By July 10, the *St. Paul* rounded the eastern end of Cuba along the Windward Passage, the same straits that buccaneers and pirates from the island of Tortuga frequented over 200 years earlier. At around 6 A.M. the ship moved into Santiago Bay on the southern coast. Ames reported that word had reached vessels in the bay that the US garrison might need evacuation. "Evidentially their situation is getting serious." Instead of continuing his diary, Ames sent it back to the United States with the ship's mail. He and his son disembarked at 10 A.M. Once on the ground, the general reported to the local army telegraph office to await instruction from Major General Shafter. Ames did not find the office in good order, and he thought that perhaps Henry's criticism of the way things were handled in Cuba was accurate after all. "The office was run in a stupid, ignorant, irresponsible way. It was typical of the management," Ames wrote Blanche.²⁹ Impatient, he borrowed a horse and rode to General Shafter's headquarters with one of General Henry's aides as a guide.

When he found Shafter, Ames was even less impressed. The ponderous general weighed over 300 pounds, he surmised: "His immense abdomen hung down, yes, actually hung down between his legs." Ames had kept his trim, military physique at sixty-three, and although Shafter was the same age, he was morbidly obese and suffering from gout. His raiment did not help his appearance either, Ames noted. Shafter did not wear a complete uniform, his suspenders were dirty, and the placket of his trousers "were forced to its lowest point."³⁰

Shafter was equally unhappy upon seeing Ames, as he thought the brigadier had brought his troops with him. Although the Eighth Ohio Volunteers had been on board the *St. Paul*, Ames did not command them. Puzzled, Shafter and a staff officer tried to figure out what had happened as Ames waited impatiently. According to Ames, the V Corps commander at length decided to give him a brigade of regulars in the First Division, under Brig. Gen. Jacob Ford Kent. Ames's brigade consisted of the Ninth, Thirteenth, and Twenty-Fourth US Infantry, the last unit being an all-Black regiment. All three units had seen combat prior to Ames's arrival. At the Battle of San Juan Hill, the brigade served admirably and played a pivotal role in seizing the hill and the trench system at its peak. Ames left Shafter's headquarters and felt grateful to command regulars instead of volunteers, who had not had time to receive proper training. Still, he had doubts about the campaign and remained unimpressed by the shoddy organization he encountered during his first day in Cuba.³¹

By July 9, the V Corps completely sealed off Santiago de Cuba from the rest of the island. Forces under Brig. Gen. Henry Lawton defeated 500 Spanish defenders at El Caney on July 1, then returned to the main body of the V Corps to ensnare Santiago de Cuba and 12,000 Spanish troops inside. Taking El Caney and pushing back Spanish defenders on San Juan and Kettle Hills proved costly. Shafter's corps suffered 200 dead and 1,100 wounded. At El Caney alone, Lawton's division lost 81 men and 360 wounded. Even though the Americans outnumbered the defenders ten to one, Spanish forces suffered only 38 dead. The casualties on the battlefield, moreover, paled to the number of US servicemen dying from tropical diseases. Ames wanted to remedy their misery as quickly as he could. "As the yellow fever is here the Spaniards can depend on an efficient ally," he observed.³²

Ames's brigade at that moment occupied an important position at the American center, just to the south of Kettle Hill, which the Rough Riders of the First US Volunteer Cavalry had ascended two weeks before. Roughly

Brig. Gen. Adelbert Ames in Cuba, 1898 (Ames Family and Smith College)

1,000 yards in front of his men lay Fort Canovar, the most forward Spanish entrenchment protecting Santiago de Cuba. On July 12 both sides exchanged volleys, with Ames's men smothering the Spanish line with rifle fire. With his men thus engaged, Ames scoffed at the overall incompetency of the force's leadership. "Shafter is reticent," he wrote his wife from his headquarters, "so neither Gen. Wheeler nor Gen. Kent, who have tents side by side, know anything of what is going on. I cannot learn that Shafter has any confidant or that he speaks with anyone." To Ames, poor generalship at the corps and division level trickled down and adversely influenced every aspect of the military excursion. "No general plan, no system, no method seems to have been followed.... Transportation is quite inadequate to supply the troops for which state of affairs there is no excuse.... What inextricable confusion should and does result from such generalship!" To make matters worse, Ames had lost nearly all of his baggage, and his headquarters consisted of a single tent shared between himself, his son, and two other officers.[33]

Ames's attitude slightly improved when word reached his line that Major General Miles had arrived in Cuba to assume command. Miles demanded an expedient conclusion to the fighting and intended to force the surrender of Santiago or else swiftly take the city. He oversaw a ceasefire on July 13 and orchestrated a summit between the two sides, meeting under a large tree between the lines to discuss terms. Ames believed that Spain would rather let its soldiers suffer annihilation than suffer the disgrace of surrendering. In reality, Spain wanted to preserve its manpower rather annihilate it. The American navy had destroyed the Spanish fleet outside of Santiago harbor just before Ames's arrival, and the Spanish preferred to minimize future losses.[34]

During the ceasefire, Ames wrote to Blanche daily. He promised her he was keeping Adelbert Jr. safe from both gunfire and unsanitary water. Ames added that their son only neared the frontline rifle pits of Ames's brigade after the ceasefire came into effect. "He is much pleased with his situation," he wrote her. "He is very helpful."[35]

On July 14 Ames received word from Kent to prepare an assault on the city. Peace talks appeared stalled, and Secretary of War Alger, who had fought under George Custer during the Civil War, wanted the V Corps to take the city if the Spanish-American parlay broke down. The news did not invite a positive response. Sick and exhausted, Ames's men did not have enough food. Rain fell day and night, causing streams in the area to rise "some eight feet and spread." Supplies could not reach his men, and they could not receive full rations. Ames nonetheless called a meeting with his regimental commanders to prepare for their assault. All three of the officers had displayed courage during the campaign, but none of them had any desire to throw their downtrodden regiments against Santiago. His subordinates "look with disfavor on the bald purpose of the Sec. of War," Ames wrote. "No one has confidence."[36]

After Ames concluded his meeting, a cheer broke out throughout the camp. Rumors reached the men that General Wheeler reported the Spanish had surrendered. "The information was not satisfactory to me," recalled Ames. He went to see Wheeler, who showed Ames a message from Shafter saying that the prospect of surrender looked promising. According to Lawton, however, Shafter told him that surrender was not imminent. Miles had no new information. With contradictory news, Kent ordered Ames to take his troops out of the trenches at 1 P.M. to await further instructions. Two hours later word reached Ames that the Spanish had in fact agreed to surrender terms. After waiting for days and receiving telegrams from both the United States and Spain, Santiago's defenders intended to lay down their arms.

The surrender ceremony took place on July 17. Ames and his son attended the ceremony and met José *Toral* y Velázquez, the commander of the Spanish troops in Santiago de Cuba. "The [enlisted] men seemed indifferent and happy. Then the Spanish soldiers marched by us to our rear a short distance when they stacked their arms and were formally held in a line of the 13th U.S. Infantry, a regiment of my brigade." Afterward, US forces entered the city to find it full of dead horses and shallow graves.[37]

Ames and the other American generals met the mayor and the city's archbishop, Francisco Sáenz de Urturi. Afterward, the Americans entered the governor's palace, and at noon they observed the US flag raised over the city's cathedral. Even though everyone enjoyed the revelry of the victory, Ames claimed that no one thought Shafter deserved credit. "Not one officer here whom I have met accredits Shafter with anything more than having a very grand army and—luck. His military management has been most deplorable, hence the delights of this army in this happy issue." The combat was over, and in a few days, Ames reported to Blanche, "the excitement of the situation here has passed away."[38]

Ames committed himself to working harder than ever to keep his men safe from illness now that the Spanish had capitulated. The shooting had ended, but not the dying. "Many men are sick, many others are ailing, while comparatively few are in the first-class condition," the general wrote as he relocated his brigade nearer to a source of clean water. Yellow fever claimed numerous victims, and Ames realized that typhoid fever and dysentery were taking over his camp. The hot and humid climate exacerbated the men's predicament, but Ames made it clear that he believed military incompetence primarily had devastated his brigade. "The troops have been deprived of so many necessities and exposed to the sun and rain so needlessly that they have been broken down before their time." Adelbert Jr. became sick on July 19, possibly with malaria. Ames wanted his son to return to the States, but the army quartermasters and ship captains he contacted refused. Incandescent with anger, the general fired a message to Adjutant J. C. Gilmore to see if he could help. Gilmore replied that he could get Adelbert Jr. on board the vessel *Concho* for a return passage to the United States. Ames also attempted to get some Michigan volunteers who had been transferred to his command back to the States. Pulling strings because Secretary of War Alger and General Shafter were from Michigan, Ames endeavored to get them home. The rest of his men, however, still had to incur the heat of Cuba.[39]

Near the end of July, Ames reported that 35 percent of his men were down with illness. Instead of getting his sick command off the island, he discovered that Shafter was transporting prisoners instead. To Ames, the surrender of Santiago de Cuba meant that his men should go home to the United States. Instead, he received orders to march the brigade to a new camp and await further instructions. "We could not march five miles without disorganizing," Ames remembered. His men procured better rations in their new camp, but Ames was still piqued, and his criticism of Alger and Shafter continued. The corps commander did not want to send any men home until their fevers abated, yet Ames was adamant that the only way to quell the illness was to get the men back to the States. On August 3 Shafter held a meeting in which all but two of the generals under his command attended. Ames told the group, "if I had authority I would ship my sick on board the transport now in port today—tomorrow and send them home."[40]

Ames thought Shafter was beginning to understand the gravity of the situation, but he wanted a quicker resolution. He joined a bevy of officers in circumventing Shafter entirely and sending a telegram to Adj. Gen. Henry C. Corbin after the meeting on August 3. Absolving themselves of blame, ten generals and other senior officers, including Lt. Col. Theodore Roosevelt, wrote that they were "of the unanimous opinion that this army must be at once taken out of the island of Cuba and sent to some point on the northern seacoast of the United States." To mitigate fear of an outbreak in the United States, they informed Corbin that yellow fever was not the primary culprit but rather malarial fever. Moving to the interior of Cuba was not an option because of the poor condition of the men. "Moreover, the best medical authorities in the island say that without our present equipment we could not live in the interior during the rainy season without losses from malarial fever almost as badly as from yellow fever. This army must be moved at once or it will perish." Ames and his fellow officers believed that the men were able to board ships and leave. "Persons responsible for preventing such a move will be responsible for the unnecessary loss of many thousands of lives."[41]

The telegram provoked the desired outcome. The War Department received the message at 1:13 A.M. on August 4. On August 5 at 11 A.M., Corbin instructed Shafter: "Take advantage of all our transports in Santiago to send your troops north. . . . [W]e are sparing no effort to send to you all that we can get."[42] While department officials scrambled to get ships to Cuba, they also worked on transferring regiments with tropical immunities to replace the woebegone troops in Santiago.

"It seems our report of Shafter has had good results," wrote Ames. "He has received orders to take this army to the U.S. at once." Progress, however, was slow, which did not surprise Ames. "His [Shafter's] capacity to effect results is not great, so, like everything else he attempts, our going will be slow." The process required tedious planning to get sick men moved. At the time the

War Department approved of the army's departure, 23 percent of the soldiers were ill. Ames hoped his men could escape Cuba by August 20 but finally received a pleasant surprise when Kent told him that he would accompany the Thirteenth Infantry to Santiago de Cuba's port and await a transport on August 7. The following day Ames and the Thirteenth Infantry boarded the *Vigilencia* and departed for Montauk Point, Long Island.[43]

The army designated Montauk Point's Camp Wikoff as a recuperation site for men leaving Cuba. Ames reported that his health was sound, although the scorching Caribbean sun had nearly made him wilt. He wrote Blanche that the ship he was on thankfully did not have yellow fever and she should not worry about his condition. The dissipation of illness among the troops coincided with the evaporation of the men's depression. Unlike some troops during the Civil War, the professional soldiers in Ames's brigade appreciated having a senior, military-trained officer who cared for the well-being of his men, he claimed. "The regulars under me are constantly rejoicing that they have me as a commander. . . . I am accorded by all what I attained over 1/3 century ago." As for the senior officers and fellow generals, Brig. Gen. Philip Reade told Ames that every one of those in the field "respected and feared me—whatever that means."[44]

Ames and his men stayed at Camp Wikoff for five days. His staff, which the general bragged about because of their competence and activeness, made sure that everything in the camp ran smoothly. While those men worked dutifully, Ames oversaw the recuperation of his regiments and himself. He also received word that his son Butler had served admirably in Puerto Rico and earned the rank of colonel in the Massachusetts militia. If he kept the rank for five years, he would become a general in the state's militia, the elder Ames noted with delight.[45]

Although the convalescence helped his men, Ames continued to thrash the incompetency of the army, especially Shafter. He wrote to Blanche on August 21 that the camp lacked enough supplies to care for the indisposed soldiers. Sick men from Cuba as well as Tampa Bay, Florida, arrived on Montauk after Ames's brigade, and the hospitals lacked enough tents and nurses to care for all of them. Ames particularly blamed Shafter for sending US regulars and healthier men to the United States first, even though it benefited him personally. The veteran general bristled at the situation and venomously assailed Secretary of War Alger too: "He had no heads and consequently cannot select men with heads."[46] Decades after his service during the Civil War, Ames was still meticulous and intolerant of what he perceived as incompetence.

On August 25 Ames assumed command of the First Division, V Corps. The new responsibility kept him at Camp Wikoff longer than he projected. Due to his appointment, Ames had to write to the veterans organization of his old regiment, the Twentieth Maine, and inform them that he could not attend a reunion they planned to host because he was in quarantine. In October the army transferred him to Camp Meade, outside of Harrisburg, Pennsylvania. While stationed there, Ames helped lead a peace parade in Philadelphia on October 25, attended by President McKinley. "Nominally it was the active opening of the peace jubilee," the *Scranton Tribune* observed. "Actually it was a thunderous greeting of praise, welcome, and thanks."[47] Shortly after the celebration, the army transferred the general one last time, to Summerville, South Carolina. In close proximity to Charleston, Ames described a different sentiment than the last time he was in the state: "In this town there are two or three union flags on residences. Some of its young men are in [the] South Carolina Regiment. One or two natives are at home on furlough wearing our uniform. I am treated with great courtesy and the City of Charleston is grieving, apparently, that I passed through it without being entertained by its officials.... The outward respect for our flag and uniform is worth millions to our country."[48]

Ames received an honorable discharge in January 1899. He made one final report as a soldier, retelling his experience to McKinley's War Investigating Commission in Washington. Initially, Ames did not want to say anything negative about the military; the war was over and successful. But commission members wanted to learn about the role that illness played in affecting the army overseas. Ames recalled his experiences for them, although adding, "At the same time I have no doubt that the official records, if thoroughly studied and properly interpreted, would reveal the cause of the delinquencies now under investigation."[49]

Ames considered the rank-and-file soldiers blameless. They merely followed orders, and those orders put them in unhealthy noncombat situations. But the highest-ranking officers, Ames believed, demonstrated neglect and incompetency. He posited that the lessons learned during the Civil War were "not utilized in the expedition to Santiago, Cuba." Sanitation was poor and organization horrendous, then he berated the military's strategy and tactics. El Caney, for example, was a senseless battle that did not need to happen since artillery could have destroyed the Spanish position in lieu of a direct infantry assault. He claimed that brave soldiers died because of bad leadership and planning there as well as during the entire campaign. Well researched and citing reports and correspondence, his testimony concluded that the nation

Adelbert and Blanche in Massachusetts, 1898 (Ames Family and Smith College)

needed its army and navy to cooperate, its soldiers cared for, and its military led by men who were able.[50]

Ames returned to civilian life with his health in good standing and as a minor celebrity. His conduct, and that of his sons, impressed people in New England social circles, who were eager to lend an ear to anything that was happening abroad and far away from their quaint lives. Local organizations asked Ames to speak about his time in Cuba and how it differed from his service as a Civil War soldier. In these talks, he maintained that the greatest similarity was the prevalence of disease. Such speaking engagements soon dwindled, however, which satisfied Ames; he could spend more time with his family now. To his rapture, the final contract that the Northfield mill had neared completion in 1899. The mill continued operations, but Ames had no more part in it. He could leave the industry behind and enjoy his later years with a growing family and sizable wealth.[51]

Although Ames did not seek any further recognition, his Civil War legacy continued to garner minor acclaim in his later years. He eventually published a book in 1897 about his experiences during the First and Second Battles of Fort Fisher, but his connection to Reconstruction and civil rights continued to surface with less favorable acclamation. At the end of the century, Reconstruction was slipping into historical disrepute, especially in the eyes of Columbia University professor William A. Dunning and his students, who described the era as a disaster. Historians credited Dunning and his disciples for portraying the Civil War as unjust and Reconstruction as being exploitative of freedmen and white citizens in the South. As this "Dunning School" emerged, with its defenses of southern whites and the Democratic Party accompanied by condemnations of Radical Republicans, Ames increasingly defended his actions, energetically engaging with historians who painted him in a less-than-stellar light.[52]

Elisha Andrews, president of Brown University, was the first. In 1895 he published an essay entitled "The Downfall of the Carpet-Bag Regime." Andrews discussed the debts accumulated under Republican carpetbaggers, claiming that Mississippi accumulated a massive debt of $20,000,000. Ames did not appreciate this error, as the actual debt was only $500,000. He wrote a letter to the article's publisher, *Scriber's Magazine,* asking them to forward a letter to Andrews. In a lengthy message Ames cited the Tenth US Census Report and his state address in 1876 to provide the real figures. "A careful analysis of my message will show that our management was not only honest but eminently economical."[53]

Ames also complained that Andrews had presented Attorney General Pierrepont and the Grant administration too positively. Extolling Pierrepont, Andrews depicted the moral fiber of Mississippi Republicans as decrepit. Ames especially did not appreciate the way the article exonerated racist Democratic behavior in the state because it painted him as corrupt. "Have you not done injustice, in your History, to the white people of Mississippi in failing to show adequate cause for their lawlessness? There was no corruption as the statistics prove." Andrews responded apologetically: "I beg now to say that it was and is my wish in my History not to deal unjustly by any man, State or Section. I heartily thank you for the facts you give me and shall use them." The two men continued writing each other, and Andrews made amends to his original research.[54]

In August 1899 Ames received a letter from historian James Wilford Garner, a native Mississippian who was working toward his doctorate under Dunning at Columbia. Garner planned to write on Reconstruction in Mississippi and requested Ames's help. The former governor gladly complied, sharing his papers with him and answering all of the historian's questions. He hoped that Garner would "be free from the prejudices and animosities of other days, and that you will be able to understand the integrity of my purpose at all times; that you will examine the matter from every standpoint and set forth in charity, as well as justice, your findings without fear or favor." In the preface of his work, Garner admits that he felt his own prejudices during his project but made "an earnest effort to divest himself of every influence."[55]

Garner's published his monograph, *Reconstruction in Mississippi*, in 1901, months before he received his doctorate, with edits and advice from Dunning. The book portrays Ames as a man of integrity. The collapse of his governorship had nothing to do with his being malfeasant, Garner adds. Instead, he describes the threats of violence made by Democrats and notes that any freedmen who voted Democratic in 1875 likely did so under duress. Nevertheless, Garner writes that the Republican Party as a whole was ruled by carpetbaggers and brigands, with ethical pursuits being secondary. One mistake that plagued Ames's political career, Garner argues, was when he declared himself an elected senator by his power as provisional governor. "There is no evidence that General Ames was not regularly and legally elected by the legislature," Garner notes. "But there can be little doubt, on the other hand, that he was guilty of bad taste.... [I]t was discreditable to him and the profession."[56]

Garner's book ultimately gives credence to the taxpayers leagues and their campaign throughout Mississippi. White Liners too evade criticism, while Ames's decisions, and Republican activity more generally, receive the blame for creating more burdens for the people of Mississippi. When approached about Garner's less-than-glowing interpretation of Mississippi's Reconstruction era, Ames reportedly handled it calmly, stating, "He did the best he knew how."[57]

Other members of the Dunning School took aim at Ames's career with more alacrity. C. Mildred Thompson, an Atlanta native and instructor at Vassar College, was another student of Dunning's, graduating with her Ph.D. in 1915. Her essay "Carpet-baggers in the United States Senate," published as a chapter in a 1914 Dunning festschrift, discusses Republicans and their Reconstruction efforts with contempt. She maintains that carpetbaggers, like Ames, benefited from having carpetbag allies in the Senate. In and of itself, that is not an inaccurate statement, but she further elucidates that carpetbaggers were only motivated by patronage and greed. Ames and his colleagues would "raise their voices on behalf of the rights of the negro" merely to retain power and oppress southern civilians.[58]

Claude G. Bowers, a Democrat and columnist who wrote best-selling books on American history, thoroughly hammered Ames's Reconstruction record and, unlike Garner, thrashed his character. In his 1929 work *The Tragic*

Era: The Revolution after Lincoln, Bowers states that Ames was a "soldier of fortune" and "worse than mediocre." He calls the former governor a weakling and pathetic, asserting that the "darkest days of Mississippi" dawned because of him. According to Bowers, Ames was "arrogant, insolent, tyrannical towards the courts, naming incompetents to the bench, and presuming to dictate their decisions."[59]

By this time, Ames felt less defensive about his time in Mississippi. He chose not to defend himself against the mockery of his senatorial or gubernatorial record or to respond to academic critics of Reconstruction and civil rights. Perhaps he had put the past behind him. When asked if he felt bitterness, Ames said he did not because he understood why Mississippians had turned on him. "I was a damn Yankee, an abolitionist and a [pro-]Black Republican. I had fought against them in the War. They saw their former slaves made equal to them in the eyes of the law."[60]

Ames and his wife were settled in Lowell as the twentieth century arrived. He favored that community and settled down at the Butlers' Bay View estate. By 1906, Ames and Blanche moved into their newly built estate in nearby Tewksbury. Affectionately called "the Castle," the home was only a few short miles from Lowell, but it was a place Ames could call his own. Mentally and physically at peace at last, he regularly attended the town's Episcopal church and welcomed his children for social calls. By all accounts, the New Englander was comfortable in his familiar surroundings. Ames focused most of his attention on relishing the finer things in life. He also became fascinated with genealogy and joined historical organizations that studied early American history. His daughter Blanche later wrote that the only time she saw him irate during this period was when he read a segment of Morris Schaff's *The Spirit of Old West Point*. Schaff was a West Pointer from Ohio and a Civil War veteran, but according to fellow graduate Ames, the book impugned the integrity and valor of New Englanders during the Civil War. He sent the author a ten-page letter. "Justice prompts me to assert that it is only by death's harvest of witnesses for nearly half a century that you have gathered courage to utter the worst, the most uncalled for slander I ever saw in print," Ames scribbled.[61]

The aging veteran also attended military reunions wherever he could. Ames tried to appear at large and small functions alike, such as the fiftieth anniversary of the Grand Review in Washington, DC, and the annual Twentieth Maine reunions. Ellis Spear, his former subordinate in the Twentieth Maine, wrote to Ames how much his legacy ultimately meant to the old regiment—a stark contrast from 1862, when Ames was considered a perfectionistic, brash young officer. "As time has gone on we have all realized, more and more, what you did for the regiment, in fact that you made it, and that all of us are indebted to you for all we learned."[62]

Adelbert and Blanche would leave Lowell each winter and travel to warmer climates. Sometimes they would go to California, but they preferred Florida, staying at Ormond and Daytona Beach. At first they were seasonal guests at the Hotel Ormond, but later on Blanche oversaw the purchase of the "Captain Wardell" home and updated the house and grounds. While there, Ames became an avid golfer. One his golfing friends was John D. Rockefeller, the famed business magnate and philanthropist. According to observers, Ames, even in his eighties, could play thirty-six holes at the Ormand Beach golf course without tiring. "I usually beat him [Rockefeller] and he never bet with me," Ames recalled in an interview in 1931. "I'd often say to him, 'I'll bet you a nickel on this one,' but he'd never take me up." When the Ames's were not sunning themselves in Florida, the couple traveled to Europe, often visiting the Villa del Balbianello, a home built in the 1780s on Lake Como in Italy. Butler Ames purchased the villa; it remained in the family for decades.[63]

When the United States entered World War I in 1917, Ames was eighty-two years old, but both of his sons served in the military. Butler Ames already had served as a congressman for Massachusetts's Fifth District, but he now offered his services to the Woodrow Wilson administration and became a general. Adelbert Ames Jr., who had graduated law school but quit to study physiological optics, flew reconnaissance missions for the US military. Ames's sons survived the war and would die old men.[64]

With all of his and Blanche's children married, Ames saw his grandchildren multiply, living long enough to see all eighteen of them born. Unfortunately, his daughter Sarah lost her son, Ames Borden, in 1926 at the age of seventeen; the young man reportedly suffered from infantile paralysis. Five years later Sarah herself died at the age of fifty-six. Her loss shocked the family. Ames and Blanche had lost matriarchs and patriarchs, as well as his brother, John, in 1915, but Sarah's death stung. Despite her passing, the Ameses recovered thanks to their other children visiting them regularly when the elderly couple was in Lowell. In 1929 the family evaded financial woes from the great crash since most of their wealth was safe from the turbulent stock market. While the United States entered a season of uncertainty, Ames entered his ninety-fourth year.[65]

In the face of old age, Ames's health remained relatively strong. He kept a lean physique and a good military posture, whether sitting or standing. The elderly man went on daily walks and took outings in his automobile with regularity. As he continued to enjoy life, most of his comrades and colleagues,

Ames taking a stroll while in his nineties (Ames Family and Smith College)

including Howard in 1909 and Chamberlain in 1914, passed away. It was not until Ames was in his mid-nineties that maladies began to present themselves. The first was his left eyelid, which drooped over his left eyeball like a patch and impeded his vision. He then injured his leg shortly thereafter, putting an end to his long walks. When he was ninety-four, he had multiple surgeries at Massachusetts General Hospital to regain better mobility, but his impairments effectively ended his games of golf with Rockefeller as well. "There's no use living to be 95," Ames told a reporter. "You can't eat candy any longer, can't see or hear very well, and you become more or less a curiosity."[66]

On April 13, 1933, Adelbert Ames died at the age of ninety-seven. He was not suffering from any obvious malady at the time other than old age. The longest-living non-brevet general from the Civil War to die, Ames had outlived all his army friends, colleagues, and adversaries. The sea captain's son was buried in the Butler family plot in Lowell, Massachusetts. Blanche Ames lived six more years, dying on December 16, 1939, at the age of ninety-two. She too was interred in the family burial plot.[67]

News of the general's death received front-page coverage in newspapers from Key West, Florida, to Bismarck, North Dakota. Papers printed obituaries that highlighted a lengthy and respectable career. He was one of nine Union generals to serve as a US senator and a state governor. He was one of the celebrated boy generals, the only one to serve in three branches of the military (artillery, topographical engineers, and infantry), and one of two to win the Medal of Honor, all after having graduated near the top of his class from West Point. Ames had been a senator, a governor, and a successful businessman who, in his later years, volunteered to fight for his country once again, this time against Spain in Cuba. His record garnered general, if no universal, applause. In Mississippi the press responded to Ames's passing coldheartedly and without fanfare. His governorship there had ended fifty-seven years earlier, but the *Lexington Advertiser* nonetheless described his time in office as an "unfortunate reign of sorrow and depravity." Writer Radford Killebrew wished that God would not judge Ames the way he had judged "noble men" who had seceded from the Union and later taken the state back from Republicans.[68]

Regardless of the way the media or scholarship portrayed Ames, his place within his family's history remained pristine. Unsurprisingly, the his and his wife's legacy became storied, unblemished, and nearly mythic within the family and the books they wrote. Their daughter wrote of them, "And into the future each child, in his or her way, carried on the ideals of Adelbert and Blanche; their example and teachings, jealous of their heritage and his name."[69]

CONCLUSION

The life and career of Adelbert Ames offers a glimpse into a turbulent period in American history. Most importantly, it addresses his place as an essential, contributary figure to the Union's victory during the Civil War, the postwar Republican Party, Reconstruction, and civil rights. Even now his name is mentioned scantly in discussing nineteenth-century American history, with the particulars of his strengths and weaknesses, achievements and mishaps during the Civil War and Reconstruction scattered throughout the historiography in mostly small snippets. The Dunning School and its interpretation of Reconstruction did not paint Ames in a flattering light. This academic movement dominated history and educational circles for decades after his death, cementing a misinterpretation of his legacy. He was an opportunistic carpetbagger, according to Dunningites, and Reconstruction was an embattled and corrupt takeover of the former Confederate states. The conversation about Ames's legacy thereafter decreased and remained relatively dormant until the 1960s.

While the general was not alive to fight for himself, one of his daughters was. Blanche Ames strenuously defended her father's public career, an unwavering and unyielding force who would not accept any shortcoming in accuracy. Her efforts to protect her father's vestige in the 1950s and 1960s offers an intriguing postscript to the soldier's story (while also serving as the springboard for this book). Like many members in her family, Blanche became a reputable and accomplished public figure. She graduated from Smith College with her bachelor's degree in art history, at a time when most women did not even attend university, and was even president of her class of 1899. The following year she married a botany professor from Harvard University named Oakes Ames, unrelated to her father's family but hailing from a storied New England family in Massachusetts. Although Blanche Ames Ames was a dedicated wife to her husband and mother to their four children, she ably managed to accomplish numerous feats. She held multiple patents for inventions and became a prolific artist. Influenced by her art education, her preferred medium was oils, but she also created sketches and drawings. Helping her husband, she began to illustrate Oakes's botanical publications and especially his multiple volumes on orchids. Additionally, Blanche began to produce widely circulated political cartoons supporting women's suffrage that gained her notoriety within the movement.

Likewise, Blanche committed herself to important women's crusades in the early twentieth century. Beginning in 1915, she attended rallies throughout Massachusetts promoting female equality and women's suffrage. She led the suffrage league in Easton, Massachusetts, from 1915 until 1918, continuing a lengthy tradition of female activists from the Bay State. In 1916 she founded the Birth Control League of Massachusetts, and her organization grew in prominence, later affiliating with Margaret Sanger's American Birth Control League. The two organizations, and the two women, worked in unison and created a pioneering partnership.

This alliance progressed until the Ameses elected to distance their league from Sanger. For one thing, Blanche disapproved of Sanger's opposition to Roman Catholic medical practices advocating the rhythm method. She thought that Sanger was blossoming into a "persecutor" on an antireligious crusade. Was preventing unwanted pregnancies not their primary objective? If so, Blanche wondered, did it matter if someone elected to use artificial birth control or a natural method? In addition, Sanger's support for eugenics and reports about her public speaking engagements at sister organizations of the Ku Klux Klan convinced Blanche that she needed to sever her ties with the founder of Planned Parenthood. Afterward, she continued to promote birth control measures, including universal access to birth control for women in Massachusetts and all of New England.[1]

As Blanche dedicated her life to her career and activism, she also became the chief defender of her father's legacy. According to the dominant school of thought at the time, Adelbert Ames was part of a carpetbagging contingent epitomizing the corruption that Reconstruction brought to the South. The policies such men promoted destabilized the region and harmed white citizens. Arguably, the most important work on Mississippi and Reconstruction up to that point remained Garner's book, which did not portray Ames as the right man for Mississippi. The greatest affront to her father's legacy, however—it prompted Blanche's most visceral response—came from then senator John F. Kennedy.

Published in 1956, *Profiles in Courage: Decisive Moments in the Lives of Celebrated Americans* highlighted eight notable senators who demonstrated bravery and defied the opinions of their party to do what they believed was right, although they faced consequences and lost popular support as a result. Reportedly, Kennedy decided to write the book shortly after he became the junior senator from Massachusetts in 1952. Impressed with the courage of past US senator and US president John Quincy Adams of Massachusetts, he asked his speechwriter Ted Sorensen to scrounge up more examples of senators acting boldly in the face of opposition. Sorensen compiled copious data, and Kennedy decided that a full-length book was needed to properly detail everything his assistant had found. From 1954 into 1955, the senator, with Sorenson's assistance, wrote the book. When it was finally published in 1956, it became a best seller. Looking at men from the 1820s to the 1940s, the book introduced the American public to an assortment of senatorial heroes worthy of admiration. Kennedy claimed that the book was meant to show that heroism has, and still is, "performed almost daily in the Senate Chamber." Although Sorensen claimed that he had done the yeoman's work and was essentially a ghostwriter, the book was a passion project for Kennedy. The monograph won the Pulitzer Prize for biography in 1957.[2]

Ames was not one of the eight senators selected by Kennedy and Sorensen, but he was mentioned by them. On page 181 Kennedy describes Ames as a power-driven and unwanted denizen in Mississippi who hurt the state. "No state suffered more from carpetbag rule than Mississippi. Adelbert Ames, first Senator and then Governor, was a native of Maine, a son-in-law of the notorious 'butcher of New Orleans,' Ben Butler." The book further argued that Ames was an interloper, only staying in Mississippi for political benefit, and placed the burden for its economic turmoil and corruption on Ames's shoulders. Davis's and Cardozo's impeachments, taxation, war debts, and intimidation all stemmed from Ames, especially since he held varying degrees of power in the state from 1867 to 1876.[3]

This depiction of her father incensed Blanche Ames Ames. "Apart from the historical inaccuracies," she wrote, "it is indeed ironic that an officer who fought with outstanding gallantry and courage throughout the entire period of the 'War to save the Union' should be maligned in a book bearing the title

Profiles in Courage." While acknowledging that the paragraph was brief, she found it offensive that her father would suffer slander in such an immensely popular book. To make matters even worse, the chapter in which Kennedy mentions Ames is about Lucius Q. C. Lamar. Rather than portraying the Mississippian as an opponent of civil rights, *Profiles in Courage* lauds Lamar as courageous because he praised Sen. Charles Sumner in a eulogy in Congress and opposed the free coinage of silver in the Bland-Allison Act of 1878. Blanche was beside herself. Lamar, a man who fought for the Confederacy and worked to undermine Reconstruction—at one point stoking tensions and even threatening to lynch her father—was praised for courage in part at the expense of the patriarch of her family, who had received no positive scholarly attention or public acclaim. Kennedy's portrayal had relied on esteemed historians like Harvard's Arthur N. Holcombe and Arthur M. Schlesinger Jr., but to Blanche, they perpetuated falsehoods and vilification about her immaculate father. She decided to remedy the situation.[4]

On June 6, 1956, Blanche wrote to Kennedy. She first introduced herself and stated that she was the daughter of Adelbert Ames. Transitioning to the true reason for her letter, Blanche asked if it was "possible in future editions of it [*Profiles in Courage*] to make some corrections of errata for your own sake as well as mine, particularly those embodied in the paragraph about General Adelbert Ames." Before diving into the particulars of what Kennedy got wrong about her father, Blanche drew his attention to an article published in the *Boston Herald* on May 20, 1956. John M. Lynch, chair of the Massachusetts Democratic Party, claimed that Kennedy had bought the election that won him his seat, that his interest in going to the US Senate was driven by crookedness. She doubted that the young senator would appreciate historians seizing such slander and repeating it "over and over in varying forms to defame your good name." Yet according to Blanche, "this is the method you have used in writing about General Ames. . . . [B]y implication and inuendo you indicate that he was responsible for the suffering in Mississippi."[5]

Ames's daughter then sent another lengthy letter factually refuting Kennedy. She cited the congressional report on the Vicksburg Troubles and Boutwell's 1876 committee report. She used exact quotations from Ames's testimony, words he used to defend himself, contending that his motivation for serving as governor and senator was not wholly self-interested. Tackling more than just the slander against her father, Blanche now scolded Kennedy for calling her grandfather the "butcher of New Orleans" and propping up a narrative that featured Bourbon Democrats in a positive light but looked down upon "Ames, Butler, and their fellow patriots" who had fought for the Union and for civil rights. She encouraged the senator to "right the wrong you have done" and to have the integrity and fortitude that her father had to do what was right regardless of the circumstance.[6]

Senator Kennedy replied on July 13, 1956. His letter, far more succinct than Blanche's, applauded her for "proper and commendable" concern about her family's legacy. He confessed that writing about the Civil War and Reconstruction was remarkably difficult. "I appreciate, too, your awareness that 'in a work as ambitious as *Profiles in Courage* which seeks to approach the problems of politics in American history there are bound to be some viewpoints to arouse controversy.'" After expressing an understanding of her position, Kennedy defended the book. He told her that he had to rely on the works of writers who were "recognized as reputable authorities in their fields." Their research is what Kennedy relied upon, and he trusted those sources, many of them in agreement with Dunning. He said that he did not intended to slander her father, or anyone else, and was sorry she felt that he had. Kennedy concluded his letter with his doubts that *Profiles in Courage* would go through another printing. "There will be no opportunity to make changes in the text," Kennedy told her. "However, your letter has succeeded in stimulating me to further research with respect to the matters your mention. I hope to be able to pursue their investigations sometime after the adjournment of Congress."

The problem was that as Kennedy's star rose, so did the fame of *Profiles in Courage*. When Kennedy became the thirty-fifth president of the United States in 1960, the popularity of the book spiked again so that it became a best seller a second time. Blanche loathed its resurgence in popularity. In 1963 NBC announced that it planned to televise a special dedicated to *Profiles in Courage*, which provoked Blanche to write to Kennedy once more. "The announcement of the plans by the National Broadcast Company to televise Profiles in Courage prompts me to appeal to you again to correct the errata in your account of *Lucious Quintus Cincinnatus Lamar*," she penned on July 18. It was hard enough dealing with the shame of her father's name being tarnished in a book printed and distributed all over the world, she complained, but now the public would see it on television. "A visual representation of *Profiles in Courage*, it seems to me, offers you time and authority to bring your views into accord," she advised the president. Blanche concluded her letter by praising him for his opposition to Democratic leaders who had pushed back against desegregation and hoped that even though he was busy, he could rectify this slight against her father's record.[7]

On this occasion Kennedy did not reply, but Sorensen, now a special counsel to the president, did. He noted that the president appreciated her letter but could not personally fulfil her request. Kennedy could not reassess his book, Sorenson said, but "we will bring to the attention of the producers of the televised version any material which you wish to submit. I am certain that they will judge it fairly and satisfactory."[8]

At the time of her correspondence with Kennedy and Sorenson, Blanche was eighty-five years old. Nevertheless, she decided to defend her father's legacy and give a different assessment of his life's story since no one else would. She adored her father, revered his service, and thought his legacy deserved better representation; she did not waver from the mammoth undertaking. The biography of her father would primarily address several slanders that she believed *Profiles in Courage* had unjustly directed at General Ames: that Mississippi suffered more than other states under carpetbaggers and that Ames wrecked the state's finances, abused expenditures, raised taxes, and oppressed its citizens.[9]

In 1964 Blanche finished writing a 625-page biography about Adelbert Ames. She wanted the book to epitomize accuracy and tried to avoid heavy bias by emphasizing her own scholarly diligence to primary sources and official records. Furthermore, she boasted about her family's immense support: "Behind me stood my family, at first tolerant of my efforts—and finally rendering every assistance, each in his or her own way, as opportunity arose—all with understanding of the deep desire for justice which prompted the making of this book."[10]

Her final product contains a wealth of content. The biography is laden with useful sources and invaluable information about Ames's formative years that only a daughter would know, having heard her father talk about his life on the Maine shoreline—something especially helpful since he did not maintain a journal for most of his life. It depicts Ames as a noteworthy figure who served from the beginning of the Civil War to the near end of Reconstruction, making claims about his courage that has stood the test of time. She also provides appendixes that reveal both her correspondence with Kennedy and important federal and private documents that justify Ames's actions in Mississippi. Her copious footnotes and wide assortment of family photographs brought the life of Adelbert Ames more attention than ever before.

For all its positive attributes, the biography, perhaps understandably, drifts into hagiography. Nothing Ames did was ever wrong. He did not make mistakes as an impetuous young general, nor did he distrust his subordinates or infuriate them with his perfectionism. Ames was perpetually humble and never boastful. In Mississippi he was essentially a martyr. Blanche never discusses his turbulent emotional state, his occasional depressed apathy to chaos in the Magnolia State, or his hardline dogma that alienated citizens. In addition, the book frequently takes detours to explain superfluous details about American culture and politics that do not relate to Ames's experiences or service. When more attention could have been spent on his West Point education, training the Twentieth Maine, defending Cemetery Hill at Gettysburg, or his debates on the floor of the Senate, Blanche Ames instead focuses on the Declaration of Independence, Abraham Lincoln, and Ames's minor banking interests as a young man. Although "academic," the book lacks the polish of other historical monographs that would later discuss the Civil War and Reconstruction. Its shortcomings aside, the biography does make one crucial argument: Adelbert Ames's life, experiences, and actions do not deserve anonymity or only negative portrayal.

Adelbert Ames is a figure worthy of attention as an integral individual in an important period of American history. His life serves as a microcosm of the Civil War from the early shots on the plains of Manassas until the last vestiges of Reconstruction. From 1861 until 1876, Ames was rarely absent from divisive the issues that plagued the United States. Beyond that, his presence and participation in a modernizing America makes him an ideal guide to better comprehending the complex issues and dramatic developments of the nineteenth century.

NOTES

INTRODUCTION

1. "Last Civil War General Observes 96th Birthday," *Washington (DC) Evening Star*, Oct. 31, 1931, A-4.
2. Hall, "Long Civil Rights Movement and the Political Uses of the Past."
3. Cha-Jua and Lang, "'Long Movement' as Vampire"; Tilghman, "Debating the Long Civil Rights Movement"; Dierenfield, *Civil Rights Movement*; McGuire and Dittmer, *Freedom Rights*; Brooker, *American Civil Rights Movement*.
4. Blanche Ames married botanist Oakes Ames. While there was no family connection between them, Blanche's maiden and married names were identical.
5. Catton, *Glory Road*; Catton, *Mr. Lincoln's Army*; Catton, *Stillness at Appomattox*.
6. Wert, *Sword of Lincoln*.
7. Eicher and Eicher, *Civil War High Commands*; Castel and Simpson, *Victors in Blue*; Rafuse, *Corps Commanders in Blue*.
8. Jordan and Lavery, *Iron Brigade General*; Barthel, *Abner Doubleday*.
9. Martin, *Kill-Cavalry*; Alberts, *General Wesley Merritt*; Wittenberg, *Gettysburg's Forgotten Cavalry Actions*; Longacre, *Custer*; Davis, *Most Desperate Acts of Gallantry*; Fitzpatrick, *Emory Upton*; Ambrose, *Upton and the Army*.
10. Trulock, *In the Hands of Providence*; Desjardin, *Joshua L. Chamberlain*.
11. Pullen, *Twentieth Maine*. See also, for example, Desjardin, *Stand Firm Ye Boys from Maine*.
12. Historian Gregory P. Downs, who heralded the notion of the long Civil War, has noted that the fighting did not end with Confederate forces capitulating in the spring of 1865. Ex-soldiers remained committed to the former Confederacy, albeit in dwindling numbers. The violence that Downs has described is comparable to the insurgency documented by other historians. Like Downs, George C. Rable has noted the prevalence of violence in southern communities, especially in Mississippi, after the war. Contending that southerners saw militant activity as being counterrevolutionary, Rable has argued that federal postwar policies, and the troops used to enforce them, faced daunting chal-

lenges. See Downs, *After Appomattox*; and Rable, *But There Was No Peace*. For more on the Freedman's Bureau, see Cimbala, *Freedman's Bureau*; Farmer-Kaiser, *Freedwomen and the Freedman's Bureau*; and Litwack, *Been in the Storm So Long*.

13. Current, *Those Terrible Carpetbaggers*.

14. See Harris, *Presidential Reconstruction in Mississippi*; Perman, *Emancipation and Reconstruction*; and Lemann, *Redemption*.

1. FROM THE ROCKLAND WATERFRONT TO THE POTOMAC RIVER

1. US Census Office, "Maine," in *Seventh Census*, 5; Coolidge and Mansfield, *History and Description of New England*, 284–85.

2. By 1595, the West Country, of which Dorset was a part, had developed a reputation of producing pirates—a reputation that would continue to grow. Within a year of Anthony Eames's birth, famed English privateers Sir John Hawkins and Sir Francis Drake both died at sea. Sugden, *Sir Francis Drake*, 308–14.

3. Ames, *Adelbert Ames*, 1. As noted by Adelbert Ames's granddaughter Pauline Ames Plimpton: "The ancestry of Adelbert Ames is much more nebulous than that of the Butler family [his future in-laws]. The words 'very little known' or 'of uncertain proof' are used frequently." Plimpton, *Ancestry of Blanche Butler Ames and Adelbert Ames*, 154–55. For further information about the origination, location, and settlers of Hingham, see *Hingham: A Story of its Early Settlement and Life*, 28.

4. Bouve, *History of the Town of Hingham*, 10, 208. Bozoan Allen was actually a business partner of Anthony Ames. They set up a corn mill for the town in June 1643. Plimpton, *Ancestry of Blanche Butler Ames and Adelbert Ames*, 159. Allen did not remain captain for long. Reverend Hobart's brother would eventually assume command of the town militia, leading them both before and after the King Philip's War in 1675. *Hingham: A Story of Its Early Settlement and Life*, 12.

5. Plimpton, *Ancestry of Blanche Butler Ames and Adelbert Ames*, 162.

6. Ames, *Adelbert Ames*, 1.

7. Coolidge and Mansfield, *History and Description of New England*, 285.

8. Shore Village Historical Society, *Around Rockland*, 12; MacLachlan, et al., *Rockland Area Lime Industries*, 43.

9. "Launched in Rockland," *Eastern Times* (Bath, ME), Nov. 3, 1853, 2; Coolidge and Mansfield, *History and Description of New England*, 285.

10. Ames, *Adelbert Ames*, 1.

11. Ames, *Adelbert Ames*, 3.

12. Ames, *Adelbert Ames*, 4.

13. Webb, "Party Development and Political Conflict in Maine," 177; "Convention of the Democratic Whigs," *Lincoln Telegraph* (Wiscasset, ME), Aug. 13, 1840, 2. The Webster-Ashburton Treaty in 1842 resolved the Aroostook War, a conflict between Maine and New Brunswick over their shared border. The agreement resulted in Maine losing more territory than the state claimed. Webb, "Party Development and Political Conflict in Maine," 181. Also see Le Duc, "Maine Frontier and the Northeastern Boundary Controversy," 30–31; and Jones, "Anglophobia and the Aroostook War."

14. Ames, *Adelbert Ames*, 1.

15. Webb, "Party Development and Political Conflict in Maine," 198; Theodore Foster, ed., "The Wilmot Proviso in Maine," *Signal of Liberty* (Liberty, ME), Aug. 14, 1847, 1.

16. Ames, *Adelbert Ames*, 14.

17. Ames, *Adelbert Ames*, 23.

18. Benson, "Public Career of Adelbert Ames," 85.

19. Morrison, *Best School*, 39–40.

20. Benson, "Public Career of Adelbert Ames," 24.

21. Benson, "Public Career of Adelbert Ames," 15; Vandervort, *Indian Wars of Canada, Mexico, and the United States*, 56.

22. Morrison, *Best School*, 41.

23. Waugh, *Class of 1846*, 14–15, 20.

24. Allen, *Origins of the Dred Scott Case*, 1–2, 211.

25. Hsieh, "Old Army in War and Peace," 176.

26. Hsieh, "Old Army in War and Peace," 175.

27. Morrison, *Best School*, 118.

28. Kirshner, *Class of 1861*, 6–7. One of the books Ames borrowed was *Aristotle's Rhetoric*.

29. Boatner, *Civil War Dictionary*, 12; Cullum, *Biographical Register of the Officers and Graduates of the U.S. Military Academy*, 2:772; Heitman, *Historical Register and Dictionary of the United States Army*, 316–17, 12; Kirshner, *Class of 1861*, 4–6.

30. Bush, *Army of the US Historical Sketches*, 376; War Department commission, May 11, 1861, Ames Family Papers, Smith College; Benson, "Public Career of Adelbert Ames," 23; Adjutant General's Office, General Orders No. 21, May 17, 1861, Ames Family Papers, Smith College; Adjutant General's Office, Special Orders No. 88, May 20, 1861, Ames Family Papers, Smith College.

31. Gould, *Major General Hiram G. Berry*, 34.

32. Krick, *Civil War Weather in Virginia*, 28.

33. Adelbert Ames to O. O. Howard, May 12, 1861, Oliver Otis Howard Papers, Bowdoin College.

34. Benson, "Public Career of Adelbert Ames," 23; Adelbert Ames to O. O. Howard, May 12, 1861, Howard Papers.

35. Newell and Shrader, *Of Duty Well and Faithfully Done*, 39, 53–54; Newell, *Regular Army before the Civil War*, 52–53.

36. Bush, *Army of the US Historical Sketches*, 376.

37. Ames, *Adelbert Ames*, 59–60; Huntington, *Maine Roads to Gettysburg*, 34.

2. FRESH LIEUTENANT TO SEASONED COLONEL

1. Benson, "Public Career of Adelbert Ames," 23, 85; Rafuse, *Single Grand Victory*, 73–74.

2. Hennessy, *First Battle of Manassas*, 7–10.

3. Longacre, *Early Morning of War*, 295; James B. Fry, "McDowell's Advance to Bull Run," in Johnson and Buel, *Battles and Leaders*, 1:183.

4. US War Department, *War of the Rebellion*, ser. 1, 2:383–85, 394 (hereafter cited as *O.R.*; all citations from ser. 1 unless otherwise stated); Fry, "McDowell's Advance," 1:188–89; Longacre, *Early Morning of War*, 381–82.

5. *O.R.*, 2:394.

6. *O.R.*, 2:188–89; Casler, *Four Years in the Stonewall Brigade*, 36; Longacre, *Early Morning of War*, 410.

7. Casler, *Four Years in the Stonewall Brigade*, 38; *O.R.*, 2:188–89; Longacre, *Early Morning of War*, 449; "War News: The Battle of Bull Run, Latest Particulars," *Baltimore Sun*, July 23, 1862.

8. Ames, *Adelbert Ames*, 68; *O.R.*, 2:398.

9. Ames, *Chronicles from the Nineteenth Century*, 1:2–3, 8.

10. Adelbert Ames to Martha and Jesse Ames, Oct. 3, 1861, Ames Family Papers, Smith College. From October 1861 to the end of the war, Ames wrote letters to his loved ones with relative consistency although he did not keep a diary. Benson, "Public Career of Adelbert Ames," 24. Ames was a brevet (honorary) major but referred to himself as a first lieutenant in this letter; he preferred to reference his regular-army rank.

11. Adelbert Ames to Martha and Jesse Ames, Dec. 31, 1861, Ames Family Papers, Smith College.

12. Ames, *Adelbert Ames*, 71.

13. Adelbert Ames to Martha and Jesse Ames, Dec. 4, 1861, Ames Family Papers, Smith College.

14. Adelbert Ames to Martha and Jesse Ames, Dec. 21, 1861, Ames Family Papers, Smith College; Ames, *Chronicles from the Nineteenth Century*, 1:5.

15. Ames, *Chronicles from the Nineteenth Century*, 1:3.

16. Adelbert Ames to Martha and Jesse Ames, Dec. 21, 1861, Ames Family Papers, Smith College.

17. Dougherty and Moore, *Peninsula Campaign of 1862*, 40–41.

18. George B. McClellan, "The Peninsular Campaign," in Johnson and Buel, *Battles and Leaders*, 2:167–69; Dougherty and Moore, *Peninsula Campaign of 1862*, 40–41.

19. Adelbert Ames to Jesse and Martha Ames, Jan. 14, 1862, Ames Family Papers, Smith College; Adelbert Ames to Jesse and Martha Ames, Jan. 21, 1862, Ames Family Papers, Smith College.

20. Ames, *Chronicles from the Nineteenth Century*, 1:8–9.

21. Ames, *Chronicles from the Nineteenth Century*, 1:8–9.

22. Sears, *To the Gates of Richmond*, xi.

23. Adelbert Ames to Martha and Jesse Ames, Apr. 18, 1862, Ames Family Papers, Smith College.

24. *O.R.*, 11(2):352; Adelbert Ames to Martha and Jesse Ames, Apr. 18, 1862, Ames Family Papers, Smith College; Eicher, *Longest Night*, 217; Ames, *Adelbert Ames*, 81.

25. Adelbert Ames to Martha and Jesse Ames, May 14, 1862, Ames Family Papers, Smith College.

26. Broadwater, *Battle of Fair Oaks*, 6; Sears, *To the Gates of Richmond*, 147.

27. Adelbert Ames to Martha and Jesse Ames, June 3, 1862, Ames Family Papers, Smith College; Ames, *Chronicles from the Nineteenth Century*, 1:12.

28. Ames, *Chronicles from the Nineteenth Century*, 1:12.

29. R. E. L. Krick, "The Men Who Carried This Position Were Soldiers Indeed: The Decisive Charge of Whiting's Division at Gaines's Mill," in Gallagher, *Richmond Campaign of 1862*, 181.

30. Krick "Men Who Carried This Position," 182.

31. Burton, *Extraordinary Circumstances*, 143; *O.R.*, 11(2):252, 704, 748.

32. *O.R.*, 11(2):252, 545, 747.

33. *O.R.*, 11(2):252, 259, 748; Burton, *Extraordinary Circumstances*, 144; Fitz John Porter, "Hanover Court House and Gaines Mill," in Johnson and Buel, *Battles and Leaders*, 2:343.

34. Brian K. Burton notes that Porter's command lost 6,837 men, with 2,836 of them captured. *Extraordinary Circumstances*, 136.

35. *O.R.*, 11(2):252–53; Sears, *To the Gates of Richmond*, 250–51, 311–12; Burton, *Extraordinary Circumstances*, 306.

36. Burton, *Extraordinary Circumstances*, 308–9.

37. Burton, *Extraordinary Circumstances*, 308.

38. Sears, *To the Gates of Richmond*, 314; Burton, *Extraordinary Circumstances*, 308; Benson, "Public Career of Adelbert Ames," 41; *O.R.*, 11(2):252–53, 287.

39. *O.R.*, 11(2):252–53, 260.

40. *O.R.*, 11(2):252–53.

41. *O.R.*, 11(2):240; Benson, "Public Career of Adelbert Ames," 41; Ames, *Chronicles from the Nineteenth Century*, 1:13.

42. Adelbert Ames to Gov. Israel Washburn, July 11, 1862, Civil War Regimental Correspondence, State Archives of Military Records, Maine State Archives.

43. Schubert, *Nation Builders*, 1, 24–25, 43–47, 75–78.

44. Excerpt from E. D. Townsend, Assistant Adjutant General, Special Orders No. 190, Aug. 14, 1862, Ames Family Papers, Smith College; Maine, Civil War Enlistment Papers, Box 58, Digital Collections, Maine State Archives, 18, 30, 300, 102.

45. Pullen, *Twentieth Maine*, 1.

46. Pullen, *Twentieth Maine*, 2.

47. Whitman and True, *Maine in the War for the Union*, 490; Pullen, *Twentieth Maine*, 5. Joshua Lawrence Chamberlain was a professor of rhetoric at Bowdoin College in Maine. He was able to teach all but two classes offered in the curriculum and knew ten languages.

48. Trulock, *In the Hands of Providence*, 16.

49. Spear and Spear, *20th Maine at Fredericksburg*, 142–44, Kindle; Pullen, *Twentieth Maine*, 8, 9, 16. Unfortunately, Ames did not chronicle this time in letters or in a journal. Perhaps he simply did not have the time.

50. Trulock, *In the Hands of Providence*, 14–16; Benson, "Public Career of Adelbert Ames," 43.

51. Benson, "Public Career of Adelbert Ames," 43.

52. Whitman and True, *Maine in the War for the Union*, 491.

53. Pullen, *Twentieth Maine*, 16; Assistant Quartermaster's Office, Boston, to Col. Adelbert Ames, Aug. 29, 1862, Ames Family Papers, Smith College.

54. Total wartime casualties for the Twentieth Maine, from its activation in 1862 to its mustering out of the service on July 16, 1865, was 689 men. Of those, 147 were killed or died of wounds, 381 were wounded, 146 died of disease or from the elements, and 15 died as prisoners of war. Records indicate that, 1,621 men served in the regiment at one time or another during the war. 20th Maine Regiment, Box 23, Department of Defense, Veterans, and Emergency Management, State Archives of Military Records, Maine State Archives.

55. Whitman and True, *Maine in the War for the Union*, 491.
56. Pullen, *Twentieth Maine*, 18–19.
57. Gerrish, *Army Life*, 25.
58. Gerrish, *Army Life*, 25.

3. COLONEL AMES, HIS REGIMENT, AND SMALLPOX

1. Second Bull Run, or Second Manassas, took place August 28–30, 1862. The rear guard of the Union army prevented a panicked retreat similar to First Bull Run. Hennessy, *Return to Bull Run*, 467–69; Sears, *Landscape Turned Red*, 338.

2. Antietam Battlefield Board, *Map of the Battlefield of Antietam, No. 1: This Map Shows the Position of the Union and Confederate Forces on the Morning of Sept. 17th 1862, prior to the Battle of Antietam which Opened at Daybreak* (Washington, DC: Norris Peters, photo-litho, 1893), Library of Congress, https://www.loc.gov/item/99447384 (accessed Apr. 3, 2020); Sears, *Landscape Turned Red*, 362; Long, *Hard Times, Hard Bread, and Harder Coffee*, 5; Ames, *Chronicles from the Nineteenth Century*, 1:14. The Twentieth Maine remained roughly two miles east of Antietam Creek and the Middle Bridge.

3. McGrath, *Shepherdstown*, 44; Ames, *Chronicles from the Nineteenth Century*, 1:14–15.

4. *O.R.*, 19(1): 204, 813, 19(2):70, 330; McPherson, *Crossroads of Freedom*, 3.

5. Long, *Hard Times, Hard Bread, and Harder Coffee*, 10; Ames, *Chronicles from the Nineteenth Century*, 1:14.

6. Ames, *Chronicles from the Nineteenth Century*, 1:14; Benson, "Public Career of Adelbert Ames," 46; 37th Congress (1861–1863), Congress Profiles, History, Art, and Archives, Congress Profiles, US House of Representatives, https://history.house.gov/Congressional-Overview/Profiles/37th/ (accessed Nov. 7, 2020); 38th Congress (1863–1865), Congress Profiles, History, Art, and Archives, Congress Profiles, US House of Representatives, https://history.house.gov/Congressional-Overview/Profiles/38th/ (accessed Nov. 7, 2020).

7. *O.R.*, 19(1): 557; William Marvel, "The Making of a Myth: Ambrose E. Burnside and the Union High Command at Fredericksburg," in Gallagher, *Fredericksburg Campaign*, 2–3.

8. Joseph Hooker to Hannibal Hamlin, Nov. 16, 1862, Ames Family Papers, Smith College.

9. Hiram Berry to Hannibal Hamlin, Nov. 24, 1862, Ames Family Papers, Smith College.

10. Lt. Col. Joshua L. Chamberlain and Maj. Charles D. Gilmore to Gov. Israel Washburn, Nov. 15, 1862, "1862-11-16 Chamberlain and Gilmore Recommend Adelbert Ames for Promotion," 20th Maine Regiment, no. 35, Digital Maine Repository, https://digitalmaine.com/chamberlain_corr/35 (accessed Apr. 4, 2020).

11. Rable, *Fredericksburg! Fredericksburg!*, 59; *O.R.*, 19(2):579.

12. *O.R.*, 19(2):581, 21(1):551; Eicher, *Longest Night*, 397.

13. Gerrish, *Army Life*, 63.

14. Spear and Spear, *20th Maine at Fredericksburg*, 1, Kindle; *O.R.*, 21(1):64–65, 411; O'Reilly, *Fredericksburg Campaign*, 36, 79–81; James Longstreet, "The Battle of Fredericksburg", in Johnson and Buel, *Battles and Leaders*, 3:75.

15. Palfrey, *Antietam and Fredericksburg*, 141, Sutherland, *Fredericksburg and Chancellorsville*, 76.

16. *O.R.*, 21(1):71.

17. Krick, *Civil War Weather in Virginia*, 78; Sutherland, *Fredericksburg and Chancellorsville*, 50.

18. Longstreet, "Battle of Fredericksburg," 3:79; Palfrey, *Antietam and Fredericksburg*, 143.

19. Trulock, *In the Hands of Providence*, 77.

20. Spear and Spear, *20th Maine at Fredericksburg*, 80, Kindle.

21. Trulock, *In the Hands of Providence*, 95.

22. Gerrish, *Army Life*, 77. Capt. Ellis Spear, who became a brigadier general in 1865, dismissed various parts of Chamberlain's story about Fredericksburg and called them fictitious. Notably, he questioned Chamberlain's description of the artillery volume the regiment faced both crossing the river and charging Marye's Heights. See Spear and Spear, *20th Maine at Fredericksburg*, 78–80, Kindle.

23. Chamberlain, "My Story of Fredericksburg"; O'Reilly, *Fredericksburg Campaign*, 382.

24. Carter, *Four Brothers in Blue*, 196.

25. Carter, *Four Brothers in Blue*, 196.

26. Chamberlain, "My Story of Fredericksburg," 153–56.

27. *O.R.*, 21(1):411–12; Sutherland, *Fredericksburg and Chancellorsville*, 61.

28. Nathan S. Clark, "Nathan S. Clark Diary, 20th Maine," Historical Documents, no. 2, Digital Maine Repository, 81, 411–12, https://digitalmaine.com/hist_docs/2/ (accessed Mar. 12, 2020); Pullen, *Twentieth Maine*, 55; Spear and Spear, *20th Maine at Fredericksburg*, 2, Kindle.

29. Spear and Spear, *20th Maine at Fredericksburg*, 2, Kindle; Pullen, *Twentieth Maine*, 55.

30. *O.R.*, 21(1):136, Pullen, *Twentieth Maine*, 55–56; Chamberlain, "My Story of Fredericksburg," 156–57.

31. *O.R.*, 21(1):136; Benson, "Public Career of Adelbert Ames," 49; Pullen, *Twentieth Maine*, 55–56; Chamberlain, "My Story of Fredericksburg," 156–57; Ames, *Chronicles from the Nineteenth Century*, 1:16.

32. "From the 20th Maine Regiment, Camp near Falmouth, VA., December 19, 1862," *Portland (ME) Daily Press*, Dec. 31, 1862, 1; Palfrey, *Antietam and Fredericksburg*, 190.

33. Rable, *Fredericksburg! Fredericksburg!*, 421, Pullen, *Twentieth Maine*, 63–68.

34. Adelbert Ames to Martha and Jesse Ames, Jan. 10, 1863, Ames Family Papers, Smith College.

35. Longacre, *Commanders of Chancellorsville*, 205.

36. Ames, *Adelbert Ames*, 109; Gerrish, *Army Life*, 86.

37. Long, *Hard Times, Hard Bread, and Harder Coffee*, 47.

38. Ames, *Chronicles from the Nineteenth Century*, 1:17; Adelbert Ames to Daniel Butterfield, Apr. 10, 1863, Ames Family Papers, Smith College.

39. Ames, *Chronicles from the Nineteenth Century*, 1:17, 19; O. O. Howard to Joseph Hooker, Apr. 19, 1863, Ames Family Papers, Smith College.

40. Sears, *Chancellorsville*, 117–18; John J. Hennessy, "We Shall Make Richmond Howl: The Army of the Potomac on the Eve of Chancellorsville," in Gallagher, *Chancellorsville*, 9; Eicher, *Longest Night*, 474.

41. Trulock, *In the Hands of Providence*, 95.

42. Eicher, *Longest Night*, 475; [Battle of Chancellorsville], map 2, *Dispositions of Union and Confederate Forces at 4:00 P.M., 2nd May, 1863*, Library of Congress Geography and Map Division (Washington, 1863), https://www.loc.gov/item/99439121.

43. Doubleday, *Chancellorsville and Gettysburg*, 34, 55; Eicher, *Longest Night*, 479; *O.R.*, 25(1):183.

44. Stackpole, *Chancellorsville*, 283; Sears, *Chancellorsville*, 441; Doubleday, *Chancellorsville and Gettysburg*, 29–34; Beattie, Cole, and Waugh, *Distant War Comes Home*, 44; *O.R.*, 25(1):179.

45. *O.R.*, 25(1):806–9.

46. *O.R.*, 25(1):308, 394, 672.

47. *O.R.*, 25(1):509, 519. After the Chancellorsville Campaign, Ames's college friend Charles Cross, who was shot by a sharpshooter while constructing a bridge, died of his wound. "Cross, the best beloved of our class, was killed by a rebel bullet," Ames wrote. He graduated third in Ames's class. Kirshner, *Class of 1861*, 49.

48. Stevens, *1863*, 193; Brager, *Grant's Victory*, 71–72; *O.R.*, 25(2):320.

4. BOY GENERAL

1. Wert, *Glorious Army*, 219–20.

2. Ames, *Chronicles from the Nineteenth Century*, 1:9.

3. Trulock, *In the Hands of Providence*, 111.

4. Cullum, *Biographical Register of the Officers and Graduates of the U.S. Military Academy*, 2:772; Desjardin, *Stand Firm Ye Boys from Maine*, 18. Edmund Kirby, who graduated five spots behind Ames, was another "boy general" who received a promotion to brigadier general at the age of twenty-three, although he died that same day (May 23, 1863). President Lincoln approved the promotion of Kirby, a highly regarded officer in his own right, to award his widowed mother a larger pension. See Boatner, *Civil War Dictionary*, 465.

5. Long, *Hard Times, Hard Bread, and Harder Coffee*, 47.

6. A. Wilson Greene, "From Chancellorsville to Cemetery Hill: O. O. Howard and Eleventh Corps Leadership," in Gallagher, *Three Days at Gettysburg*, 47; Doubleday, *Chancellorsville and Gettysburg*, 218; *O.R.*, 25(2):582; Benson, "Public Career of Adelbert Ames,"

52. One of the soldiers in the Seventeenth Connecticut was Pvt. Anthony Comstock, who would later be responsible for the well-known Comstock Law of 1873. See Anna Louise Bates, *Weeding in the Garden of the Lord: Anthony Comstock's Life and Career* (Lanham, MD: Univ. Press of America, 1995).

7. L. L. Crounse, "The Army of the Potomac: . . . The Conduct of Gen. Schurz's Corps in the Battle at Chancellorsville," *New York Times,* May 28, 1863.

8. *O.R.*, 27(3):16–17.

9. Wittenberg, *Union Cavalry Comes of Age,* 432; Wittenberg and Davis, *Out Flew the Sabres,* 16; Doubleday, *Chancellorsville and Gettysburg,* 80.

10. *O.R.*, 27(3):1043.

11. *O.R.*, 27(1):170, 27(3):1044.

12. "Hooker's Army: The Cavalry Fight on the Rappahannock," *New York Herald,* June 11, 1863, 1; "The Recent Fight at Brandy Station," *North Carolina Weekly Standard* (Raleigh), June 17, 1873, 1.

13. *O.R.*, 27(1):903–4.

14. *O.R.*, 27(3):1046.

15. *O.R.*, 27(3):70; Doubleday, *Chancellorsville and Gettysburg,* 84.

16. *O.R.*, 27(1):4, 60, 27(3):59, 70; Sears, *Gettysburg,* 123; Doubleday, *Chancellorsville and Gettysburg,* 84; Guelzo, *Gettysburg,* 128.

17. Sears, *Gettysburg,* 156–58.

18. Howard, *Autobiography,* 408; *O.R.*, 27(1):701–5; Sears, *Gettysburg,* 189.

19. John B. Bachelder, *Map of the Battlefield of Gettysburg: July 1st, 2nd, 3rd,* 1879, Geography and Map Division, Library of Congress, Washington, DC; *O.R.*, 27(1):701–5, 717, 720; Culp, *25th Ohio Vet. Vol. Infantry,* 78; Howard, *Autobiography,* 416–18.

20. *O.R.*, 27(1):703, 712, 729.

21. *O.R.*, 27(1):712–13; Howard, *Autobiography,* 418.

22. Sears, *Gettysburg,* 221; *O.R.*, 27(1):719; Howard, *Autobiography,* 407, 418–19.

23. *O.R.*, 27(1):485; O. O. Howard, "General Howards Official Report," in Johnson and Buel, *Battles and Leaders,* 3:289; Pfanz, *Gettysburg: Culp's Hill & Cemetery Hill,* 242. The number of captured or missing men from Ames's division for July 1–3, 1863, was 670. *O.R.*, 27(1):182, 485.

24. Pfanz, *Gettysburg: Culp's Hill & Cemetery Hill,* 28.

25. Pfanz, *Gettysburg: Culp's Hill & Cemetery Hill,* 242.

26. Mingus, *Louisiana Tigers in the Gettysburg Campaign,* 136; *O.R.*, 27(1):716, 720.

27. Mingus, *Louisiana Tigers in the Gettysburg Campaign,* 136–38; Jones, *Cemetery Hill,* 82–83.

28. *O.R.*, 27(1):429. Other reports from XI Corps officers reaffirm Howard's statement. See *O.R.*, 27(1):722–28.

29. *O.R.*, 27(1):720, 27(2):486, 761.

30. Pfanz, *Gettysburg: Culp's Hill & Cemetery Hill,* 273.

31. Sears, *Gettysburg,* 274, 340.

32. Doubleday, *Chancellorsville and Gettysburg,* 182–83; Pfanz, *Gettysburg: Culp's Hill & Cemetery Hill,* 279.

33. *O.R.*, 27(1):182, 27(2):474–75; Ames, *Adelbert Ames,* 135.

34. Howard, *Autobiography*, 43; Meade, *Life and Letters*, 103.

35. Doubleday, *Chancellorsville and Gettysburg*, 190–96; Howard, *Autobiography*, 437; Pfanz, *Gettysburg: Culp's Hill & Cemetery Hill*, 357, 367.

36. Adelbert Ames to Martha and Jesse Ames, Aug. 1863, Ames Family Papers, Smith College.

37. H. S. Melcher, "The 20th Maine at Little Round Top," in Johnson and Buel, *Battles and Leaders*, 3:315; Desjardin, *Stand Firm Ye Boys from Maine*, 51; Pullen, *Twentieth Maine*, 125; *O.R.*, 27(1):179.

38. Desjardin, *Stand Firm Ye Boys from Maine*, 91; Ames, *Chronicles from the Nineteenth Century*, 1:20.

39. *O.R.*, 27(1):917, 994–95.

40. *O.R.*, 27(1):996, 27(3):660.

41. Huntington, *Searching for George Gordon Meade*, 205; "Abraham Lincoln to George G. Meade, July 14, 1863, letter draft, Library of Congress, https://www.loc.gov/item/ma12480600 (accessed Mar. 1, 2020).

42. *O.R.*, 28(2):74.

43. Brennan, *Assault on Charleston*, 243; C. R. P. Rodgers, "Du Pont's Attack at Charleston," in Johnson and Buel, *Battles and Leaders*, 4:32.

44. *O.R.*, 28(2):74–76, 210–12, 406.

45. Ames, *Chronicles from the Nineteenth Century*, 1:22.

46. Benson, "Public Career of Adelbert Ames," 59.

47. Ames, *Chronicles from the Nineteenth Century*, 1:21; *O.R.*, 28(2):73, 724–26, 35(1):464; Whitman and True, *Maine in the War for the Union*, 499.

48. Samuel Jones, "Battle of Olustee or Ocean Pond," in Johnson and Buel, *Battles and Leaders*, 4:76; Broadwater, *Battle of Olustee*, 175.

49. *O.R.*, 35(1):491.

50. Adelbert to Martha and Jesse Ames, Mar. 8, 1864, Ames Family Papers, Smith College; Adelbert Ames to Martha and Jesse Ames, Mar. 27, 1864, Ames Family Papers, Smith College; Adelbert to Martha and Jesse Ames, Apr. 24, 1864, Ames Family Papers, Smith College.

51. Benson, "Public Career of Adelbert Ames," 62–63; Ames, *Adelbert Ames*, 146.

52. Adelbert Ames to Martha and Jesse Ames, Apr. 24, 1864, Ames Family Papers, Smith College.

5. FUTILITY ALONG THE JAMES RIVER

1. Grimsley, *And Keep Moving On*, 94.
2. Boatner, *Civil War Dictionary*, 458, 531, 818; *O.R.*, 5:19–32, 36(1):106–16.
3. Hogan, *Overland Campaign*, 8–12.
4. Robertson, *Back Door to Richmond*, 14, 20; Grimsley, *And Keep Moving On*, 7–8.
5. Longacre, *Army of Amateurs*, 33–39.
6. Longacre, *Army of Amateurs*, 33–39; Grimsley, *And Keep Moving On*, 120.
7. Longacre, *Army of Amateurs*, 39–40.
8. Longacre, *Army of Amateurs*, 23, 35, 42.

9. Longacre, *Army of Amateurs*, 61–62; "The Opposing Forces at the Beginning of Grant's Campaign against Richmond," in Johnson and Buel, *Battles and Leaders*, 4:181–82.

10. Longacre, *Army of Amateurs*, 24–30; Robertson, *Back Door to Richmond*, 9–10.

11. Adelbert Ames to Martha and Jesse Ames, May 4, 1864, Ames Family Papers, Smith College; Adelbert Ames to Martha and Jesse Ames, May 7, 1864, Ames Family Papers, Smith College.

12. Longacre, *Army of Amateurs*, 76.

13. Longacre, *Army of Amateurs*, 79.

14. *O.R.*, 36(1):36; Grimsley, *And Keep Moving On*, 122.

15. Grimsley, *And Keep Moving On*, 124, 171–72.

16. *O.R.*, 36(2):36, 620–21, 623; Robertson, *Back Door to Richmond*, 127; *Union Army*, 274.

17. Robertson, *Back Door to Richmond*, 145.

18. *O.R.*, 36(2):775.

19. Longacre, *Army of Amateurs*, 91; Robertson, *Back Door to Richmond*, 149–51, 175; *O.R.*, 36(2):776.

20. Robertson, *Back Door to Richmond*, 198–203; *O.R.*, 36(2):39, 834–35.

21. *O.R.*, 36(2):837.

22. *O.R.*, 36(2):837–38; Longacre, *Army of Amateurs*, 99; Robertson, *Back Door to Richmond*, 213–14.

23. [P.] G. T. Beauregard, "The Defense of Drewry's Bluff," in Johnson and Buel, *Battles and Leaders*, 4:204; Longacre, *Army of Amateurs*, 99–101; *O.R.*, 36(2):40, 43–44.

24. Robertson, *Back Door to Richmond*, 217; *O.R.*, 36(2):898.

25. Dickey, *Eighty-Fifth Regiment Pennsylvania Volunteer Infantry*, 324; *O.R.*, 36(2):192, 36(3):33–35.

26. Adelbert Ames to Martha and Jesse Ames, May 19, 1864, Ames Family Papers, Smith College; *O.R.*, 36(3):203.

27. Robertson, *Back Door to Richmond*, 225; Longacre, *Army of Amateurs*, 325.

28. Ames, *Adelbert Ames*, 161; Young, *Around the World with General Grant*, 304.

29. Ames's former regiment, the 20th Maine, saw action in every engagement leading up to Totopotomoy Creek. By June 1, Maj. Ellis Spear reported that the unit had suffered 139 casualties—24 dead, 97 wounded, and 18 missing or captured. *O.R.*, 36(1):573–74.

30. *O.R.*, 36(3):282–83.

31. *O.R.*, 36(3):285; Rhea, *Cold Harbor*, 154–56.

32. Rhea, *Cold Harbor*, 196–97.

33. Grimsley, *And Keep Moving On*, 200–203.

34. Grimsley, *And Keep Moving On*, 206; Furgurson, *Not War but Murder*, 95; Rhea, *Cold Harbor*, 318.

35. William Farrar Smith, "The Eighteenth Corps at Cold Harbor," in Johnson and Buel, *Battles and Leaders*, 4:225.

36. Ames, *Adelbert Ames*, 165; John G. Nicolay and John Hay, *Abraham Lincoln: A History, the Full and Authorized Record of His Private Life and Public Career*, vol. 8 (Washington, DC: American Historical Foundation, 1914), 404.

37. Price, *Ninety-Seventh Regiment, Pennsylvania Volunteer Infantry*, 287–89; Longacre, *Army of Amateurs*, 139; O.R., 36(1):180; Benson, "Public Career of Adelbert Ames," 65.

38. Adelbert Ames to Martha and Jesse Ames, June 9, 1864, Ames Family Papers, Smith College. Grant's forces reported 54,926 casualties for May 5–June 24, 1864. O.R., 36(1):188; Martin T. McMahon, "Cold Harbor," in Johnson and Buel, *Battles and Leaders*, 4:213, 220.

39. Butler had permission from Grant to try another attack on Petersburg but declined. Butler felt dispirited by both his army failing again and learning that he only received 28 votes at the National Union Convention in Baltimore; Lincoln, the presumptive favorite, won 484. Longacre, *Army of Amateurs*, 138.

40. O.R., 40(1):212; Hess, *In the Trenches at Petersburg*, 32–37.

41. Adelbert Ames to Martha and Jesse Ames, July 10, 1864, Ames Family Papers, Smith College; Adelbert Ames to Martha and Jesse Ames, July 21, 1864, Ames Family Papers, Smith College; Benson, "Public Career of Adelbert Ames," 66.

42. Ames, *Chronicles from the Nineteenth Century*, 1:24.

43. Ames, *Chronicles from the Nineteenth Century*, 1:24. It is unknown why Ames could not potentially vote, and he does not reference who his preferred candidate was. Considering his political philosophy and criticism of Lincoln in 1864, Ames may have preferred a candidate with military experience. U. S. Grant, Benjamin Butler, Lovell Rousseau, and William S. Rosecrans are all possible, albeit completely speculative, persons that Ames might have supported.

44. Hess, *Crater*, 3; Levin, *Remembering the Battle of the Crater*, 11.

45. Hess, *Crater*, 26; Bonekemper, *Ulysses S. Grant*, 201.

46. Bonekemper, *Ulysses S. Grant*, 32–34, 55; Levin, *Remembering the Battle of the Crater*, 11–12.

47. Charles H. Houghton, "In the Crater," in Johnson and Buel, *Battles and Leaders*, 4:561, 567; O.R., 40(1):719.

48. McPherson, *Battle Cry of Freedom*, 760; O.R., 40(1):108–9.

49. Longacre, *Sharpshooters*, 252; Axelrod, *That Horrid Pit*, 236; O.R., 40(1):387, 515, 42(2):52; Adelbert Ames to Martha and Jesse Ames, Sept. 1, 1864, Ames Family Papers, Smith College. A significant number of Ames's command fell ill during this time after overseeing the construction of earthworks.

50. U. S. Grant, "General Grant on the Siege of Petersburg," in Johnson and Buel, *Battles and Leaders*, 4:577.

51. O.R., 42(3):801–2.

52. Benson, "Public Career of Adelbert Ames," 73.

53. O.R., 42(1):146, 42(3):190; Randolph, *Civil War Soldier's Diary*, 241.

54. O.R., 42(1):149, 152; Trudeau, *Last Citadel*, 247.

55. O.R., 42(3):553.

56. *Bvt. Maj. Gen. Adelbert Ames and Staff, Army of the James, Nov. 1864*, photograph, Prints and Photographs Division, Library of Congress, https://loc.gov/item/2013647577/.

57. O.R., 43(3):52, 514, 553, 1105.

6. THE FINAL STRUGGLE FOR VICTORY

1. Ames, *Capture of Fort Fisher*, 1; Gragg, *Confederate Goliath*, 3.
2. Gragg, *Confederate Goliath*, 13–14, 18–19; Harkness, *Expeditions against Fort Fisher and Wilmington*, 149–50.
3. Fonvielle, *Wilmington Campaign*, 43–45.
4. Kummer, *U.S. Marines in Battle*, 4–5.
5. Gragg, *Confederate Goliath*, 40; Grant, *Personal Memoirs*, 570.
6. Kummer, *U.S. Marines in Battle*, 7; Ames, *Capture of Fort Fisher*, 1–2.
7. Grant, *Personal Memoirs*, 571; Butler, *Butler's Book*, 783; Porter, *Incident and Anecdotes*, 262–63; Fonvielle, *Wilmington Campaign*, 103–6.
8. US Navy Department, *Official Records of the Union and Confederate Navies*, ser. 1, 11:222 (hereafter cited as *O.R.N.*).
9. Porter, "Campaigning with Grant," 359; *O.R.N.*, ser. 1, 11:207–14.
10. Ames, *Capture of Fort Fisher*, 2; Gragg, *Confederate Goliath*, 40; *O.R.N.*, ser. 1, 11:219.
11. Ames, *Capture of Fort Fisher*, 2–3; Gragg, *Confederate Goliath*, 36.
12. Gragg, *Confederate Goliath*, 36; Ames, *Capture of Fort Fisher*, 2. Scholars at Eastern Carolina University have conducted surveys to find the wreckage. They were unable to find it in the 1990s, but Brian T. Clayton, using a marine magnetometer, later located a large dipolar magnetic anomaly aligning with the supposed location of the wreckage given on a map produced in 1866 by John S. Bradford. See Clayton, "Applying GIS to Locate the USS *Louisiana*: A Study of the Fort Fisher Civil War Battlefield" (master's thesis, East Carolina Univ., 2013).
13. Ames, *Capture of Fort Fisher*, 4; Fonvielle, *Wilmington Campaign*, 145.
14. Fonvielle, *Wilmington Campaign*, 148.
15. Fonvielle, *Wilmington Campaign*, 149–50.
16. Fonvielle, *Wilmington Campaign*, 154; Gragg, *Confederate Goliath*, 86.
17. Fonvielle, *Wilmington Campaign*, 158–60; Gragg, *Confederate Goliath*, 88–89.
18. *Report of the Joint Committee on the Conduct of the War*, iii; Gragg, *Confederate Goliath*, 88–89.
19. Gragg, *Confederate Goliath*, 89.
20. Gragg, *Confederate Goliath*, 89.
21. Fonvielle, *Wilmington Campaign*, 162.
22. *Report of the Joint Committee on the Conduct of the War*, 40.
23. Gragg, *Confederate Goliath*, 90–94; Ames, *Capture of Fort Fisher*, 6; Fonvielle, *Wilmington Campaign*, 162–63, 165.
24. Fonvielle, *Wilmington Campaign*, 165.
25. *Report of the Joint Committee on the Conduct of the War*, 40.
26. *Report of the Joint Committee on the Conduct of the War*, 40; *O.R.N.*, ser, 1, 11:333; Gragg, *Confederate Goliath*, 95–96; Ames, *Adelbert Ames*, 165; Ames, *Capture of Fort Fisher*, 6; Fonvielle, *Wilmington Campaign*, 178–79.
27. Shiver, "Gross and Culpable Failure of Leadership," 60–61; Adelbert Ames to Martha and Jesse Ames, Jan. 2, 1865, Ames Family Papers, Smith College; Fonvielle, *Wilmington Campaign*, 186.
28. Kummer, *U.S. Marines in Battle*, 23; Fonvielle, *Wilmington Campaign*, 198–99.

29. *O.R.*, 46(1): sec. 2, 415; Fonvielle, *Wilmington Campaign*, 203, 224; Curtis, *Capture of Fort Fisher*, 306.

30. Fonvielle, *Wilmington Campaign*, 205; *O.R.*, 46(1): sec. 2, 395; Gragg, *Confederate Goliath*, 95–96, 110, 116.

31. Curtis, *Capture of Fort Fisher*, 306; McCaslin, *Last Stronghold*, 67–68.

32. *O.R.*, 46(2):1048, 1056; Fonvielle, *Wilmington Campaign*, 201, 221.

33. Fonvielle, *Wilmington Campaign*, 223–26.

34. Fonvielle, *Wilmington Campaign*, 231.

35. Gragg, *Confederate Goliath*, 135, 158–67; Robinson, *Hurricane of Fire*, 160–61, 170. Of those in Porter's diversionary force, 393 men fell. Fonvielle, *Wilmington Campaign*, 221.

36. Fonvielle, *Wilmington Campaign*, 45.

37. Robinson, *Hurricane of Fire*, 172–75; Lockwood, "Capture of Fort Fisher," 46–47.

38. Robinson, *Hurricane of Fire*, 172–75.

39. Ames, *Capture of Fort Fisher*, 12.

40. Ames, *Capture of Fort Fisher*, 45.

41. Curtis, *Capture of Fort Fisher*, 321; McCaslin, *Last Stronghold*, 81; Ames, *Capture of Fort Fisher*, 44; Adelbert Ames to Martha and Jesse Ames, Jan. 30, 1865, Ames Family Papers, Smith College; Thomas, *Story of Fort Fisher*, 11.

42. Gragg, *Confederate Goliath*, 210; Lockwood, "Capture of Fort Fisher," 54; *O.R.*, 46(1):399.

43. Lockwood, "Capture of Fort Fisher," 53.

44. Fonvielle, *Wilmington Campaign*, 290.

45. Ames, *Capture of Fort Fisher*, 16; *O.R.*, 46(1): sec. 2, 405, 416, 46(2):140; Gragg, *Confederate Goliath*, 227.

46. Grant, *Papers*, vol. 18, *November 16, 1864–February 20, 1865*, 230; *O.R.*, 46(1): sec. 1, 400.

47. A survey using the Library of Congress's Chronicling America website shows only twenty instances in which the phrase "General Ames" exists in archived newspapers during the week after the Second Battle of Fort Fisher. The phrase "General Terry" can be found eighty-six times. Chronicling America, Library of Congress, https://chroniclingamerica.loc.gov/.

48. Ames, *Adelbert Ames*, 199.

49. *O.R.*, 51(1):1200; Ames, *Adelbert Ames*, 199.

50. Adelbert Ames to Martha and Jesse Ames, Feb. 9, 1865, Ames Family Papers, Smith College.

51. Ames, *Capture of Fort Fisher*, 23; Gragg, *Confederate Goliath*, 228, 266–67; Curtis, *Capture of Fort Fisher*, 326; Lockwood, "Capture of Fort Fisher," 48.

52. *O.R.*, 46(1):416; Ames, *Capture of Fort Fisher*, 23.

53. *O.R.*, 47(1):149, 924, 47(2): sec. 1, 498.

54. *O.R.*, 47(1):151, 214; Fonvielle, *Wilmington Campaign*, 428.

55. Adelbert Ames to Martha and Jesse Ames, Feb. 23, 1865, Ames Family Papers, Smith College; Fonvielle, *Wilmington Campaign*, 430–35; *O.R.*, 47(1):924.

56. Adelbert Ames to Martha and Jesse Ames, Mar. 26, 1865, Ames Family Papers, Smith College; Cullum, *Biographical Register of the Officers and Graduates of the U.S. Military Academy*, 2:773.

57. Benson, "Public Career of Adelbert Ames," 85; Gragg, *Confederate Goliath*, 265; *O.R.*, 47(1):1.

58. Benson, "Public Career of Adelbert Ames," 85.

59. Adelbert Ames to Martha Ames, May 26, 1865, Ames Family Papers, Smith College; Records of United States Army Continental Commands, 1821–1920 (Record Group 393), 1817–1940 (bulk 1817–1940), 393.14, Guide to Federal Records; National Archives, https://www.archives.gov/research/guide-fed-records/groups/393.html#393.14 (accessed June 6, 2023).

60. *O.R.*, 47(3):615, 675; Ames, *Adelbert Ames*, 218; Wineapple, *Impeachers*, 126; Gordon-Reed, *Andrew Johnson*, 115–16.

61. Adelbert Ames to Martha and Jesse Ames, Sept. 6, 1865, Ames Family Papers, Smith College.

62. Ames, *Adelbert Ames*, 225.

63. Adelbert Ames to Martha and Jesse Ames, Nov. 24, 1865, Ames Family Papers, Smith College.

64. Ames, *Chronicles from the Nineteenth Century*, 1:29. The remainder of this letter is missing after the word "wrath." Ames also wrote home that he had befriended a "Mr. Caldwell" who represented a pro-Union contingent within Columbia.

65. Ames, *Adelbert Ames*, 225.

66. Ames, *Adelbert Ames*, 32–33.

67. Ames, *Adelbert Ames*, 32–33.

7. TRAVELS ABROAD

1. Ames, *Chronicles from the Nineteenth Century*, 1:36.

2. Dupont, Gandhi, and Weiss, *American Invasion of Europe*, 3, 47; Stowe, *Going Abroad*, 8.

3. Stowe, *Going Abroad*, 5–8. Ames's total monthly pay in 1866 was $170.00, or roughly $2,688.68 when accounting for inflation. *Official Army Register for 1865* (Washington, DC: Adjutant General's Office, 1865), 112.

4. Adelbert Ames, "Ames' Journal while Abroad," Ames Family Papers, Smith College, 1; Wawro, *Franco-Prussian War*, 312; Hudson, "Formation of the North German Confederation," 425.

5. Stowe, *Going Abroad*, 5.

6. Ames, "Ames' Journal while Abroad."

7. Wawro, *Austro-Prussian War*, 40–43; Wetzel, *Duel of Giants*, 21; Ames, "Ames' Journal while Abroad," 1.

8. Ames, "Ames' Journal while Abroad," 4.

9. Ames, "Ames' Journal while Abroad," 2.

10. Ames, "Ames' Journal while Abroad," 3.

11. Ames, "Ames' Journal while Abroad," 7–8. John Van Buren died a few months later and was interred in Albany, New York. "Funeral of John Van Buren," *Tiffin (OH) Tribune*, Oct. 25, 1866, 2.

12. Ames, "Ames' Journal while Abroad," 9.

13. Ames, "Ames' Journal while Abroad," 10–11.

14. Ames, "Ames' Journal while Abroad," 11, 29. Ames's travels took him to Europe during the 1866–67 spike of the nineteenth century's fourth cholera epidemic (1863–75). Beginning on the Indian subcontinent, the disease entered the United States in 1866 via New Orleans and spread all over the world by 1869. Hays, *Epidemics and Pandemics,* 268. For more on this, see Rosenberg, *Cholera Years;* and Snowden, *Epidemics and Society.*

15. Ames, "Ames' Journal while Abroad," 12–13.

16. Ames, "Ames' Journal while Abroad," 20–21.

17. Ames, "Ames' Journal while Abroad," 27–29; Boulard, *Swing around the Circle,* 112; Guelzo, *Reconstruction,* 37–38.

18. Guelzo, *Reconstruction,* 27, 29.

19. Ames, "Ames' Journal while Abroad," 34.

20. Ames, "Ames' Journal while Abroad," 30–31.

21. Shaw, *Personal Memoirs and Correspondence,* 44.

22. Ames, "Ames' Journal while Abroad," 37.

23. Ames, "Ames' Journal while Abroad," 42–44.

24. Ames, "Ames' Journal while Abroad," 48, 55.

25. Strauss-Schom, *Shadow Emperor,* 230; Ames, "Ames' Journal while Abroad," 52.

26. Ames, "Ames' Journal while Abroad," 62.

27. Ames, "Ames' Journal while Abroad," 71.

28. Ames, "Ames' Journal while Abroad," 81–83.

29. Ames, "Ames' Journal while Abroad," 81; Adelbert Ames, "Ames' Journal while Abroad, Journal No. II," Ames Family Papers, Smith College, 24. The Tuileries Palace would not exist long after Ames left France. Marxist revolutionaries burned it to the ground after Napoleon III was captured and the French lost the Franco-Prussian War in 1870. A socialist government, the Paris Commune, held power in the city March–May 1871. See Merriman, *Massacre.*

30. Ames, "Ames' Journal while Abroad, Journal No. II," 22–23; Hanser, *Architecture of France,* 117; Pickney, *Napoleon III and the Rebuilding of Paris,* 78.

31. Ames, "Ames' Journal while Abroad, Journal No. II," 55.

32. Ames, "Ames' Journal while Abroad, Journal No. II," 55.

33. Ames, "Ames' Journal while Abroad, Journal No. II," 39, 55–56, 66; Raudzens, "British Ordnance Department"; Spurgeon, *Complete Works,* 2, 5.

34. Ames, "Ames' Journal while Abroad, Journal No. II," 75.

35. Beale, *Charles Hallé,* 239; Ames, "Ames' Journal while Abroad, Journal No. II," 79.

36. Ames, "Ames' Journal while Abroad, Journal No. II," 79.

37. Mackworth-Young, *History & Treasures of Windsor Castle,* 75; Ames, "Ames' Journal while Abroad, Journal No. II," 87. Penn's democratic principles that he helped instill in Pennsylvania's founding served as an inspiration for the US Constitution. The home in England Ames toured was where Penn died after returning penniless from North America. For a biography of Pennsylvania's founder, see Fantel, *William Penn.*

38. Adelbert Ames, "Ames' Journal while Abroad, Journal No. III," Ames Family Papers, Smith College, 1–4; Hobhouse, *Crystal Palace and the Great Exhibition,* 18.

39. Ames, "Ames' Journal while Abroad, Journal No. III," 5.
40. Ames, "Ames' Journal while Abroad, Journal No. III," 6.
41. Ames, "Ames' Journal while Abroad, Journal No. III," 8.
42. Ames, "Ames' Journal while Abroad, Journal No. III," 11–13.
43. Ames, "Ames' Journal while Abroad, Journal No. III," 13–15.
44. Ames, "Ames' Journal while Abroad, Journal No. III," 26–25, 31.

8. A MILITARY MAN WEARING POLITICAL HATS

1. Harris, *Presidential Reconstruction in Mississippi*, 7, 19.
2. Woodrick, *Civil War Siege of Jackson*, 112.
3. Ballard, *Vicksburg*, 52, 385, 414–15; Hall, Nowell, and Childress, *Washington County, Mississippi*, 8.
4. Foner, *Reconstruction*, 15.
5. Foner, *Reconstruction*, 15; Messner, *Mississippi Black Codes*, 82. Mississippi did not approve the Thirteenth Amendment until 1995.
6. Foner, *Forever Free*, 117; Satcher, *Blacks in Mississippi Politics*, 19.
7. Sanger, *U.S. Statutes at Large*, 507–9.
8. Egerton, *Wars of Reconstruction*, 289; Ames, *Adelbert Ames*, 255. Forrest was integral in the growth of the supremacist organization during the late 1860s. But by the 1870s, he had renounced the Klan, testifying before Congress about the group. During the last five years of his life, Forrest actively criticized Klan activity. In a turn of events, the former Confederate general offered to track down those who had lynched four men in Tennessee. In his last public event, Forrest gave a speech before a convention of Black southerners, promoting equal rights for all people and advocating harmony. Hurst, *Nathan Bedford Forrest*, 357–84.
9. Ames, *Adelbert Ames*, 264, 266; Turkel, *Heroes of the American Reconstruction*, 15.
10. Satcher, *Blacks in Mississippi Politics*, 18–19.
11. Satcher, *Blacks in Mississippi Politics*, 27–29.
12. "Gen. Gillem's Election Report," *Weekly Panola (MS) Star*, July 25, 1868, 2; Lemann, *Redemption*, 34; Satcher, *Blacks in Mississippi Politics*, 28–29.
13. "The Election in Mississippi," *American Citizen* (Canton, MS), July 25, 1868, 3; "A Prompt Rebuke," *Jackson (MS) Daily Clarion*, July 3, 1868, 1.
14. Grant, *Papers*, vol. 18, *October 1, 1867–June 30, 1868*, 279.
15. Grant, *Papers*, vol. 18, *October 1, 1867–June 30, 1868*, 280; Ames, *Chronicles from the Nineteenth Century*, 1:34–35.
16. Ames, *Adelbert Ames*, 271.
17. Ames, *Adelbert Ames*, 272–73; "Gov. Humphrey's Ejected from the Executive Mansion by Military Force," *Oxford (MS) Falcon*, July 18, 1868, 1.
18. "Off With His Head," *Grenada (MS) Sentinel*, June 20, 1868, 2.
19. Lemann, *Redemption*, 28.
20. Lemann, *Redemption*, 34–35.
21. Downs, *After Appomattox*, 108, 142.
22. Downs, *After Appomattox*, 187; Ames, *Chronicles from the Nineteenth Century*, 1:36–37.

23. Ames, *Chronicles from the Nineteenth Century*, 1:36–37.
24. Grant, *Papers*, vol. 18, *October 1, 1867–June 30, 1868*, 530–31, 541; Fairman, *Reconstruction and Reunion*, 581–83.
25. Adelbert Ames, "Ames' Journal while Abroad," Ames Family Papers, Smith College, 24; Ames, *Chronicles from the Nineteenth Century*, 1:37.
26. Ames, *Adelbert Ames*, 267.
27. Grant, *Papers*, vol. 18, *October 1, 1867–June 30, 1868*, 172, 402, 416.
28. French, *Two Wars*, 342–43; Grant, *Papers*, vol. 18, *October 1, 1867–June 30, 1868*, 468.
29. Satcher, *Blacks in Mississippi Politics*, 34.
30. Ames, *Adelbert Ames*, 281; "Election Order, Headquarters 4th Military District, Department of Mississippi," *Jackson (MS) Weekly Clarion*, Nov. 4, 1869, 3.
31. McPherson, *Political History of the United States*, 481; Satcher, *Blacks in Mississippi Politics*, 34.
32. "The Reason Why the Alcorn-Ames Faction Cannot Be Trusted," *Jackson (MS) Weekly Clarion*, Nov. 4, 1869, 2.
33. Lemann, *Redemption*, 38.
34. Grant, *Papers*, vol. 18, *October 1, 1867–June 30, 1868*, 262.
35. Kalb, *Congressional Quarterly's Guide to U.S. Elections*, 1707; "Information Wanted," *Jackson (MS) Weekly Clarion*, Dec. 2, 1869, 2; "The Great Election," *Macon (MS) Beacon*, Dec. 4, 1869, 2; "General Alcorn Refuses to be Provisional Governor," *Vicksburg (MS) Weekly Herald*, Jan. 1, 1870, 3.
36. State of Mississippi, *Constitution and Ordinances of the State of Mississippi* (Jackson: Mississippi Historical Society, 1870), 1.
37. "The Admission of Mississippi," *Jackson (MS) Weekly Clarion*, Feb. 24, 1870, 2.
38. Ames, *Adelbert Ames*, 286.
39. Ames, *Adelbert Ames*, 285, 42–43.
40. Ames, *Adelbert Ames*, 294.
41. Current, *Those Terrible Carpetbaggers*, 182–83; *Congressional Globe*, 41st Cong., 2nd sess., 1870, 42(3):2129.
42. *Congressional Globe*, 41st Cong., 2nd sess., 1870, 42(3):2129.
43. *Congressional Globe*, 41st Cong., 2nd sess., 1870, 42(3):2129.
44. *Congressional Globe*, 41st Cong., 2nd sess., 1870, 42(3):2128.
45. *Congressional Globe*, 41st Cong., 2nd sess., 1870, 42(3):2128.
46. *Congressional Globe*, 41st Cong., 2nd sess., 1870, 42(3):2131–33.
47. *Congressional Globe*, 41st Cong., 2nd sess., 1870, 42(3):2161.
48. *Congressional Globe*, 41st Cong., 2nd sess., 1870, 42(3):2151, 2162–67.
49. *Congressional Globe*, 41st Cong., 2nd sess., 1870, 42(3):2314, 2341.
50. James H. Pierce to Adelbert Ames, Apr. 3, 1870, Ames Family Papers, Smith College.

9. SENATOR FROM MISSISSIPPI

1. Ames, *Adelbert Ames*, 316.
2. Martha Ames to Adelbert Ames, Apr. 5, 1870, Ames Family Papers, Smith College.

3. Martha Ames to Adelbert Ames, Apr. 5, 1870; Blanche Butler to Adelbert Ames, May 7, 1870, Ames Family Papers, Smith College.

4. Ames, *Adelbert Ames*, 316.

5. Adelbert Ames to Blanche Butler, May 24, 1870, Ames Family Papers, Smith College; Adelbert Ames to Blanche Butler, June 21, 1870, Ames Family Papers, Smith College; Adelbert Ames to Blanche Butler, June 28, 1870, Ames Family Papers, Smith College.

6. Ames, *Adelbert Ames*, 325–26.

7. Blanche Ames to Sarah Butler, Sept. 1870, Ames Family Papers, Smith College; Ames, *Adelbert Ames*, 327–29.

8. Ames, *Adelbert Ames*, 330.

9. Ames, *Adelbert Ames*, 331.

10. Ames, *Adelbert Ames*, 331.

11. *Congressional Globe*, 42nd Cong., 1st sess., 1871, 44(1):194, 197.

12. *Congressional Globe*, 42nd Cong., 1st sess., 1871, 44(1):195, 197.

13. *Congressional Globe*, 42nd Cong., 1st sess., 1871, 44(1):198.

14. *Congressional Globe*, 42nd Cong., 1st sess., 1871, 44(1):198.

15. *Congressional Globe*, 42nd Cong., 1st sess., 1871, 44(1):198.

16. Ames, *Adelbert Ames*, 340.

17. "Untitled Article," *Ouachita Telegraph* (Monroe, LA), May 20, 1871, 2.

18. "A Hideous Picture," *Weekly Caucasian* (Lexington, MO), Apr. 8, 1871, 1; "The New Principle," *Anderson Intelligencer* (Anderson Court House, SC), June 1, 1871, 1.

19. Ames, *Adelbert Ames*, 337; Posey, *Succeeding against Great Odds*, i.

20. Foner, *Reconstruction*, 298.

21. *Congressional Globe*, 42nd Cong., 1st sess., 1871, 44(2):app., 13.

22. *Congressional Globe*, 42nd Cong., 1st sess., 1871, 44(2):app., 73; Ames, *Adelbert Ames*, 342.

23. *Congressional Globe*, 42nd Cong., 1st sess., 1871, 44(2):app., 127, 128.

24. *Congressional Globe*, 42nd Cong., 1st sess., 1871, 44(2):569.

25. "Waving the bloody shirt" became a phrase that highlighted southern contempt against northern politicians and former Union soldiers who bemoaned the violence and struggle that white residents in ex-Confederate states perpetrated against the US military, freedmen, freedwomen, and white Republicans. See Budiansky, *Bloody Shirt*, 3.

26. *Congressional Globe*, 42nd Cong., 1st sess., 1871, 44(2):569.

27. *Congressional Globe*, 42nd Cong., 1st sess., 1871, 44(2):569.

28. *Congressional Globe*, 42nd Cong., 1st sess., 1871, 44(2):571.

29. *Congressional Globe*, 42nd Cong., 1st sess., 1871, 44(2):571.

30. Ames, *Chronicles from the Nineteenth Century*, 1:297–98.

31. Ames, *Chronicles from the Nineteenth Century*, 1:298.

32. Ames, *Chronicles from the Nineteenth Century*, 1:260, 266,

33. Ames, *Chronicles from the Nineteenth Century*, 1:271.

34. *Treaty between the United States and Great Britain*, 1–4. The Great Rapprochement, a term coined by historians like Bradford Perkins, refers to the developing unity between the United States and Great Britain from 1895 to 1915. After the Spanish-American War, a conflict in which Ames fought, Britain and the United States frequently

sided with each other during geopolitical troubles. See Burton, *British-American Diplomacy*, chaps. 1–3.

35. Ames, *Chronicles from the Nineteenth Century*, 1:279, 285.

36. Ames, *Chronicles from the Nineteenth Century*, 1:307.

37. Ames, *Chronicles from the Nineteenth Century*, 1:315, 319, 342.

38. Untitled article, *Macon (MS) Beacon*, Oct. 7, 1871, 1; "Radical War upon Mississippians," *Jackson (MS) Weekly Clarion*, Oct. 5, 1871, 1.

39. Ames, *Chronicles from the Nineteenth Century*, 1:332, 351; Lemann, *Redemption*, 50.

40. *Report of the Joint Select Committee to Inquire into the Condition of Affairs in the Late Insurrectionary States*, 424, 505, 581. Plenty of witnesses noted the political complexion of Reconstruction violence, with one interviewee stating, "I have never heard of anybody else other than Republicans suffer at the hands of hooded louts," while Democratic commentators usually dismissed these connections. *Report of the Joint Select Committee to Inquire into the Condition of Affairs in the Late Insurrectionary States*, 302.

41. *Congressional Globe*, 42nd Cong., 2nd sess., 1872, 45(2):1109.

42. *Congressional Globe*, 42nd Cong., 2nd sess., 1872, 45(6):403.

43. *Congressional Globe*, 42nd Cong., 2nd sess., 1872, 45(6):403.

44. Benson, "Public Career of Adelbert Ames," 190, app., 393–95.

45. Benson, "Public Career of Adelbert Ames," 190, app., 393–95.

46. Rawley, "General Amnesty Act of 1872," 480.

47. Ames, *Chronicles from the Nineteenth Century*, 1:366–70.

48. Ames, *Chronicles from the Nineteenth Century*, 1:379.

49. Ames, *Chronicles from the Nineteenth Century*, 1:380–81.

50. Ames, *Chronicles from the Nineteenth Century*, 1:384.

51. Ames, *Chronicles from the Nineteenth Century*, 1:384; Benson, "Public Career of Adelbert Ames," 196.

52. "A Representative Granite Exposes the Cloven Foot of Radicalism," *Jackson (MS) Weekly Clarion*, Sept. 12, 1872, 2; "The Liberal Ticket, for President, Horace Greely," *American Citizen* (Canton, MS), Sept. 7, 1872, 2.

53. "The Election," *Jackson (MS) Weekly Clarion*, Nov. 14, 1872, 1.

54. "The Presidential Election," *American Citizen* (Canton, MS), Nov. 9, 1872, 1.

55. Ames, *Chronicles from the Nineteenth Century*, 1:412, 416.

56. Plimpton, *Ancestry of Blanche Butler Ames and Adelbert Ames*, 1.

57. Blanche Ames to Sarah Butler, May 21, 1873, Ames Family Papers, Smith College; Ames, *Adelbert Ames*, 377.

58. Benson, "Public Career of Adelbert Ames," 204; Ames, *Chronicles from the Nineteenth Century*, 1:524.

59. Benson, "Public Career of Adelbert Ames," 206.

60. Benson, "Public Career of Adelbert Ames," 206.

61. Benson, "Public Career of Adelbert Ames," 536, 540.

62. Ames, *Chronicles from the Nineteenth Century*, 1:597; Benson, "Public Career of Adelbert Ames," 211.

63. Ames, *Chronicles from the Nineteenth Century*, 1:597.

64. Benson, "Public Career of Adelbert Ames," 214.

65. Ames, *Chronicles from the Nineteenth Century*, 1:624, 625.
66. Current, *Those Terrible Carpetbaggers*, 309; Adelbert Ames to Blanche Ames, Nov. 7, 1873, Ames Family Papers, Smith College.
67. Ames, *Chronicles from the Nineteenth Century*, 1:630.

10. THE HEIGHT OF THE PARTY AND THE HEIGHT OF PREJUDICE

1. Ames, *Chronicles from the Nineteenth Century*, 1:635; Current, *Those Terrible Carpetbaggers*, 309.
2. Ames, *Chronicles from the Nineteenth Century*, 1:642, 644; Current, *Those Terrible Carpetbaggers*, 310.
3. Ames, *Adelbert Ames*, 385; Ames, *Chronicles from the Nineteenth Century*, 1:636; Benson, "Public Career of Adelbert Ames," 222.
4. Ames, *Chronicles from the Nineteenth Century*, 1:637.
5. Ames, *Chronicles from the Nineteenth Century*, 1:638.
6. Ames, *Chronicles from the Nineteenth Century*, 1:640.
7. Ames, *Chronicles from the Nineteenth Century*, 1:638, 640. Butler congratulated Ames for this and several other speeches, noting, "I am very much pleased with their tone, their substance, and the manner in which they are framed." Ames, *Chronicles from the Nineteenth Century*, 1:659.
8. Smith, *Mississippi in the Civil War*, 91–92.
9. Smith, *Mississippi in the Civil War*, 95.
10. Summers, *Railroads, Reconstruction, and the Gospel of Prosperity*, 4; Willis, *Forgotten Time*, 15–16.
11. Railroads represented 80 percent of the total stock market capitalization on the eve of the crash. Eighty-nine railroads defaulted on their bonds by the end of 1873, a total that grew to 108 by 1874. See Morris, *Tycoons*, chap. 4.
12. Current, *Those Terrible Carpetbaggers*, 311; Mixon, "Crisis of 1873," 722; Morris, *Tycoons*, 100–101; Skrabec, *Henry Clay Frick*, 51.
13. Ames, *Adelbert Ames*, 388.
14. Ames, *Adelbert Ames*, 390; Ames, *Chronicles from the Nineteenth Century*, 1:664.
15. "Message of Governor Ames on the Vicksburg and Nashville Railroad," *National Republican* (Washington, DC), Mar. 14, 1874, 4; Ames, *Chronicles from the Nineteenth Century*, 1:665.
16. "The Conservative Press on the Governor's Reform Recommendations," *Jackson (MS) Weekly Clarion*, Mar. 12, 1874, 4; Benson, "Public Career of Adelbert Ames," 225.
17. Ames, *Chronicles from the Nineteenth Century*, 1:659, 667–69; Lemann, *Redemption*, 64.
18. "The Governor's Address," *American Citizen* (Canton, MS), Jan. 31, 1874, 2; Benson, "Public Career of Adelbert Ames," 227.
19. Lemann, *Redemption*, 64; Ames, *Chronicles from the Nineteenth Century*, 1:667, 671, 673.
20. Lemann, *Redemption*, 65.
21. Ames, *Chronicles from the Nineteenth Century*, 1:677; Benson, "Public Career of Adelbert Ames," 236.

22. Blanche Ames to Sarah Butler, May 9, 1874, Ames Family Papers, Smith College; Lemann, *Redemption*, 64, 70–71; Ames, *Chronicles from the Nineteenth Century*, 1:671, 673.

23. Benson, "Public Career of Adelbert Ames," 237–38.

24. Benson, "Public Career of Adelbert Ames," 238.

25. Benson, "Public Career of Adelbert Ames," 238.

26. Ames, *Adelbert Ames*, 397; Rable, *But There Was No Peace*, 147.

27. Current, *Those Terrible Carpetbaggers*, 314–15; Rable, *But There Was No Peace*, 147; Grant, *Papers*, vol. 25, *1874*, 158.

28. Grant, *Papers*, vol. 25, *1874*, 158–59.

29. Gillette, *Retreat from Reconstruction*, 150.

30. Ames, *Chronicles from the Nineteenth Century*, 1:693.

31. Current, *Those Terrible Carpetbaggers*, 314.

32. Gillette, *Retreat from Reconstruction*, 150; Rable, *But There Was No Peace*, 150.

33. Ames, *Chronicles from the Nineteenth Century*, 2:1; Lemann, *Redemption*, 75.

34. Ames, *Chronicles from the Nineteenth Century*, 2:702, 707.

35. "Cardozo Arrested," *Greenville (MS) Times*, Aug. 29, 1874, 2; Benson, "Public Career of Adelbert Ames," 250; Gillette, *Retreat from Reconstruction*, 150.

36. Ames, *Chronicles from the Nineteenth Century*, 1:695, 706, 2:10, 23–28; Lemann, *Redemption*, 75.

37. Mayes, *Lucius Q. C. Lamar*, 29, 94.

38. Lemann, *Redemption*, 69–70.

39. "Lamar on Sumner," *Chicago Daily Tribune*, Apr. 29, 1874.

40. Ames, *Adelbert Ames*, 392–93; Ames, *Chronicles from the Nineteenth Century*, 1:661; Lemann, *Redemption*, 70.

41. "L. Q. C Lamar," *American Citizen* (Canton, MS), Apr. 18, 1874.

42. Leman, *Redemption*, 29, 32, 42–43, 79; Ames, *Adelbert Ames*, 402.

43. Ames, *Chronicles from the Nineteenth Century*, 2:52; Lemann, *Redemption*, 79.

44. Lemann, *Redemption*, 83–84.

45. Lemann, *Redemption*, 85; *Vicksburg Troubles*, in *House Reports*, 43rd Cong., 2nd sess., US Congressional Serial Set 1659 (Washington, DC: Government Printing Office, 1875), 23; Current, *Those Terrible Carpetbaggers*, 316.

46. Lemann, *Redemption*, 86, 87; Ames, *Adelbert Ames*, 405; Dorsey, "'Vicksburg Troubles,'" 101–2.

47. Dorsey, "'Vicksburg Troubles,'" 102.

48. Dorsey, "'Vicksburg Troubles,'" 97.

49. Dorsey, "'Vicksburg Troubles,'" 102–3, 147; Current, *Those Terrible Carpetbaggers*, 316; Gillette, *Retreat from Reconstruction*, 150. Owen evaded injury by jumping into a muddy ditch; Miller's men found him and took him prisoner. Lemann, *Redemption*, 88.

50. Benson, "Public Career of Adelbert Ames," 252; Lemann, *Redemption*, 91.

51. Ames, *Chronicles from the Nineteenth Century*, 2:72.

52. Ames, *Chronicles from the Nineteenth Century*, 2:72; Current, *Those Terrible Carpetbaggers*, 316.

53. Ames, *Chronicles from the Nineteenth Century*, 2:77, 92. Nicholas Lemann attributes Grant's uncharacteristically rapid response to the uncomplicated aggression that

brought about Crosby's deposition. Inaction "would mean permitting a force of armed rebels to install itself in the seat of government in an American county." Lemann, *Redemption*, 91.

54. Ames, *Chronicles from the Nineteenth Century*, 2:81, 92; Lemann, *Redemption*, 96; "Rates of Subscription (Headlines)," *Jackson (MS) Daily Clarion*, Jan. 7, 1875, 1.

55. Lemann, *Redemption*, 98.

56. Satcher, *Blacks in Mississippi Politics*, 141; Coffey, *Reconstruction Years*, 157, 290.

57. Bradley, *Army of Reconstruction*, 69; Lemann, *Redemption*, 104; Holloway, *Black Rights in the Reconstruction Era*, 14–16.

58. "Riot in Yazoo City: A Republican Meeting Broken Up," *American Citizen* (Canton, MS), Sept. 4, 1875, 2.

59. The editor of one newspaper would later claim that a Black official started the fight when he tried to stop some young white men from drinking. "The Clinton Riot," *Copiahan* (Copiah, MS), Sept. 11, 1875, 3.

60. "The Clinton Riot: The Beginnings, the Results, Casualties, Incidents," *Jackson (MS) Weekly Clarion*, Sept. 8, 1875, 2; "Bloodshed and Riot in Hinds," *Greenville (MS) Times*, Sept. 11, 1875, 2; Lemann, *Redemption*, 110–16.

61. Ames, *Adelbert Ames*, 424; Ames, *Chronicles from the Nineteenth Century*, 2:166.

62. Ames, *Chronicles from the Nineteenth Century*, 2:183; Lemann, *Redemption*, 123, 427.

63. Augur's men were instructed to protect state property, not to serve as ad hoc law enforcement. Moreover, Augur could only lend assistance if so ordered by his superiors. Ames, *Chronicles from the Nineteenth Century*, 2:195.

64. Ames, *Chronicles from the Nineteenth Century*, 2:191; Stauffer and Jenkins, *State of Jones*, 268; Lemann, *Redemption*, 125.

65. Lemann, *Redemption*, 126.

66. Ames, *Adelbert Ames*, 434; Ames, *Chronicles from the Nineteenth Century*, 2:215; Lemann, *Redemption*, 127.

67. Pierrepont had already cautioned Chase "not to be misled" by the governor. Ames, *Chronicles from the Nineteenth Century*, 2:230.

68. Lemann, *Redemption*, 129. Barksdale's older brother, William, was a Confederate general who had been killed at Gettysburg while fighting in the same area as Ames's former command, the 20th Maine. Tucker, *Barksdale's Charge*, 249.

69. Ames, *Chronicles from the Nineteenth Century*, 2:150–51.

70. Ames, *Chronicles from the Nineteenth Century*, 2:218; Current, *Those Terrible Carpetbaggers*, 323.

71. Ames, *Chronicles from the Nineteenth Century*, 2:245.

72. Foner, *Short History of Reconstruction*, 236; Lemann, *Redemption*, 147.

73. Ames, *Chronicles from the Nineteenth Century*, 2:249; Benson, "Public Career of Adelbert Ames," 300–301; Lemann, *Redemption*, 150.

11. A GOVERNOR AND RECONSTRUCTION ON TRIAL

1. "A Clean Sweep," *Star of Pascagoula* (Pascagoula, MS), Nov. 6, 1875, 1; "It Is Finished," *Greenville (MS) Times*, Nov. 6, 1875, 2; "Gov. Ames," *Jackson (MS) Weekly Clarion*, Nov. 3, 1875, 2.

2. "Crooked Whiskey," *Easton (OH) Democrat,* Nov. 25, 1875, 2; "Pease on the Warpath," *Indiana State Sentinel* (Indianapolis), Nov. 18, 1875, 6.

3. Ames, *Chronicles from the Nineteenth Century,* 2:257.

4. Lemann, *Redemption,* 148.

5. "Impeachment or No Impeachment," *Jackson (MS) Weekly Clarion,* Dec. 8, 1875, 2; "The Tidal Wave: The Voice of the Press on Impeachment," *Jackson (MS) Daily Clarion,* Jan. 4, 1876, 1.

6. "The Impeachment Bugbear," *New Orleans Republican,* Nov. 14, 1875, 4.

7. Benson, "Public Career of Adelbert Ames," 312; Ames, *Chronicles from the Nineteenth Century,* 2:261.

8. Ames, *Chronicles from the Nineteenth Century,* 2:266–70.

9. Lemann, *Redemption,* 161.

10. Ames, *Chronicles from the Nineteenth Century,* 2:281; Benson, "Public Career of Adelbert Ames," 313.

11. Benson, "Public Career of Adelbert Ames," 314; Lemann, *Redemption,* 157–59.

12. "Whither Are We Drifting," *Canton (MS) Mail,* Mar. 11, 1876, 2; "Impeachment," *Jackson (MS) Weekly Clarion,* Jan. 26, 1876, 1.

13. Benson, "Public Career of Adelbert Ames," 312.

14. Ames, *Chronicles from the Nineteenth Century,* 2:339.

15. *Preliminary Proceedings: The Testimony in the Impeachment of Adelbert Ames, as Governor of Mississippi* (Jackson, MS: Power & Barksdale, 1877), 19; Ames, *Chronicles from the Nineteenth Century,* 2:351.

16. "Mississippi Legislature, Senate—Court of Impeachment," *Jackson (MS) Daily Clarion,* Mar. 17, 1876; "The Impeachment of Gov. Ames—What Outsiders Say," *Jackson (MS) Daily Clarion,* Mar. 11, 1876.

17. Untitled article, *Jackson (MS) Times,* Mar. 2, 1876.

18. *Preliminary Proceedings,* 1.

19. Benson, "Public Career of Adelbert Ames," 322.

20. Ames, *Chronicles from the Nineteenth Century,* 2:351.

21. *Journal of the Senate of the State of Mississippi, Sitting as a Court of Impeachment in the Trials of Adelbert Ames,* 28 (hereafter cited as Ames Impeachment Trials Journal).

22. Ames Impeachment Trials Journal, 29.

23. Ames Impeachment Trials Journal, 5.

24. Ames Impeachment Trials Journal, 6.

25. Ames Impeachment Trials Journal, 9.

26. Ames Impeachment Trials Journal, 31.

27. Ames Impeachment Trials Journal, 32.

28. Ames, *Chronicles from the Nineteenth Century,* 2:315.

29. Ames Impeachment Trials Journal, 15.

30. Ames Impeachment Trials Journal, 15.

31. Ames Impeachment Trials Journal, 33.

32. Ames Impeachment Trials Journal, 33.

33. Ames Impeachment Trials Journal, 33.

34. Ames, *Chronicles from the Nineteenth Century,* 2:316.

35. Ames Impeachment Trials Journal, 34.
36. Ames Impeachment Trials Journal, 35.
37. Ames, *Chronicles from the Nineteenth Century*, 2:317–18.
38. Ames Impeachment Trials Journal, 36.
39. Ames Impeachment Trials Journal, 39.
40. Ames Impeachment Trials Journal, 323.
41. Ames Impeachment Trials Journal, 39.
42. Ames Impeachment Trials Journal, 41.
43. Ames, *Chronicles from the Nineteenth Century*, 2:330.
44. Ames Impeachment Trials Journal, 41.
45. Ames, *Chronicles from the Nineteenth Century*, 2:332–35.
46. *Preliminary Proceedings*, 13–14.
47. Ames, *Chronicles from the Nineteenth Century*, 2:334.
48. Ames Impeachment Trials Journal, 41.
49. Ames, *Chronicles from the Nineteenth Century*, 2:336–37.
50. Ames, *Chronicles from the Nineteenth Century*, 2:337.
51. Ames Impeachment Trials Journal, 42–45.
52. Ames, *Chronicles from the Nineteenth Century*, 2:348; Ames Impeachment Trials Journal, 51.
53. Ames Impeachment Trials Journal, 37.
54. Ames, *Chronicles from the Nineteenth Century*, 2:351.
55. Ames, *Chronicles from the Nineteenth Century*, 2:352–53.
56. Ames, *Chronicles from the Nineteenth Century*, 2:347, 351.
57. Ames Impeachment Trials Journal, 58–59, 61.
58. "Ames's Resignation," *Greenville (MS) Times*, Apr. 1, 1876.
59. Ames, *Chronicles from the Nineteenth Century*, 2:354.
60. "Ames' Resignation," *Greenville (MS) Times*, Apr. 1, 1876, 2.
61. Ames, *Chronicles from the Nineteenth Century*, 2:310.
62. *Report of Committees of the Senate of the United States*, iii.
63. Senator McMillan replaced Republican senator Richard J. Oblesby on April 25. *Report of Committees of the Senate of the United States*, iii.
64. *Report of Committees of the Senate of the United States*, v.
65. Ames, *Chronicles from the Nineteenth Century*, 2:355–56.
66. *Report of Committees of the Senate of the United States*, 5.
67. *Report of Committees of the Senate of the United States*, 2.
68. *Report of Committees of the Senate of the United States*, 5.
69. *Report of Committees of the Senate of the United States*, 5, 9–12.
70. *Report of Committees of the Senate of the United States*, 8.
71. *Report of Committees of the Senate of the United States*, 17–19.
72. *Report of Committees of the Senate of the United States*, 20.
73. *Report of Committees of the Senate of the United States*, 20.
74. *Report of Committees of the Senate of the United States*, 25.
75. *Report of Committees of the Senate of the United States*, 29–36.
76. Ames, *Chronicles from the Nineteenth Century*, 2:373, 379.

77. *Report of Committees of the Senate of the United States*, ix–x.
78. *Report of Committees of the Senate of the United States*, x, xii.
79. *Report of Committees of the Senate of the United States*, xiv.
80. *Report of Committees of the Senate of the United States*, xiv–xv.
81. "The Governor's Resignation," *American Citizen* (Canton, MS), Apr. 1, 1876, 2.
82. "Rejoicing over the Resignation," *Jackson (MS) Daily Clarion*, Mar. 30, 1876, 1.
83. Foner, *Short History of Reconstruction*, 223.
84. Foner, *Forever Free*, 197–98; Ferrell, *Reconstruction*, 59.
85. Guelzo, *Reconstruction*, 109–10.
86. Rehnquist, *Centennial Crisis*, 201–2; Foner, *Second Founding*, 126.

12. LIFE REFUSING TO SLOW

1. Ames, *Chronicles from the Nineteenth Century*, 2:398–401.
2. Blegen, *Minnesota*, 344; David L. Nass, "The Rural Experience," in Clark, *Minnesota in a Century of Change*, 131; Noe, *Howling Storm*, 164, 327–29, 417–19.
3. John Younger was briefly a member of the gang, but he died more than two years before his brothers raided Northfield after being shot through the throat following an ambush that went awry. See Younger, *Story of Cole Younger*, 89–90.
4. Stiles, *Jesse James*, 324; Fanebust, *Chasing Frank and Jesse James*, 27.
5. Younger, *Story of Cole Younger*, 104; Yeatman, *Frank and Jesse James*, 172; Stiles, *Jesse James*, 325.
6. Stiles, *Jesse James*, 326–27; Ames, *Chronicles from the Nineteenth Century*, 2:403.
7. Stiles, *Jesse James*, 327–29, 331; Fanebust, *Chasing Frank and Jesse James*, 37.
8. Ames, *Chronicles from the Nineteenth Century*, 2:403–4.
9. Younger, *Story of Cole Younger*, 109; Ames, *Chronicles from the Nineteenth Century*, 2:403–4.
10. Ames, *Chronicles from the Nineteenth Century*, 2:403–4.
11. Ames, *Chronicles from the Nineteenth Century*, 2:404–5.
12. Stiles, *Jesse James*, 334; Ames, *Chronicles from the Nineteenth Century*, 2:404–5.
13. Fanebust, *Chasing Frank and Jesse James*, 46; Ames, *Chronicles from the Nineteenth Century*, 2:404–6.
14. Ames, *Chronicles from the Nineteenth Century*, 2:443.
15. Ames, *Chronicles from the Nineteenth Century*, 2:449, 459.
16. Ames, *Chronicles from the Nineteenth Century*, 2:473, 503; Ames, *Adelbert Ames*, 495.
17. Plimpton, *Ancestry of Blanche Butler Ames and Adelbert Ames*, 162; Ames, *Adelbert Ames*, 495.
18. Butler, *Butler's Book*, 81, 495–597; Sinnett, *Our Family in Maine*, 55.
19. "Bravery Awarded: The President Given Medals to Gallant Men," *Washington (DC) Evening Star*, June 22, 1894, 1.
20. Ames, *Chronicles from the Nineteenth Century*, 2:605.
21. Ames would become the president of the Union Land and Grazing Company, started by Benjamin Butler. He and his son, Butler, would oversee the growth of the

ranch. Still owned by Butler-Ames ancestors, the cattle ranch currently comprises 95,315 acres northwest of Las Vegas, New Mexico.

22. Ames, *Chronicles from the Nineteenth Century*, 2:613.

23. O'Toole, *Spanish War*, 12, 171–73.

24. "Movement for a National Volunteer Reserve, with General Schofield at Its Head," *Copper Country Evening News* (Calumet, MI), Apr. 6, 1898, 3.

25. Ames, *Chronicles from the Nineteenth Century*, 2:613; *Journal of the Executive Proceedings of the Senate of the United States of America*, vol. 31, *Fifty-Fifth Congress, from March 15, 1897, to March 3, 1899*, pt. 1 (Washington, DC: Government Printing Office, 1909), 928; Kirshner, *Class of 1861*, 107.

26. Ames, *Chronicles from the Nineteenth Century*, 2:615.

27. Ames, *Chronicles from the Nineteenth Century*, 2:614.

28. Ames, *Chronicles from the Nineteenth Century*, 2: 616.

29. Ames, *Chronicles from the Nineteenth Century*, 2: 617.

30. Ames, *Chronicles from the Nineteenth Century*, 2:617.

31. Ames, *Chronicles from the Nineteenth Century*, 2:617.

32. Konstam, *San Juan Hill 1898*, 76; Nofi, *Spanish-American War*, 137; Ames, *Chronicles from the Nineteenth Century*, 2:620.

33. Ames, *Chronicles from the Nineteenth Century*, 2:617–19.

34. Konstam, *San Juan Hill 1898*, 79, 84; Ames, *Chronicles from the Nineteenth Century*, 2:619, 621; Hendrickson, *Spanish-American War*, 14.

35. Ames, *Chronicles from the Nineteenth Century*, 2:619.

36. Ames, *Chronicles from the Nineteenth Century*, 2:621–22.

37. Ames, *Chronicles from the Nineteenth Century*, 2:624; O'Toole, *Spanish War*, 350–51.

38. Ames, *Chronicles from the Nineteenth Century*, 2:626–28.

39. Ames, *Chronicles from the Nineteenth Century*, 2:626, 628–30.

40. Ames, *Chronicles from the Nineteenth Century*, 2:631, 633, 638.

41. US Adjutant General's Office, *Correspondence Relating to the War with Spain*, 202.

42. US Adjutant General's Office, *Correspondence Relating to the War with Spain*, 205.

43. US Adjutant General's Office, *Correspondence Relating to the War with Spain*, 20; Ames, *Chronicles from the Nineteenth Century*, 2:640, 641. Ames's Twenty-Fourth Infantry had to remain in the town of Siboney because of a yellow fever outbreak. Ames, *Chronicles from the Nineteenth Century*, 2:204.

44. Ames, *Chronicles from the Nineteenth Century*, 2:645.

45. Ames, *Chronicles from the Nineteenth Century*, 2:646.

46. Ames, *Chronicles from the Nineteenth Century*, 2:649.

47. Ames, *Adelbert Ames*, 519; "Philadelphia Welcomes War Heroes," *Scranton (PA) Tribune*, Oct. 26, 1898, 1.

48. Ames, *Adelbert Ames*, 519.

49. Ames, *Chronicles from the Nineteenth Century*, 2:664.

50. Ames, *Chronicles from the Nineteenth Century*, 2:665–67, 678.

51. Ames, *Adelbert Ames*, 521; Ames, *Chronicles from the Nineteenth Century*, 2:664.

52. Smith and Lowrey, *Dunning School*, i.

53. Ames, *Adelbert Ames*, 503.

54. Ames, *Adelbert Ames*, 506.
55. Adelbert Ames to James W. Garner, Jan. 17, 1900, Ames Family Papers, Smith College; Garner, *Reconstruction in Mississippi*, viii.
56. Garner, *Reconstruction in Mississippi*, 229, 276, 393.
57. Garner, *Reconstruction in Mississippi*, ix, 414; Ames, *Adelbert Ames*, 503, 527.
58. Thompson, "Carpet-baggers in the United States Senate," 165–66.
59. Bowers, *Tragic Era*, 413–14, 449.
60. Ames, *Adelbert Ames*, 535.
61. Ames, *Adelbert Ames*, 528; Adelbert Ames to Morris Schaff, Mar. 1908, Ames Family Papers, Smith College.
62. "To Celebrate the 50th Anniversary of Grand Review," *New Britain (CT) Herald*, Sept. 18, 1915, 9; Ames, *Adelbert Ames*, 533.
63. "Ormond," *Daytona (FL) Daily News*, Mar. 31, 1915; "Last Civil War General Observes 96th Birthday," *Washington (DC) Evening Star*, Oct. 31, 1931, A-4; Ames, *Adelbert Ames*, 530, 535.
64. Ames, *Adelbert Ames*, 531.
65. Plimpton, *Ancestry of Blanche Butler Ames and Adelbert Ames*, 260.
66. Ames, *Adelbert Ames*, 531; "Rockefeller Buoyed by 125-Yard Golf Drive," *Washington (DC) Evening Star*, Dec. 14, 1930, 24.
67. Ames, *Adelbert Ames*, 531.
68. Radford Killebrew, "New and Views," *Lexington (MS) Advertiser*, Apr. 20, 1933, 4.
69. Ames, *Adelbert Ames*, 540.

CONCLUSION

1. Clark, "My Dear Mrs. Ames," 215, 224, 229.
2. Kennedy, *Profiles in Courage*, 2.
3. Kennedy, *Profiles in Courage*, 181.
4. Ames, *Adelbert Ames*, 552.
5. Ames, *Adelbert Ames*, 556.
6. Ames, *Adelbert Ames*, 561.
7. Ames, *Adelbert Ames*, 566.
8. Ames, *Adelbert Ames*, 567.
9. Ames, *Adelbert Ames*, 563–65.
10. Ames, *Adelbert Ames*, vi.

BIBLIOGRAPHY

ARCHIVAL SOURCES

Bowdoin College, Brunswick, Maine
   O. O. Howard Papers
Maine State Archives, Augusta
   State Archives of Military Records
Smith College, Northampton, Massachusetts
   Ames Family Papers

PUBLISHED PRIMARY SOURCES

Ames, Adelbert. *Capture of Fort Fisher*. Washington, DC: Library of Congress, 1897.
Ames, Blanche Butler, ed. *Chronicles from the Nineteenth Century: Family Letters of Blanche Butler and Adelbert*. 2 vols. Clinton, MA: Colonial, 1957.
Butler, Benjamin F. *Butler's Book: Autobiography and Personal Reminisces of Major General Benjamin Butler*. Boston: A. M. Thayer, 1892.
Carter, Robert G. *Four Brothers in Blue; or, Sunshine and Shadows of the War of the Rebellion*. Washington, DC: Gibson Brothers, 1913.
Chamberlain, Joshua L. "My Story of Fredericksburg." *Cosmopolitan* 54, Dec. 1912, 148–59.
Clark, Nathan S. "Nathan S. Clark Diary, 20th Maine." *Historical Documents*, Digital Maine. https://digitalmaine.com/hist_docs/2/.
Curtis, Newton M. *The Capture of Fort Fisher*. Boston: Military Order of the Loyal Legion, 1900.
French, Samuel G. *Two Wars: An Autobiography of General Samuel G. French*. . . . Nashville: Confederate Veteran, 1901.
Gerrish, Theodore. *Army Life: A Private's Reminiscences of the Civil War*. Portland, ME: Hoyt, Fogg, and Donkham, 1882.
Grant, Ulysses S. *The Papers of Ulysses S. Grant*. Vol. 13, *November 16, 1864–February 20, 1865*. Edited by John Y. Simon. Carbondale: Southern Illinois Univ. Press, 1991.

———. *The Papers of Ulysses S. Grant*. Vol. 18, *October 1, 1867–June 30, 1868*. Edited by John Y. Simon. Carbondale: Southern Illinois Univ. Press, 1991.

———. *The Papers of Ulysses S. Grant*. Vol. 25, *1874*. Edited by John Y. Simon. Volumes of the Papers of Ulysses S. Grant, Mississippi State Univ. Libraries Digital Collections. https://scholarsjunction.msstate.edu/usg-volumes/24/.

———. *Personal Memoirs of U. S. Grant: Two Volumes in One*. Old Saybrook, CT: Konecky and Konecky, 1994.

Heitman, Francis B. *Historical Register and Dictionary of the United States Army, from Its Organization, September 29, 1789, to March 2, 1903*. Washington, DC: Government Printing Office, 1903.

Howard, O. O. *Autobiography of Oliver Otis Howard*. New York: Baker and Taylor, 1907.

Johnson, Robert Underwood, and Clarence Clough Buel, eds. *Battles and Leaders of the Civil War*. 4 vols. Secaucus: Castle Books, 1887.

Journal of the Senate of the State of Mississippi, Sitting as a Court of Impeachment in the Trials of Adelbert Ames, Governor; Alexander K. Davis, Lieutenant Governor; Thomas W. Cardozo, Superintendent of Public Education. Jackson, MS: Power and Barksdale State Printers, 1876.

Lockwood, Henry C. "The Capture of Fort Fisher." *Atlantic Monthly* 27, no. 163 (May 1871): 622–36.

———. "A Man from Maine: A True History of the Army at Fort Fisher." *Maine Bugle* 1, no. 1 (Jan. 1894): 29–71.

Long, Hezekiah. *Hard Times, Hard Bread, and Harder Coffee*. Northport, ME: Richardson's Civil War Roundtable, 2008.

Meade, George G. *Life and Letters of George Gordon Meade, Major-General United States Army*. 2 vols. New York: Charles Scriber, 1913.

Porter, David. *Incident and Anecdotes of the Civil War*. New York: D. Appleton, 1885.

Porter, Horace. "Campaigning with Grant." *Century Illustrated Monthly Magazine*, 54, new ser. 32 (May–October 1897): 98–114, 201–18, 353–69, 584–602, 737–54, 879–98.

Report of Committees of the Senate of the United States for the First Session of the Forty-Fourth Congress, 1875–1876. Vol. 1. Washington, DC: Government Printing Office, 1876.

Report of the Joint Committee on the Conduct of the War: Red River Expedition, Fort Fisher Expedition, Heavy Ordnance. Washington, DC: Government Printing Office, 1865.

Report of the Joint Select Committee to Inquire into the Condition of Affairs in the Late Insurrectionary States. . . . Vols. 11 and 12, *Mississippi*. Washington, DC: Government Printing Office, 1872.

Sanger, George P., ed. *U.S. Statutes at Large, Treaties, and Proclamations of the United States of America*. Vol. 13. Boston: Little and Brown, 1866.

Shaw, Charles. *Personal Memoirs and Correspondence of Colonel Charles Shaw*. Vol. 1. London: Henry Colburn, 1837.

Spear, Ellis, and Abbot Spear. *The 20th Maine at Fredericksburg: The Conflicting Accounts of General Joshua Lawrence Chamberlain and General Ellis Spear*. Union, ME: Union Publishing, 1989. Kindle.

Spurgeon, Charles H. ed. *The Complete Works of C. H. Spurgeon*. Vol. 13, *Sermons 728 to 787*. Harrington, DE: Delmarva Publicans, 2013.

Thomas, Leonard R. *The Story of Fort Fisher*. [Ocean City, NJ?], 1915.

Treaty between the United States and Great Britain: Claims, Fisheries, Navigation of the St. Lawrence, etc., American Lumber on the River St. John, Boundary, May 8, 1871. Washington, DC: Government Printing Office, 1871.

US Adjutant General's Office. *Correspondence Relating to the War with Spain and Conditions Growing out of the Same, including the Insurrection in the Philippine Islands and the China Relief Expedition, . . . April 15, 1898, to July 30, 1902.* Washington, DC: Government Printing Office, 1902.

US Census Office. "Maine." In *Seventh Census of the United States of America, 1850. . . .* Washington, DC: Robert Armstrong, 1850.

US Congress. *Congressional Globe.* 46 vols. Washington, DC, 1834–73.

US Navy Department. *Official Records of the Union and Confederate Navies in the war of the Rebellion.* 30 vols. Washington, DC: Government Printing Office, 1894–1922.

US War Department. *War of the Rebellion: Official Records of the Union and Confederate Armies.* 129 vols. Washington, DC: Government Printing Office, 1894–1901.

Younger, Cole. *The Story of Cole Younger, by Himself.* Chicago: Henneberry, 1903.

NEWSPAPERS

American Citizen (Canton, MS)
Anderson Intelligencer Anderson Court House, SC)
Baltimore Sun
Bangor (ME) Whig and Courier
Chicago Daily Tribune
The Copiahan (Copiah, MS)
Copper Country Evening News (Calumet, MI)
Daily Davenport (ME) Democrat
Daytona (FL) Daily News
Eastern Times (Bath, ME)
Easton (OH) Democrat
Greenville (MS) Times
Grenada (MS) Sentinel
Jackson (MS) Daily Clarion
Jackson (MS) Weekly Clarion
Lexington (MS) Advertiser
Lincoln Telegraph (Wiscasset, ME)
Macon (MS) Beacon
National Republican (Washington, DC)
New Britain (CT) Herald
New Orleans Republican
New York Herald
New York Times
North Carolina Weekly Standard (Raleigh)
Ouachita Telegraph (Monroe, LA)
Oxford (MS) Falcon

Portland (ME) Daily Press
Scranton (PA) Tribune
Signal of Liberty (Liberty, ME)
Washington (DC) Evening Star
Weekly Caucasian (Lexington, MO)
Weekly Panola (MS) Star

SECONDARY SOURCES

Alberts, Don E. *General Wesley Merritt: Brandy Station to Manila Bay.* Memphis: General's Books, 2001.
Allen, Austin. *Origins of the Dred Scott Case: Jacksonian Jurisprudence and the Supreme Court, 1837–1857.* Athens: Univ. of Georgia Press, 2006.
Ambrose, Stephen E. *Upton and the Army.* Baton Rouge: Louisiana State Univ. Press, 1993.
Ames, Blanche Ames. *Adelbert Ames: General, Senator, Governor, 1835–1933.* London: MacDonald, 1964.
Axelrod, Alan. *That Horrid Pit: The Battle of the Crater.* New York: Carroll and Graff, 2007.
Ballard, Michael B. *Vicksburg: The Campaign That Opened the Mississippi.* Chapel Hill: Univ. of North Carolina Press, 2004.
Barthel, Thomas. *Abner Doubleday: A Civil War Biography.* Jefferson, NC: McFarland, 2010.
Beale, Robert. *Charles Hallé: A Musical Life.* New York: Routledge, 2007.
Beatie, Russel H. *Army of the Potomac: Birth of Command, November 1860–September 1861.* New York: Da Capo, 2002.
———. *Army of the Potomac: McClellan's First Campaign, March–May 1862.* El Dorado Hills, CA: Savas Beatie, 2007.
———. *Army of the Potomac: McClellan Takes Command, September 1861–February 1862.* New York: Da Capo, 2004.
Beattie, Donald W., Rodney M. Cole, and Charles G. Waugh, eds. *A Distant War Comes Home: Maine in the Civil War Era.* Camden, ME: Down East Books, 1996.
Benson, Harry King. "The Public Career of Adelbert Ames, 1861–1876." PhD diss., Univ. of Virginia, Charlottesville, 1975 (Proquest/UVA).
Blegen, Theodore C. *Minnesota: A History of the State.* Minneapolis: Univ. of Minnesota, 1975.
Boatner, Mark M., III. *The Civil War Dictionary.* New York: David McKay, 1959.
Bonekemper, Edward H. *Ulysses S. Grant: A Victor, Not a Butcher: The Military Genius of the Man Who Won the Civil War.* Washington, DC: Regency, 2004.
Boulard, Garry. *The Swing around the Circle: Andrew Johnson and the Train Ride That Destroyed a Presidency.* Bloomington, IN: iUniverse, 2008.
Bouve, Thomas T. *The History of the Town of Hingham, Massachusetts.* Cambridge, MA: John Wilson and Son, 1893.
Bowers, Claude G. *The Tragic Era: The Revolution after Lincoln.* New York: Blue Ribbon, 1929.
Bradley, Mark L. *The Army of Reconstruction, 1865–1877.* Washington, DC: Center of Military History, 2015.
Brager, Bruce L. *Grant's Victory: How Ulysses S. Grant Won the Civil War.* New York: Stackpole, 2020.

Brennan, Patrick. *Assault on Charleston*. Boston: Da Capo, 1996.

Broadwater, Robert P. *The Battle of Fair Oaks: Turning Point of McClellan's Peninsula Campaign*. Jefferson, NC: McFarland, 2011.

———. *The Battle of Olustee: The Final Union Attempt to Seize Florida*. Jefferson, NC: McFarland, 2006.

Brock, Euline W. "Thomas W. Cardozo: Fallible Black Reconstruction Leader." *Journal of Southern History* 47, no. 2 (1981): 183–206.

Brooker, Russell. *The American Civil Rights Movement: Black Agency and People of Good Will*. Lanham, MD: Lexington Books, 2018.

Budiansky, Stephen. *The Bloody Shirt: Terror after Appomattox*. New York: Viking, 2008.

Burnham, Walter Dean. *Presidential Ballots, 1836–1892*. Baltimore: John Hopkins Univ. Press, 1955.

Burton, Brian K. *Extraordinary Circumstances: The Seven Days Battles*. Bloomington: Univ. of Indiana Press, 2010.

Burton, David Henry. *British-American Diplomacy, 1895–1917: Early Years of the Special Relationship*. Malabar, FL: Krieger, 1999.

Bush, James C. *The Army of the US Historical Sketches of Staff and Line with Portraits of Generals-in-Chief through 1894*. New York: Maynard, Merrill, 1896.

Casler, John Overton. *Four Years in the Stonewall Brigade*. Columbia: Univ. of South Carolina Press, 2005.

Castel, Albert, and Brooks D. Simpson. *Victors in Blue: How Union Generals Fought the Confederates, Battled Each Other, and Won the Civil War*. Lawrence: Univ. Press of Kansas, 2015.

Catton, Bruce. *Glory Road*. New York: Doubleday, 1952.

———. *Mr. Lincoln's Army*. New York: Doubleday, 1951.

———. *A Stillness at Appomattox*. New York: Anchor Books, 1953.

Cha-Jua, Sundiata Keita, and Clarence Lang. "The "Long Movement" as Vampire: Temporal Fallacies in Recent Black Freedom Studies." *Journal of African American History* 92, no. 2 (Spring 2007): 265–88.

Cimbala, Paul A. *The Freedman's Bureau: Reconstructing the American South after the Civil War*. Huntington, NY: Krieger, 2005.

Clark, Anne Biller. "My Dear Mrs. Ames: A Study of the Life of Suffragist Cartoonist and Birth Control Reformer Blanche Ames Ames, 1878–1969." PhD diss., Univ. of Massachusetts at Amherst, 1996.

Clark, Clifford E., Jr., ed. *Minnesota in a Century of Change: The State and Its People since 1900*. St. Paul: Minnesota Historical Society, 1989.

Coffey, Walter. *The Reconstruction Years: The Tragic Aftermath of the War between the States*. Bloomington, IN: AuthorHouse, 2014.

Coolidge, A. J., and J. B. Mansfield. *A History and Description of New England, General and Local*. Boston: Austin J. Coolidge, 1859.

Cullum, George W., ed. *Biographical Register of the Officers and Graduates of the U.S. Military Academy, at West Point, N. Y. . . .* 2 vols. New York: D. Van Nostrand, 1868.

Culp, Edward C. *25th Ohio Vet. Vol. Infantry in the War for the Union*. Topeka, KS: Geo. W. Crance, 1885.

Current, Richard Nelson. *Those Terrible Carpetbaggers: A Reinterpretation*. New York: Oxford Univ. Press, 1988.

———. *Three Carpetbag Governors*. Baton Rouge: Louisiana State Univ. Press, 1967.

Davis, Daniel T. *The Most Desperate Acts of Gallantry: George A. Custer in the Civil War*. El Dorado Hills, CA: Savas Beatie, 2018.

DeBlack, Thomas. *With Fire and Sword: Arkansas, 1861–1874*. Fayetteville: Univ. of Arkansas Press, 2003.

Desjardin, Thomas A. *Joshua L. Chamberlain: A Concise Biography*. Lanham, MD: Downeast Books, 2014.

———. *Stand Firm Ye Boys from Maine: The 20th Maine and the Gettysburg Campaign*. New York: Oxford Univ. Press, 2009.

Dickey, Luther Samuel. *History of the Eighty-Fifth Regiment Pennsylvania Volunteer Infantry, 1861–1865*. New York: J. C. and W. E. Powers, 1915.

Dierenfield, Bruce J. *The Civil Rights Movement: Revised Edition*. Oxfordshire, UK: Taylor and Francis, 2013.

Donnelly, Ralph W. "Federal Batteries on the Henry House Hill, Bull Run, 1861." *Military Affairs* 21, no. 4 (1957): 188–92.

Dorsey, Albert, Jr. "'Vicksburg Troubles': Black Participation in the Bloody Politic and Land Ownership in the Age of Redeemer Violence." PhD diss., Florida State Univ., 2012.

Doubleday, Abner. *Chancellorsville and Gettysburg*. New York: Charles Scribner's Sons, 1882.

Dougherty, Kevin, and J. Michael Moore. *The Peninsula Campaign of 1862: A Military Analysis*. Oxford: Univ. of Mississippi Press, 2005.

Downs, Gregory P. *After Appomattox: Military Occupation and the Ends of War*. Cambridge, MA: Harvard Univ. Press, 2015.

Dupont, Brandon, Alka Gandhi, and Thomas Weiss. *The American Invasion of Europe: The Long Term Rise in Overseas Travel, 1820–2000*. Boston: National Bureau of Economic Research, 2008.

Egerton, Douglas R. *The Wars of Reconstruction*. New York: Bloomsbury, 2014.

Eicher, David J. *The Longest Night: A Military History of the Civil War*. New York: Simon and Schuster, 2001.

Eicher, John H., and David J. Eicher. *Civil War High Commands*. Stanford, CA: Stanford Univ. Press, 2001.

Ellem, Warren A. "The Overthrow of Reconstruction in Mississippi," *Journal of Mississippi History* 54, no. 2 (1992): 175–201.

Fairman, Charles. *Reconstruction and Reunion, 1864–1868*. New York: Macmillan, 1971.

Fanebust, Wayne. *Chasing Frank and Jesse James: The Bungled Northfield Bank Robbery and the Long Manhunt*. Jefferson, NC: McFarland, 2018.

Fantel, Hans. *William Penn: Apostle of Dissent*. New York: Morrow, 1974.

Farmer-Kaiser, Mary J. *Freedwomen and the Freedman's Bureau: Race, Gender, and Public Policy in the Age of Emancipation*. New York: Fordham Univ. Press, 2010.

Ferrell, Claudine L. *Reconstruction*. Westport, CT: Greenwood, 2003.

Fitzpatrick, David J. *Emory Upton: Misunderstood Reformer*. Norman: Univ. of Oklahoma Press, 2017.

Foner, Eric. *Forever Free: The Story of Emancipation & Reconstruction.* New York: Harper and Row, 2010.

———. *Reconstruction: America's Unfinished Revolution, 1863–1877.* New York: Harper and Row, 1988.

———. *The Second Founding: How the Civil War and Reconstruction Remade the Constitution.* New York: W. W. Norton, 2019.

———. *A Short History of Reconstruction.* New York: Harper and Row, 1990.

Fonvielle, Chris E., Jr. *Fort Anderson: Battle for Wilmington.* Cambridge, MA: Da Capo, 1999.

———. *The Wilmington Campaign: Last Rays of Departing Hope.* Mechanicsburg, PA: Stackpole Books, 2001.

Furgurson, Ernest B. *Not War but Murder: Cold Harbor.* New York: Random House, 2000.

Gallagher, Gary W., ed. *Chancellorsville: The Battle and Its Aftermath.* Chapel Hill: Univ. of North Carolina Press, 1996.

———, ed. *The Fredericksburg Campaign: Decision on the Rappahannock.* Chapel Hill: Univ. of North Carolina Press, 1995.

———, ed. *The Richmond Campaign of 1862: The Peninsula and the Seven Days.* Chapel Hill: Univ. of North Carolina Press, 2008.

———. ed. *Three Days at Gettysburg: Essays on Confederate and Union Leadership.* Kent, OH: Kent State Univ. Press, 1999.

Garner, James W. *Reconstruction in Mississippi.* New York: Macmillan, 1901.

Gillette, William. *Retreat from Reconstruction, 1869–1879.* Baton Rouge: Louisiana State Univ. Press, 1979.

Gordon-Reed, Annette. *Andrew Johnson.* American President Series. New York: Times Books, 2011.

Gould, Edward K. *Major General Hiram G. Berry.* Rockland, ME: Press of the Courier-Gazette, 1899.

Gragg, Rod. *Confederate Goliath: The Battle of Fort Fisher.* New York: HarperCollins, 1991.

Greenberg, Kenneth S. *Honor and Slavery: Lies, Duels, Noses, Masks, Dressing as a Woman, Gifts, Strangers, Death, Humanitarianism, Slave Rebellions, the Proslavery Argument, Baseball, Hunting, and Gambling in the Old South.* Princeton, NJ.: Princeton Univ. Press, 1996.

Grimsley, Mark. *And Keep Moving On: The Virginia Campaign, May–June 1864.* Lincoln: Univ. of Nebraska Press, 2002.

Guelzo, Allen C. *Gettysburg: The Last Invasion.* New York: Alfred A. Knopf, 2013.

———. *Reconstruction: A Concise History.* New York: Oxford Univ. Press, 2018.

Hall, Jacquelyn Dowd. "The Long Civil Rights Movement and the Political Uses of the Past." *Journal of American History* 91, no. 4 (2005): 1233–63.

Hall, Russell S., Princella W. Nowell, and Stacy Childress. *Washington County, Mississippi.* Charleston, SC: Arcadia, 2000.

Hanser, David A. *Architecture of France.* Westport, CT: Greenwood, 2006.

Harkness, E. J. *The Expeditions against Fort Fisher and Wilmington.* Chicago: Military Order of the Loyal Legion of the United States, Commandery of the State of Illinois, 1894.

Harris, William C. "The Creed of the Carpetbaggers: The Case of Mississippi." *Journal of Southern History* 40, no. 2 (1974): 199–224.

———. *Presidential Reconstruction in Mississippi*. Baton Rouge: Louisiana State Univ. Press, 1967.
Hays, J. N. *Epidemics and Pandemics: Their Impacts on Human History*. Santa Barbara, CA: ABC-CLIO, 2005.
Hendrickson, Kenneth E., Jr. *The Spanish-American War*. Westport, CT: Greenwood, 2003.
Hennessy, John J. *The First Battle of Manassas: An End to Innocence, July 18–21, 1861*. Mechanicsburg, PA: Stackpole Books, 2015.
———. *Return to Bull Run: The Campaign and Battle of Second Manassas*. 1993. Reprint, Norman: Univ. of Oklahoma Press, 2012.
Hess, Earl J. *The Crater: The Mine Attack at Petersburg*. Columbia: Univ. of South Carolina Press, 2010.
———. *In the Trenches at Petersburg: Field Fortifications & Confederate Defeat*. Chapel Hill: Univ. of North Carolina Press, 2009.
Hingham: A Story of Its Early Settlement and Life, Its Ancient Landmarks, Its Historic Sites and Buildings. Hingham, MA: Old Colony Chapter, DAR, 1911.
Hobhouse, Hermione. *The Crystal Palace and the Great Exhibition: Science, Art, and Productive Industry: A History of the Royal Commission for the Exhibition of 1851*. London: Athlone, 2002.
Hogan, David W., Jr. *The Overland Campaign 4 May–15 June 1864*. Washington, DC: Department of the Army, 2014.
Holloway, Vanessa. *Black Rights in the Reconstruction Era*. New York: Hamilton Books, 2018.
Hsieh, Wayne Wei-siang. "The Old Army in War and Peace: West Pointers and the Civil War Era, 1814–1865." PhD diss., Univ. of Virginia, Charlottesville, 2004 (Proquest/UVA).
Hudson, Richard. "The Formation of the North German Confederation." *Political Science Quarterly* 6, no. 3 (1891): 424–38.
Huntington, Tom. *Maine Roads to Gettysburg: How Joshua Chamberlain, Oliver Howard, and 4,000 Men from the Pine Tree State Helped Win the Civil War's Bloodiest Battle*. Guilford, CT: Stackpole Books, 2018.
———. *Searching for George Gordon Meade: The Forgotten Victor of Gettysburg*. Mechanicsburg, PA: Stackpole Books, 2013.
Hurst, Jack. *Nathan Bedford Forrest: A Biography*. New York: Vintage, 1994.
Jones, Howard. "Anglophobia and the Aroostook War." *New England Quarterly* 48, no. 4 (1975): 519–39.
Jones, Terry L. *Cemetery Hill: The Struggle for the High Ground, July 1–3, 1863*. Cambridge, MA: Da Capo, 2003.
Jordan, Mark H., and Dennis Lavery. *Iron Brigade General: John Gibbon, a Rebel in Blue*. Westport, CT: Praeger, 1993.
Kalb, Deborah. *Congressional Quarterly's Guide to U.S. Elections*. Washington, DC: C.Q., 2016.
Kennedy, John F. *Profiles in Courage*. New York: Pocket Books, 1957.
Kirshner, Ralph. *The Class of 1861: Custer, Ames, and Their Classmates after West Point*. Carbondale: Univ. of Southern Illinois Press, 1999.
Konstam, Angus. *San Juan Hill 1898: America's Emergence as a World Power*. Oxford: Osprey, 2004.

Krick, Robert K. *Civil War Weather in Virginia*. Tuscaloosa: Univ. of Alabama Press, 2007.

Kummer David W. *U.S. Marines in Battle: Fort Fisher, December 1864–January 1865*. Washington, DC: Marine Corps History Division, 2012.

Le Duc, Thomas. "The Maine Frontier and the Northeastern Boundary Controversy." *American Historical Review* 53, no. 1 (1947): 30–41.

Lemann, Nicholas. *Redemption: The Last Battle of the Civil War*. New York: Farrar, Straus, and Giroux, 2006.

Levin, Kevin M. *Remembering the Battle of the Crater: War as Murder*. Lexington: Univ. Press of Kentucky, 2012.

Litwack, Leon F. *Been in the Storm So Long: The Aftermath of Slavery*. New York: Vintage, 1980.

Longacre, Edward G. *Army of Amateurs: General Benjamin F. Butler and the Army of the James, 1863–1865*. Mechanicsburg, PA: Stackpole Books, 1997.

———. *The Commanders of Chancellorsville: The Gentleman vs. the Rogue*. Nashville: Rutledge Hill, 2005.

———. *Custer: The Making of a Young General*. New York: Skyhorse, 2018.

———. *The Early Morning of War: Bull Run, 1861*. Norman: Univ. of Oklahoma Press, 2014.

———. *The Sharpshooters: A History of the Ninth New Jersey Volunteer Infantry*. Lincoln, NE: Potomac Books, 2017.

Mackworth-Young, Robin. *The History & Treasures of Windsor Castle*. London: British Tourist Authority, 1991.

MacLachlan, Courtney C., et al. *Rockland Area Lime Industries*. Charleston, SC: Arcadia, 2006.

Martin, Samuel J. *Kill-Cavalry: The Life of Union General Hugh Judson Kilpatrick*. Mechanicsburg, PA: Stackpole Books, 2000.

Mayes, Edward. *Lucius Q. C. Lamar: His Life, Times, and Speeches. 1825–1893*. Nashville: Methodist Episcopal Church, 1896.

McCaslin, Richard B. *The Last Stronghold: The Campaign for Fort Fisher*. Abilene, TX: McWhiney Foundation, 2003.

McGrath, Thomas A. *Shepherdstown: Last Clash of the Antietam Campaign, September 19–20, 1862*. Lynchburg, VA: Schroeder, 2007.

McGuire, Danielle L., and John Dittmer, eds. *Freedom Rights: New Perspectives on the Civil Rights Movement*. Lexington: Univ. of Kentucky Press, 2011.

McPherson, Edward. *The Political History of the United States from April 15, 1865, to July 15, 1870*. 1875. Reprint, Carlisle, MA: Applewood Books, 2009.

McPherson, James M. *The Battle Cry of Freedom: The Civil War Era*. New York: Oxford Univ. Press, 1988.

———. *Crossroads of Freedom: Antietam, the Battle That Changed the Course of the Civil War*. New York: Oxford Univ. Press, 2002.

Merriman, John. *Massacre: The Life and Death of the Paris Commune of 1871*. New Haven, CT: Yale Univ. Press, 2014.

Messner, William F., ed. *Mississippi Black Codes of 1865*. Madison: Univ. of Wisconsin Madison, 1968.

Mingus, Scott L., Jr. *The Louisiana Tigers in the Gettysburg Campaign, June–July 1863*. Baton Rouge: Louisiana State Univ. Press, 2009.

Mixon, Scott. "The Crisis of 1873: Perspectives from Multiple Asset Classes." *Journal of Economic History* 68, no. 3 (2008): 722–57.

Morris, Charles R. *The Tycoons: How Andrew Carnegie, John D. Rockefeller, Jay Gould, and J. O. Morgan Invented the American Supereconomy.* New York: Henry Holt, 2006.

Morrison, James L. *The Best School: West Point, 1833–1866.* Kent, OH: Kent State Univ. Press, 1998.

———. "Educating the Civil War Generals: West Point, 1833–1861." *Military Affairs* 38, no. 3 (1974): 108–11.

Newell, Clayton R. *The Regular Army before the Civil War, 1845–1860.* Washington, DC: Center of Military History, 2014.

Newell, Clayton R., and Charles R. Shrader. *Of Duty Well and Faithfully Done: A History of the Regular Army in the Civil War.* Lincoln: Univ. of Nebraska Press, 2011.

Noe, Kenneth W. *The Howling Storm: Weather, Climate, and the American Civil War.* Baton Rouge: Louisiana State Univ. Press, 2020.

Nofi, Albert A. *The Spanish-American War, 1898.* Boston: Da Capo, 1997.

O'Reilly, Francis Augustin. *The Fredericksburg Campaign: Winter War on the Rappahannock.* Baton Rouge: Louisiana State Univ. Press, 2006.

O'Toole, G. J. A. *The Spanish War: An American Epic—1898.* New York: W. W. Norton, 1984.

Palfrey, Francis Winthrop. *The Antietam and Fredericksburg.* New York: Charles Scribner's Sons, 1882.

Perman, Michael. *Emancipation and Reconstruction.* Hoboken, NJ: Wiley-Blackwell, 2003.

Pfanz, Harry W. *Gettysburg: Culp's Hill & Cemetery Hill.* Chapel Hill: Univ. of North Carolina Press, 1993.

Pickney, David H. *Napoleon III and the Rebuilding of Paris.* Princeton, NJ: Princeton Univ. Press, 2019.

Plimpton, Pauline Ames. *The Ancestry of Blanche Butler Ames and Adelbert Ames.* New York: Wizard Graphics, 1977.

Posey, Josephine McCann. *Succeeding against Great Odds: Alcorn State University in Its Second Century.* Oxford: Univ. Press of Mississippi, 2017.

Price, Isaiah. *History of the Ninety-Seventh Regiment, Pennsylvania Volunteer Infantry during the War of the Rebellion, 1861–1865.* Philadelphia: the author, 1875.

Pullen, John J. *The Twentieth Maine: A Volunteer Regiment in the Civil War.* Philadelphia: J. B. Lippincott, 1957.

Rable, George C. *But There Was No Peace: The Role of Violence in the Politics of Reconstruction.* Athens: Univ. of Georgia Press, 1984.

———. *Fredericksburg! Fredericksburg!* Chapel Hill: Univ. of North Carolina Press, 2002.

Rafuse, Ethan S. *Corps Commanders in Blue: Union Major Generals in the Civil War.* Baton Rouge: Louisiana State Univ. Press, 2014.

———. *A Single Grand Victory: The First Campaign and Battle at Manassas.* Lanham, MD: Rowman and Littlefield, 2002.

Rainwater, P. L. "Letters of James Lusk Alcorn." *Journal of Southern History* 3, no. 2 (1937): 196–209.

Randolph, Valentine C. *A Civil War Soldier's Diary: Valentine C. Randolph, 39th Illinois Regiment.* Edited by David D. Roe. Ithaca, NY: Cornell Univ. Press, 2006.

Raudzens, George. "The British Ordnance Department, 1815–1855." *Journal of the Society for Army Historical Research* 57, no. 230 (1979): 88–107.

Rawley, James A. "The General Amnesty Act of 1872: A Note." *Mississippi Valley Historical Review* 47, no. 3 (1960): 480–84.

Rehnquist, William H. *Centennial Crisis: The Disputed Election of 1876.* New York: Vintage Books, 2005.

Rhea, Gordon C. *Cold Harbor: Grant and Lee, May 26–June 3, 1864.* Baton Rouge: Louisiana State Univ. Press, 2007.

Robertson, William Glenn. *Back Door to Richmond: The Bermuda Hundred Campaign, April–June 1864.* Baton Rouge: Louisiana State Univ. Press, 1987.

Robinson, Charles M. *Hurricane of Fire: The Union Assault on Fort Fisher.* Annapolis: Naval Institute Press, 1998.

Rosenberg, Charles E. *The Cholera Years: The United States in 1832, 1849, and 1866.* Chicago: Univ. of Chicago Press, 2009.

Satcher, Buford. *Blacks in Mississippi Politics, 1865–1900.* Lanham, MD: Univ. Press of America, 1978.

Schubert, Frank N., ed. *The Nation Builders: A Sesquicentennial History of the Corps of Topographical Engineers, 1838–1863.* Washington, DC: Government Printing Office, 1989.

Sears, Stephen W. *Chancellorsville.* New York: Houghton Mifflin, 1996.

———. *Gettysburg.* New York: Houghton Mifflin, 2003.

———. *Landscape Turned Red: The Battle of Antietam.* Boston: Houghton-Mifflin, 1983.

———. *To the Gates of Richmond: The Peninsula Campaign.* New York: Ticknor and Fields, 1992.

Shiver, Joshua. "A Gross and Culpable Failure of Leadership in the First Fort Fisher Expedition, December 23–27, 1864." *North Carolina Historical Review* 93, no. 1 (2016): 58–83.

Shore Village Historical Society. *Around Rockland.* Charleston, SC: Arcadia, 1996.

Sinnett, Charles Nelson. *Our Family in Maine.* Lewiston, ME: Journal Printshop, 1911.

Skrabec, Quentin R., Jr. *Henry Clay Frick: The Life of the Perfect Capitalist.* Jefferson, NC: McFarland, 2014.

Smith, John David. *Black Soldiers in Blue: African American Troops in the Civil War Era.* Chapel Hill: Univ. of North Carolina Press, 2003.

Smith, John David, and J. Vincent Lowery, eds. *The Dunning School: Historians, Race, and the Meaning of Reconstruction.* Lexington: Univ. Press of Kentucky, 2013.

Smith, Timothy B. *Mississippi in the Civil War: The Home Front.* Jackson: Univ. Press of Mississippi, 2010.

Snowden, Frank M. *Epidemics and Society: From the Black Death to the Present.* New Haven: Yale Univ. Press, 2019.

Stackpole, Edward J. *Chancellorsville: Lee's Greatest Battle.* 2nd ed. Harrisburg, PA: Stackpole Books, 1988.

Stauffer, John, and Sally Jenkins. *The State of Jones: The Small Southern County That Seceded from the Confederacy.* New York: Knopf, 2010.

Stevens, Joseph E. *1863: The Rebirth of a Nation.* New York: Bantam, 1999.

Stiles, T. J. *Jesse James: The Last Rebel of the Civil War.* New York: Knopf, 2003.

Stowe, William W. *Going Abroad: European Travel in Nineteenth-Century American Culture.* Princeton, NJ: Princeton Univ. Press, 1994.

Strauss-Schom, Alan. *The Shadow Emperor: A Biography of Napoleon III.* New York: St. Martin's, 2018.

Sugden, John. *Sir Francis Drake*. New York: Random House, 2012.
Summers, Mark Wahlgren. *Railroads, Reconstruction, and the Gospel of Prosperity: Aid under the Radical Republicans, 1865-1877.* Princeton, NJ: Princeton Univ. Press, 2014.
Sutherland, Daniel E. *Fredericksburg and Chancellorsville: The Dare Mark Campaign*. Lincoln: Univ. of Nebraska Press, 1998.
Symonds, Craig L. *History of the Battle of Gettysburg*. New York: HarperCollins, 2001.
Thompson, C. Mildred. "Carpet-baggers in the United States Senate." In *Studies in Southern History and Politics Inscribed to William Archibald Dunning, Ph.D., LL.D., Lieber Professor of History and Political Philosophy in Columbia University, by His Former Pupils the Authors*. New York: Columbia University Press, 1914.
Tilghman, John R. "Debating the Long Civil Rights Movement: Exploring Multiracial Alliances and Disputes." *Journal of Urban History* 40, no. 6 (2014): 1168-73.
Trudeau, Noah Andre. *The Last Citadel: Petersburg, June 1864-April 1865*. Baton Rouge: Louisiana State Univ. Press, 1993.
Trulock, Alice Rains. *In the Hands of Providence: Joshua Lawrence Chamberlain and the American Civil War*. Chapel Hill: Univ. of North Carolina Press, 1992.
Tucker, Phillip Thomas. *Barksdale's Charge: The True High Tide of the Confederacy at Gettysburg, July 2, 1863*. Philadelphia: Casemate, 2013.
Turkel, Stanley. *Heroes of the American Reconstruction: Profiles of Sixteen Educators, Politicians, and Activists*. Jefferson, NC: McFarland, 2005.
The Union Army: A History of Military Affairs in the Loyal States, 1861-65. . . . Vol. 6, *Cyclopedia of Battles*. Madison, WI: Federal Publishing, 1908.
Vandervort, Bruce. *Indian Wars of Canada, Mexico, and the United States, 1812-1900*. New York: Routledge, 2006.
Waugh, John C. *The Class of 1846: From West Point to Appomattox—Stonewall Jackson, George McClellan, and Their Brothers*. New York: Ballantine Books, 1999.
Wawro, Geoffrey. *The Austro-Prussian War: Austria's War with Prussia and Italy in 1866*. Cambridge: Cambridge Univ. Press, 1996.
———. *The Franco-Prussian War: The German Conquest of France in 1870-1871*. Cambridge: Cambridge Univ. Press, 2003.
Webb, Lee D. "Party Development and Political Conflict in Maine, 1820-1860, from Statehood to the Civil War." PhD diss., Univ. of Maine, Orono, 2017 (DigitalCommons/UM).
Wert, Jeffry D. *A Glorious Army: Robert E. Lee's Triumph, 1862-1863*. New York: Simon and Schuster, 2011.
———. *The Sword of Lincoln: The Army of the Potomac*. New York: Simon and Schuster, 2006.
Wetzel, David. *A Duel of Giants: Bismarck, Napoleon III, and the Origins of the Franco-Prussian War*. Madison: Univ. of Wisconsin Press, 2001.
Whitman, William E. S., and Charles H. True. *Maine in the War for the Union: A History of the Part Borne by the Maine Troops in the Suppression of the American Rebellion*. Lewiston, ME: Nelson Dingley Jr., 1865.
Willis, John C. *Forgotten Time: The Yazoo-Mississippi Delta after the Civil War*. Charlottesville: Univ. Press of Virginia, 2000.
Wineapple, Brenda. *The Impeachers: The Trial of Andrew Johnson and the Dream of a Just Nation*. New York: Random House, 2019.

Wittenberg, Eric J. *The Battle of Brandy Station: North America's Largest Cavalry Battle.* Stroud, UK: History Press, 2010.

———. *Gettysburg's Forgotten Cavalry Actions: Farnsworth's Charge, South Cavalry Field, and the Battle of Fairfield, July 3, 1863.* El Dorado Hills, CA: Savas Beatie, 2011.

———. *The Union Cavalry Comes of Age: Hartwood Church to Brandy Station, 1863.* Charleston, SC: History Press, 2002.

Wittenberg Eric J., and Daniel T. Davis. *Out Flew the Sabres: The Battle of Brandy Station, June 9, 1863.* El Dorado Hills, CA: Savas Beatie, 2016.

Woodrick, Jim. *The Civil War Siege of Jackson, Mississippi.* Charleston, SC: Arcadia, 2016.

Yeatman, Ted P. *Frank and Jesse James: The Story behind the Legend.* Nashville: Cumberland House, 2000.

Young, John Russell. *Around the World with General Grant.* Vol. 2. New York: American News, 1879.

INDEX

Page numbers in *italics* refer to illustrations.

107th Ohio, 73–75, 79
117th New York, 116

V Corps (Spanish-American War), 243, 245, 249
V Corps (Union Army), 37–39; Ames and, 61; at Antietam, 47; at Bermuda Hundred, 96; at Boteler's Ford, 48; at Chancellorsville, 63; at Fredericksburg, 54; Twentieth Maine and, 46
X Corps (Union Army), 84, 88–89, 91–92, 94, 129; at Chaffin's Farm, 103; at Petersburg, 105
XI Corps (Union Army), 61–62, 134; Ames and, 65–66; at Gettysburg, 70–71, 75
XVIII Corps (Union Army), 103, 105
XXIV Corps (Union Army), 105
XXV Corps (Union Army), 107

Abbott, Joseph C., 120, 125
Aberdeen, Mississippi, 227
Abgeordnetenhaus (Prussia), 134
abolitionism, 18, 130
Adams, Charles Quincy, 145
Adams, John, 145
Adams, John Quincy, 145, 259
Adelbert Ames, 4
Aesop's Fables, 16
African Americans: activism by, 202–4; Adelbert Ames and, 19, 138, 190, 212; in the Army, 91–92, 102, 105, 107, 243; Blanche Butler Ames and, 194; education and, 175; in elected office, 173, 187, 196–97, 202, 218; in Mississippi, 150, 157–58, 185; mobilization of, 208–9, 223; rights of, 21, 152, 155–56, 170–72, 190; threats against, 211–13; violence against in Mississippi ,151, 181–82, 199, 207, 215, 228; violence against in the South, 130; violence against in Vicksburg, 197–99, 204–7, 223; voting by, 161–62, 173, 195, 198; voting rights of, 170–72, 211–13, 226, 230. *See also* freedpeople
African Methodist Episcopal Church, 162
agriculture, 191–92
Alabama, CSS (ship), 100, 179
Albert (Prince), 144
Alberts, Don E., 6
Alcorn, James Lusk, 160–61, 173–76, *180*, 186–88, 223; Ames and, 180–81, 191–92; as senator, 181–83; supporters of, 195
Alcorn State University, 175, 181
Alexandria, Virginia, 34, 45
Alger, Russell A., 241, 245–48
Allen, Bozoan, 13
Alley, Cadmus H., 171
Alloway, Scotland, 145
Ambrose, Stephen E., 6
American Birth Control League, 258
American Citizen (Clanton, Mississippi), 153, 186, 194, 231
American Revolution, 16, 35
Ames, Adelbert, 1–2, *18*, 22, 65, 99, *104*, *128*, *169*, *171*, *239*, *244*, *250*, *255*; at Antietam, 47–48; in

Ames, Adelbert (*cont.*)
the Army, 23–27, 86, 88, 248–49; at Bermuda Hundred, 96–97; biographies of, 262–63; Blanche Butler and, 152; at Brandy Station, 67–69, *67*; career plans of, 131; at Chancellorsville, 63; children of, 180–81, 184, 186, 237–38; civil rights and, 158, 176–78, 183, 250; at Cold Harbor, 98–99; combat wound, 29–30; as commander of Fourth Military District, 156–57; death of, 256; drawings of, *106*; election to the Senate, 162–66; at First Bull Run, 27, *28*, 263; in Florida, 83–84; at Fort Fisher, 110, 113–27, *123*; at Fredericksburg, 51, 53–58, *55*; at Gettysburg, 70–77, *74*, 263; as governor of Mississippi, 189–203, 205–6, 208–14; at Hagerstown, 79; historical reputation of, 3–5, 7–11, 252–53, 257–61; impeachment of, 213–18, 220–24; in Lowell, 253–54; marriage to Blanche Butler, 167–70, *169*, 179, 180–81, 184, 186; Medal of Honor and, 239–40; in Minnesota, 104, 233–34, 237; in Mississippi, 148, 151; in New York, 238–39; Northfield robbery and, 235–37; in the Overland Campaign, 85, 89–94; at Petersburg, 99–105, *104*, *106*, 107–8; political policies of, 170–72, 183, 190–92, 232; political views of, 100–101, 137–38, 176–78, 186, 214, 237–38; promotion to general, 50, 59, 64, 66; promotion to major, 31; as provisional governor of Mississippi, 154–55, 159, 161; Reconstruction and, 129–30; resignation as governor, 225–26, 231; role in Civil War, 6, 128–29; role in history, 263; run for governor, 185–88; as senator, 170–84; in the Seven Days' Battles, 37–41; at Shepherdstown, 48; smallpox outbreak and, 60–61; soldiers and, 84, 248; in South Carolina, 80–81, 83; in the Spanish-American War, 241–48, 250; testimony to Congress, 227–29, 249–50, 260; travels in Europe, 131–37, 139–47; travels of, 19, 254; Twentieth Maine and, 42–47, 49, 65, 78, 253–54; upbringing of, 12–16; views of Civil War, 32–34, 36, 100, 126–27, 250; views of Reconstruction, 130–31, 172–74, 183, 198–200, 251–53; views of slavery, 17–18, 199; at West Point, 19–22; at Yorktown, 35
Ames, Adelbert, Jr., 238, 239, *239*, 242, 245–46; in the military, 254
Ames, Anthony, 12–13
Ames, Blanche Ames, 176, *239*; activism of, 258; birth of, 238; education, 239; writings, 4, 253, 256–57, 259–63
Ames, Blanche Butler, 152, *152*, 163, 165, *169*, 199–200, 202, *239*, 250, 256; children of, 180–81, 184, 186, 237–38; correspondence with Adelbert Ames, 211, 230, 236–37, 240, 245–46, 248; in Lowell, 253–54, 256; marriage to Adelbert Ames, 167–70, *169*, 179, 180–81, 184, 186; in Minnesota, 237; in Mississippi, 189, 194–96, 209; in New York, 238; travels of, 254; views of impeachment, 224–26; views of politics, 188–89, 205–6, 210, 213, 216, 218; views of Spanish-American War, 242; visits with family, 196; in Washington, DC, 171
Ames, Butler, 237, 239–42, *239*; in the Army, 248; childhood of, 180–81, 184, 188; in Congress, 254
Ames, David, 16–17
Ames, Ebenezer, 13
Ames, Edith, 186, 237, 239–40, *239*
Ames family, ancestry of, 12–13
Ames, Hanna, 13
Ames, Jesse, 12–17, *14*, 32–33, 104, 131, 240; correspondence with Adelbert Ames, 163; farming, 233; flour mill and, 170, 230, 238; move to Minnesota, 36; Northfield robbery and, 237; travels of, 18–19; views of slavery, 18
Ames, Jessie, 238, 239
Ames, John, 13, 31–32, 34, 233, 236–37, 254
Ames, Mark, 13
Ames, Martha Tolman, 12, 15–16, *16*, 104, 129; beekeeping, 170; Blanche Butler Ames and, 167, 189; correspondence with Adelbert Ames, 162–63; move to Minnesota, 36; travels, 18–19; views of slavery, 18
Ames, Oakes, 258
Ames, Sarah, 237, 239, *239*, 254
Ames's Battery, 31–32
Amite County, Mississippi, 228
Amnesty Act of 1872, 183
Anderson, Richard, 98, 104–5
Anderson Intelligencer, 174
Andover, Massachusetts, 239
Andrews, Elisha, 251
animals: Ames's views of, 33–34, 130, 134; in the Civil War, 79
Annapolis, Maryland, 119
Antietam, Battle of, 47–49, 66
Antietam Creek, 47
Appomattox River, 86, 94, 103
Arkansas, 151, 156
Arlington, Virginia, 25
Arlington Heights, Virginia, 46
Army of the James, 84, 86, 93–96; at Fort Fisher, 110; officers of, 89, 105, tactics of, 88, 90
Army of Northeastern Virginia, 26
Army of Northern Virginia, 36, 59, 86; at Antietam, 47; at Chancellorsville, 62; Fort Fisher

and, 115; after Gettysburg, 79; movements of, 64; at Petersburg, 107; tactics of, 69
Army of the Potomac, 9; Ames and, 84; Ames's views of, 34–35; assembly of, 33; casualties in, 99; at Chancellorsville, 61–63; in combat, 36; commanders of, 3, 49, 59, 69; founding of, 31; at Gettysburg, 72–74, 77–79; at Malvern Hill, 41; media coverage of, 66; morale of, 58; movements of, 99; officers in, 5–6, 50, 85–86; in the Overland Campaign, 96; tactics of, 39, 51, 64, 88–89; Twentieth Maine and, 45–46
Army of Virginia, 47
art: Adelbert Ames and, 146, 163; Blanche Ames Ames and, 258; in France, 140–41
artillery: at First Bull Run, 27–29; at Fort Fisher, 121–24; at Fredericksburg, 51, 56; at Gettysburg, 70; in the Seven Days' Battles, 37–41
Atlanta, Georgia, 252
Atlantic (ship), 119
Atlantic District (Union Army), 129
Atlantic Ocean, 14, 80, 108, 113, 132, 143
Augur, C. C., 208
Augusta, Maine, 17
aurora borealis, 57
Austin, Mississippi, 199
Austria, 133–35
Austro-Prussian War, 133–34
Avery, Isaac E., 73

Baden, Duchy of, 134
Bailey, Dennis, 204
Bailey, George, 42
Bailey, John, 164
Baltic (ship), 113
Baltimore, 69, 86
Baltimore Sun, 30
bands (Twentieth Maine), 444, 46
Bangor, Maine, 43
Bangs, Isaac, 44
Baptist Church, 143
Barbary Pirates, 16
Barksdale, Ethelbert, 209–10, 213
Barlow, Francis Channing, 66, 70–71
Barnard, John G., 19
Barrantine, Thomas H., 218
Barry, William F., 29, 31
Barton, Clara, 89
Battery A (Fifth US Artillery), 31; movements of, 34–35; in the Seven Days' Battles, 37–39, 41
Battery Anderson (Fort Fisher), 114, 120
Battery D (Fifth US Artillery), 23, 25, 40; at First Bull Run, 27, 29–30; movements of, 26
Battery Holland (Fort Fisher), 116

Bayard, Thomas F., 175, 227–29
bayonets, 78, 127
Bay Saint Louis, 200
Bay View (Butler residence), 196, 253
Beaufort, North Carolina, 113, 120
Beauregard, P. G. T., 26, 91–94, 99
bees, 170
Belfast, 145
Belknap, William W., 198
Bell, Louis, 120, 124
Benson, Harry King: on Alcorn, 183; on Ames, 4–5, 45, 81, 100, 128–29; on the Twentieth Maine, 45, 58
Berkshire, England, 144
Berlin, 134–35
Bermuda Hundred, Virginia, 87, 88–89, 91, 93–94, 103, 111, 119
Bermuda Hundred Campaign, 95, 96–97
Bern, Switzerland, 137
Berry, Hiram G., 23, 49, 59; at Chancellorsville, 62
Beverly's Ford, 67–68
Bible, 16, 176
Biddle, James, 155
Birney, David B., 54
Birney, William, 104
birth control, 258
Birth Control League of Massachusetts, 258
Bismarck, North Dakota, 256
Bismarck, Otto von, 134
"Black Codes," 150
Blackstone (ship), 119
Blaine, James G., 207
Blair, Francis P., Jr., 175–77, 182
Bland-Allison Act, 260
Blocher's Knoll (Gettysburg), 70–71
blockade runners, 108, 117
Bohemia, 136
Bois de Boulogne (Paris), 139–40
Bombardment and Capture of Fort Fisher, N.C. Jany. 15th 1865, The (drawing), 122
Borden, Ames, 254
Boston, 45
Boston Herald, 260
Boteler's Ford, Battle of, 48
Bourbons (Mississippi political faction), 195, 200–201, 206, 260
Boutwell, George S., 152, 226–30, 241–42, 260
Boutwell Committee, 233, 240
Bowers, Claude G., 252–53
"boy generals" (US Civil War), 64, 66, 79, 256
Bragg, Braxton, 110, 120–21, 127
Brandenburg Gate, 134
Brandy Station, Battle of, 9, 67–69, 67
Brickyard Lane (Gettysburg), 72–73

Bridgeport, Connecticut, 66
Britain: Ames's views of, 141, 147; rule of Ireland, 145–46; trade with Maine, 17; United States and, 179. *See also* England; Scotland; Wales
British Army, 144
Brooklyn (ship), 114
Brooks, Noah, 63
Brown, Albert G., 162
Brown, John, 21
Brown University, 251
Bruce, Blanche K., 186
Brunswick, Maine, 42–43
Bryn Mawr College, 239
Buchanan, James, 142
Buchanan County, Virginia, 240
Buckingham Palace, 144
Buford, John, 67–68; at Gettysburg, 69
bullets, physical properties of, 2
Bull Run (stream), 27
Bull Run, First Battle of, 27–30, *28*, 49, 127–28, 154, 263; Ames at, 1–2, 9, 27–30, 127–28, 154, 263; historiography of, 11; Medal of Honor and, 240
Bull Run, Second Battle of, 47, 64
Burns, Robert, 145
Burnside, Ambrose E., 49–54, 85, 88; at Fredericksburg, 57–58; at Petersburg, 101–2; tactics of, 58–59
Butler, Benjamin Franklin, 9, 84, *97*, 152, 202, 206; Ames and, 163, 165, 167, 171, 195, 229–30, 238; Ames impeachment and, 214, 217–18, 224, 226; at Bermuda Hundred, 94–96; Butler Ames and, 188, 239; in Congress, 184; death of, 240; at Fort Fisher, 111–13, 115–19; in the Overland Campaign, 86, 88–93; at Petersburg, 99, 105; reputation of, 11, 174, 197, 234, 259; role in Johnson impeachment, 152; views of KKK, 151
Butler, Blanche. *See* Ames, Blanche Butler
Butler, Sarah Hildreth, 167–68, 170, 195–96, 205–6, 216, 227
Butler's Book, 152
Butterfield, Daniel, 46, 59–61, 64–65, 69; orders of, 66

Caldwell, Charles, 209–14
Caldwell, Sam, 214
California, 154, 254
Cambridge University, 145
Cameron, Angus, 227–28
Camp Duncan, 30–31
Camp Hooker, Maryland, 32
Camp Mason, Maine, 43, 45
Camp Meade, Pennsylvania, 249

Camp Wikoff, New York, 248
Canada, 17, 108
Canton, Mississippi, 194
Canton Mail, 215
Cape Elizabeth, Maine, 43
Cape Fear River, 108, 110, 117, 120, 123, 127
Cape Hatteras, 119–20
Cape Horn, 13
Cape Lookout, 113
"Captain Wardell" home (Florida), 254
Cardozo, Thomas W., 187, 196, 200, 218–19, 259
Caribbean region, 108, 241
Carlton, Charles A., 121–22
Carpenter, Matthew H., 165
"Carpet-baggers in the United States Senate" (essay), 252
"carpetbaggers" (Reconstruction), 4–5, 7, 152, 170, 178; historiography of, 251–52
Carroll, Samuel S., 75
Carter, Robert G., 56
Cassidy, Hiram, Jr., 221
Castel, Albert, 5
"Castle, the" (Ames residence), 253
Catholicism: Ames's views of, 135–37, 142–43; Blanche Ames Ames and, 258
cattle, 83, 191
Catton, Bruce, 5
cavalry, 66–69; at Gettysburg, 79; in Prussia, 134
Cemetery Hill (Gettysburg), 9, 71–73, *72*, 75–77, 263
Cemetery Ridge (Gettysburg), 76–77
Chadwell, Bill, 234, 236–37
Chaffin's Farm, Battle of, 103–4
Chamberlain, Joshua Lawrence, 6–7, 43, *44*, 241, 256; as acting commander, 61; Ames and, 50, 63–64; at Boteler's Ford, 48; at Fredericksburg, 55–57; at Gettysburg, 78; historical reputation of, 10
Chancellorsville, Battle of, 61–64, 66
Charleston, South Carolina, 80–81, 88, 129, 131, 231, 249
Chase, George K., 209–10
Chase, Salmon P., 157
Chattanooga, Siege of, 88
Chattanooga, Tennessee, 201
Chesapeake Bay, 33
Chester Station, Battle of, 91
Chester Station, Virginia, 90–91
Chicago, 137
Chicago Daily Tribune, 201
Chickahominy River, 36–37, 39, 99
Chickasaw County, Mississippi, 224
Chickasaw Messenger, 215

Christian, Thomas, 222
Christianity, 58; Ames and, 147; in Europe, 143
Christmas, 142
City of Antwerp (ship), 147
City of Cork (ship), 133
City Point (Petersburg), 89–90
civil rights, 4–5; Ames and, 151, 183, 185, 195, 250; Ames's views of, 130, 162, 201; historiography of, 260; in Mississippi, 157–58, 170, 186
Civil Rights Act (1866), 137–38, 150
Civil Rights Act of 1871, 177
Civil Rights Act of 1875, 207
Clancey, Michael A., 218, 225
Clanton, Mississippi, 153
Clark, Charles, 192
Clark, Nathan S., 57
Cleveland, Grover, 239
Clinton, Mississippi, 207, 214, 230
Coahoma County, Mississippi, 187
Coburn, Abner, 19
Cold Harbor, Battle of, 97–98, 131, 242
Cole, Joseph Foxcroft, 140–41, 147
Colfax, Schuyler, 177
Coliseum (Rome), 143
Colquitt, Alfred H., 231
Columbia, South Carolina, 129–31
Columbia University, 251–52
Compromise of 1877, 231
Comstock, Cyrus, 117
Concho (ship), 246
Confederate Army, 25; Alcorn and, 160, 175; at Chancellorsville, 62; at Cold Harbor, 98; deserters from, 150, 208; at First Bull Run, 2, 28–29; in Florida, 83; at Fort Fisher, 108, 115–16, 120–25, 127; at Fredericksburg, 57, 59; at Gettysburg, 70–73, 76–77; at Malvern Hill, 40; in Mississippi, 148; in the Overland Campaign, 90–93; at Petersburg, 101–4; at Second Bull Run, 47; slavery and, 81; tactics of, 26–27, 61; veterans of, 158, 171–72, 183, 209, 218, 260; at Yorktown, 35
Confederate Navy, 113
Confederate States of America: Ames's views of, 30, 34–35, 176; Britain and, 179; defeat of, 127–29, 148, 190; economy of, 192; Europe and, 138; historiography of, 7; James-Younger Gang and, 234; newspapers in, 110; secession of, 23; supplies for, 117
Congress (US): Reconstruction and, 129–30, 137, 148, 150, 157; representation of Mississippi in, 161
Conkling, Roscoe, 163–65
Conner, W. M., 219–20

conservatism, 201, 206, 217, 231; in Mississippi, 160, 186, 194
convict labor, 192, 221
Corbett, Henry, 180
Corbin, Henry C., 247
Corinth, Mississippi, 231
Cork, Ireland, 146
Corps of Topographical Engineers, 41–42
Cotton, 191–92
Cragin, Aaron, 165
Crane, Joseph G., 157
Crater, Battle of the, 102–3
Crimean War, 110
Cromwell, Oliver, 146
Crosby, Peter, 197–98, 202–5, 221, 224
Crounse, L. L., 66
Crystal Palace, 145
Cuba, 240–44, *244*, 246–48, 250, 256
Cuban War for Independence, 240
Culpeper County, Virginia, 64
Cumming, J. B., 38
Cummings, Arthur C., 29
currency, 193, 260
Current, Richard N., 7
Currier, Nathaniel, *122, 173*
Currier and Ives, *122, 173*
Curtis, Newton M., 114–16, 121–27
Custer, George Armstrong, 6, 64, 245

Daggett, Rufus, 116
Daily Clarion (Jackson, Mississippi), 153, 206, 209, 217, 231
Daily Davenport Democrat, 126
Dakota County, Minnesota, 234
Dakota Territory, 238
Darbytown Road, Battle of, 104–5
David Kimball (ship), 15
Davis, Alexander Kelso, 187, 195–98, 222; impeachment of, 218, 259
Davis, Daniel, 6
Davis, Garrett, 165
Davis, Jefferson, 108, 138, 162, 201; West Point and, 20
Daytona Beach, Florida, 254
Deason, J. B., 221
Declaration of Independence, 174, 263
Deep Bottom, First Battle of, 101–2
Delafield, Richard, 19–20, 111–12
Democratic Party, 7–8; in 1862 elections, 49; in 1868 elections, 156; in 1869 elections, 160–61; in 1872 elections, 184, 186; in 1874 elections, 202; in 1875 elections, 211–12, 227–28; in 1876 elections, 231; Ames and, 163, 165, 173–75, 178,

Democratic Party (*cont.*)
    185, 194–95, 213–14; Ames impeachment and, 215–17, 219–24, 226; Butler and, 86; Dunning School and, 251–52; John F. Kennedy and, 260–61; in Maine, 17; in Mississippi, 10, 152–53, 155, 232; Reconstruction and, 181–82; Revels and, 162; in Vicksburg, 197–99; violence in Mississippi and, 3, 170–72, 206–7, 209–11, 230
Denmark, 133–34
Dent, Louis, 160–61
Department of the Gulf (US Army), 205
Department of the South (Union Army), 79–80, 84, 88
Department of West Virginia (Union Army), 86
Desjardin, Thomas A., 6–7
Devens, Charles, Jr., 96, 131
Devin, Thomas, 70
Dickens, Charles, 143–44
diphtheria, 237
Dix, John Adams, 142
Dixon, Henry, 207
Dorset, England, 12, 143
Doubleday, Abner, 6
Douglass, Frederick, 133
"Downfall of the Carpet-Bag Regime, The" (essay), 251
Downs, Gregory, 156
Drake, Jeremiah C., 89, 91
Dred Scott v. Sandford, 21
Drennan, W. A., 222
Dresden, Germany, 135
Drewry's Bluff, Virginia, 91–94
Dublin, 145–46
Dudley, Thomas, 13
dueling, 174
Duncan, John, 158
Dunning, William, 251–52, 261
Dunning School, 8, 251–52, 257
Du Pont, Francis, 80–81
Durant, Thomas J., 218–22, 223–25
Durham Station, North Carolina, 128
dysentery, 246

Eames, Anthony, 12–13, 133
Eames, Margery, 12
Early, Jubal, 70–73
East Cemetery Hill (Gettysburg), 74, 76
Easton, Massachusetts, 258
East Thomaston, Maine, 14–15
Ecole Polytechnique (France), 19
Edinburgh, 146
Edinburgh, Duke of, 146
Edson, Theodore, 168–69

education, 191
Edward II (the Black Prince), 146
Edwards, Mississippi, 209
Eggleston, Beroth B., 152–53
Eicher, David, 5
Eicher, John, 5
El Caney, Cuba, 243, 249
elections: of 1862, 49; of 1864, 100–101, 118; of 1868, 156; of 1869, 159–60; of 1872, 184–85; of 1873, 186–88; of 1874, 201–2, 206; of 1875, 211–12, 226–27; of 1876, 231
Ellis Ford, 58
Ely's Ford, 61
Emancipation Proclamation, 5
engineering, 20; at Fort Fisher, 110–12
engineers: Adelbert Ames and, 41–42; Butler Ames as, 241; in the Civil War, 35, 51, 77
England, 12; Ames in, 133, 138, 141, 144–46; trade with Maine, 14
Enterprise, Mississippi, 231
environment, in Minnesota, 234
Episcopalian Church, 12, 253
Essex, England, 143
eugenics, 258
Eugénie (French empress), 140
Europe: Ames family in, 254; Ames's travels in, 9, 131–32, 135, 138–47, 163, 233; tourism in, 132–33; US economy and, 193
Ewell, Richard S., 70–71, 73, 76, 79
Ex Parte Yerger, 157

Fairfax, Virginia, 25
Fair Oaks, Battle of. *See* Seven Pines, Battle of
Fair Oaks, Second Battle of, 105
Falmouth, Maine, 46, 52
Falmouth, Virginia, 51
Fargo, North Dakota, 238
Farnsworth, Elon, 6, 64
Featherston, Winfield S., 216, 224, 226
Federalist Papers, 16
Federal Point (Fort Fisher), 108, 114–15, 120–21
feminism, 258
Fenians, 145
Ferrero, Edward, 102
Fifteenth Amendment, 160–61
Fifth US Artillery, 2, 23, 31; at Malvern Hill, 40; movements of, 35
fireflies, 24
First Brigade (X Corps), 89, 91
First Brigade (XI Corps): at Gettysburg, 75; at Hagerstown, 79
First Colored Senators and Representatives, in the 41st and 42nd Congress of the United States (drawing), 173

First Division (XXIV Corps), 105
First English Civil War, 145
First National Bank (Northfield), 234–35
First Rhode Island, 24
First US Artillery, 27
fishing, 13–14, 16, 170; international policy and, 179–80
Fitzpatrick, David J., 6
Flanagan, A. J., 205, 221
Florence, Italy, 143
Florida, 1, 254; Civil War in, 83–84, 128; politics of, 231
flour mill, Ames family's, 104, 131, 170, 230, 233, 239, 250
Folly Island, South Carolina, 83
food, at West Point, 21
Forrest, Nathan Bedford, 151
Fort Anderson, 127
Fort Atkinson, Iowa, 184
Fort Canovar, Cuba, 244
Fort Craig, Virginia, 46
Fort Darling, 91–94
Fort Donelson, 34
Fort Fisher, Battles of, 9, 108, *109*, 241; historiography of, 11, 250
Fort Fisher, First Battle of, 110–19, *112*
Fort Fisher, Second Battle of, 119–27, *122*, *123*
Fort Gilmer, 103
Fort Harrison, 103
Fort Henry, 34
Fort Monroe, Virginia, 33–34, 80, 86, 89, 96, 115
Fort Sumter, 23, 81, 83
Fort Union, New Mexico, 240
Fort Wagner, South Carolina, 81
Foster, R. S., 103
Fourteenth Amendment, 150–51, 153, 155–56, 160–61, 177
Fourth Maine Volunteer Infantry, 23
Fourth Military District (Reconstruction), 151, 154
France, 139–40, 143, 146–47
Franco-Prussian War, 193
Franklin, William B., 54, 86
Fredericksburg, Battle of, 9, 51–58, *55*, 64, 171; historiography of, 11
Fredericksburg, Virginia, 51–55, 61–62
Freedman's Bureau, 129–30, 151, 238; Ames and, 7, 162
freedpeople: Ames and, 7, 10, 157–58, 162, 226; Ames's views of, 138, 146, 177, 195; historiography of, 251; mobilization of, 204, 223; in politics, 200–201; rights of, 150, 190, 195, 206; violence against, 130; voting by, 156, 160–61, 182, 210–11, 252; voting rights of, 172, 210–11. *See also* African Americans

Free-Soil movement, 22
Frémont, John C., 101
French, O. C., 221
French, Samuel G., 158–59
French language, 139
Fry, James B., 158
Fulton (ship), 84

Gaines, William F., 37
Gaines's Mill, 37–38
Garner, James Wilford, 8, 251–52, 258–59
Gayer, Henry, 42
General Orders No. 33, 158
Genoa, 142
Genthner, Llewellyn, 42
George, James Z., 207, 209–10, 212
Georgia: Civil War in, 111, 127; politics of, 156, 231
German Americans, 62, 66, 71, 134
German language, 134–35, 138–39
Germanna Ford, 61
Germany, 133–35, 147
Gerrish, Theodore, 46, 51–52, 56
Getchell, George, 42
Getty, George W., 37–38, 41
Gettysburg, Battle of, 69–77, *72*, *74*, 86, 134, 213; Ames at, 9, 11, 263; historiography of, 6–7
Gettysburg, Pennsylvania, 69–72, 76–78
Gibbon, John, 6, 54
"Gibraltar Brigade," 75
Gillem, Alvin C., 151–52, 154, 159
Gillette, William, 198
Gillmore, Quincey A., 79, *80*, 81, 83, 99, 129; in the Overland Campaign, 88–92, 94–96
Gills family, 170
Gilmore, Charles D., 43, 50
Gilmore, J. C., 246
Gladstone, William, 179
Glasgow, 145
Gloucester Point, Virginia, 84
golf, 254
Gordon, George H., 79, 81
governor's mansion (Mississippi), 154–55, 189, *190*
Graham, Charles, 115
Graham, Robert, 90
grain, 191
Grand Review, 253
Grant, Julia, 168, 179
Grant, Ulysses S., 2, 5, 84; Ames and, 151, 157–59, 168, 198–99, 214; at Cold Harbor, 97–99; command of Army of the Potomac, 6; Fort Fisher and, 110–11, 114, 118–19; historical reputation of, 251; as lieutenant general, 86; at Petersburg, 101–3, 107; presidency of, 156,

Grant, Ulysses S. (*cont.*)
198–99, 205, 208–10, 227, 231; Reconstruction and, 153–54; reelection as president, 184–86; relatives of, 160; tactics of, 85, 88–89, 96, 108, 127; at Vicksburg, 148; views of Mississippi elections, 161; views of tactics, 95
grapes, 233
Grear, Charles David, *123*
Great Lakes, 41–42
Greeley, Horace, 184–86
Greenville, Mississippi, 149, 187
Greenville Times, 207–8, 212, 226
Griffin, Charles, 23, 27–30, 65, 240; Ames and, 60; at Fredericksburg, 54, *55*; promotion of, 31
Gustafson, Nicholas, 236

Habsburg dynasty, 136
Hagerstown, Maryland, 79
Hagood, Johnson, 90
Hall, Jacquelyn Dowd, 4
Hallé, Charles, 144
Halleck, Henry W., 51–53, 84
Hamburg, Germany, 138
Hamilton, Alexander, 16
Hamlin, Hannibal, 49–50
Hampton Roads, Virginia, 89, 113, 118–19
Hancock, Winfield S., 101
Harper's Ferry, West Virginia, 21, 26, 47–48
Harris, Andrew L., 71
Harris, G. E., 221
Harris, William C., 7
Harrisburg, Pennsylvania, 69–70, 249
Harrisburg Road (Gettysburg), 70
Harrison, William Henry, 17
Harrison's Landing, 41
Harvard University, 239, 258, 260
Havana, 240, 242
Hay, John, 98
Hayes, Rutherford B., 231, 237
Hays, Harry T., 73, 75
Head, George, 205
Heckman, Charles A., 90
Heidelberg, Germany, 137
Heintzelman, Samuel, 85–86
Henry, Guy V., 242–43
Henry House Hill (Bull Run), 27
Herod (King), 176
Hess, Earl J., 101
Heth, Henry, 70
Heywood, Joseph Lee, 235–36
Hico, Arkansas, 178
Hill, James, 187, 196
Hill, P. H., 93

Hills, Julia, 36
Hilton Head, South Carolina, 129
Hincks, Edward B., 89–91
Hinds County, Mississippi, 207, 209, 223, 227
Hinds County Gazette, 194
Hingham, Massachusetts, 12–13
Hobart, Rev. Peter, 13
Hoke, Robert, 115, 120–21
Holcombe, Arthur N., 260
Holland, M. L., 221
Holly Springs, Mississippi, 170, 187, 198
Holyrood Castle, 145
Holy Spirit, 137
Homestead Act, 233
Hooker, C. E., 155
Hooker, Joseph, 49–50, *55*, 59–64, 85; orders of, 67, 69
horses: captured at Gettysburg, 79; in the Civil War, 29, 65; as combat casualties, 236, 246; in Northfield robbery, 234–36; in Prussia, 134; in the Thirty Years' War, 136
House of Representatives (US), 49
Howard, Jacob H., 164–65
Howard, Oliver Otis, 24, 59–60, 65–66, 238, 241, 256; at Chancellorsville, 62; at Gettysburg, 70–71, 73–74, 76, 79
Howlett Line, 94
Hsieh, Wayne, 21
Hudson Valley, 21
Hughes, Adelbert, 178
Hughes, Nathan, 178–79
Humphreys, Benjamin G., 150, 153–55
Hunt, Henry, 35; at Fredericksburg, 52; at Malvern Hill, 40
Hunter, David, 26
hunting, 16, 170

impeachment: of Ames, 10, 213–18, 220–26; of Andrew Johnson, 151–52, 213
Independence Day, 77, 197
infantry: Ames and, 41; cavalry and, 66, 68
Inspection of the 2nd Pennsylvania Artillery by Gen Ames (drawing), *106*
inventions, by Ames, 238
Iowa, 180, 184
Ireland, 19, 145–46
Italy, 142–43, 147, 254
Iuka, Mississippi, 231
Ives, James Merritt, *122, 173*

Jackson, Mississippi, 159, 204, 206, 227; Ames in, 180, 189; Ames family in, 194, 213; as capital, 156, 195–96; Civil War in, 148, 192; con-

stitutional convention in, 152–53; impeachment in, 215; militia in, 208–9; newspapers in, 160; refugees in, 210; violence in, 157
Jackson, Thomas J. "Stonewall," 27, 29, 37; at Chancellorsville, 61–62; at Fredericksburg, 51, 53–54
Jackson County, Mississippi, 212
Jackson Times, 217
Jacksonville, Florida, 83–84
Jacque, Charles, 140
James, Frank, 234–35
James, Henry, 133
James, Jesse, 10, 234–36
James Island, South Carolina, 80
Jameson, Charles Davis, 50
James River, 37, 39, 41, 87, 91, 94–96; crossing of, 99, 103
James-Younger Gang, 234–37
Jesus Christ: in Christian practices, 142–43; in religious art, 135
Joachim, Joseph, 144
John (King of England), 144
"John Brown's Body" (song), 145
Johnson, Andrew, 129–31, 137–38, 148, 150; Ames and, 154; impeachment of, 151–52, 213; supporters of, 157
Johnston, Joseph E., 26–27, 33, 128; at Seven Pines, 36; at Williamsburg, 35
Joint Committee on the Conduct of the War, 119
Jordan, Mark H., 6
Joseph (Nez Perce chief), 238
Judaism, 135
judiciary, in Mississippi, 216, 222–23
Juliet (Shakespearean character), 143

Kansas, 234
Kautz, August, 154
Keene, Samuel T., 52, 57–58
Kennebunk, Maine, 42
Kennedy, John F., 259–62
Kent, Edward, 17
Kent, Jacob Ford, 243–45
Kettle Hill, Cuba, 243
Keyes, Erasmus, 85
Key West, Florida, 256
Killarney, Ireland, 146
Killebrew, Radford, 256
Killer Angels, The, 6
Kilpatrick, Hugh Judson, 6, 64, 79
Kingsbury, Henry W., 40
Kirby, Edmund, 36
Knight, Newton, 208
Knox, John, 145

Krick, Robert K., 54
Krzyżanowski, Włodzimierz, 75
Ku Klux Klan, 7, 151–52, 174, 181–83; Ames's views of, 170, 172, 185, 237–38; Blanche Ames Ames on, 258; Congressional debates about, 176; prosecution of, 173

Lake Como, Italy, 254
Lamar, Lucius Quintus Cincinnatus, 200–201, 207, 209, 214, *215*, 260–61
Lamb, William, 110, 120–21, 125
Lambinet, Émile, 140
Langley, James W., 217
Lathrop, Isaac, 42
Lavery, Dennis S., 6
Law, Evander M., 78
Lawton, Henry W., 242–43, 245
Ledlie, James H., 102
Lee, Robert E., 36–37, 63, 96; at Chancellorsville, 61–62; at Cold Harbor, 97, 99; at Fredericksburg, 50–53; at Gettysburg, 73, 78–79; at Malvern Hill, 39–40; at Petersburg, 99, 101, 105, 107; retreat from Maryland, 48; at Second Bull Run, 47; tactics of, 64, 69; Union Army and, 59–61, 67, 85–86, 88–89
Lee, Stephen D., 38
Lee County, Mississippi, 194
Leister, Lydia, 76
Lemann, Nicholas, 8
Lexington Advertiser, 256
lime, 15
Lincoln, Abraham: administration of, 6, 176; Ames and, 84, 101; assassination of, 128–29; biographies of, 98; Blanche Ames Ames on, 263; Fort Fisher and, 111, 118; Grant and, 86; McClellan and, 48–49; military policy of, 24, 41, 69; military strategies of, 33, 51, 83; Reconstruction policy of, 129–30; southerners' views of, 30; views of Chancellorsville, 63; views of Gettysburg, 79
Lincoln County, Maine, 12
literature, 16
Little, A. W., 223
Littlefield, Daniel, 42
Little Round Top (Gettysburg), 78
Liverpool, England, 133, 146
livestock, 234; in art, 140
Lockwood, Henry C., 121–22, 124–27
logging, 14
London: Ames in, 141, 143–45; tourism in, 133
Long, Hezekiah, 48–49, 60, 65
Longacre, Edward G., 6, 95
Long Civil War, 233

Long Island, New York, 248
Longstreet, James, 64; at Chancellorsville, 61; at Fredericksburg, 51, 53–54; at Gettysburg, 73, 78
Louisiana (ship), 112–15
Louisiana, 174, 205; Civil War in, 86; politics of, 156, 231
Louisiana Donaldsonville Artillery, 56
Louisiana Tigers, 73–74
Louvre, 141–42
Lowell, Massachusetts: Ames-Butler wedding in, 168; Ames family in, 186, 188, 195, 227, 237, 253–54, 256; Blanche Butler Ames in, 179, 184; Butler family in, 233, 240
Lowndes County, Mississippi, 211
Luther, Martin, 135
Lutheranism, 135
Lutz, John M., 74
Lynch, John M., 260

Macon Beacon, 161, 181
Madison, James, 16
Madrid, 133
Magna Carta, 144
Magruder, John B., 35, 38–39
Mahan, Alfred Taylor, 21
Mahan, Denis Hart, 21
Maine (ship), 240–42
Maine: abolitionism in, 18; Adelbert Ames in, 2, 43, 164, 229, 262; Ames family in, 13–14, 16, 36; in the Civil War, 6, 23; economy of, 15; politics of, 17, 49–50; soldiers from, 41–42, 45–46, 58, 89
malaria, 246–47
Malvern (ship), 121
Malvern Hill, Battle of, 11, 39–41
Manassas Junction, Virginia, 25–27, 33
Manning, Anselm, 235–36
marriage: of Adelbert Ames and Blanche Butler, 167–70; Ames's views of, 32
Marseilles, 142
Marshfield, Massachusetts, 13
Marston Moor, Battle of, 145
Martin, Samuel J., 6
Mary I (of Scotland), 145
Marye's Heights (Fredericksburg), 53, 55–56, 58
Maryland, 46–48, 69
Massachusetts, 168–69, 195, 200, 248, 258–60; politics of, 202, 241, 254
Massachusetts Bay Colony, 12–13
Massachusetts Institute of Technology, 239
Massie, John L., 38
Maurin, Victor, 56

McClellan, George: Ames's views of, 36; criticism of, 47; Lincoln and, 48–49; policies of, 85; staff of, 31; tactics of, 33, 35, 37, 39–41
McCook, Andrew McDowell, 241
McDonald, Joseph E., 227–28
McDowell, Irvin, 26–27, 85, 154
McKee, George C., 229
McKinley, William, 241, 249
McLaws, Lafayette, 38
McLean, Lucy, 32
McLean, Nathaniel C., 65–66
McMillan, Samuel J. R., 227, 229
Meade, George G., 86, 88–89, 96; Ames and, 61, 63, 84; after the Civil War, 129; at Cold Harbor, 98; command of Army of the Potomac, 69; at Fredericksburg, 54; at Gettysburg, 70, 76, 78–79; at Petersburg, 99, 102
Mechanicsville, Battle of, 37
Medal of Honor, 126, 239–40, 242, 256
Mediterranean Sea, 143
Memphis, Tennessee, 199
Meridian, Mississippi, 148
Merrimac (ship), 45
Merritt, Wesley, 6, 64
Mexican-American War, 17, 23–24
Mexico, 17, 108
Michigan, 246
Milan, 142
Miles, Nelson A., 242, 244–45
Miller, Clell, 234–37
Miller, Horace, 203–4
Minnesota: Adelbert Ames in, 179, 230, 233; agriculture in, 234; Ames family in, 36, 104, 130–31, 164, 170
Mississippi: Adelbert Ames in, 1, 149, 163–66, 170, 180–84; Ames family in, 186; Ames as governor of, 9–10, 185–86, 190–92, 206, 229–30, 233; Ames impeachment in, 213–14, 217, 226; Ames as provisional governor of, 154–55; Ames's reputation in, 256; Civil War in, 148–49; constitutional convention in, 152–53; courts in, 223; debt of, 251; economy of, 192–94; elections in, 159–62, 186–88, 211–13, 226–29; historiography of, 3, 5, 251–53, 258–59, 262–63; politics of, 175, 195, 200–201, 206, 226, 231–32; Reconstruction in, 7–8, 150–51, 156–58, 161–63, 171–77, 199; Vicksburg Troubles in, 197–98, 204–5, 221; violence in, 177–78, 181, 207–10, 214–17, 227–29, 237
Mississippi Board of Levee Commissioners, 159
Mississippi Constitution, 161, 163
Mississippi Legislature, 161–62, 165, 195–97, 214,

218–19, 222; elections to, 188, 211; historiography of, 252; impeachment of Ames by, 216, 218–20, 222, 224–26
Mississippi militia, 208–10, 223
"Mississippi Plan," 207
Mississippi Railroad, 192
Mississippi River, 42, 149, 156
Mississippi Supreme Court, 189, 217
Missouri, 174, 234
Monroe County, Mississippi, 228
Monroe, N. P., 60
Montauk Point, New York, 248
Morgan, Albert T., 207
Morrell, George W., 41
Morrill, Lot M., 30, 165–66
Morris Island, South Carolina, 81, 82, 83
Morse, Freeman Harlow, 145
Morton, Oliver P., 214
mules, 66, 79
Musgrove, Henry, 187
music, 144–45
Myers, Jasper, 155

Naples, 143
Napoleon III, 139–40, 142
Natchez, Mississippi, 170, 181, 186, 188
National Union Republican Party (NURP), 160
National Volunteer Reserve, 241
Native Americans, 20, 238
Navesink Highlands, New Jersey, 238
NBC, 261
Nebraska, 138
New Castle Ferry, 97
New England, 1, 250; Ames's views of, 24
New Englanders, 253
Newington, London, 143
New Inlet, North Carolina, 110, 113, 120
New Jersey, 238
New Orleans, 19, 86, 111, 196
New Orleans Republican, 213
New Testament, 176
New York (US state), 168–70; elections in, 49; politics of, 213
New York City, 83, 132–33, 184, 218, 238, 241
New York Herald, 68, 126
New York Times, 66
New York Tribune, 174
New York World, 217
Nez Perce people, 238
Nice, France, 142
Nicolay, John, 98
Noble, William H., 83
Norfolk, England, 13

Northampton, Massachusetts, 239
North Anna River, 96
North Carolina: Civil War in, 111, 113, 127–28; politics of, 231; Reconstruction in, 129
North Carolina Weekly Standard, 68
Northfield, Minnesota, 184, *236*; Ames family in, 131, 170, 179, 233, 240; Ames flour mill in, 131, 230, 233; robbery in, 234–37
North Fox Island, Maine, 13–14
North Yorkshire, England, 145
Notre Dame Cathedral, 141
Noxubee County, Mississippi, 161, 219–20

Oak Grove, Battle of, 37
Okolona, Mississippi, 148
Old Cold Harbor, 97–98
O'Leary, Richard, 203
Olustee, Battle of, 83
Ord, Edward O. C., 103–5, 151–52, 154
Oregon, 231
Ormond, Florida, 254
Ouachita Telegraph, 174
Overland Campaign, 85–91
Owen, Andrew, 204
Oxford, Mississippi, 200
Oxford Falcon, 155
Oxford University, 145
oystercatchers, 121
oysters, 200

Packer, A. G., 202
Paine, Charles, 120, 137
Pamunkey River, 96–97
Paris, *140*; Ames in, 139–42, 146; tourism in, 133
Parsons, Frederick, 216, 220, 223
Pattinson, Robert, 26
Pease, Henry R., 178, 212–13, 229
Pegram's Salient, 101
Pelham, John, 23
pelicans, 121
Pendleton, William N., 48
Peninsula Campaign, 34–41, 43, 85
Penn, William, 144
Pennsylvania, 239; Civil War in, 69; elections in, 49; founding of, 144
Pennypacker, Galusha, 122, 125
Penobscot Bay, 8, 13–14
Perman, Michael, 7
Perth, Scotland, 145
Petersburg, Siege of, 11, 99–104, *100*, *104*, *106*, 107
Petersburg, Virginia, 88–92, 111
Pettus, John J., 192
Peyton, E. G., 217

Philadelphia, 218, 249
Philips Academy, 239
Piatti, Carlo Alfredo, 144
Pickett, George E., 77
Pickwick Papers, The, 143
Pierce, James H., 166
Pierrepont, Edwards, 208–10, 251
pirates, 15–16, 242
Pitts, Charlie, 234–36
Pittsburgh, 184, 193
Pius IX (Pope), 143
Pleasanton, Alfred, 66–69, 84
Pleasants, Henry, 101
Plymouth Colony, 12–13
Pope, John, 47
Porter, Andrew, 26–28
Porter, David D., 110–11, 113–14, 118–21
Porter, Fitz John, 37–40, 85; at Antietam, 47; at Boteler's Ford, 48
Porter, Horace, 159
Portland, Maine, 43, 45
Portland Daily Press, 58, 126
Port Walthall Junction, 90–93, 120
potatoes, 192
Potomac River, 25, 31, 33, 46, 51, 69
Potsdam, Germany, 134
Potter, Robert, 101
Powers, Ridgely, 181, 186, 188, 192, 194–95
Prague, 135–36, *136*
Profiles in Courage (book), 259–62
Prospect Hill (Fredericksburg), 53
Protestantism, 135, 143, 147
Prussia: Ames in, 133–35, 138–40; military training in, 66
Pryor, Roger Atkinson, 218, 224–25
"Public Career of Adelbert Ames, The, 1861–1876" (dissertation), 4–5
Puerto Rico, 248
Pulitzer Prize, 259
Pullen, John J., 7, 43, 45–46, 78

Quakerism, 144
Quarantine Hill, 60, 64

racism: of James-Younger Gang, 234; in Mississippi, 150, 178, 190, 209, 219, 223; in politics, 162; in the South, 130
Radical Republicans, 176, 201, 206–7; Ames and, 130, 172, 175 186–88; historiography of, 251; Johnson and, 137; in Mississippi, 183; Reconstruction policies of, 150, 154; support for, 194; views of Lincoln, 101
Rafuse, Ethan S., 5

railroads, 192–94, 196
Raleigh, North Carolina, 129
Ransom, Robert, 92
Rapidan River, 61
Rappahannock River, 33, 51–53, 59, 61–63, 65, 67–68
rats, 33–34
Raymond, John B., 221
Reade, Philip, 248
Reconstruction, 129–31; Ames and, 2, 7, 9–10, 182–84, 250–51, 257; civil rights and, 4; conclusion of, 231–32; debates about, 137, 148, 176, 201, 206–7, 219; historiography of, 5, 8, 251–52, 258–63; judiciary and, 216; Ku Klux Klan and, 170; in Mississippi, 150, 154, 159, 161–63, 171–75, 226; violence and, 195, 199, 208–9
Reconstruction Acts, 150–52, 155
Reconstruction in Mississippi (book), 8, 252
Redeemers, 206–7, 209–10, 212–14, 216, 218–19, 230
Red Jacket (ship), 15
"Red Shirts" (Mississippi), 206, 209
relics, of saints, 141
Republican Party, 3, 101, 180–81; in 1862 elections, 49; in 1868 elections, 156; in 1869 elections, 159–60; in 1872 elections, 184; in 1874 elections, 201–2; in 1875 elections, 210–11, 228; in 1876 elections, 231; Ames and, 162–66, 173–74, 184, 212, 238, 257; congressional investigations and, 227; Dunning School and, 252; factions of, 153, 175, 196–97, 201, 210; impeachment and, 215–20, 223, 226; Ku Klux Klan and, 170; in Maine, 19, 30; in Mississippi, 10, 200–201, 205, 228, 230, 232; policies of, 192, 194–95; race and, 190; Reconstruction policy of, 129–30, 137–38, 150–51, 198, 207; supporters of, 153, 195, 226; Vicksburg Troubles and, 205, 207–9; violence against in Mississippi, 214, 228, 230
Revels, Hiram, 162–63, 175, 181, 212
Reynolds, John F., 70
rice, 192
Rice, Benjamin F., 164
Rice, John, 30
Richards Ford, 58
Richmond, Virginia, 26, 85, 88–90, 96–97, 127; combat at, 36, 104; as Confederate capital, 33–34, 51; military defenses of, 86
Richmond Dispatch, 34
Ricketts, James B., 27–29
Rock Creek, 70
Rockefeller, John D., 254, 256

Rockland, Maine, 12, 142, 147; history of, 14–15; soldiers from, 23, 48, 52
Rockland Gazette, 12
Rockland Guard, 23
Rolling Fork, Mississippi, 215
Rome, 143
Roosevelt, Theodore, 247
Rosser, Thomas Lafayette, 23
Rough Riders, 243
rowing, 145
Royal Arsenal (Britain), 144
Runnymeade, England, 144
Ruscombe, England, 144
Russell, David Allen, 69

Sáenz de Urturi, Francisco, 246
Saint Anne's Episcopal Church (Lowell), 168
Saint James Hall (London), 143–44
Saint Maria Degli Angeli (basilica), 143
Saint Paul, Minnesota, 36, 234, 237
Saint Peter's (Rome), 143
Salon (Paris), 141
Sanger, Margaret, 258
San Juan Hill, Battle of, 243
Santiago Bay, 242
Santiago de Cuba, 241–49
Savannah, Georgia, 110, 120
Saxony, Germany, 135
Schaff, Morris, 253
Schlesinger, Arthur M., Jr., 260
Schleswig-Holstein, 133–34
Schofield, John A., 119
Schurz, Carl, 71
Scotland, 12, 145–46
Scott, Dred, 21
Scott, Winfield, 24, 26
Scranton Tribune, 249
Scriber's Magazine, 251
Sears, Stephen, 6
Second Amendment, 150
Second Brigade (X Corps), 89
Second Brigade (XI Corps), 65–66
Second Division (XVIII Corps), 103
Second Rhode Island, 24
Second US Artillery Regiment, 23
Sedgwick, John, 61–62, 79
Seine River, 142
Senate (US): 1862 elections to, 49; Ames and, 241; Ames in, 170–84, 189; Ames's election to, 162–66; historiography of, 259–60; impeachment of Andrew Johnson and, 152; investigation of Mississippi elections, 226–30
Senate Judiciary Committee, 163–65

Senate Military Committee, 171
Seven Days' Battles, 37, 86, 98
Seven Pines, Battle of, 36
Seymour, Horatio, 156
Seymour, Truman, 83
Shaara, Michael, 6
Shaeffer, J. W., 92
Shafter, William R., 241–48
Shakespeare, William, 143, 146, 167
Sharpsburg, Maryland, 46–47
Shaw, Charles, 138
Shenandoah Valley, 26, 64, 86
Shepherdstown, Battle of, 48
Sheridan, Philip H., 2, 86, 119, 205
Sherman, John, 165
Sherman, William Tecumseh, 2, 110–11, 127–28, 130, 165; in Mississippi, 148, 192
shipbuilding, 15
shrimp, 200
Sickles, Daniel, 59; at Chancellorsville, 62–63; at Gettysburg, 70, 73, 78
Sigel, Franz, 86
Sigsbee, Charles Dwight, 242
Simpson, Brooks D., 5
Simrall, Horatio F., 217–18, 225–26
Skinkers Neck on the Rappahannock below Fredericksburg, VA (drawing), 52–53
slavery: abolition of, 177, 190; Ames's views of, 17–18, 199–200; Confederate war effort and, 81, 108; debates about, 21–22
Slocum, Henry Warner, 70
smallpox, 59–61
Smith, Alexander, 224–25
Smith, William Farrar "Baldy," 35, 88–92, 95–98; at Petersburg, 103
Smith College, 239, 257
Sorenson, Ted, 259, 262
South Ayrshire, Scotland, 145
South Carolina, 135, 174; Civil War in, 80–81, 127; Reconstruction in, 129–32; violence in, 231
Southerners: Ames's views of, 30; at West Point, 22
Spain, 240–45, 249, 256
Spanish-American War, 10, 241–46
Spear, Ellis, 44, 55, 253–54
Spirit of Old West Point, The, 253
Spotsylvania Court House, Battle of, 96
Spurgeon, Charles, 143
Stanberry, Henry, 157
Stanton, Edwin, 94, 126, 152
Stark, Peter Burwell, 171
Star of Pascagoula (newspaper), 212
Stephens, Alexander, 176
Stevens, Joshua, 219–20

Stevens, Thaddeus, 152
Stockton, T .B., 47; at Fredericksburg, 57
Stone, John Marshall, 231
Stoneman, George, 61
Stowe, Harriet Beecher, 18
Stowe, William W., 132
St. Paul (ship), 241–43
Stratford-upon-Avon, England, 146
Stuart, J. E. B., 64, 67–69
sugarcane, 192
Sugar Loaf (Fort Fisher), 120, 127
Summerville, South Carolina, 249
Sumner, Charles, 165, 180, 201, 206, 260
Sumner County, Mississippi, 196
Supreme Court of Massachusetts, 18
Surrey, England, 144
Swift Creek, 90
Switzerland, 137
swords: ceremonial, 78; in combat, 74, 121, 124, 127; in training, 44

Tampa Bay, Florida, 248
Taney, Roger B., 21
Tate, Samuel, 74
"taxpayers convention" (Mississippi), 206
"Taxpayers' Leagues," 202–3, 205, 252
Tennessee: Civil War in, 119; Reconstruction in, 150–51
Tenth US Census Report, 251
Tenure of Office Act, 152
Terry, Alfred H., 89–91, 94, 105, *118*, 119–22, 125–27
Terry's Provisional Corps, 119
Tewksbury, Massachusetts, 253
Texas, 17, 108
Thabor (ship), 143
Thayer, John Milton, 165
Thayer, Sylvanus, 19
Thirteenth Amendment, 150, 156, 159
Thirty-Third Virginia Infantry, 29
Thirty Years' War, 136
Thomas, Leonard R., 124
Thompson, C. Mildred, 252
Thorne, John L., 42
Thurman, Allen, 175
Tilden, Samuel J., 213, 231
Toombs, Robert, 38
Toral y Velázquez, José, 245
Tortuga, 242
Totopotomoy Creek, 96–97
Tower of London, 143
Tragic Era, The (book), 252–53
travelogues, 133
Treasury Department (Mississippi), 220–21
Treasury Department (US), 130

Treaty of Washington, 179–80
Trulock, Alice Rains, 6–7
Tuileries Palace, 142
Tunica County, Mississippi, 199
Tupelo, Mississippi, 187
Turner, John W., 89, 91, 96; at Petersburg, 102
Twain, Mark, 133
Twelfth New York Militia, 24
Twentieth Maine Regiment, 3, 7; Ames and, 9, 42, 65–66, 253–54; at Antietam, 47–48; at Fredericksburg, 51–52, 54–58, 171; at Gettysburg, 77–78; movements of, 59; reunions of, 249, 253; smallpox outbreak in, 60–61; training of, 43–45, 47, 263; views of Ames, 49; in Washington, 45–46
Twenty-Fifth Ohio, 71, 73
Twenty-Fourth Infantry (Union Army), 148
Twenty-Fourth US Infantry (Spanish-American War), 242
Twyford, England, 155
Tyler, John, 17
typhoid fever, 246

Uncle Tom's Cabin, 18
Underground Railroad, 18
Underwood, Ballou, 66
Union Army: Ames and, 2, 84, 129–30; Ames's views of, 32; at Bermuda Hundred, 93–94; at Chancellorsville, 62; Charleston and, 80; at Cold Harbor, 98; commanders of, 86; at First Bull Run, 29–30; at Fort Fisher, 116–17, 120–25, 127; at Fredericksburg, 54, 57; generals in, 1, 3, 5–6, 256; after Gettysburg, 79; at Gettysburg, 70–73, 76–77; historiography of, 7; logistics of, 35; in Mississippi, 148, 156–57; at Morris Island, 81, *82;* in the Peninsula Campaign, 34, 37–40; at Petersburg, 99, 101–2; tactics of, 61; training of, 24–25; veterans of, 162; views of war in, 26
United States: Ames in history of, 8, 11, 257, 263; Ames's views of, 139; Britain and, 141; civil rights in, 4–5, 137–38; Civil War in, 23; economy of, 192–93, 239; elections in, 156; military history of, 20; politics of, 21, 148; Reconstruction in, 210; Rockland in, 15; Spain and, 241; travelers from, 132–33, 138–39, 141–42, 145; in World War I, 254
United States Democrat (newspaper), 12
Upton, Emory, 6
Urbanna, Virginia, 33
US Army, 129–30; Ames and, 147, 151, 239; interest in Europe, 146; in Mississippi, 198; supplies from, 209
US Christian Commission, 89

US Civil War: aftermath of, 3; Ames in, 2, 8, 10–11, 257, 262; armies in, 25; beginning of, 23; Britain and, 179; conclusion of, 128–29; expectations of, 26; historiography of, 5–6, 250–51, 261, 263; in Minnesota, 234; photography and, 105; Reconstruction and, 172; soldiers in, 248; tourism and, 132; veterans of, 233, 241, 253, 256; West Point and, 22–24
US Constitution, 18, 174, 185, 205
US Marshals Service, 166
US Military Academy, 19. *See also* West Point
US Navy, 80–81, 83, 241, 245; at Fort Fisher, *112*, 115, 117, 119–21
US Sanitary Commission, 89
US Supreme Court, 157
US Volunteers, 64, 128–29

Van Buren, Anna, 135
Van Buren, John, 135
Van Buren, Martin, 135
Vassar College, 252
Venice, 143
Verona, Italy, 143
Vicksburg, Mississippi, 156, 187, 199–200, *203*; Civil War in, 101, 148–49; violence in, 197–98, 202–6, 223
Vicksburg Troubles, 204–6, 217, 221, 223, 230, 260
Vicksburg Weekly Herald, 161
Victoria (Queen), 144–45
Vienna, 135–36
Vigilencia (ship), 248
Villa del Balbianello (Lake Como), 254
Virginia, 2, 35, 79, 84–85, 91, 127
Virginia Peninsula, 33
von Gilsa, Leopold, 66, 70–73
von Wallenstein, Albrecht, 136
voting rights, 153, 156, 159–60, 172, 210–11, 226–30

Wainwright, Charles S., 72
Wales, 146
Wallenstein Palace, 136, *136*
War Department, 23, 41–42, 198, 247–48
Ware Bottom Church, 94
War Investigation Commission, 249
Warren, Gouverneur, 77, 96
Warren, Maine, 55
Warren County, Mississippi, 199, 202–6, 217, 221, 224
Warren County Courthouse (Mississippi), 149, 203
Warrenton Junction, Virginia, 80
Warwick, England, 146
Washburn, Israel, 41, 50
Washington (DC) Evening Star, 1

Washington, DC, 25–26, 30–32, 69, 126; Adelbert Ames in, 83, 151, 163, 171, 181, 227–30; Ames family in, 179–80, 195; Butler family in, 167; Civil War in, 128; Congressional hearings in, 249; military defenses of, 33, 86; Twentieth Maine at, 45–47; veteran's reunions in, 253; voting rights in, 138
Washington, George, 41
Waterloo, Battle of, 138
Waterville, Maine, 42
Waud, Alfred A., *52–53*
Waud, William, *106*
Webb, Alexander S., 63
Webster, Daniel, 18
Webster County, Mississippi. *See* Sumner County, Mississippi
Weekly Caucasian (newspaper), 174
Weekly Clarion, 160–62, 185–86, 207; on Ames, 161, 188, 194, 212–13, 217
Weitzel, Godfrey, 110–11, 114–19
Wellington, Duke of, 138
Wert, Jeffrey P., 5
West Point, 1, 3, 8; Adelbert Ames at, 20–23, 164, 169–70, 256, 263; Butler Ames at, 239; engineers from, 35; graduates of, 31, 117, 155, 242; historiography of, 253; history of, 19
West Point Battery, 23
West Virginia, 48
wheat, 233
Wheeler, Henry, 235–36
Wheeler, Joseph, 242
Whig Party, 16–17, 19, 175
White, Richard, 89–91
White House, 25
White House, Virginia, 96–97
White Leagues, 209, 217
"White Line," 197–98, 202, 205–6, 211, 228; historiography of, 252
white supremacism, 172, 182, 197–98
Whiting, William H. C., 92–93, 120–21, 125
Wilderness (ship), 113
Wilderness, Battle of the, 89, 96, 99
Wilhelm I (of Prussia), 134
Williams, Seth, 31
Williamsburg, Battle of, 35
Wilmington, Delaware, 113
Wilmington, North Carolina, 110, 113, 115, 117, 120; Confederate trade and, 108, 117; Union capture of, 127
Wilmot, David, 17
Wilmot Proviso, 17
Wilson, Woodrow, 254
Windsor Castle, 144
Windward Passage, 242

Winthrop, John, 13
Wisconsin, 180
Wittenberg, Eric J., 6
Wittenberg, Germany, 135
women: education of, 257; as tourists, 132–33
women's suffrage, 258
Woolfolk, James, 38
Woolwich, London, 144
World War I, 254
Wyman, Frank, 237

"Yankee Doodle" (song), 127
Yazoo City, Mississippi, 207

Yazoo County, Mississippi, 207, 228
yellow fever, 181, 243, 246–48
Yerger, Edward M., 157
York, England, 145
York, Pennsylvania, 69
York River, 33, 96
Yorktown, Virginia, 35
Younger, Bob, 234–36
Younger, Cole, 234–36
Younger, Jim, 234

Zurich, Switzerland, 137

www.ingramcontent.com/pod-product-compliance
Lightning Source LLC
Chambersburg PA
CBHW020007241225
37250CB00015B/118